READING DEATH IN ANCIENT ROME

Reading Death in Ancient Rome

MARIO ERASMO

THE OHIO STATE UNIVERSITY PRESS • COLUMBUS

Library of Congress Cataloging-in-Publication Data
Erasmo, Mario.
  Reading death in ancient Rome / Mario Erasmo.
    p. cm.
  Includes bibliographical references and index.
  ISBN-13: 978-0-8142-1092-5 (cloth : alk. paper)
  ISBN-10: 0-8142-1092-9 (cloth : alk. paper)
  1. Death in literature. 2. Funeral rites and ceremonies—Rome. 3. Mourning cus-
toms—Rome. 4. Latin literature—History and criticism. I. Title.
  PA6029.D43E73 2008
  870.9'3548—dc22
                                              2008002873

This book is available in the following editions:
Cloth (ISBN 978-0-8142-1092-5)
CD-ROM (978-0-8142-9172-6)

Cover design by DesignSmith
Type set in Adobe Garamond Pro by Juliet Williams
Printed by Thomson-Shore, Inc.

∞ The paper used in this publication meets the minimum requirements of the American
National Standard for Information Sciences—Permanence of Paper for Printed Library
Materials. ANSI 39.48-1992.
9 8 7 6 5 4 3 2 1

Contents

List of Figures   vii

Preface and Acknowledgments   ix

INTRODUCTION   Reading Death   1

CHAPTER 1   Playing Dead   13

CHAPTER 2   Staging Death   35

CHAPTER 3   Disposing the Dead   75

CHAPTER 4   Disposing the Dead?   108

CHAPTER 5   Animating the Dead   154

CONCLUSION   205

Notes   209

Works Cited   243

Index   253

LIST OF FIGURES

1. Funerary altar of Cornelia Glyce. Vatican Museums. Rome. 161
2. Sarcophagus of Scipio Barbatus. Vatican Museums. Rome. 167
3. Sarcophagus of Scipio Barbatus (background). Vatican Museums. Rome. 168
4. Epitaph of Rufus. Capitoline Museums #4520. Rome. 178
5. Capitoline Venus. Capitoline Museums. Rome. 179
6. Portrait of Flavian Woman as Venus. Capitoline Museums. Rome. 180

PREFACE AND ACKNOWLEDGMENTS

WHILE ordering a new tombstone for my father, the cemetery director nonchalantly mentioned that the old tombstone would be moved and placed "out of view" on a field in the country once the new one arrived. His words had a jarring effect: the old tombstone is now out of context, no longer marking where my father is buried, but is now an out-of-place inscribed piece of stone intruding on the landscape in a way that recalls Poussin's painting *Et in Arcadia Ego.* The old tombstone is still on my mind while viewing the new one now in place in the cemetery and the meaning of the Greek word for a grave—*sema,* the basis of semiotics—took on personal meaning as I wondered: who, if anyone, is reading the inscription of the old one? Is someone reading the inscription of the old one as someone reads the inscription of the new one? Which of the two will last longer?

The question of how long anyone will remember the existence of the original points to the time limits inherent in cultural memory and memorialization. There are literally two markers dedicated to the same person in two different locations, the new one now in the cemetery and the old one in a field now only in the memory of those who saw it. When I am not in the cemetery, however, both are figurative memorials that are even prioritized as emotional markers: the first tombstone, the former localizer/grave marker of my initial grief, has been replaced by another that represents a later stage of grief. Therefore, I as viewer and reader reify a meaning to a slab of stone which itself gives meaning to a person and site as it identifies the deceased and defines space. From another's perspective unaware of the existence of the first tombstone, the second one simply marks the place where my father is buried.

This semiotic exercise involving the associations between two grave markers commemorating my father in two distinct physical settings led me to reread descriptions of funerary rituals in Latin literature that had often seemed to operate on many narrative levels to engage the reader in a similar interplay between physical and figurative allusions. As with my work on Roman drama, the theory of performance semiotics that examines the physical and figurative relation between the stage, actors, and the audience/reader informs my approach to funerals as staged events with participants and audience members.

"Reading death" offers a reading strategy for analyzing literary descriptions and allusions to death ritual, rather than a reconstruction of the evidence for funeral and burial ritual in ancient Rome. In fact, authorial agendas should make us cautious about treating these descriptions and allusions as evidence for Roman burial practices. I focus, in particular, on the associative reading process—the extent to which literary texts allude to funeral and burial ritual, the narrative role played by the allusion to recreate a fictive version of the ritual (to turn reading, in some cases, into a performative and ritualistic act), and how the allusion engages a reader's knowledge of the ritual or previous literary intertexts. Since I analyze a series of case studies, the conclusions of each specific case vary. Examples, therefore, are illustrative: no ancient source offers complete information regarding funerary and burial rituals and no attempt has been made to include every literary reference to funerary ritual or to place literary passages within a wider cultural shift in ritual practice. This book is aimed at an interdisciplinary audience, so I have translated all Greek and Latin passages in the main text.

My approach complements those of recent literary and archeological studies that focus on the figurative interpretation of Roman death ritual, such as Basil Dufallo's *The Ghosts of the Past: Latin Literature, the Dead, and Rome's Transition to a Principate* (2007); Maureen Carroll's *Spirits of the Dead: Roman Funerary Commemoration in Western Europe* (2006); Geoffrey Sumi's *Ceremony and Power. Performing Politics in Rome between Republic and Empire* (2005); Penelope J. E. Davies's *Death and the Emperor. Roman Imperial Funeral Monuments from Augustus to Marcus Aurelius* (2000); Donald G. Kyle's *Spectacles of Death in Ancient Rome* (1998); and John Bodel's influential publications which have increased our knowledge of the importance of figurative interpretations of the archeological record of burials. Christiane Sourvinou-Inwood's *Reading Greek Death* (1995) is wider in scope of Greek cultural material, but her analysis of literary texts is relevant to my study. Catharine Edwards's *Death in Ancient Rome* (2007) is more concerned with the act of dying than death ritual, but our different approaches to, at times, the same literary evidence highlight the range of cultural and interpretive agendas at work in narratives on dying, the dead, and their disposal. Parts of my book *Roman Tragedy: Theatre to Theatricality* (2004a) considered the metatheatricality of funerals and the political significance of the attempted restaging of Accius' *Brutus* following the funeral of Julius Caesar as did my article on Pompey's cremation in Lucan's *Bellum Civile* that appeared in *Studies in Latin Literature and Roman History: Collection Latomus* 12: vol. 287. I build upon these earlier analyses of the theatricality of funerary presentation and representation of the dead.

Modern funerary practices are contributing to opportunities for the (self-) representation of the deceased as is the Internet which is emerging as a forum for the communication of grief and bereavement with virtual wakes, and the reciprocal communication between the dead and the living. Increasingly, websites make grieving universal and perpetual in a way that visiting a grave in a cemetery or erecting a tombstone is not. These modern cultural developments provide interesting intertexts to my analysis of Latin descriptions and allusions to Roman death ritual and point to the enduring need for communication with the dead.

I have benefited greatly from the interdisciplinary focus of the International Conference on the Social Context of Death, Dying, and Disposal sponsored by the Centre for Death and Society (CDAS) at the University of Bath and its affiliated journal, *Mortality*, and the support of Glennys Howarth and Peter C. Jupp. I owe much to the audiences and fellow panelists (especially Penelope Davies, Eric Varner, Naomi Norman, and James C. Anderson Jr.), of my lectures delivered at the conferences in Glasgow (1998): "Among the Dead: The Symbolic Participation of the Dead in Ancient Rome"; London (2000): "Playing Dead: Death Ritual and the Dead in the Roman Theatre"; York (2002): "The Poetics of Latin Epitaphs"; Bath (2005): "Cremating Pallas: The Poetics of Cremation in Vergil's *Aeneid*"; and again in Bath (2007): "Ausonius' *Parentalia:* Walking among the Dead." I would also like to thank the audiences of my lectures for their helpful questions and comments at the 126th APA Annual Meeting (1994): "The Dead and Divine as Actor and Audience at Rome"; the 129th APA Annual Meeting (1997): "Death and the Roman Imperial Court"; the fourth annual Boston University Roman Studies Conference (1998): "Reading Death in Roman Poetry"; Classical Association of the Midwest and South (2000): "Picking Up the Pieces: Seneca *Phaedra* 1262–68"; and the University of Georgia (2005): "Playing Dead in

Seneca's *Troades*." I would also like to thank Eugene O'Connor, the anonymous readers, and the editorial staff at The Ohio State University Press for making this a better book in every way. I am grateful to the Willson Center for Humanities and Arts at the University of Georgia for a grant that allowed me release time from teaching in spring 2006 to work on this book.

Reading Death

As Poussin's shepherds contemplate the meaning of the epitaph inscription *Et in Arcadia ego,* in the painting of the same name, the viewer/ reader considers the impact that death and the shepherds' contemplation of death has on their picturesque pastoral landscape and the self.[1] The inscription is both syntax and iconography imposed on nature which the viewer (the shepherds and the viewers of the painting) must interpret against the backdrop of and within the context of nature. The tombstone situates the dead (physically and figuratively) and allows a viewer to read the dead (epitaph) as a cultural and textual marker.[2] A proper name is not given on the epitaph and any attempt at (self) representation is avoided, thus a universality and timelessness result that even make Death itself a possible referent, rather than a person unknown to the shepherds.

Deciphering the name of the deceased, even if it were inscribed on an epitaph, may be just as challenging a semiotic exercise. Like Poussin's shepherds, Ausonius' inability to identify the deceased in *Epigram* 37 leads to contemplation of mortality and the anonymity of the dead (with or without identifying markers on their tombstones):

> Lucius una quidem, geminis sed dissita punctis
>   littera; praenomen sic nota sola facit.
> post M incisum est. puto sic, non tota videtur;
>   dissiluit saxi fragmine laesus apex.
> nec quisquam, Marius seu Marcius anne Metellus
>   hic iaceat, certis noverit indiciis.

truncatis convulsa iacent elementa figuris,
    omnia confusis interiere notis.
miremur periisse homines? monumenta fatiscunt,
    mors etiam saxis nominibus venit.[3]

Lucius is definitely one letter, but divided off by two points;
    thus, this is how one letter makes the praenomen.
Next, an M is inscribed. At least I think so, but it is not entirely clear;
    the top is damaged chipped from a break in the stone.
Nor can anyone know certainly whether a Marius, a Marcius
    or even a Metellus lies here.
The shapes of the letters lie disfigured, with their forms mangled,
    all have fallen in the confusion of marks.
Are we surprised that men die? Tombstones decay,
    and death comes even to inscribed stones.

Ausonius' epigram emphasizes the reading process of an epitaph which seems to change in appearance the more he studies the inscription. The identity of the letters inscribed on the tombstone are as elusive as the identity of the actual corpse buried beneath it. Despite commemoration in stone, not even a famous lineage guarantees remembrance by later generations who cannot read the name of the deceased on the grave that suffers the same fate as those which it commemorates: *monumenta fatiscunt, / mors etiam saxis nominibus venit.*[4]

The tomb and epitaph may mark the location where someone is buried, but Ausonius demonstrates that the living give it meaning, whether as an identifying marker of a specific person or the symbol of a universal fate which befalls all humans whether their remains or their tombstones are even identifiable.[5] The description of the stone's damage in terms that evoke a battle scene (*truncatis convulsa iacent elementa figuris / omnia confusis interiere notis*) only heightens the pathos of the current anonymity of the stone and the deceased it once identified.

The tombstone can also be read as an unnatural imposition on nature/ landscape in which a tomb and epitaph physically, literally, and figuratively redefine their surroundings. The redefined landscape that now becomes associated with someone dead and buried takes on the aesthetics of mortality. The aesthetics of morality are also involved: representation by a tomb and epitaph that mark the location of one's remains can be seen as an act of arrogance by the deceased who tries to exert control beyond death and stretch the limits of their biological life. *Cepotaphia,* graves surrounded by orchards, owned by the deceased, which are harvested and the profits of which were used to celebrate the deceased illustrate the human desire to impact the landscape even after death.[6] The epitaph of Hostius Pamphilus (*CIL* VI 9583), for example, defines the tomb as an eternal home, farm, orchard, and funeral monument that demarcates the landscape as the property of the deceased to specific measurements and functions:

> C. Hostius C. 1Pamphilus
> medicus hoc monumentum
> emit sibi et Nelpiae M.1.Hymnini
> et libertabus omnibus
> posterisque eorum.
> Haec est domus aeterna, hic est
> fundus, heis sunt horti, hoc
> est monumentum nostrum.
> In fronte p. XIII, in agrum p. XXIIII.

> Gaius Hostius Pamphilus freedman of Gaius
> a doctor, bought this monument for himself
> and for Nelpia Hymnis freedwoman of Marcus
> and for all of their freedmen and their descendants.
> This is our eternal home, here is our farm,
> these our are gardens, this is our monument.
> Frontage 13 feet, depth 24 feet.

The dead are agents of transformation (of self and imposed on nature) whose desire for permanence, even in death, transforms the landscape by their burial and by their cultivation of the land for their own commemoration. The living continue to interact with the dead who in turn continue to assert their presence and even exert their influence in death.

Nature becomes transformed into a landscape of death, through the burial and (temporary) commemoration of humans, but it can also play an active role in transforming itself by turning death and death ritual into a reified experience as spectacle, or as the setting for poetic inspiration. Reification of a grave (physical and figurative) is important to poet and reader as a source of poetic inspiration and interpretation.[7] Just as he does at *Silvae* 4.4 where Vergil's tomb is a source of poetic inspiration, Statius laments the death of his father in *Silvae* 5.3 at his grave; the grave becomes part of the poetic landscape of death as Statius combines poetic inspiration with the aesthetics of mortality:

tuus ut mihi vultibus ignis
irrubuit cineremque oculis umentibus hausi,
vilis honos studiis. vix haec in munera solvo
primum animum tacitisque situm depellere chordis
nunc etiam labente manu nec lumine sicco
ordior acclinis tumulo quo molle quiescis
iugera nostra tenens, ubi post Aeneia fata
stellatus Latiis ingessit montibus Albam
Ascanius, Phrygio dum pingues sanguine campos
odit et infaustae regnum dotale novercae.
hic ego te (nam Sicanii non mitius halat
aura croci, dites nec si tibi rara Sabaei
cinnama odoratas nec Arabs decerpsit aristas)
inferiis cum laude datis heu carmine plango
Pierio; sume <en> gemitus et vulnera nati
et lacrimas, rari quas umquam habuere parentes!

since your (cremation) fire reddened my face
and with streaming eyes I took in your ashes,
I treated my writing as nothing. Scarcely, do I free
my mind, for the first time, and begin to remove dust from
silent chords, even now with a failing hand and a
teary eye, leaning against the grave mound in which you rest,
occupying our fields, where after Aeneas' death, starry
Ascanius set Alba among the Latian hills, since he hated
the fields enriched by Phrygian blood and the kingdom
given as a dowry to his unfortunate stepmother.
Here, do I mourn you with my Pierian song (for the fragrance of the
Sicanian crocus is not softer nor if the wealthy Sabaeans plucked
the rare cinnamon or Arabs their perfumed blooms),
alas, offerings given with praise; ah! receive the groans and
heartache of your son, even his tears, which few fathers
have ever received! (5.3.31–46)[8]

Death ritual and mourning are both sources of hindrance and inspiration for poetic composition. Statius composes as he mourns, but outward signs of death ritual such as the ash from his father's pyre on the strings of his lyre offer an objective backdrop to his subjective mourning. Statius leans on his father's tomb to compose poetry of lamentation against the mythic and geographical backdrop of Vergil's Latium. The *Aeneid* is subtext to Statius' text as referent and as subject since Statius' expression of grief is the subject of his poem. No other tombs are described in the vicinity, so it takes on added significance as both a foreign and exclusive structure that is yet in harmony with its surroundings. While Statius does not record the words on his father's tombstone, his lament and landscape of death (*hic ego te*) serve as an epitaph that links father with son as the poem retains focus on the son's grief.

If burial and commemoration are statements and representations of one's individuality or need for permanence, then the refusal to bury oneself expresses an equally powerful sentiment and disavowal of such an ambition or even the need for solace.[9] A poetic fragment of Horace's patron Maecenas reflects this epicurean perspective: *nec tumulum curo: sepelit natura relictos.*[10] / "I do not care for a tomb: nature buries those forsaken." The phrases of three words each are balanced: human thought is contrasted with nature's actions. The human indifference over burial/proper death ritual seems to express a certain trust that nature will dispose of his remains properly (and those of others), but there is also an element of studied neglect on the part of the poet and on survivors who neglect to bury the dead with the implication that nature is performing a duty that should be performed by humans. Despite his statement to the contrary, the poet is, in fact, thinking about burial and the role of nature in disposing the dead. Maecenas' famous garden on the Esquiline, which was either on the site or the former site of a cemetery, also causes the reader to question his sincerity.[11]

Unlike Poussin's pastoral landscape, burials and memorials in an urban setting require an interpretive adjustment to account for successive layers of habitation by an ever changing populace. The cultural memory of space attaches a group recollection of a site or an event associated with that site, including the commemoration of death ritual.[12] Livy, for example, describes the place where many Gauls died from famine and disease following their thwarted attack on the Capitol in 386 BCE:

Quorum intolerantissima gens umorique ac frigori adsueta cum aestu et angore vexati volgatis velut in pecua morbis morerentur, iam pigritia singulos sepeliendi promisce acervatos cumulos hominum urebant, bustorumque inde Gallicorum nomine insignem locum fecere.

Of these conditions, the race accustomed to damp and cold was most intolerant and vexed by heat and suffocation. They were dying as diseases spread as if among a herd of cattle. Soon when tired of burying each body separately, they burned a pile of men, heaping them indiscriminately. From

that time, they made the location famous with the name of Gallic Pyres.
(5.48.3).[13]

It is remarkable that four centuries later, up to Livy's day, Romans still
marked the spot where the dead were cremated with the name "Gallic Pyres."
Death ritual separates the living from the dead but recollection of its practice
also unites generations. Thus, the site, permanently associated with death
and death ritual, transformed an urban setting into an urban setting of
death.[14]

The living define what it means to be properly cremated or buried,
according to religious or legislative requirements, regardless of whether the
deceased has already been cremated or buried. Funerary rituals and tombs
were defined by a combination of physical and religious attributes that point
to a grave as a social construct in ancient Rome.[15] In the *De legibus,* Cicero
discusses the religious character of burial rituals, such as the festival of the
Parentalia (2.22.55–69), but he claims that it is unnecessary to describe
rituals that are commonly practiced by Romans (*neque necesse est edisseri a
nobis . . . ,*2.22.55) such as the appropriate length of mourning, appropriate
sacrifices to the Lar, the ritual mutilation of a corpse by which a finger was
cut before cremation and placed in the urn with the ashes (*ossilegium*), the
sacrifice of a pig, and the time when a grave becomes a grave and is gov-
erned by the rules of religion (*quo tempore incipiat sepulchrum esse et religione
teneatur*).[16] Thus, the inhumation of a corpse or cremated remains must meet
religious requirements before the burial is accepted as a proper burial.[17]

Cicero's discussion next focuses on the antiquity of inhumation, starting with King Numa and continuing to the present day with the Cornelii
(2.22.56–57). Sulla was the first member of his gens to be cremated and
Cicero wonders whether the reason was political rather than religious: it
was cruel for Sulla to dig up and scatter remains of Marius into the Anio
river and Sulla feared a similar fate for his own remains.[18] Even in the case
of inhumation burials, the sacrifice of a pig was needed for the grave to be
given legal status (*nec tamen eorum ante sepulchrum est, quam iusta facta et
porcus caesus est*). Cicero claims that the term inhumation later applied to
all burials, including cremations and signified by the expression *humati.* In
the case of cremation inhumations, only when earth was cast on bones did
the place where cremated remains were placed become sacred.[19]

Cicero proceeds to discuss burial laws in the Twelve Tables, which outlined the legal, rather than the religious, status of graves and proper funerary and mourning rituals in Table Ten (*Leg.* 2.23.58–59; 2.24.60–62).[20]
The laws, for example, forbid burial and cremation within the pomerium

of the city (*hominum mortuum in urbe ne sepelito neve urito*), which Cicero attributes to the danger of fires, but he is more concerned about the legal definition of those buried (*sepulti*) and he deduces that the term refers to inhumation, rather than cremation burials. Cicero notes exceptions to the rule prohibiting burial within the city, but he does not mention that the gens Valeria was allowed cremation within the walls (on the Velian Hill) but refused the privilege and, instead, performed a symbolic cremation for family members.[21] The prohibition against holding multiple funerals for the same person (*homini mortuo ne ossa legito quo post funus faciat*), was intended to limit the perpetuation of grief, but the inclusion of the law implies that it was once a custom for some to rebury the dead and thereby also perpetuate an ambiguous status for the dead who would not be located where their tombstone indicates during their subsequent funeral ceremonies.

A grave is a social construct that was interpreted variously, literally, and figuratively by ancient Romans. Cicero's *De legibus* illustrates interest in the antiquity and definition of funerary rituals, from disposal to mourning and commemoration, that defines the dead in relation to the customs practiced by the living. Despite laws that separated the living from the dead, death ritual and the dead formed an important part of the living fabric of Rome. While the living define what it means to be buried, the dead themselves (re)define what it means to be dead. The dead are mourned, but they also become symbols.[22] As symbols, the dead themselves, in funerary rituals or literary allusions to those rituals, can be read as self-represented individuals who continue to participate in the world of the living and who define their survivors by the very means used by them to dispose and identify their remains and commemorate their life.[23]

Cicero claims that it was unnecessary to explain burial rituals practiced by Romans to a Roman audience, but an explanation by a Roman of rituals practiced by foreigners reveals as much about foreign rituals as it does about Roman reaction to those rituals. After describing burial laws contained in the Twelve Tables, Cicero describes the burial practices of the Athenians and the reforms of Solon (*Leg.* 2.25.62–64; 2.26.64–66; 2.27.67–68) that affected Roman funerary practices.[24] Cicero is concerned with the role of legislation in defining inhumation burials and attendant ritual ceremonies at the grave and, although it follows his discussion of Roman practices, the Greek section gives precedence and context to Roman burials.

Other foreign burial practices differed significantly from those practiced at Rome. The ghost of Appius Claudius in Silius Italicus' *Punica* asks Scipio not to embalm his corpse to be conveyed back to Rome for a proper burial, but to cremate it immediately (13.463–465). In response, Scipio promises to cremate Appius' corpse without delay and then describes the burial rituals of non-Romans in a geographic survey (13.468–87):

> "Namque ista per omnis
> discrimen servat populos variatque iacentum
> exequias tumuli et cinerum sententia discors.
> Tellure—ut perhibent, is mos antiquus—Hibera
> exanima obscoenus consumit corpora vultur.
> Regia cum lucem posuerunt membra, probatum est
> Hyrcanis adhibere canes. Aegyptia tellus
> claudit odorato post funus stantia saxo
> corpora et a mensis exanguem haud separat umbram.
> Exhausto instituit Pontus vacuare cerebro
> ora virum et longum medicata reponit in aevum.
> Quid, qui reclusa nudos Garamantes harena
> infodiunt? Quid qui saevo sepelire profundo
> exanimos mandant Libycis Nasamones in oris?
> At Celtae vacui capitis circumdare gaudent
> ossa, nefas, auro ac mensis ea pocula servant.
> Cecropidae ob patriam Mavortis sorte peremptos
> decrevere simul communibus urere flammis.
> At gente in Scythia suffixa cadavera truncis
> lenta dies sepelit, putri liquentia tabo."[25]

"Among all people, there is a distinction
observed about these matters and differing opinion on funerals,
the burial and cremation of the dead. On Spanish soil, this custom is
ancient, so they claim, that a foul vulture consumes dead bodies.
When a royal body is laid to rest, it is a custom
among the Hyrcanians to set dogs on it. In the land
of Egypt, after death, they enclose bodies, standing, in a
fragrant tomb and rarely separate the bloodless shades from
their meals. It is the custom in Pontus to empty the head
of men by draining out the brain and after embalming,
to preserve it for centuries. What to make of the Garamantes
who bury their dead naked in a hole in the sand? What about the
Nasamones who, on Libyan shores, order the dead to be
buried in the savage sea? But the Celts take pleasure in scooping
out the bones of an empty head and, shocking, preserve it in gold and
these are their drinking cups at meals. Athenians decreed to burn

in a communal cremation those who died in war defending their country. But among the Scythians, cadavers are attached to trees, and slow days consume them, melting into a putrid slime."

Silius and Scipio assume that both the reader and Appius know traditional Roman burial practices and the cursory description of foreign burial rituals is intended to inform the reader unaware of foreign customs, but some practices, such as the exposure, mutilation of corpses, and Egyptian banquets with a skeleton at the feast to represent the symbolic participation of the dead (476), are more exotic than inhumation or the mass cremation of fallen Athenian warriors. The contrast between traditional and foreign burial rituals, however, serves a narrative purpose: Appius wants to forego a traditional funeral and transportation of his corpse back to Rome so that he can proceed to the underworld more quickly. Scipio's summary of foreign practices, therefore, is intended to illustrate to the reader, since Appius pleads for a break from tradition and needs no convincing, that the various forms of burial justify an untraditionally Roman (and hasty) funeral that would still be less barbaric than some of the other burial methods that he describes.[26]

Silius' description of various burial practices also illustrates that reactions to practices foreign to one's own culture are relative. Burial rituals dispose of corpses, but they also signify a figurative transformation that affects both the corpse and the place of burial. Corpses consumed by animals (471–74) signify the temporary participation of humans in the natural life cycle and contrast with the unnatural prolonging of humans through embalming (474–78). The mass cremation of Athenians (484–85), finds parallels in Latin epic, as symbols of unity or anonymity, but the symbolic burial of an empty coffin for those soldiers whose bodies could not be recovered, which Thucydides describes (2.34), points to a figurative disposal that benefits mourners more than the actual deceased who would still lack a proper burial. The inhumation burial of a naked corpse by the Garamantes (479–80) compares a tomb to the metaphorical womb of Mother Earth and reverses the birthing process.[27]

Texts like Silius' that allude to Roman funerary ritual present only an illusion of that ritual.[28] Denis Feeney describes the interpretative process of association and (re) performance that a text elicits as part of an authorial agenda to mediate and manipulate the reader's perception of reality:

> Tibullus at once involves us in his representation and reminds us that it is just that, a representation. This carefully created sense of our distance from

the reality of the performed rite helps to set up another kind of distance, the distance of the performance of the rite from reality. The poem is not only highly self-conscious about its own fictive nature, it is also highly self-conscious about the fictive nature of the rite which it is evoking. The powerful fictiveness of the rite comes from its insistence on the fact that this day is different, that its creation of a moment and area of security and tranquility is a fantasy.[29]

Feeney focuses on the description of the *Ambarvalia* in Tibullus 2.1; however, his formulation of the fictive nature of a description of a ritual that is itself fictive applies to descriptions of funerary rituals. When reading narratives of funerals, cremations, burials, and the commemoration of the dead, the readers are positioned between their own experience as performers of the rituals and the author's performative description of those rituals that may lead to the questions: "Have I experienced this before?" and "Have I read a similar treatment before?" The questions become interconnected in a reader's response to ritual that further blends the reader's reality with the fictional reality of the text. Since all readers bring their own experiences to a text, one cannot generalize on the ability of a passage to evoke a particular funeral recollection from past experiences or even a reader's knowledge of the tradition behind various rituals. One can, however, make general assumptions about readers who share a common culture even if their individual experiences of death and dying differ.

In the following chapters, I consider both actual funerary rituals and their literary depictions as a form of participatory theater in which the performers of the rituals and the depicters of rituals in literature are engaging in strategies to involve the viewer/reader in the process of the ritual and are doing so specifically by invoking and playing upon their cultural associations at a number of levels simultaneously. Thus the depiction of funerary ritual could advance a range of authorial agendas by inviting the reader, through its use of allusions, to read and reread assumptions both about the surrounding Roman culture and about earlier literature that the authors invoke through intertextual referencing. By (re)defining their relation to the dead, the reader assumes various roles in an ongoing communion with the dead: survivor, mourner, disposer, audience member, spectator, and commemorator.

I examine the semiotic and moral implications of the living corpse in chapter 1, "Playing Dead." Propertius' self-representation as a corpse at his own funeral and the funeral rehearsals of Pacuvius and Trimalchio illustrate how allusions to funerary ritual are used by authors to blur the boundary between life and death. This blurring casts doubt on the character's mortality and allows the reader to consider the moral implications of a character's appearance or behavior as a living corpse when that character is presented as dead but alive or alive when they should be dead. In the case of figuratively dead widows, fictional and historic, the ambiguity of their mortality and their abuse of funerary ritual condemns their behavior as immoral.

Chapter 2, "Staging Death," examines further the implications of playing dead, in particular, the dramatization of death ritual as conscious theater. The reciprocity between theatricality and funerary rituals turns a funeral into a theater of the dead to make viewing and reading performative acts: mourners become audience members seated among the figurative dead who extend the metaphor as mourners and actors. I begin with an analysis of the funeral of Julius Caesar that turned his cremation into a spectacle and representations of Caesar into actors performing to a mourning audience. I then focus on the inherent theatricality of funerals and reciprocity with the theater: playing dead and death ritual as spectacle in Seneca's *Troades;* reassembling the dead in Seneca's *Phaedra;* and the theatricalizing of funerary ritual that results in a cast of corpses, such as representations of Augustus at his funeral and a reader who assumes the changing roles of spectator and mourner. The revival of the dead as actor and audience further enhances reading as participatory theater as the dead participate in their own and others' funerals before a spectator reader/audience.

Chapter 3, "Disposing the Dead," focuses on funerary ritual as text and intertext in the epics of Vergil and Ovid and the associative reading process. Starting with the cremation of Pallas, I examine how successive additions to the trope of cremations increases the intertextuality within and between texts but distances the ritual further from reality and the experiences of the reader. In Ovid's *Metamorphoses,* cremations are vehicles for further transformations that link stories within the poem, but they can also distance narratives from intertexts through hyperbolic treatment of the trope. The narrative of Hecuba's sorrows following the fall of Troy, for example, is presented as a tragedy within the epic that turns pathos into bathos as Hecuba prepares Polyxena's corpse for burial only to corrupt the ritual when she find Polydorus' corpse on the shores of Troy. Ovid's descriptions of funerary ritual, however, can also distance the reader from a text that is removed from their experience or historical fact: the description of the cremation of Julius Caesar serves as the teleological focus of the poem, as it reverses the formulation of apotheosis through cremation, but Ovid leaves out many historic details to arrive at his reformulation of his apotheosis. Caesar's transformation into a god foreshadows Ovid's own immortality, effected through his poetry and expressed through funerary ritual.

In chapter 4, "Disposing the Dead?" I focus on the descriptions of cremation in the epics of Lucan, Statius, and Silius Italicus. Successive treatments
of the epic trope of funerals and cremations further engage and frustrate the
reader's (and character's) experience with those rituals and their familiarity
with the trope. Lucan's description of the death and cremation of Pompey
takes Ovid's narrative style to more grotesque levels. Narratives, such as
the cremation of Opheltes in Statius' *Thebaid,* engage more with literary
intertexts than associations with actual funerary ritual. Argia and Antigone's
search for the corpses of Polynices and Eteocles and Statius' abandoning of
his description of the funeral and cremation of Creon serve as metaphors for
the trope in search of a narrative. Readers of these descriptions of cremations
and burials in post-Vergilian and Ovidian epic become further distanced as
participants or readers who can identify elements of the ritual as realistic
as they simultaneously sympathize with the narrative (mis)treatment of the
deceased's death and funeral. The reader thus becomes a mourner and participant of the funeral ritual through and despite the narrative.

Chapter 5, "Animating the Dead," analyzes epitaphs as grave and textual
markers, actual and illusory, for the (self) representation of the dead who
may or may not be buried where their epitaphs indicate. Self-representation
of the dead competes with the authorial voice of narratives as the dead take
control of their future commemoration. The revival of the dead in elegiac
texts leads to reciprocity with epitaphs that give the dead further opportunity for self-representation. The blurring of the boundaries between the
living and the dead through epitaphs in Ausonius' *Parentalia* turns reading
into a ritualistic act (and the reification of an illusory epitaph). Narratives
of funerary ritual have come full circle as the dead are not actually dead and
mourners have become audience members competing with both the author
and the dead.

CHAPTER 1

Playing Dead

This living hand, now warm and capable
Of earnest grasping, would, if it were cold
And in the icy silence of the tomb,
So haunt thy days and chill thy dreaming nights
That thou would wish thine own heart dry of blood,
So in my veins red life might stream again,
And thou be conscience-calm'd. See, here it is—
I hold it towards you. (John Keats)[1]

KEATS'S self-representation as a living corpse in the setting of a tomb dramatizes an exchange between the living and the dead and between poet and an unnamed interlocutor/reader. Even if he is a corpse, death will not come to the poet who will hasten the death of his interlocutor/reader as an escape from his haunting. The poet's hand dominates the poem and seems to reach out beyond the page to assault the reader spatially and psychologically, as it forms a ring composition, now alive, now dead and alive. The interlocutor/reader's death, however, will not destroy the poet whose corpse and poem will live on. In a variation of the theme of poetry as a vehicle for immortality, both poet and the poet's corpse live on in a poem that seeks to destroy the very reader who is instrumental in securing the poet's immortality.

The allusion to death ritual in Keats's poem results in the figurative blurring of the living and the dead and the theatricalization of death ritual that produces many effects, including: narrative tension as to whether a character is dead or alive; the denial or removal of narrative closure that makes it more difficult to interpret a process rather than a completed act, especially in the case of someone in the act of living or dying who should otherwise be dead (or alive); the questioning of nature in the reversal of biological experience or fact and the questioning of death ritual. Biological or veristic ambiguity

leads to a moral ambiguity: is a character dying or staying alive in a "morally correct" way? Should they be dead or are they cheating death? Are they
fooling the living or betraying the dead?

Sallust's description of the dead Catiline, for example, calls his mortality (and morality) into question through allusion to death ritual: *Catilina
vero longe a suis inter hostium cadavera repertus est, paululum etiam spirans
ferociamque animi, quam habuerat vivos, in voltu retinens.* (61.4)[2] /. "Catiline was found far from his own men among the corpses of the enemy, still
breathing a little and retaining the violent expression on his face which he
had when alive." Sallust focuses the narrative on Catiline's face which is
lifelike (still breathing and retaining a violent expression) but it is described
in terms that evoke an *imago.*[3] Thus, Catiline's face serves as metonymy for
his entire body but presents the reader with a paradox: Catiline is a cadaver
and yet not a cadaver, but he is at once lifelike and funereal. Moreover, he
seems to defy the narrative by continuing to live even beyond his death and
the reader is confronted with a living corpse that is neither dead nor alive
but whose description anticipates its appearance at his funeral.[4]

Seneca (*Ep.* 12.8–9) makes his condemnation of playing dead explicit
when he describes the funerals which Pacuvius, the governor of Syria, held
for himself:

> Pacuvius, qui Syriam usu suam fecit, cum vino et illis funebribus epulis sibi
> parentaverat, sic in cubiculum ferebatur a cena, ut inter plausus exoletorum
> hoc ad symphoniam caneretur: βεβίωται, βεβίωται. Nullo non se die
> extulit. Hoc, quod ille ex mala conscientia faciebat, nos ex bona faciamus
> et in somnum ituri laeti hilaresque dicamus:
> *Vixi et quem dederat cursum fortuna, peregi.*
>
> Crastinum si adiecerit deus, laeti recipiamus. Ille beatissimus est et
> securus sui possessor, qui crastinum sine sollicitudine expectat. Quisquis
> dixit "vixi," cotidie ad lucrum surgit.[5]

> Pacuvius, who from habit made Syria his own, with wine and funeral feasts
> commemorated himself, thus he was carried into his room from the dinner
> table, while, among the applause of boys, this was sung to the accompani-
> ment of music: "He lived, he lived." Not just on this one day was he carried
> out to burial. Let us do this from a good motive and not from a bad one
> as he used to do, and going to sleep, let us say joyfully:
> *I lived and what course Fortune gave, I completed.*
>
> If God adds a tomorrow, we should accept it joyfully. That man is most
> fortunate and confident in self-possession who looks forward to the next

day without worry. Anyone who has said, "I lived" will rise each day to advantage.

In playing dead, Pacuvius takes on a number of roles simultaneously: host, actor, and corpse as dinner guests (and musicians) willingly play mourners. Pacuvius mimics a commemorative death ritual (*Parentalia*) to anticipate his future death which Seneca attributes to a bad motive (*ex mala conscientia*), but it is not clear whether Seneca finds the imitation of the deceased itself more amoral than Pacuvius' repeated role playing as a corpse as part of some *carpe diem* entertainment.[6]

Clarity on the morality of playing dead, however, emerges from Seneca's condemnation, since he self-identifies with the dying Dido in his quotation of *Aeneid* 4.653 which is in the form of an epitaph. Seneca imagines himself close to death in order to appreciate life (rather than to entertain his dinner guests) but, ironically, his quotation of Dido comes as he is about to fall asleep and thus play dead himself. Thus, to Seneca's mind, one's motive defines the morality of playing dead and not just the imitation of the dead.

Recent developments in the American funeral industry point to the growing theatricality of modern funerary practices that mirror Pacuvius' "living funeral" (or the extending of the theatricality inherent in displaying the deceased in a formal living room setting at a funeral home which is neither a living room nor a recreation of an activity common in many American living rooms) that mirror the theatricalized funerals of ancient Rome. The range of unique funeral services varies from the personal (such as the selection of music or a reading), to the representational (unique choice of funeral service or burial setting), and self-representational (the corpse as actor in their former role and setting).

These contemporary practices offer a useful perspective when considering the figurative impact of theatricalized elements of Roman funerals, in particular, role playing by the deceased, mimes imitating the deceased, and mourners who are spectators and actors in the illusion that blurs the distinction between the living and the dead. Wakes are staged as a theater experience by funeral directors who perform like stage directors and design sets for the deceased to act out their former identities even though their displayed bodies break the illusion of a reanimated corpse.[7] Mourners extend the theatricalized experience: they become an audience entertained by the stage props, but they also emerge as actors perpetuating the dramatic illusion. At the Wade Funeral Home in Saint Louis, for example, staged funerals include "Big Momma's Kitchen" in which mourners find the deceased in

a family dinner setting with such props as a loaf of Wonder Bread on top
of the refrigerator and real fried chicken on the stove. The website for the
Funeral Home reveals other themes such as "The Woodsman," "Military,"
"Jazz," and "The Gardener." These various *tableaux vivants* feature corpse
actors in the starring role of their own recreated biographies for an audience
who joins in the dramatic illusion.

The dead continue to role play as they assume their former identities
and favorite activities in familiar settings in which mourners recreate their
own relationships and interactions with the deceased as they simultaneously
mourn and celebrate the deceased. The deceased, however, is not limited to
role playing during a funeral wake—the "Celebrate Life Program" turns the
ashes of the deceased into a firework display in which the deceased literally
becomes the entertainment and not just a participant in the dramatic illusion of wakes.[8]

This chapter explores the living corpse, the dead represented as alive and
the living (self) represented as dead through physical or figurative referents
from funerary ritual. I focus on the author's use of death ritual to call both
the mortality and the morality of a literary character/historical personality
into question, such as funeral rehearsals like Pacuvius' and the figuratively
dead widow, fictional and historic, which results in a text in which the referents themselves take on their own figurative (re)interpretations.[9]

The Living Corpse

In Propertius, 2.13B. 17–58, the poet plays dead as he describes his own
cremation and epitaph to an uncaring Cynthia:

> Quandocumque igitur nostros mors claudet ocellos,
>   accipe quae serves funeris acta mei.
> nec mea tunc longa spatietur imagine pompa,
>   nec tuba sit fati vana querela mei;
> nec mihi tunc fulcro sternatur lectus eburno,
>   nec sit in Attalico mors mea nixa toro.
> desit odoriferis ordo mihi lancibus, adsint
>   plebei parvae funeris exsequiae.
> sat mea sat magna est, si tres sint pompa libelli,
>   quos ego Persephonae maxima dona feram.
> tu vero nudum pectus lacerata sequeris,
>   nec fueris nomen lassa vocare meum,

osculaque in gelidis pones suprema labellis,
  cum dabitur Syrio munere plenus onyx.
deinde, ubi suppositus cinerem me fecerit ardor,
  accipiat Manis parvula testa meos,
et sit in exiguo laurus super addita busto,
  quae tegat exstincti funeris umbra locum,
et duo sint versus: QUI NUNC IACET HORRIDA PULVIS,
  UNIUS HIC QUONDAM SERVUS AMORIS ERAT.
nec minus haec nostri notescet fama sepulcri,
  quam fuerant Pthii busta cruenta viri.
tu quoque si quando venies ad fata, memento,
  hoc iter ad lapides cana veni memores.
interea cave sis nos aspernata sepultos:
  non nihil ad verum conscia terra sapit.
atque utinam primis animam me ponere cunis
  iussisset quaevis de Tribus una Soror!
nam quo tam dubiae servetur spiritus horae?
  Nestoris est visus post tria saecla cinis:
cui si longaevae minuisset fata senectae
  †Gallicus† Iliacis miles in aggeribus,
non ille Antilochi vidisset corpus humari,
  diceret aut 'O mors, cur mihi sera venis?'
tu tamen amisso non numquam flebis amico:
  fas est praeteritos semper amare viros.
testis, cui niveum quondam percussit Adonem
  venantem Idalio vertice durus aper;
illis formosus iacuisse paludibus, illuc
  diceris effusa tu, Venus, isse coma.
sed frustra mutos revocabis, Cynthia, Manis:
  nam mea quid poterunt ossa minuta loqui?[10]

Therefore, whenever death may close my eyes,
  hear how you should carry out my funeral arrangements.
let there be no long procession that winds its way with my image,
  nor a trumpet that vainly mourns my death;
nor let the posts of a couch be covered in ivory for me,
  nor should my corpse lie on a bed in Attalic style.
nor let there be a sequence of fragrant plates for me,
  rather, there should be the modest rites of a common funeral.
Enough, great even, if there were a procession of my three books,

my greatest gifts, which I will make to Persephone.
Of course you will follow with your breasts bared and beaten,
    nor will you tire from calling out my name,
and you will place final kisses on my cold lips,
    when the onyx jar full of Syrian oil is given.
Then, when the fire placed underneath has made me ash,
    let a small clay urn receive my shade,
and let a laurel be planted near my small pyre,
    that will cover the place of my cremation with shade,
and these two verses: HE WHO NOW LIES HERE AS CRUDE DUST,
    ONCE WAS THE SLAVE OF A SINGLE LOVE.
Nor will the fame of my grave be less famous
    than was the bloody tomb of the Phthian.
And whenever you arrive at your end, remember, white haired,
    the way to these commemorative stones and come.
Meanwhile, be careful not to despise my buried remains:
    Earth, aware of all, knows not a little about the truth.
I wish that one of the Three Sisters had decreed that
    I would stop breathing in my child's seat.
For why is the spirit saved for a doubtful hour?
    The ash of Nestor was seen after three generations:
if some soldier on the ramparts of Troy had
    reduced the term of his old age,
he would not have seen the corpse of Antilochus buried,
    or asked, "O death, why do you come to me so late?"
Sometimes, however, you will weep for your dead friend:
    it is right always to love men who have passed.
Witness, the savage boar who once pierced snow white
    Adonis on the peaks of Mount Ida;
beautiful as he lay on those reeds where they say
    you, Venus, went with disheveled hair.
But, in vain, Cynthia, will you call back my senseless shade:
    for how will my diminished bones be able to speak?

The tone of the elegy is ironic as the poet describes his death, mock-funeral, cremation, burial, and epitaph as future events that seem to be unfolding in the present. The "fictiveness of the rite," as described by Feeney in relation to Tibullus' poetry in the Introduction, reveals Propertius' authorial agenda in alluding to funerary ritual: to contrast Cynthia's future peformance of funerary ritual in the poem with her present neglect of the poet. The poet directs her response and our interpretation of her actions: the poet is both corpse and funeral director as the narrator and reader focus on Cynthia's fictive performance of funerary ritual (27 ff.), in which Propertius depicts his mistress as his wife, but that also adds to the illusion and irony of her performance. Cynthia's reaction to the poet's role playing as a dead lover is not described but the tone of his performance as corpse, while ironic in its allusion to death ritual, is playful and not intended to offend the reader.

The epitaph does not identify the poet by name, but rather he uses it to self-identify as a *servus amoris* who was faithful to one lover alone. Nonetheless, the grave will be famous, but whether because it will be associated with the poet specifically or appeal to a visitor/reader's sympathy is not stated. While there is no mention of his beloved in the epitaph, the expression *servus* implies his love for a *domina* who may or may not take notice of his suffering and death. The epitaph is both text and pretext to communicate the poet's love which will be read by Cynthia as she makes commemorative visits to his grave and reads the words of the dead (40–41).

Mythological allusions add to the tragic (and comic) tone. The poet's tomb is compared to Achilles', which was where Polyxena was slaughtered as Achilles' bride (36–37). The poet also expresses a wish for an earlier death than that which came to Nestor who lived for three generations (43–50). Self-identification with two diverse mythological characters—the one died young, the other in extreme old age—adds to the irony. Propertius uses the expression, *fas est praeteritos semper amare viros* (52), with its pun on the verb to esteem and to love, that even makes it a religious and moral imperative to love the dead. Other mythological referents, such as Venus' mourning of Adonis, provide an example, or even a script, for Cynthia to follow when performing her fictive rituals.

The last two lines of the poem call attention to the joke that Propertius' corpse is currently animated and will continue to impact and engage Cynthia's life after the poet's death, much like Keats' hand that defies time and space to haunt the living. Despite playing dead and alluding to death ritual, however, the elegiac context keeps the tone playful rather than offensive, by situating Propertius' mock funeral and burial within the context of his elegies as a lover with a persona who is at the mercy of a *domina*.

Trimalchio's Funeral Rehearsal

Pacuvius' prestaging of his funeral as entertainment receives fuller treatment as a *carpe diem* topos in Petronius' *Satyricon*. The freedman Trimalchio

invites guests to his house for a dinner party, including the novel's protago-
nists Encolpius, Ascyltus, and Giton. Trimalchio's house becomes a source
of conversation that constantly reacts to an ever-changing environment that
requires ever-changing interpretations of the setting by characters and readers alike. Descriptions of funeral preparations accompany dinner courses in
a complex interplay between conversation and food, as Trimalchio, obsessed
with death, outlines details of his funeral and burial to his dinner guests
(71–78).[11] Since the meal begins before Trimalchio's description and enactment of his funeral, guests unwittingly become participants of Trimalchio's
funeral in a reversal of Trimalchio's modern corpse actors, like those at the
Wade Funeral Home, who provide "entertaining" wakes and present themselves as literal spectacles for mourners who arrive at a funeral home to
participate in the dramatic illusion and allusion. By feasting a living man
who imitates his future dead-self, the guests participate in a reversal of the
Parentalia, the festival in which Roman honored the dead with ritual meals
at their graves.[12]

Among conversation on the brevity of life, Trimalchio gives directions
for his tomb and epitaph, including plot size, an area for the cultivation
of fruit and wine (*cepotaphium*), and a marker addressed to passersby that
reads more like an entry in a will: *Hoc monumentum heredem non sequatur* /
"Let this monument not accede to an heir.[13] After describing measures that
will be taken to ensure that no one will defecate on his tomb, Trimalchio
describes the monument itself as a ship, with a statue of himself seated
as a magistrate accompanied by a statue of his wife and various pets. The
passerby is imagined as a reluctant or hostile visitor since Trimalchio takes
measures to ensure that his name is tied to the monument: *Horologium in
medio, ut quisquis horas inspiciet, velit nolit, nomen meum legat* / "In the
middle a sundial, so that anyone wanting to see the time will read my name,
whether he wants to or not."

Trimalchio's epitaph marks the location where his remains are buried and
lists his accomplishments (71.12):

C. Pompeius Trimalchio Maecenatianus hic requiescit. Huic seviratus
absenti decretus est. Cum posset in omnibus decuriis Romae esse, tamen
noluit. Pius, fortis, fidelis, ex parvo crevit, sestertium reliquit trecenties, nec
umquam philosophum audivit. Vale: et tu.

Here lies Gaius Pompeius Trimalchio Maecenatianus. He was voted a priest
of Augustus in his absence. Although he was able to be enrolled in every
office in Rome, he refused. Devoted, brave, faithful, he grew from humble

origins, he left thirty million sesterces, he never listened to a philosopher. Farewell: even to you.

The epitaph implies membership to political clubs which Trimalchio took no interest in attending. The listing of his virtues mix moral qualities with his financial success and pride in his lack of education. Trimalchio addresses the passerby and even writes a response to ensure a dialogue with the living after death.

After describing his funeral monument and epitaph, and filling the dining room with funereal lamentation, Trimalchio asks, *"ergo" inquit "cum sciamus nos morituros esse, quare non vivamus?"* / "'Therefore, he said, 'since we know that we are all going all die, why not enjoy life?'" (72.2). The question is far from philosophical musing since the tasteless dinner conversation takes a turn for the worse when Trimalchio enacts his own funeral and turns his dinner guests into mourners (77.7–78.1–7):

"[. . .] Interim, Stiche, profer vitalia in quibus volo me efferri. Profer et unguentum et ex illa amphora gustum ex qua iubeo lavari ossa mea."

Non est moratus Stichus sed et stragulam albam et praetextam in triclinium attulit iussitque nos temptare an bonis lanis essent confecta. Tum subridens "vide tu" inquit "Stiche, ne ista mures tangant aut tineae; alioquin te vivum comburam. Ego gloriosus volo efferri, ut totus mihi populus bene imprecetur." Statim ampullam nardi aperuit omnesque nos unxit et "spero" inquit "futurum ut aeque me mortuum iuvet tamquam vivum." Nam vinum quidem in vinarium iussit infundi et "putate vos" ait "ad parentalia mea invitatos esse." Ibat res ad summam nauseam cum Trimalchio ebrietate turpissima gravis novum acroama, cornicines, in triclinium iussit adduci fultusque cervicalibus multis extendit se super torum extremum et "fingite me" inquit "mortuum esse. Dicite aliquid belli."

Consonuere cornicines funebri strepitu. Unus praecipue servus libitinarii illius qui inter hos honestissimus erat tam valde intonuit ut totam concitaret viciniam. Itaque vigiles qui custodiebant vicinam regionem, rati ardere Trimalchionis domum, effregerunt ianuam subito et cum aqua securibusque tumultari suo iure coeperunt.

"[. . .] In the meantime, Stichus, bring out the shroud in which I want to be buried. Bring the ointment and a taste of wine from that jar from which I ordered my bones to be washed."

Stichus did not delay but brought the white cloth and bordered toga into the dining room and Trimalchio ordered us to test whether they were made of good wool. Then smiling, he said, "Stichus, don't let mice or moths touch it or I will burn you alive. I want to be carried out for burial magnificently so that everyone will say a kind prayer for me." Immediately, he opened a jar of nard and smeared all of us, then said, "I hope that this will be equally as pleasant in death as it is to me alive." Next he ordered wine to be poured into a bowl and said, "Pretend that you have been invited to my *parentalia*." The whole thing was reaching a nauseating level when Trimalchio, grounded in his shameful drunkenness, ordered new entertainment and horn players to be led into the dining room. Propped up on many cushions and stretched out along the length of his couch, he said, "Pretend that I am dead. Say something nice."

The horn players made a mess of the funeral music. Especially one, the slave of the undertaker and the most respectable man among them, blew so loudly that he woke up the whole neighborhood. So the watchmen who were guarding a neighboring region, thinking that Trimalchio's house was on fire, quickly broke the door open and, like always, began to cause a commotion with their water and axes.

Trimalchio's directions to his slaves to produce items that would be used in his cremation and burial place him in the alternating roles of corpse and funeral director. Trimalchio's directions, however, are not given in a chronological order that reflects funerary practice; rather they are given in random order from cremation, burial preparation, wake, graveside commemoration, to laid-out corpse: Trimalchio asks for items that would be used to quench his cremation fire and describes the collection of his cremated remains (*ossilegium*) before he describes his pre-cremated appearance in his funeral shroud. Guests are then invited to pay respects at his tomb in an enactment of the *parentalia*. Finally, Trimalchio stretches out on a couch and imitates his own future corpse and asks his guests to pretend that he is dead and pay him compliments. The arrival of the fire brigade puts a comic end to Trimalchio's funeral rehearsal and allows some of his guests to escape. Trimalchio's "rescue" by the fire brigade simulates his resurrection in yet another inversion of funerary ritual.

Intertexts also marginalize Trimalchio's funeral enactment: Seneca's condemnation of Pacuvius, the governor of Syria, who acted out his own funeral as entertainment, points to the amorality of playing dead.[14] Claudius, who witnesses his own funeral cortege in Seneca's *Apocolocyntosis* (12), as Mercury leads him from heaven to the underworld, is already dead and does not take an active role in directing the rituals. The description of the funeral and public lamentation mock Claudius' deification and the intelligence of the emperor himself: *Claudius, ut vidit funus suum, intellexit se mortuum esse* (12.12–13).[15] In Suetonius' narrative of Nero's final moments before his death (discussed in chapter 5), Nero gives burial directions to his slaves out of expediency and his concern for the size of the grave and his impromptu epitaph reflect his cowardice and fear of decapitation and his vanity. Unlike Trimalchio, however, Nero does not play dead in anticipation of his imminent death.

Trimalchio, like his counterpart Pacuvius, alternates between his roles as host, a corpse, and a funeral director. Dinner guests are turned into mourners and actors since Trimalchio observes their actions and gauges their sincerity. The chronological confusion of ritual elements and the sensory assault on his guests magnify the vulgarity and absurdity of Trimalchio's behavior. Despite the melodramatic humor of the scene, from an aesthetics of mortality perspective, Trimalchio's enactment or even rehearsal of his funeral is a perversion of death ritual and his request that his guests and household staff demonstrate the grief that they would show for him after his death, while he is watching, exemplify his amoral character. This moral lapse and the impropriety of his behavior are reminiscent of Pacuvius' own and Seneca's condemnation of it as originating *ex mala conscientia*. Literary intertexts place Trimalchio's behavior within a satiric topos but in a class all his own.

The Entombed Widow

Petronius uses funerary ritual as a literal backdrop in the tale of the Widow of Ephesus (111–113) which Eumolpus recites (as reported by Encolpius) on Lichas' ship to intercede on behalf of Encolpius and Giton who have been discovered by their former patrons, Tryphaena and Lichas, from whose amorous attentions they escaped earlier in the novel. The story revolves around a widow who figuratively plays dead, by mourning the death of her husband in his tomb, until she gives in to temptation and has sex with the soldier who was guarding the crucified bodies of criminals nearby, and with whom she flees at the end of the tale.[16]

The widow's husband is buried in a "mausoleum crypt in the Greek manner" (*in hypogaeo Graeco more corpus* (111.2) which means that the body is not cremated in the Roman custom but laid to rest intact.[17] The mausoleum provides a dramatic setting that focuses the narrative on three characters (the widow, her maid, and the soldier) within an enclosed space whose actions take place within view of the husband's corpse (and perhaps the corpses/sarcophagi of others). The reader (and Eumolpus' audience) is

introduced to the widow first by reputation (her public display of grief is
described as a spectacle, *spectaculum* [111.1] that turns her mourning into a
performance before an audience), and then by a demonstration of her deep
grief through excessive ritual mourning as she occupies the mausoleum with
her husband. The widow becomes a figurative corpse in her constant mourning and shunning of life:

> Sic afflictantem se ac mortem inedia persequentem non parentes potuerunt
> abducere, non propinqui; magistratus ultimo repulsi abierunt, complo-
> rataque ab omnibus singularis exempli femina quintum iam diem sine ali-
> mento trahebat.

> Neither her parents nor her relatives were able to lead her away, a woman
> so shattered and following death through starvation; finally the magistrates,
> after being rejected, left. This woman was mourned by all as a unique
> example who already let five days go by with any food. (111.3)

Therefore, after playing the widow in public, the widow plays dead in
her husband's mausoleum, and even looks the part as she is symbolically
entombed/buried alive in order to continue to mourn the death of her husband until (presumably) death also comes to her.

After the soldier, who is guarding the bodies of crucified criminals,
notices a light among the *monumenta,* he investigates the cause and discovers the widow and her maid (111.7–9):

> Descendit igitur in conditorium, visaque pulcherrima muliere primo quasi
> quodam monstro infernisque imaginibus turbatus substitit. Deinde ut et
> corpus iacentis conspexit et lacrimas consideravit faciemque unguibus sec-
> tam, ratus scilicet id quod erat, desiderium extincti non posse feminam pati,
> adtulit in monumentum cenulam suam coepitque hortari lugentem ne per-
> severaret in dolore supervacuo et nihil profuturo gemitu pectus diduceret:
> omnium eandem esse sedem et domicilium, et cetera quibus exulceratae
> mentes ad sanitatem revocantur. At illa ignota consolatione percussa lacera-
> vit vehementius pectus ruptosque crines super pectus iacentis imposuit.

> Therefore, he went down into the tomb and when the most beautiful woman
> was first seen he stood still as though disturbed by some apparition from
> the underworld [*imagines*]. Then when he saw the corpse and studied the
> tears and her face scratched from her nails, he took the situation for what
> it was, the woman was not able to endure the loss of her dead husband.

He brought his own dinner into the tomb and began to urge the grieving woman not to persist in her useless grief or harm her breasts in lamentation: the same end and resting spot awaits us all, and other things with which troubled minds are recalled to health. But she, uncaring of consolation, struck and tore her breast more violently and laid the hair that she pulled from her head onto the chest of her dead husband.

The soldier, after mistaking the widow for an apparition from the under-world, sees physical signs of mourning and tries to get her to eat and drink to rejoin the living. The practical maid accepts the wine and food and then works on getting the widow to drink and eat by quoting Anna's advice to Dido in Vergil's *Aeneid* in which she urges her sister not to be a widow who does not remarry (*univira*) out of loyalty to her husband's memory: *Id cinerem aut manes credis sentire sepultos?* / "Do you think that ashes and the buried shades can feel this?" (4.34). The maid quotes a second line from the same scene in the *Aeneid*, but this time from Anna's advice to Dido to consider remarriage for the security of her kingdom: *Placitone etiam pugnabis amori, / nec venit in mentem quorum consederis arvis?* / "Do you even resist a pleasant love, nor has it entered your mind whose lands you have settled?" (4.38–39). The maid's second allusion draws attention to the setting and political reality of Dido's refusal to remarry, but in the widow's case, the set-ting is her husband's tomb which should provoke the opposite response. The initial quote from the *Aeneid* momentarily raises the tone of the story and the dignity of the widow, but the second quote causes the reader to rethink the allusion and the tone of the comparison.

The widow gives in to the arguments of food and then her lust for the soldier. The text is not explicit whether the widow and the soldier have sex within view of the husband's corpse, but there is a double entendre to the mourner's assumption that the widow was expiring over the corpse of her husband (112.3):

> Iacuerunt ergo una non tantum illa nocte qua nuptias fecerunt sed postero etiam ac tertio die, praeclusis videlicet conditorii foribus, ut quisque ex notis ignotisque ad monumentum venisset putaret expirasse super corpus viri pudicissimam uxorem.

So they lay together, and not just on this one night did they make love but also on the next night and even the third day. The doors of the tomb were naturally closed, so that any relative or stranger who came to it would think that this most chaste woman had died over the corpse of her husband.

Thus, the widow betrays her husband and her reputation by not observing his death for a decent length of time and failing to do so in his very tomb. The widow also betrays her epic intertext since allusions to the *Aeneid* add a mock epic tone which may also cause the reader to question Dido's commitment to her dead husband.

Meanwhile, one of the bodies of the crucified criminals was removed while the soldier was having sex with the widow in the tomb. When the soldier threatens to commit suicide to avoid punishment, the widow offers to place the body of her husband on the cross (112.7–8):

> Mulier non minus misericors quam pudica "nec istud" inquit "dii sinant ut eodem tempore duorum mihi carissimorum hominum duo funera spectem. Malo mortuum impendere quam vivum occidere." Secundum hanc orationem iubet ex arca corpus mariti sui tolli atque illi quae vacabat cruci adfigi. Usus est miles ingenio prudentissimae feminae posteroque die populus miratus est qua ratione mortuus isset in crucem.

> But the woman was no less compassionate than she was chaste. "The gods," she said, "do not allow me to look on the two deaths of the two men most dear to me at the same time. I prefer to hang a dead man than to kill a man who is alive." Following this speech, she ordered the body to be taken out of his tomb and to be attached to the cross which was empty. The soldier took advantage of this idea of the most thoughtful woman and on the next day, the people marveled at how the dead man had climbed onto the cross.

The resourcefulness of the widow and the reversal of death ritual at the end of the story give the ending its humor: she unburies her husband (and subjects his corpse to a criminal's punishment) while she undergoes a metaphorical rebirth/resurrection from his tomb to marry the soldier. The confusion of the populace only adds to her amoral victory since it is their (incorrect) interpretation of her character and actions while mourning that lead to her cunning departure with her sterling reputation seemingly intact.

The paradoxical ending of the tale depends on death ritual: the widow plays dead in her grief but she betrays her husband's memory in his own tomb within days of his burial. Moreover, she leaves his body unburied and on a criminal's crucifix as she secretly leaves town with the soldier. The widow's amoral yet humorous disregard for her dead husband, in favor of her new lover, contrasts with her reputation and outward signs of mourning. It also contrasts with her epic intertext, Dido, since Petronius' allusions to the *Aeneid* suggest commonality between the characters of the widow and

Dido.[18] The tomb as backdrop to the widow's mourning and her disrespect for her former husband serve as an aesthetic focal point to her amorality. The sailors listening to Eumolpus laugh at the widow's cleverness but not Lichas (113.2), who interprets himself as an intertext to the betrayed husband of the tale and the target of Eumolpus' authorial aim.

The tomb of the widow's husband is the setting of both his burial and her subsequent wedding, which is a reversal of the literary topos of the virgin Polyxena, daughter of Priam and Hecuba, who is sacrificed on Achilles' tomb on her wedding day, thus turning her wedding into her funeral (see discussion below of Seneca's *Troades*). The story is a Milesian tale designed to shock through irony and paradox, but the story employs complex narrative strategies: Although Eumolpus claims that the story happened in his lifetime, it alludes to literary intertexts from Homer's *Odyssey* to Vergil's *Aeneid;* thus it is and is not a tale based on reality (the fictional reality of the novel) and it is and is not a literary topos. The setting is Ephesus but the focus is on the universality of the characters' actions rather than their locale. Neither the widow nor the soldier is named, and thus the story becomes an Everyman's tale that exploits the folly of human behavior.

Seneca's Dead Widow

Narratives on the deaths of prominent men (*exitus illustrium virorum*) were popular at the beginning of Nero's reign and Tacitus incorporates noteworthy suicides in his *Annales* following the Pisonian conspiracy. The suicide of Seneca in 65 CE, in particular, provided Tacitus with a subject whose philosophical writings often contrasted with his political activities. Tacitus extends the irony between Seneca's moralistic persona and his expedient/self-serving behavior to the narrative of his death to exemplify his hypocrisy and pomposity. Seneca's wife, Paulina, does not escape the scathing indictment of hypocrisy leveled at Seneca; Tacitus uses a description of her attempted suicide and allusion to death ritual to cast her as a living corpse who cheats death amorally to remain among the living.[19]

The theatricality of Tacitus' narrative, as with his earlier account of the death of Agrippina that is framed as a tragedy, turns characters into actors and the reader into an audience member:

> Ubi haec atque talia velut in commune disseruit, complectitur uxorem et
> paululum adversus praesentem fortitudinem mollitus rogat oratque temperaret dolori neu aeternum susciperet, sed in contemplatione vitae per
> virtutem actae desiderium mariti solaciis honestis toleraret. illa contra sibi

quoque destinatam mortem adseverat manumque percussoris exposcit. tum
Seneca gloriae eius non adversus, simul amore, ne sibi unice dilectam ad
iniurias relinqueret, 'vitae' inquit 'delenimenta monstraveram tibi, tu mortis
decus mavis: non invidebo exemplo. Sit huius tam fortis exitus constantia
penes utrosque par, claritudinis plus in tuo fine.' post quae eodem ictu brachia ferro exolvunt. Seneca, quoniam senile corpus et parco victu tenuatum
lenta effugia sanguini praebat, crurum quoque et poplitum venas abrumpit;
saevisque cruciatibus defessus, ne dolore suo animum uxoris infringeret
atque ipse visendo eius tormenta ad impatientiam delaberetur, suadet in
aliud cubiculum abscedere. et novissimo quoque momento suppeditante
eloquentia advocatis scriptoribus pleraque tradidit, quae in vulgus edita eius
verbis invertere supersedeo.

At Nero nullo in Paulinam proprio odio, ac ne gliscèret invidia crudeli-
tatis, iubet inhiberi mortem. hortantibus militibus servi libertique obligant
brachia, premunt sanguinem, incertum an ignarae. nam ut est vulgus ad
deteriora promptum, non defuere qui crederent, donec implacabilem Nero-
nem timuerit, famam sociatae cum marito mortis petivisse, deinde oblata
mitiore spe blandimentis vitae evictam; cui addidit paucos postea annos,
laudabili in maritum memoria et ore ac membris in eum pallorem albenti-
bus ut ostentui esset multum vitalis spiritus egestum.

When he had said these and similar things as if for public hearing, he
embraced his wife and, somewhat contrary to his current show of strength,
he gently asked and begged that she limit her grief and not endure it for
long, but to bear it in dignified solace through contemplation of her husband's life conducted with virtue. Instead, she resolutely demanded to die
with him and asked for the executioner's stroke. Seneca was not opposed
to her aspiration and at the same time out of love, did not want to leave to
harm one so cherished by himself. "I offered the attractions of life to you"
he said, "but you prefer the glory of death: I will not begrudge you becoming an example. May this resolve of so brave a death be shared by us both
but there will be more fame in your death" After he spoke, they cut their
arms with the same stroke of the blade. Seneca, because his body was old
and slight through austere living, released a slow flow of blood so he also
cut the veins in his shins and behind his knees. Worn out from the brutal
pain and so that he would not weaken his wife's resolve through his own
suffering and lose his own determination in seeing her agony, he asked her
to go to another room. But even in his final moments, his eloquence was at
hand and he recited many things to summoned secretaries which I will not
relate since they are in circulation, published in his own words.

But Nero, since he did not hate Paulina personally, and so that his reputation for cruelty would not spread, ordered her death to be prevented. At
the urging of soldiers, slaves and freedmen tied up her arms and staunched
the blood, but it is unclear whether she was unconscious. The public, however, is drawn to less favorable versions and there were some who believed
that as long as she feared that Nero was implacable, she sought the glory
of a shared death with her husband, then was persuaded when offered the
brighter prospect of a pleasant life; she lived on for a few years afterwards,
in praiseworthy memory of her husband; on her face and limbs was a pallor
that showed how much vital blood she had lost. (*Ann.* 15.63–64).[20]

In Tacitus' account of Seneca's suicide, Seneca is the initial protagonist who
directs his own and his wife's suicide and interprets them in-progress. Seneca
is both emperor and author: although condemned to die, he takes control
of his suicide and the narrative which he interprets, in particular Paulina's
seemingly faithful and voluntary decision to die with her husband. How
could he not? The *exemplum* of Seneca's life has made Paulina morally virtuous, so Seneca accepts her offer to commit suicide with him immediately
without doubting her sincerity. Seneca is aware of the posthumous glory of
her deed to his own reputation if she accompanied him in death and it was
seen as her choice.[21] The direct words of Paulina to her husband are not
reported, however, which gives Tacitus' narrative an intentionally ambiguous quality: the reader must accept her intentions and his interpretation as
sincere or both as examples of self-aggrandizement.

Although a character in the scene, Paulina is relegated to a supporting
role and the reader, as does Seneca, loses sight of her when Seneca orders that
she be moved to another room. Paulina, therefore, does not witness Seneca's
suicide and she is figuratively in the wings or backstage while Seneca enacts
the final moments of Socrates. Nero's prevention of Paulina's death interrupts the dramatic action in time for her to survive and thus he emerges as
a *deus ex machina* figure in the narrative who can order one to die or to live.
Nero's reversal indicates that he was aware how her suicide would be "read"
by contemporaries. So Nero now controls the life and death of the characters
and the direction of the narrative. Like a dramatist, he changes the script
of Paulina's suicide. The digression on Paulina's subsequent life represents a
temporal shift of narrative events: Paulina's future after the death of Seneca
to the present suicide of Seneca. Both suicides, however, are interconnected
from a narrative and historical perspective.

The narrative lingers on the life of Paulina, following her suicide
attempt, and gives her an epilogue in which she is symbolized by her deathly

appearance, with emphasis placed on the pallor of her face and limbs. The evocation of an *imago* or ancestor mask is ironic: earlier, in saying goodbye to his friends and servants, Seneca pompously leaves the model of his life to them in his will, which Tacitus describes as an *imago: imaginem vitae suae* (*Ann.* 15.62). Seneca seems to have conferred the same model to his wife. The slaves who saved her could not tell whether she was alive or dead, and now the public (and Paulina's own ambiguous appearance) is confused as to whether she is alive or dead.

The image of a deathlike Paulina and the reporting of gossip that interprets her as a hypocrite even as she presents herself in public as a devoted widow adds a comic tone to the narrative, turning her biography into a tragicomedy. Paulina is out of context among the living and she plays dead as she is transformed from character to actor during her suicide attempt to character when allowed to live, but again to an actor after Seneca's suicide. Paulina imitates the actions of a mime at a funeral who wore an *imago* of the deceased who was imitated by him at his funeral. The funereal role playing assigned to Paulina is similar to the earlier assumed role playing of Aemilia Lepida in the *Annales* who evoked her own funeral and the *imagines* of her ancestors, when entering the Theater of Pompey, to evoke sympathy from the audience and resentment toward Tiberius, who had accused her of treason.[22]

Contemporary interpretation of Paulina's motivations and actions are reported as malicious gossip (*nam ut est vulgus ad deteriora promptum*), in which Paulina's suicide attempt and devotion to her husband was self-serving: only when condemned to die would she commit suicide and feign devotion to her husband to increase his and her own glory but, when pardoned, she chose to live. The course of action preferred by the populace seems to be that Paulina should have shown devotion to Seneca and disregarded Nero's order to live, so now, more than a testimonial of her devotion to her husband, her continued life advertises her hypocrisy instead.[23] Tacitus' narrative also questions Paulina's sincerity: comic details surround Seneca's pompous suicide and his unresponsive body, but why does it take so long for Paulina to die? When ordered to live, her mortality was still in doubt: *incertum an ignorae* raises the question, did she prolong her suicide to outlive her husband and perhaps to change her mind?

The questioning of Paulina's sincerity is related to the narrative of Octavia's death in which she is described as a living corpse (*Ann.* 14.64):

> Ac puella vicesimo aetatis anno inter centuriones et milites, praesagio malorum iam vitae exempta, nondum tamen morte adquiescebat. paucis dehinc interiectis diebus mori iubetur, cum iam viduam se et tantum soror-

em testaretur communisque Germanicos et postremo Agrippinae nomen
cieret, qua incolumi infelix quidem matrimonium sed sine exitio pertulis-
set. restringitur vinclis venaeque eius per omnis artus exolvuntur; et quia
pressus pavore sanguis tardius labebatur, praefervidi balnei vapore enecatur.
additurque atrocior saevitia quod caput amputatum latumque in urbem
Poppaea vidit.

But the girl in her twentieth year surrounded by centurions and soldiers,
with the expectation of calamity and already void of life, nevertheless, was
not yet soothed by death. Ordered to die a few days later, she claimed that
she was not Nero's wife but only his sister and invoked their shared relatives,
the Germanici, and later even invoked the name of Agrippina, under whom
she was unharmed—certainly she had experienced an unhappy marriage
but it was without death. She was bound and the veins on each of her arms
were opened; but because she was overcome with fear, the blood flowed
slowly so she was suffocated by the steam of an exceedingly hot bath. An
even crueler savagery was added: her head was cut off and brought to Rome
for Poppaea to see.

The narrative is sympathetic to Octavia who is presented as a victim of an
unjust fate.[24] Although there are similarities in the description of her death
and that of Paulina's, Octavia emerges as a victim and not an opportununist:
she is a living corpse who is not yet comforted by the release of pain in death
and her suicide is slow due to fear retarding the flow of blood. She is then
placed in a bath, like Seneca, to ease the flow of blood. As soon as the narrative pronounces her dead, Octavia is decapitated (like a military enemy)
and the fickleness and insecurity of Poppaea further shock the reader. The
severed head alludes to the ritual of *ossilegium* in which a body part, normally
a finger, was cut before cremation and placed in an urn with the cremated
remains (see discussion below). Since Octavia's death is treated as an aver-
sion of a national disaster, her decapitation can also be read as a sacrificial
act to ensure the well-being of the emperor and the state. The text does not
indicate whether Octavia's head was rejoined with the rest of her body for
cremation.

The recounting of events in Octavia's life that precedes the description
of her death (14.63) serves as an epitaph (textual marker) in which Octavia
is contextualized as a victim and a corpse before her actual death, since her
wedding day was also the day of her funeral:

huic primum nuptiarum dies loco funeris fuit, deductae in domum in qua
nihil nisi luctuosum haberet, erepto per venenum patre et statim fratre;

tum ancilla domina validior et Poppaea non nisi in perniciem uxoris nupta, postremo crimen omni exitio gravius.

To Octavia the first day of her marriage was like a funeral, led into a home in which there was nothing but misery, with her father removed by poison and soon after her brother. A maid was more powerful than her mistress and after Poppaea's engagement, there was only misery for Nero's wife. Last, the charge [of sterility] was worse than all the ruin.

The severed narrative, the epitaphic summary of her life, and her description as a living corpse before her actual death reflect Octavia's decapitation. The allusions to and the corruption of funeral ritual make Octavia an even more sympathetic character whose narrative treatment contrasts with that of Paulina.

The digression on Paulina's suicide attempt interrupts the narrative of Seneca's suicide (*Ann.* 15.60–64), and therefore prolongs it.[25] Tacitus mocks the modeling of his suicide after Socrates' (Plato, *Phaedo* 117 ff.), especially the fact that Seneca had hemlock prepared beforehand as he quotes the Athenian practice of capital punishment:

Seneca, interim, durante tractu et lentitudine mortis, Statium Annaeum, diu sibi amicitiae fide et arte medicinae probatum, orat provisum pridem venenum quo damnati publico Atheniensium iudicio extinguerentur promeret; adlatumque hausit frustra, frigidus iam artus et cluso corpore adversum vim veneni. postremo stagnum calidae aquae introiit, respergens proximos servorum addita voce libare se liquorem illum Iovi liberatori. exim balneo inlatus et vapore eius exanimatus sine ullo funeris sollemni crematur. ita codicilis praescripserat, cum etiam tum praedives et praepotens supremis suis consuleret.

Seneca, meanwhile, since his death was drawn out and lingering, called for Statius Annaeus, a longtime friend of his and his doctor, and asked for the poison, previously prepared, that killed criminals in public trials at Athens which he gave. When it was given to him, he drank it to no avail, already his limbs were cold and not conducive to the force of the poison. At last, he entered a pool of hot water and sprinkling it onto the nearby slaves said that he was making a libation to Jupiter the Liberator. Then carried into the bath, he was suffocated by its steam and was cremated without a solemn funeral as he had specified in his will which contained his final instructions, written when he was wealthy and powerful. (*Ann.* 15.64)

The syntax participates in the comically lingering death of Seneca: the inclusion of *interim* within the clause denotes a return to the subject of Seneca's suicide following the digression on Paulina, but it also implies that the suicide was still in progress during the digression and while Paulina was enjoying her post-suicide reentry into society. Alliteration also calls attention to the repeated failed suicide attempts: *adlatumque hausis frustra, frigidus iam artus et cluso corpore adversum vim veneni*. Seneca's lingering death and the slow flow of blood from his aged body give connotations of greed and hypocrisy to his suicide.[26] Seneca is presented as a living corpse in death which complements the ambiguous mortality of Paulina who is a living corpse in life.

As a living corpse, Seneca's final actions take on added signficance: the bath is an evocation of the bathing of a corpse ritual (*lustratio*) which serves as a subsitution for it since it takes place immediately prior to his cremation. Seneca, as a living corpse, seems to imitate Pacuvius, the governor of Syria, whose behavior he condemned (*Ep.* 12.8–9), and thus now contradicts his own morality about playing dead. Even death does not seem to stop Seneca's loquacity: after noting that he was cremated without ceremony, Seneca's will is mentioned to keep him "talking" even after speech was no longer possible. The writing of the will at the height of his power contrasts with his pretentious desire for a philosopher's death, for which he planned a humble funeral in advance.[27]

The narrative of Seneca's suicide in Tacitus' *Annales* illustrates the pomposity and hypocrisy of Seneca by prolonging the narrative of his suicide with details of his quoting of Socrates' death, an account of his wife's contemporaneous suicide and digression on her subsequent survival, and his body's unresponsiveness to various forms of suicide. The clinging to life of both husband and wife can also be read as a cheating of death: Seneca and his body as an autonomous agent refuse to leave the pages of history quickly and Paulina's survival is presented as a moral crime to various people: to her dying husband who thought both were committing suicide together; to society which marks her deathly appearance; and even to Tacitus and the reader. Paulina's characterization changes from virtuous to amoral through the aesthetics of mortality and the reader's moral reception and interpretation of her actions affect how Seneca's suicide is read. Tacitus emerges as a dramatist/funeral director who stages Seneca's suicide and Paulina's survival as a tragicomedy that turns the reader into an audience member.

The following chapter explores playing dead further within the context of Seneca's *Troades* in which the theatricality of death ritual—the viewing/reading death ritual in a theater context—involves and expands on the relationship between the aesthetics of mortality and the aesthetics of morality as it relates to literary texts: in addition to a figurative visual referent to funerary ritual that calls the mortality and morality of a literary character into question, such as reported descriptions and actions in speeches, the dramatization of playing dead depends on physical referents that take on their own figurative interpretations.

CHAPTER 2

Staging Death

IN HIS description of Julius Caesar's funeral, Suetonius describes the populace's role in cremating Caesar's body that turned his funeral into theater spectacle:

Funere indicto rogus extructus est in Martio campo iuxta Iuliae tumulum et pro rostris aurata aedes ad simulacrum templi Veneris Genetricis collocata; intraque lectus eburneus auro ac purpura stratus et ad caput tropaeum cum veste, in qua fuerat occisus. Praeferentibus munera, quia suffecturus dies non videbatur, praeceptum, ut omisso ordine, quibus quisque vellet itineribus urbis, portaret in Campum. Inter ludos cantata sunt quaedam ad miserationem et invidiam caedis eius accommodata, ex Pacuvi Armorum iudicio:

> Men servasse, ut essent qui me perderent?

et ex Electra Atili ad similem sententiam. Laudationis loco consul Antonius per praeconem pronuntiavit senatus consultum, quo omnia simul ei divina atque humana decreverat, item ius iurandum, quo se cuncti pro salute unius astrinxerant; quibus perpauca a se verba addidit. Lectum pro rostris in Forum magistratus et honoribus functi detulerunt. Quem cum pars in Capitolini Iovis cella cremare pars in curia Pompei destinaret, repente duo quidam gladiis succincti ac bina iacula gestantes ardentibus cereis succenderunt confestimque circumstantium turba virgulta arida et cum subselliis tribunalia, quicquid praeterea ad donum aderat, congessit. Deinde tibicines et scaenici artifices vestem, quam ex triumphorum instrumento ad praesentem usum induerant. detractam sibi atque discissam iniecere flammae et

35

veteranorum militum legionarii arma sua, quibus exculti funus celebrant; matronae etiam pleraeque ornamenta sua, quae gerebant, et liberorum bullas atque praetextas.

In summo publico luctu exterarum gentium multitudo circulatim suo quaeque more lamentata est praecipueque Iudaei, qui etiam noctibus continuis bustum frequentarunt.

When the funeral was announced, a pyre was built in the Campus Martius near the tomb of Julia and on the rostra, a golden shrine modeled after the Temple of Venus Genetrix was placed; inside was an ivory couch covered in gold and purple and at the head was a trophy with the cloak in which he was killed. It was decreed for those bearing gifts, because a day was not considered sufficient time, to bring them to the Campus by whatever street in the city each person wished, regardless of rank or order. At the funeral games, certain lines from Pacuvius' *Contest of Arms* were sung to arouse pity and resentment of his murder:

Did I save them so that they might destroy me?

and similar sentiments from Atilius' *Electra*. In the place of a eulogy, the consul Antonius recited the Senate's decree in which he was given all divine and human honors at once and also the oath sworn by which they bound themselves for the sake of his safety; to which he added a few words of his own. Magistrates and ex-magistrates carried his bier down from the rostra into the forum. Some wanted to cremate him in the cella of the Temple of Jupiter but others in the Curia of Pompey, when suddenly, two men armed with swords and carrying two javelins of burning wax set fire to it and immediately the crowd of bystanders piled dry twigs, even the seats from the tribune and whatever else was available as an offering. Next the musicians and actors tore off the robes taken from the items of his triumph and worn for the occasion, shred them and threw them on the fire and veterans of the legions their own armor which they had worn for the funeral; and many matrons threw the jewelry that they were wearing, even the amulets and robes of their children.

At the height of the public mourning a group of foreigners went around and lamented according to their own customs, especially Jews who crowded around his pyre for several nights in a row. (*Divus Iulius,* 84.1–5)[1]

The placement of Caesar's body next to a model of the Temple of Venus Genetrix (Suetonius' text is not clear on the exact location of the bier in relation to the shrine even though both were on the rostra) would effectively exploit propaganda claims connecting the Iulii with Venus and serve as a symbolic evocation of a burial in which mother earth receives her children.

The presence of the cloak that Caesar was wearing when he was murdered inside the shrine that was itelf an evocation of a divine space would also imply divine associations.[2] The various routes taken by the mourners to participate in Caesar's funeral point to the absence of a *pompa* which would have given Caesar further opportunity to advertise his illustrious family ancestry.

Suetonius' narrative gives the impression of a sequential listing of elements that focuses on the extempore actions of the participants.[3] If this account can be trusted, the public's role in changing the script of the funeral is remarkable: from cremating the remains of Caesar in the Roman Forum rather than the intended location of the Campus Martius next to the tomb of Caesar's daughter Julia or the impromptu locations suggested by the populace, the Capitoline Hill or the Curia of Pompey. The details concerning funeral games that preceded Caesar's cremation and popular quotations from tragedies show the populace's increasing role in theatricalizing the funeral even before actors and musicians threw costumes and instruments onto Caesar's impromptu pyre. If these actors were the same mimes who dressed in the robes representing four of Caesar's five triumphs during his *pompa*, then all five Caesars (including the actual Caesar) would have departed from the funeral site at the same time, and thus turned the cremation into the end of an act or script. Mourners who became spectators at the *ludi* and *laudatio* made themselves dramatists by changing the script of the funeral and now have become cremators/pyre technicians as actors themselves break the illusion of imitation by burning symbols that had temporarily transformed them into Caesar and now return to their former identities as Caesar's corpse burns.[4]

When Suetonius mentions public concern over where to cremate Caesar's body, before deciding to burn it in the Forum (Appian, *BC* 2.147 claims the populace burned the Senate house rather than the Curia of Pompey, which was the site of Caesar's assassination), he does not refer to the extraordinary claim made by Cicero, not mentioned elsewhere in his corpus and uncorroborated by other contemporary sources, that Caesar's cremation was only half-completed.[5] Even if Cicero's claim is false, it is nonetheless effective as invective: it suggests that Caesar's journey to the afterlife (before apotheosis?) would be interupted and that Caesar's corpse may revisit the living as a ghost.[6] The detail that Jews visited Caesar's *bustum*, however, suggests that the pyre burned Caesar's corpse completely and that the remnants of the burned-out pyre were still in public view.

Appian, in his *Bellum Civile*, preserves remarkable details about Caesar's funeral that connect elements of the funeral with theater spectacle more explicitly than Suetonius: Mark Antony bowed in a theatrical way and invoked the gods repeatedly before the bier in imitation of theater gestures (2.146); Caesar's corpse was dramatically unveiled by Mark Antony on the Rostra during the course of the *laudatio* and Caesar's torn and bloody robe was shown to the audience which mourned like a tragic chorus (2.146); someone, who spoke as though Caesar, listed Caesar's enemies and the benefits given to each (2.146) and who quoted from Pacuvius' tragedy as in Suetonius, seems to refer to one of the four mimes dressed in Caesar's triumphal robes.[7]

The most theatrical element was a wax likeness of Caesar complete with twenty-three bloody stab wounds to reflect the condition of his body at the time of his murder, which was raised above Caesar's bier (his body was not visible but covered) and then placed on a mechanical device that repeatedly rotated it before the entire audience (2.147):

> While they [populace] were roused and close to violence, someone raised an image of Caesar himself, made of wax, above his bier. The body as it lay on its back on the couch, was not visible. The image was turned around in every direction from a mechanical device and showed the twenty-three wounds on his entire body and on his face which had been viciously given to him. The populace could no longer bear the pitiful sight shown to them but groaned and girded themselves. They burned the senate where Caesar was killed and they searched for the murderers who had fled earlier, running here and there. They were so maddened by rage and grief, that they brutally tore to pieces Cinna the tribune from the similarity of his name with Cinna the praetor, who had publicly spoken against Caesar, not waiting to hear about the similarity of his name, and no part of him remained for burial. They carried fire to the houses of the others but their household bravely resisted them and neighbors restrained them; they checked their fires but threatened to return the next day with arms.[8]

In Appian's narrative, albeit a later source, Antony is both actor and dramatist who directs the mourners to assume the roles of actors before the wax image of Caesar literally takes over the spectacle: the mourners' role playing contrasts with the populace's assumption of these roles on their own accord in Suetonius' narrative (*Divus Iulius,* 84.1–5). The identity of the mourner who raised the image is not given but, like a marionette operator whose identity is concealed from the audience, he makes the actions of the effigy seem to be acting on its own accord as a self-representational character, even after it is placed on the spinning wheel and rotating like an automaton.[9] Caesar's actual corpse has been replaced by his wax image that represents his body in its murdered state which turns the funeral (already theatricalized) into an actual spectacle that evokes the ending of a tragedy with Caesar, soon to be cremated, appearing at his own funeral as though a *deus ex machina* and underscored by the actual rotating *machina*.[10]

The figurative effectiveness of the mechanized device is ambiguous from a dramaturgical perspective: while the device may provide dramatic closure in the theater, it may be seen as performing an opposite function at Caesar's funeral—it was used to turn Caesar, the soon to be cremated corpse, back into Caesar the murder victim—a temporal shift that would remind mourners of his murder but a prop that figuratively competed with Caesar's actual corpse. This temporal shift is also paradoxical in terms of Caesar's deification—the representation of his bloody murdered corpse as evidence of his mortality contrasts with the amorality of his killers (as interpreted by the populace) and with the divine implications of the bier's setting within a model of the Temple of Venus (Suetonius, *Divus Iulius* 84.1), but the paradox also points to Caesar's success: metamorphosis from human to god through funerary ritual that anticipates his actual deification two years later in 42 BCE.[11]

The wax image was created before the funeral, but its appearance at the funeral was made to look impromptu and unscripted and took on an identity of its own as a self-representational corpse in its own fatal charade of dramatized executions within and as theater spectacle.[12] If the intended purpose of the wax image was to relive and dramatize Caesar's murder with a wax image of his murdered corpse in front of Caesar's actual murdered corpse, there was the danger that the significance of either or both Caesars would be interpreted variously: as a punishment against Caesar in an evocation of a dramatized execution of a criminal, but whose performance comes after death and not preceding it, or, as was case, the focus of the public's sympathy in order to incite mourners to exact revenge against Caesar's assassins.[13] The mourners' memory of Caesar's murder (and his murdered body) vies with the theatricalized staging of his funeral (of his actual body and the wax image) which the populace is experiencing as mourners, viewing as spectators, and participating in as impromptu organizers. The wax image extends the theatricality of the funeral and serves as a cathartic device (like the bloody cloak held up by Mark Antony) that reopens the tragedy of Caesar's murder rather than closes the funeral of Caesar. The dramatizing of death ritual leads to an actor/audience dynamic that turns a funeral into a theater experience (like Caesar's funeral) or else turns a theater experience into a funeral with the actual dead performing at their own funeral (on bier/stage), and the figurative dead on stage, participating in dramas, or in the audience—actors imitating the deceased or his ancestors. The theater is not just an element of funerals but rather the cultural intertext of the ritual mourning and disposal processes.

This chapter focuses on the (meta)theatricality and theatricalization of death ritual, in particular the semiotic and moral implications of playing dead on stage ("Playing Dead in Seneca's *Troades*" and "Death Ritual as Spectacle within a Play"); death ritual as performance text in Seneca's *Phaedra* ("Reassembling the Dead"); and funerals from a theater/performance perspective: in which a funeral becomes a theater of the dead ("A Cast of Corpses") with a reviving of the dead at their own funeral, in the audience and possibly on-stage which blurs the distinction between the living and the dead. This blurring of life and death and the living and the dead in literary and dramatic texts assaults the metaphysical world of the reader/audience who (un)conciously extends the metaphor of playing dead as mourner/actor. Therefore, there is a reciprocal theatricality between stage and audience and between deceased and mourner and funeral ritual and the allusion/inclusion of funerary ritual on stage.

Playing Dead in Seneca's *Troades*

The *Troades* of Seneca is set among the smoldering ruins of Troy as the Trojan women await the results of an allotment that will determine their new Greek masters. Against this backdrop the Greeks effect the murder of Andromache's son Astyanax and the slaughter of Polyxena on the tomb of Achilles. The play opens with Hecuba and the Chorus mourning the dead following the destruction of Troy in a dramatic reenactment of a *conclamatio* which is normally delivered over the corpse (thus signaling from the beginning the inclusion/allusion to funerary/death ritual within the play). They weep for those already dead, especially Priam and Hector, but they also anticipate the deaths of Polyxena and Astyanax and future grieving for their deaths. We have closure and nonclosure at the play's beginning that reflects an ongoing theme of the play that suffering continues, in life and in death, but the play is about more than mourning the dead. When Andromache buries Astyanax alive in Hector's tomb in Act 3, Astyanax plays dead to avoid being caught by the Greeks.[14] The scene is pivotal to the play since Astyanax's death is demanded by Calchas with the sacrifice of Polyxena on Achilles' tomb. Emphasis on Astyanax serves as a paradigm to the events that lead up to the sacrifice of Polyxena later in the play. Astyanax does not imitate a corpse once within the tomb, but his entry and hiding inside the tomb represent a figurative burial and his metaphorical death.

The *Troades* presents literally and figuratively the ambiguity between the living and the dead: Andromache self-identifies with the dead Hector; Astyanax plays dead when he is buried alive in Hector's tomb; Polyxena's wedding day is also her funeral as she herself becomes a funeral offering to Achilles' shade in the theatricalized setting of Achilles' tomb. The living define what it means to be dead and how to dispose remains properly, but when the actions of the living are seen to imitate the actions of those disposing of the dead and the dead themselves, a social construct becomes a figurative one.

(Theater) aesthetics of morality underlie both the actions of characters and the audience's interpretation of their actions, and they also affect the visual referents of the play: Hector's tomb and Andromache's imitation/ evocation of funeral ritual situate the moral dilemmas within the text/stage scenery (whether actual or figurative) of Act 3. For example, Andromache's stage movements as she paces in front of Hector's tomb out of anxiety over whether the Greeks will find Astyanax and whether Hector's tomb was the best place to hide her son, reflect her inner torment and call attention to the tomb—Andromache's moral dilemma focuses the audience/reader's eyes on the tomb which is the aesthetic focal point of the scene and evokes the following questions: is it wrong for Andromache to use her husband's tomb as a hiding place for her son? To what extent are the affections and duties owed to the dead more important than those owed to the living and further complicated when the living are united with the dead? These questions are not limited to the stage since actors and the audience share the same meta-physical/figurative space, and the audience members/readers participate in funeral ritual by virtue of the viewing/reading process that turn them into mourners even if they do not wish to participate.

I would like to focus on Acts 3 and 5—how a dramatic text imitates funerary rituals practiced by the audience and the metatheatrical implications of the text and the theatricality of death ritual; in particular, how the living play dead and the dramatic implications of including funerary ritual, especially the tombs of Hector and Achilles both within the play and as a play within the play.[15] As he does in the *Phaedra*, Seneca evokes the pathos of the audience through death ritual: sympathy for a mother and her young son, especially in the presence of and within Hector's tomb. The sacrifice of Polyxena (as a form of funeral ritual/corruption of wedding ritual) shocks the play's characters (Agamemnon: *quis iste mos est? quando in inferias homo est / impensus hominis?* 298–99) and audience for its corruption of funeral customs.

The topography of death is also important in the play: the tomb of Hector is at once a representation and a metaphor of a tomb that provides an

aesthetic focal point for the audience in the theater to interpret the actions
of the characters on stage. When Andromache buries Astyanax alive, literally
and figuratively the audience questions the metaphorical boundaries separating the living from the dead and the morality of playing dead. Since the
audience/reader or even the other characters cannot tell whether the character is alive or dead or, if the audience/reader does know and other characters
do not, then dramatic tension/irony arises. Approaching the *Troades* from a
semiotic perspective is appropriate since the term is derived from the Greek
word for a grave, a *sema,* which marks and represents a burial; therefore, the
approach allows for a figurative reading of drama and a figurative staging
of drama, which in the case of the *Troades* is dramatized by Hector's and
Achilles' tombs.

Hector's tomb dominates Act 3 as a visual referent as much as the tower
of Troy and Achilles' tomb serve as the figurative focus in Act 5. Andromache
describes the tomb as imposing and eerie:

> est tumulus ingens coniugis cari sacer,
> verendus hosti, mole quem immensa parens
> opibusque magnis struxit, in luctus suos
> rex non avarus: optime credam patri—
> sudor per artus frigidus totos cadit:
> omen tremesco misera feralis loci.

> There is the burial mound of my dear husband, sacred
> and revered by the enemy, a huge mound his father
> built at great expense, even in his grief, the king
> was not sparing: it is best for his father to safeguard him—
> a cold sweat has brokken out over my whole body:
> in misery, I tremble at the omen of this funereal place. (483–88).[16]

The audience/reader's first introduction to the tomb is on its appearance
and the great cost to Priam to build it. The appearance of the tomb should
be definitive (physically) on stage, even if a doorway represents an entrance
to the tomb; stage directions call for an actual tomb, but the ever-changing
description of the tomb within the text (figurative) requires the audience to
look at the tomb on stage but to imagine various altered stages of its appearance throughout the play. Seneca uses a variety of terms such as *bustum,
tumulus, sepulcrum,* and *pyra* interchangeably throughout the play to refer
to Hector's (and Achilles') burial mound/tomb. Technically, the terms are
not interchangeable but, as with Vergil's adaptation of funerary customs and

use of bucolic language to describe the bier of Pallas (chapter 3), Seneca uses technical language for figurative effect: the tomb's appearance and its state of completion and/or destruction change before our eyes since Hector's pyre would have been burned, covered by a *tumulus* which contained *sepulcra,* and then the location marked by a grave. The effect is to have Hector's tomb constantly burned, built, and rebuilt in random figurative reconstructions as the actual tomb represented on stage does not change.

The shifting language to describe the tomb and its figuratively changing appearance also reflect Andromache's psychological state as she confuses the dead with the living (including herself: when she self-identifies with the dead Hector who appeared to her in a dream looking like her, therefore she, too, plays dead as though a living corpse). Andromache distorts details of the tomb's appearance as she constantly reflects and relives details of Hector's cremation: when deciding where to hide Astyanax, she refers to Hector's tomb as a *tumulus* and *sanctas parentis conditi sedes* which will become the future *sepulcrum* of her son should he be caught by the Greeks:

> Quis te locus, quae regio seducta, invia
> tuto reponet? quis feret trepidis opem?
> quis proteget? qui semper, etiamnunc tuos,
> Hector, tuere: coniugis furtum piae
> serva et fideli cinere victurum excipe.
> succede tumulo, nate—quid retro fugis?
> turpesne latebras spernis? agnosco indolem:
> pudet timere. spiritus magnos fuga
> animosque veteres, sume quos casus dedit.
> en intuere, turba quae simus super:
> tumulus, puer, captiva: cedendum est malis.
> sanctas parentis conditi sedes age
> aude subire. fata si miseros iuvant,
> habes salutem; fata si vitam negant,
> habes sepulcrum.

> What place, what location off the beaten track
> will keep you safe? Who will bring aid to the frightened?
> Who will give protection? You, as always, Hector,
> even now, watch over your loved ones: protect the
> theft of your faithful wife and welcome him in your
> protective ash so he may live.
> Go into the burial mound, son—why do you turn back?

Do you shun cowardly hiding places? I recognize your
character: to show fear is shameful. Let go of your
great pride and former attitudes, accept those that ruin
has given. Look, what a group of survivors we are:
a burial mound, a boy, a captive: we must accept misfortune.
Go, be brave to enter the sacred place of your buried father.
If the fates help those in need, you have safety;
if the fates deny you life, you have a tomb. (498–512)

Later, Andromache refers to the tomb as *bustum* (689), thus recalling an
earlier aspect of Hector's cremation in her confusion and casting into doubt
whether she is accurately seeing/interpreting events in the present. The
anachronistic reference also symbolizes the moral ambiguity of her decisions
and the ambiguous role it plays in both preserving and betraying Astyanax.
From a linguistic perspective, the tomb also represents the departed Hector:
Andromache blocks out the scene in line 508 and prioritizes the lives of her
family and herself: *tumulus, puer, captiva.* The *tumulus* stands for Hector by
metonymy and the present configuration of the family points to their collective inability to mount any defense.

The tomb stands by metonymy for Hector, but it never does so for
Astyanax: it is not his tomb but rather he is temporarily occupying Hector's
final resting place. Although playing dead, Astyanax is a visitor and not a
resident of the tomb.[17] From a semiotic perspective, however, the metonymy
of tomb equals Hector leads to confusion over the identity of Hector and the
relation of father to son. Since Andromache equates Astyanax with Hector at
659 (*utrimque est Hector*) in her debate over saving husband or son, there are
two Hectors in the same tomb at the same time, one dead, the other alive
playing dead in imitation of his father. The fact that Andromache cannot
distinguish between the two Hectors further accounts for her anguish and
confusion between a husband who is at once dead and alive and a son who
is at once alive and dead:[18]

Quid agimus? animum distrahit geminus timor:
hinc natus, illinc coniugis cari cinis.
pars utra vincet? testor immites deos,
deosque veros coniugis manes mei:
non aliud, Hector, in meo nato mihi
placere quam te. vivat, ut possit tuos
referre vultus. —prorutus tumulo cinis
mergetur? ossa fluctibus spargi sinam
disiecta vastis? potius hic mortem oppetat.—

poteris nefandae deditum mater neci
videre, poteris celsa per fastigia
missum rotari? potero, perpetiar, feram,
dum non meus post fata victoris manu
iactetur Hector. —hic suam poenam potest
sentire, at illum fata iam in tuto locant.
quid fluctuaris? statue, quem poenae extrahas.
ingrata, dubitas? Hector est illinc tuus —
erras, utrimque est Hector: hic sensus potens,
forsan futurus ultor extincti patris —
utrique parci non potest: quidnam facis?
serva e duobus, anime, quem Danai timent.

What am I doing? Twin fears tear my mind:
from this side my son, from the other, the ashes of my
dear husband. Which side will win?
I call the merciless gods to witness and the true
gods, the shades of my husband: nothing is more
pleasing, Hector, than you living on in my son.
He should live so that he may recall your features.
But, let the ashes fall, thrown from the burial mound?
Should I allow his bones to be scattered, spread over
the rough waves? Let this one seek his death, instead.
Can you, his mother, see him given over to an
unspeakable death, can you send him tumbling
from the high walls? I will be able to, I will bear it,
and I will endure it as long as my Hector is not hurled
about after death by the victor's hand. The one can
feel pain, but death keeps the other in a safe place.
Why do you waver? Decide, which one you will
extract from injury. Ungrateful woman, do you
hesitate? Your Hector is here, no, you are wrong,
Hector is on both sides: this one controls his
senses and may be the future avenger of his dead
father. Both cannot be spared: what are you doing?
Of the two, my heart, save the one whom the
Danaans fear. (642–62)

Afterward, when Ulysses threatens to destroy Hector's tomb, Andromache distinguishes father from son only after contemplating a mixing of Astyanax's corpse with Hector's cremation remains. Andromache, however, still equates

the tomb with Hector since she is afraid that Hector would be responsible
for their son's death if he is crushed by the tomb:

> Quid agis? ruina mater et natum et virum
> prosternis una? forsitan Danaos prece
> placare poteris. conditum elidet statim
> immane busti pondus: intereat miser
> ubicumque potius, ne pater natum obruat
> prematque patrem natus.

> What are you doing? In a single ruin, you, a
> mother, are scattering both son and husband.
> Perhaps you can win over the Danaans through entreaty?
> Right away the huge weight of the mound will
> press out the one hiding: let the poor boy die
> somewhere else, it is better, so that father does
> not destroy son or son crush father. (686–91)

When Andromache buries Astyanax alive, she is the metaphorical cause of
his pretended death but later, she is literally responsible for his actual death
when she hands her son over to Ulysses to be killed. Earlier in the play, upon
hearing of Achilles' ghost, Andromache had asked whether Greeks alone
could return from the underworld, but now she proves that she, too, can do
the same since she delivers/summons Astyanax back to life from the tomb.
But he will soon "return" to death because of her actions. Andromache, on a
figurative level, is the source of life and death for her son but not just once:
she has twice given birth to Astyanax and has twice acted as agent for his
death. Thus, the tomb, which is the final resting place and symbol of Hector
(and the temporary tomb of Astyanax), is also a metaphor for Andromache's
womb as she "delivers" Astyanax to the world for a second time when she
hands him over to Ulysses.[19]

The womb is also a symbol of female trickery and Andromache's choice
of Hector's tomb to hide her son strengthens the metaphor of tomb as
womb for her hiding and delivering of Astyanax. Unfortunately, Andromache, despite her deception, is outwitted by an even more sly Ulysses who
employs the tricks of a *servus callidus* in Roman comedy. It is ironic that
later in the play, Andromache wonders who will bury her son's remains (*quis
tuos artus teget / tumuloque tradet?* 1109–1110) and this question is at once
a sign of her helplessness and a declaration of her severed connection with
her son's birth and death cycle.

Since Astyanax is not killed until Act 5, his absence on stage is obscured by the arrival of Helen in Act 4 and the role she plays in initiating the sacrifice of Polyxena. The two plots are intertwined and resolved in Act 5 as a messenger reports their respective deaths to two audiences: the characters on stage and the audience in the theater who hear of the behavior and reactions of the crowds who witness the deaths of Astyanax and Polyxena. Crowds gathered to witness Astyanax' death become spectators as he is hurled from a tower, especially the *ferus spectator* who views his suicide atop Hector's tomb. Nature aids in providing sight lines to the spectacle:

> haec nota quondam turris et muri decus,
> nunc saeva cautes, undique adfusa ducum
> plebisque turba cingitur; totum coit
> ratibus relictis vulgus. his collis procul
> aciem patenti liberam praebet loco,
> his alta rupes, cuius in cacumine
> erecta summos turba libravit pedes.
> hunc pinus, illum laurus, hunc fagus gerit
> et tota populo silva suspenso tremit.
> extrema montis ille praerupti petit,
> semusta at ille tecta vel saxum imminens
> muri cadentis pressit, atque aliquis (nefas)
> tumulo ferus spectator Hectoreo sedet.

> This tower, once well known and the glory of the walls,
> now a jagged crag, from all sides, was encircled by a gathering
> crowd of leaders and people. Leaving their ships,
> the whole host assembled. A distant hill gave a clear view to some,
> to others, a high cliff, on whose peak, a crowd stood on the tips of their
>   toes.
> A pine tree bore one man, a laurel someone else, and a beech yet another;
> the whole forest nods with the suspended crowd.
> One man sought out the top of a rocky hill,
> but another stood on a burnt rooftop or even hung from part of a fallen
>   wall
> and—shocking!—a heartless spectator sat on Hector's tomb.
>   (1075–87)

Astyanax' death is a spectacle to the audience in the text and Seneca's audience/reader. The audience in the text also becomes the second focus of the audience/reader who watch them watching Astyanax. By leaping to his death on his own accord while Ulysses was still uttering prayers for his sacrifice, Astyanax emerges as the principal actor and focus of both audiences[20]:

> Per spatia late plena sublimi gradu
> incedit Ithacus parvulum dextra trahens
> Priami nepotem, nec gradu segni puer
> ad alta pergit moenia. ut summa stetit
> pro turre, vultus huc et huc acres tulit
> intrepidus animo. qualis ingentis ferae
> parvus tenerque fetus et nondum potens
> saevire dente iam tamen tollit minas
> morsusque inanes temptat atque animis tumet:
> sic ille dextra prensus hostili puer
> ferox superbit. moverat vulgum ac duces
> ipsumque Ulixem. non flet e turba omnium
> qui fletur; ac, dum verba fatidici et preces
> concipit Ulixes vatis et saevos ciet
> ad sacra superos, sponte desiluit sua
> in media Priami regna.

> Through this crowded space, with an arrogant step,
> the Ithacan walked dragging the tiny grandson of Priam
> with his right hand, nor with a hesitant step did the boy
> approach the high walls. As he stood on the
> tower's height, he bore a determined expression, here and there,
> courageous in spirit. Just as when a tiny and tender cub of a great
> beast, not yet strong enough to frighten with his teeth,
> nevertheless still rears up menacingly, tries useless bites, and
> swells with courage, so the boy, gripped by the enemy's hand,
> was fierce in his pride and moved the crowd, the leaders,
> and even Ulysses. He alone did not weep, in a crowd that wept for him.
> While Ulysses uttered the words and prayers of the
> fate-revealing prophet and invited the savage gods to the rites,
> freely, he leapt down into Priam's kingdom. (1088–1103)

Astyanax leaps (*desiluit*) and lands in the middle of Priam's kingdom, which is his by birthright but is now destroyed and, by his own choice and suicide, the home of his own destroyed body. From a dramaturgical perspective,

Astyanax changes the performance text of the characters performing the sacrifice (i.e., Seneca's dramatic text), as it were, and his unscripted suicide that spoils the ritual calls into question the unnaturalness of the sacrifice and frustrates Ulysses' role as sacrificer/priest.

Astyanax chooses death over life for himself rather than depend on his mother to make the choice for him, but he does not emerge from his suicide outside of his father's shadow (or the shadow of Hector's tomb) since, even in the mangled state of his body which the Messenger describes at 1110–1117: *iacet / deforme corpus /* "he lies a corpse without shape," 1116–17, Andromache responds, in a statement that completes line 1117, that Astyanax still looks like his father: *Sic quoque est similis patri /* "In this, too, he is like his father," 1117. The two speeches which share the same metrical line form an impromptu epitaph for Astyanax, since the "text" (*iacet; similis patri*) evokes the language of epitaphs, but sympathy gives way to tension: Andromache's comparison of the mangled body of her son with the corpse of her husband shows the continuation of her prioritizing of father over son and a certain impropriety of tone for the witticism of her remark.[21] Thus, both inside and outside of the tomb, in life and in death, Astyanax resembles his father.

Hector's tomb as a symbol for Andromache's womb, however, has been negated by Astyanax' actual death: while the text gives no explicit directions for his burial, it is clear from Andromache's speech asking who will bury her son, that she will not follow up on her figurative burial of her son with the actual burial of his corpse. The mother who tried to save her son, but who ultimately gave priority to her husband, will not grieve over her son's remains or bury him but rather will remain, as a widow and childless, permanently separated from both son and the tomb of her husband.[22] This lack of ritual finality in Seneca's text is all the more evident when one compares the explicit burial of Astyanax in Euripides' *Troades*. Not only does Hecuba give Astyanax an epitaph (1190), but he also receives a funeral on stage (1207). Therefore, Seneca makes significant changes to Euripides' treatment of Astyanax's corpse to emphasize lack of closure through death ritual and to connect Astyanax's death with Polyxena's.

Death Ritual as Spectacle within a Play

The deaths of Astyanax and Polyxena are reported by the same Messenger and linked within the same sentence between the walls of Troy from which Astyanax fell and the tomb of Achilles on which Polyxena is sacrificed. They are furthermore viewed in succession by the same gazing audience, thus turning the two deaths into a double spectacle:[23]

> Praeceps ut altis cecidit e muris puer,
> flevitque Achivum turba quod fecit nefas,
> idem ille populus aliud ad facinus redit
> tumulumque Achillis. cuius extremum latus
> Rhoetea leni verberant fluctu vada;
> adversa cingit campus, et clivo levi
> erecta medium vallis includens locum
> crescit theatri more. hi classis moras
> hac morte solvi rentur, hi stirpem hostium
> gaudent recidi; magna pars vulgi levis
> odit scelus spectatque. nec Troes minus
> suum frequentant funus et pavidi metu
> partem ruentis ultimam Troiae vident.

> Soon after the boy fell from the high walls
> and the Achaean crowd wept for a crime of its own doing,
> that same crowd turned to another crime and the
> tomb of Achilles. The waters of Rhoeteum beat
> against the far side of the tomb with a gentle wave;
> A plain faces the other side where a high bank,
> enclosing a central area, rises with a gradual slope
> just like a theater. The assembled crowd
> filled the entire shore. Some thought that the cause of
> the fleet's delay was removed by this death; others
> were glad that the offspring of the enemy was cut down.
> A great part of the fickle mob hated the crime and
> watched it. In no lesser number did the Trojans
> attend their own funeral and, shaking with fear,
> witnessed the final act of Troy's fall. (1118–31).

Like Hector's tomb, Achilles' tomb is the focal point of the audience's gaze in the text (of both Greeks and Trojans), but whereas Hector's tomb was physical, Achilles' tomb is figurative since its description is reported to the audience which does not see it on stage.[24] The contrast between the tombs, however, may be difficult to make if Hector's tomb is visible on stage or represented by a doorway, throughout the whole play, as the audience imagines Achilles' tomb. From the point of view of the aesthetics of morality, however, the tombs are different: Achilles' tomb is the site of crime and of ritual corruption and contrasts with Hector's tomb which was nurturing to Astyanax.

Whereas nature provided sight lines to the spectacle of Asytanax's suicide, the natural setting of the tomb is described in terms that evoke the architecture of a theater: one side is lashed by Rhoetus' waters and the other side faces a "valley theater" (1124–26). Achilles' tomb, therefore, is a metaphorical stage that competes with the fictional or dramatic reality of the text as witnesses become spectators/voyeurs of Polyxena's murder, drawn and repelled by her sacrifice: *magna pars vulgi levis / odit scelus spectatque* (1128–29).[25] As the theater's *cavea*, nature, too, is a spectator as she was in Astyanax's death. Polyxena's sacrifice is the final act viewed by the spectators (*partem ruentis ultimam Troiae vident,* 1131), within the final act of the play, therefore, theater competes with theater: the spectacle of Polyxena's suicide, death ritual as performance text, competes with the *Troades* for the same audience—the spectators to the two deaths within the play and the audience in the theater.[26] Death ritual as theater becomes metatheater in which actors represent themselves and defy their dramatic texts to produce new performance texts.[27]

Polyxena's wedding day is also the day of her own funeral as she literally and figuratively becomes a funereal offering to Achilles' tomb (which equals Achilles by metonymy) and the episode of her death forms a play within a play.[28] Andromache's comparison of the nuptials to a funeral (898–902)[29] is realized as Helen accompanies Polyxena to Achilles' tomb as her bridesmaid (*pronuba,* 1133).[30] Polyxena's wedding/funeral is described as a *sacrum* (1162) which emphasizes the enormity of the crime:

> Ut primum ardui
> sublime montis tetigit, atque alte edito
> iuvenis paterni vertice in busti stetit,
> audax virago non tulit retro gradum;
> conversa ad ictum stat truci vultu ferox.
> tam fortis animus omnium mentes ferit,
> novumque monstrum est Pyrrhus ad caedem piger.
> ut dextra ferrum penitus exactum abdidit,
> subitus recepta morte prorupit cruor
> per vulnus ingens. nec tamen moriens adhuc
> deponit animos: cecidit, ut Achilli gravem
> factura terram, prona et irato impetu.
> uterque flevit coetus—et timidum Phryges

misere gemitum, clarius victor gemit.
hic ordo sacri. non stetit fusus cruor
humove summa fluxit: obduxit statim
saevusque totum sanguinem tumulus bibit.

As soon as she reached the peak of the
steep hill, and the young man stood on the raised
top of his father's mound, the bold girl did not take a
step backward: fiercely, she faced the blow with
a defiant expression. Such a brave spirit moved the
minds of all—and then this strange portent: Pyrrhus
slow to slaughter. When his hand buried the
sharp sword deep into her, she received death and
blood quickly gushed out of a huge wound.
Even in death, however, she did not abandon her
courage. She lunged forward with an angry force to
make the earth heavy for Achilles.
Both sides wept, but while the Phrygians raised
timid groans, the victor groaned aloud.
This was the order of the ritual. The spilt blood
did not pool on the surface—right away the
savage mound sucked and drank all of it. (1148–64)

The emphasis on the tomb's height (described as high as a *mons* at 1149) draws a parallel to the tower from which Astyanax hurled himself, and serves as another linking device between the two deaths as Polyxena, in death, hurls her body violently against the ground to make the ground *gravem* for Achilles in a reversal of the traditional *sit tibi terra levis* wish common on epitaphs. There are no explicit directions for her funeral; therefore, both character and reader are denied ritual closure to such a violent and untimely death.

Further parallels between Polyxena and Astyanax suggest that she is "acting" like him and turning the spectacle of her wedding/funeral into a restaged production of Astyanax's death: she is described as an *audax virago* (1151), a term used to describe a girl with masculine qualities (earlier she was described as a *virgo* by the Messenger at 1063), and, like Astyanax (*ferox,* 1098), her face bears a fierce expression as she willingly approaches her death.[31] After Polyxena's death, however, there is a paradigm shift as she abandons her role as a second Astyanax and takes her cue from the young Tantalus in the *Thyestes,* who hurls his headless trunk angrily against his uncle Atreus who murdered him: [. . .] *educto stetit / ferro cadaver,*

cumque dubitasset diu / hac parte an illa caderet, in patruum cadit. / "When
the sword was pulled out, the corpse stood, as though he was hesitating for
a long time, in which direction to fall, and fell onto his uncle," 723–25.[32]
The emphasis on the young Tantalus' long indecision, as though his corpse
were tottering, now this way, now that, injects a tone of absurdity absent
in Polyxena's imitation of the same gesture. Polyxena, therefore, continues
to act in her play within a play and to defy the dramatic text and her role
within it, by continuing to communicate with other characters and the
audience even after her death (as does the personification of Achilles' tomb
which sucks her blood in disturbing imitation of a sacrificial grave offering),
and by alluding to the actions of a character from another play, thereby, like
Astyanax, producing a new performance text.[33] Polyxena as an actor within
the drama/spectacle of her own sacrifice further points to theater competing
with theater.[34]

Thus, Seneca presents death ritual as theater by dramatizing and alluding
to death ritual on stage. The result is a play in which death ritual as metatheater alters the dramatic text to create a new performance text: characters act
out their deaths in death ritual settings even as they continue to affect, even
in death, the text and tragic paradigms. The effect of this theatricalized ritual
on the audience within the *Troades* and the audience reading/watching the
play is to turn both into voyeuristic witnesses to the deaths of Astyanax and
Polyxena. The aesthetics of morality are also important to both the audience
on stage and the audience in the *cavea:* the tombs of Achilles and Hector
dominate the stage and serve important figurative roles at key moments in
the play as mourning for the dead becomes part of the theater experience.
The *Troades,* therefore, shares similarities with other texts examined thus far
that focus on playing dead: the untimely corpse and the living corpse in literary texts evoke yet challenge the audience's distinction between the living
and the dead and the moral implications of a character playing dead.

Reassembling the Dead

What are the metatheatrical implications, however, of incorporating a corpse
within the dramatic action of a play on stage? Like the *Troades,* the *Phaedra*
incorporates death ritual as a final act within the final act of the play. But,
whereas the Messenger in the *Troades* reports the description of Astyanax'
mangled corpse (1116–17), no explicit indications are given in the text
that the remains are collected, cremated, and buried.[35] The *Phaedra* goes
further in staging the metatheatricality of funeral ritual by incorporating

Hippolytus' corpse with the dramatic action of the play. As Theseus looks on the remains of his son (Andromache did not), collects and reassembles the mangled bits of Hippolytus' body, he laments:

> durate trepidae lugubri officio manus,
> fletusque largos sistite arentes genae,
> dum membra nato genitor adnumerat suo
> corpusque fingit. hoc quid est forma carens
> et turpe, multo vulnere abrumptum undique?
> quae pars tui sit dubito; sed pars est tui:
> hic, hic repone, non suo, at vacuo loco.

> Shaking hands, be steady for this funereal duty,
> and cheeks, dry up your tears,
> while a father collects the limbs of his own son and
> reassembles his body. What piece is this lacking shape,
> horrible, and ripped from all sides with many wounds?
> What part of you it is, I do not know, but it is a part of you:
> here, place it here, not the right place but one that is empty. (1262–68)[36]

Theseus performs for an audience/reader who sees him reassembling his son (before, not after cremation), but the meaning of the gesture depends on audience experience with the play's funerary and literary intertexts. By collecting the random remains of his son, Theseus participates in a variation of the traditional Roman burial ritual of *ossilegium*. Seneca alludes to the ritual and recreates it as drama with moral implications on the characters within the play and on the audience. Like Andromache's witty comment in the *Troades* that Astyanax' mangled corpse still resembles Hector, however, there is a humor to the scene that shocks one for noticing it but which nonetheless adds a subtle element by which the audience/reader may ask whether they are interpreting the scene correctly if indeed the text at once invites us to sympathize with a father's grief and to find humor in his unlikely predicament.[37]

The burial ritual of *ossilegium* involves two stages: the amputation of a body part, normally a finger, prior to cremation, which was interred with the ashes (*os resectum*) and the gathering of bone fragments and ashes following cremation (*os exceptum*).[38] Burial then entailed placing the ashes, bone fragments, and finger in an urn which could then be placed in a columbarium or interred in a sarcophagus. Theseus' gathering of Hippolytus' mangled corpse anticipates *os exceptum* as it provides an ironic example of *os resectum*.

Since Theseus orders a funeral pyre to be prepared (1277), he gives directions for the proper disposal of Hippolytus' remains (unlike Astyanax in the *Troades* or Phaedra later in the *Phaedra*). The implication is that the collected remains of Hippolytus will be cremated and then given a proper *ossilegium* before burial. Thus Hippolytus receives a "double cremation": one symbolic, the second actual. The first is alluded to on stage, but the latter will take place off-stage and after the dramatic time of the play.

There is a parallel to Hippolytus' death in the episode of Mettius Fufetius' death by quartering in Livy (1.28.10–11):

> Exinde duabus admotis quadrigis, in currus earum distentum inligat Mettium; deinde in diversum iter equi concitati, lacerum in utroque curru corpus, qua inhaeserant vinculis membra, portantes. Avertere omnes ab tanta foeditate spectaculi oculos. Primum ultimumque illud supplicium apud Romanos exempli parum memoris legum humanarum fuit: in aliis gloriari licet nulli gentium mitiores placuisse poenas.[39]

> Then, when two chariots were drawn up, he [Tullus] tied Mettius, stretched out at full length, to each chariot and the whipped horses went in different directions, carrying on either chariot the torn body whose limbs were attached by chains. All averted their eyes from such a horrible sight. This was the first and last example of this punishment among Romans which was of a type too little mindful of human laws: in other cases, we can boast that milder punishments are pleasing to no other nation.

Here, as in Seneca, we have an example of *os exceptum* prior to death and cremation, and presumably *os resectum* prior to death, although Livy does not say how Mettius' remains were disposed of.[40] The tone of Livy's passage differs from Seneca's in that the emphasis is on Roman reaction (*avertere omnes ab tanta foeditate spectaculi oculos*), rather than on Mettius' suffering.

If Mettius' punishment was too cruel for Roman tastes, how should we read Hippolytus' death? Allusions to death ritual in a dramatic production and the display of corpses of characters killed off-stage are different than the actual inclusion of a corpse being prepared for cremation and burial on stage, especially if the text calls for the reassembly of unidentifiable body parts.[41] The reciprocity between tragedy and funeral ritual points to the metatheatricality of both stage production and cremation ritual, especially those associated with women. It recalls Livia's public *ossilegium* of Augustus' remains as part of the orchestrated events of his funeral (Dio 56.42.4) and Agrippina's carrying of Germanicus' ashes into Rome (Tac. *Ann.* 3.1–2).

In Euripides' *Hippolytus,* Theseus holds the dying Hippolytus in his arms as son absolves father of his crime. Since Hippolytus is already dead when Theseus finds him in Seneca's play, Theseus is not absolved of his crime. In Euripides' *Bacchae,* Pentheus is ripped to pieces by his mother and aunts who discover their guilt after his death; therefore they are not reconciled with him at the end of the play. Theseus claims responsibility for the cutting of Hippolytus' corpse:

> morte facili dignus haud sum qui nova natum nece
> segregem sparsi per agros. . . .

> I hardly deserve an easy death, I who scattered my torn son
> through the fields in a novel death. (1209–10)

Father is cause and agent of his son's death and dismemberment. Theseus' hands are polluted, yet he alone must perform the ritual while the Chorus can serve only as witnesses of, not participants in, his punishment. It is significant that Theseus identifies himself in relation to his dead son by asking to be buried alive, thereby evoking his recent trip to the Underworld and metaphorically playing dead for a second time:

> Dehisce tellus, recipe me dirum chaos,
> recipe, haec ad umbras iustior nobis via est:
> natum sequor.

> Gape open, earth, and receive me, dire chaos,
> receive me, this trip to the shades is more just:
> I pursue my son. (1238–40)

As Theseus seeks to play dead a second time, the Chorus advises Theseus to dispose of Hippolytus' remains:

> CHO: Theseu, querelis tempus aeternum manet:
> nunc iusta nato solve et absconde ocius
> dispersa foede membra laniatu effero.

> CHO: Theseus, an eternity remains for your laments:
> now perform the rites for your son and quickly hide
> the limbs foully torn through savage ripping. (1244–46)

The Chorus, realizing the unnatural way in which Hippolytus dies, advises putting aside traditional mourning in favor of immediate washing and hiding (*absconde*), rather than burying the remains. Seneca calls attention to this unnatural death by using the rare word *laniatu* (1246) for "ripping."

Hippolytus' burial is furthermore paradoxical in its inversion of the elegiac tradition, in which the poet's mistress gathers his bones after his imagined death.[42] Propertius, for example, includes many references to *ossilegium*. In 1.17.19–24, the poet imagines his mistress collecting his cremated remains for burial:

> illic si qua meum sepelissent fata dolorem,
>   ultimus et posito staret amore lapis,
> illa meo caros donasset funere crines
>   mollitur et tenera poneret ossa rosa;
> illa meum extremo clamasset pulvere nomen,
>   ut mihi non ullo pondere terra foret.[43]

> If some fate had buried my grief there
>   and a tombstone marked my buried love,
> she would have offered her precious hair at my funeral
>   and gently have placed my bones among soft roses;
> she would have called out my name over my last ashes,
>   that the earth lie lightly over me.

The ironic tone of the poem in which Propertius flees from Cynthia and is shipwrecked extends to the allusions to burial and the wish for the earth to lie lightly, which is common on epitaphs.

A more somber tone surrounds the allusion to *ossilegium* in Propertius 1.21, in which the deceased's wife (the sister of the addressee) will return to the site of his death to perform his last rites (9–10):

> et quaecumque super dispersa invenerit ossa
> montibus Etruscis, haec sciat esse mea.

> and whatever bones she will find scattered
> on Etruscan hills, let her know these to be mine.

Pathos is achieved since the collection of bones foreshadows the collection of bone fragments following her brother's belated and substitute cremation since his flesh is no longer attached to his bones.[44]

In Propertius 2.24, a dramatic monologue is inserted into an elegy in which Propertius' mistress laments his death as she performs the rituals accompanying an *ossilegium* of his remains.

> tum mea compones et dices 'Ossa, Properti,
>   haec tua sunt? eheu tu mihi certus eras,
> certus eras eheu, quamvis nec sanguine avito
>   nobilis et quamvis non ita dives eras.'

> Then you will gather my bones and say, "Propertius,
>   are these bones yours? Alas you were faithful to me,
> faithful were you, alas, although you were were not noble
>   with ancestral blood, nor were you so wealthy." (35–38)

Cynthia's dialogue incorporates the ritualistic *versus quadratus* with its repetition in balanced cola, pointing to a performative, rather than a realistic speech. There is some doubt whether the punctuation following *haec tua sunt* should be a colon or a question mark.[45] If a colon, then we have a simple statement. If there should be a question mark, then the ambiguity reveals a paradox: that the poet's mistress may not be performing the ritual properly or even on the proper bones. The poem, however, does not provide any context under which the poet's bones might have been lost or confused for another's. The emphasis in the passage is one of time (here now are your bones, formerly, when alive, you were mine), so perhaps a colon is more appropriate.

Later in the same poem, Propertius reverses roles and claims that since no else will wish to give Cynthia her last rites, he will perform them alone:

> noli nobilibus, noli conferre beatis:
>   vix venit, extremo qui legat ossa die.
> hi tibi nos erimus: sed tu potius precor ut me
>   demissis plangas pectora nuda comis.

> Do not consort with the noble or the rich:
>   scarcely one comes who will gather your bones on your final day.
> We will be these men to you: but rather I pray that you mourn me
>   with bare breasts and disheveled hair. (49–52)

In 3.2 of the Tibullan corpus, the poet Lygdamus imagines his mistress, together with her mother, in mourning as she performs an *ossilegium* following his imagined death. The poet evokes the ritual of *ossilegium* to warn his

mistress that she will resent her present cruelty after his death—a warning
that is emphasized by the fact that she and no other mistress will have the
honor of performing these final rites:

> ergo cum tenuem fuero mutatus in umbram
> > candidaque ossa supra nigra favilla teget,
> ante meum veniat longos incompta capillos
> > et fleat ante meum maesta Neara rogum.
> sed veniat carae matris comitata dolore:
> > maereat haec genero, maereat illa viro.
> praefatae ante meos manes animamque precatae
> > perfusaque pias ante liquore manus,
> pars quae sola mei superabit corporis, ossa
> > incinctae nigra candida veste legent,
> et primum annoso spargent collecta Lyaeo,
> > mox etiam niveo fundere lacte parent,
> post haec carbaseis umorem tollere velis
> > atque in marmorea ponere sicca domo.

> And when I am changed into a slender shade
> > and black ash covers my white bones,
> let grieving Neara come with dissheveled hair
> > and cry before my bier.
> And let her come accompanied with the grief of her dear mother:
> > the one will cry for her son-in-law, the other for her husband.
> Once prayers are offered for my shades and soul
> > and perfume poured from pious hands,
> let them, wearing unbelted black robes, prepare
> > to gather my white bones, the only part of my body remaining,
> and sprinkle them with old wine,
> > and even prepare to pour white milk,
> and afterward raise them in fine linen veils,
> > and place my dry bones in a marble home. (9–22)[46]

The emphasis, in this passage, is on death ritual, rather than on the act of
dying. In the poet's imagination, Neara performs his last rites as a wife,
rather than a mistress. Neara observes full ritual mourning with heavy
emphasis on her appearance as she performs these duties. The poet's white
bones contrast with black ash and the women's mourning clothes and the
dryness of his bones/ashes (*sicca*) contrasts with the liquids being poured,
thereby emphasizing the irreversibility of death.

Theseus' performance of his symbolic *ossilegium* is an ironic inversion of elegy where the mistress gathers the bones of her lover, for here, a father, rather than a mistress, collects the pieces of a son who shunned love and sex. Since Theseus caused his son's death and moreover is responsible for the earlier death of Hippolytus' mother, no kinswomen are available to perform the rites; he alone is responsible for the improper execution of the ritual.[47] Ironically, it is Hippolytus' stepmother who plays a role in his funeral, in addition to causing his death. Phaedra, in confessing her crime and announcing her imminent suicide, gives Hippolytus' epitaph:

> iuvenisque castus crimine incesto iacet,
> pudicus, insons—recipe iam mores tuos.
>
> Here lies a youth chaste and guiltless of unchaste crime,
> modest, innocent—receive now your honor. (1194–95)

The emphasis on chastity (*castus . . . incesto . . . pudicus, insons*) rather than *virtus* reflects the virtues traditionally listed on the epitaphs of women, and reflects Hippolytus' ambiguous gender identity. The epitaph is also as much an expression of Phaedra's guilt as it is Hippolytus' innocence. It is significant that Phaedra imagines Hippolytus' corpse as lying down (*iacet*), despite her knowledge of the circumstances surrounding his death, suggesting a continued fantasizing of her beloved and perhaps denial of the repercusions of her actions if she imagines his corpse as whole.

If Hippolytus' inverted burial reflects the bizarre manner of his death, then the disposal of Phaedra's corpse reflects the enormity of her crime and further allusions to funeral rituals. Theseus does not order a burial for his wife, but rather curses her corpse by reversing the traditional "may the earth lie light" wish on epitaphs in the final lines of the play:

> —istam terra defossam premat,
> gravisque tellus impio capiti incubet.
>
> —Let soil conceal her deep,
> and let the earth lie heavy on her cursed head. (1279–80)

Theseus' curse on Phaedra's epitaph contrasts with the earlier one which she gave to Hippolytus. Role reversal between men and women extends to Theseus' relationship to his son and wife and points to a further inversion of the elegiac tradition. The emphasis on Hippolytus' funerals (the one symbolically enacted on stage and the second for performance after the end of the play) calls attention to directions not to give Phaedra a funeral, thus making Theseus' final lines against Phaedra all the more shocking.

Theseus' collection of Hippolytus' remains evokes the cremation ritual of *ossilegium* and alters the elegiac paradigm of women gathering the remains of their loved ones, and his intended abuse of Phaedra's corpse point to intertextuality with elegy to underscore the importance of death ritual to the play. Thus, just as in the *Troades,* the (theater) aesthetics of mortality extend to both performance and reception: Hippolytus' remains dominate the stage in Act 5, thus extending his role beyond his speaking parts, and they produce a mixed reaction from the audience: horror and sympathy, which is similar to the audience's (textual and actual) viewing of the deaths of Astyanax and Polyxena as spectators, more than could be effected by a Messenger speech describing Theseus' collection of his son's remains. The reassembling of Hippolytus' remains, however, like Andromache's description of Astyanax's, also introduces an ironic and absurd tone. The question of responsibility for Hippolytus' death, however, remains ambiguous—Hippolytus himself? Phaedra? Theseus? Venus? Theseus' performance of a symbolic *ossilegium* and the intertextual allusions to elegy change the focus of Euripides' play for dramatic effect and involve the audience in the play's unresolved moral dilemma, turning the theater of mortality into one of morality.

In the following section, I would like to consider further the reciprocal theatricality between stage and audience and between funeral ritual and the allusion/inclusion of funerary ritual on stage. In particular, the intertextuality between the audience, literary and dramatic texts, and playing dead that extends and reverses the figurative construct: what are the semiotic implications of a metaphorical theater of the dead in which a cast of corpses (figuratively portrayed) performs on stage or in spectacles for an actual (non-literary) audience and the implications of the (meta)theater of an audience composed of the living and (figuratively) the dead that participates in the illusion?

A Cast of Corpses

The appearance and role of the image at Caesar's funeral is interesting from a semiotic perspective: the image of the murdered Caesar was raised over the bier of the dead Caesar who was shielded from view. The two Caesars representing two different phases in the life of Caesar are in the same place at the same time. The impromptu representation of Caesar and the altering

of the funeral script by the populace contributed to the theatricalized setting
and reception of the funeral. Dio (56.34.1–4) records details of Augustus'
funeral in which images also played a central and scripted dramatic role:

> These were his instructions, but afterwards came his funeral. There was a
> couch made of ivory and gold and decorated with purple and gold cover-
> ings. His body was hidden in a coffin below but a wax image of him in a
> triumphal robe was visible. This image was carried from the palace by the
> magistrates elected for the following year; another made of gold was carried
> from the senate house, and still another on a triumphal chariot. After these,
> images of his ancestors and dead relatives were carried, except the image
> of Caesar since he was listed among the heroes (gods), and those of other
> Romans who had distinguished themselves in some way beginning with the
> image of Romulus himself. Even an image of Pompey the Great was seen
> and all of the peoples he had added, each dressed in their regional styles,
> took part in the procession. After these followed all of the items listed above.
> When the couch was placed on the rostra of the orators, Drusus read some-
> thing from there, but from the other rostra of the Julians, Tiberius delivered
> a public speech according to decree, with the following words [. . .].[48]

If the account can be trusted in a source far removed from the date of the
funeral, this description of the multiple images of Augustus is remarkable:
three images (effigies rather than masks) of Augustus originating from different points of city traveled on predetermined routes and met with his actual
corpse which was in a coffin and hidden from view.[49] Multiple representations meant that various members of the populace, in different parts of the
city, could see various representations of Augustus at the same time as the
images made their way toward each other. All four Augustuses were visible
(the actual Augustus hidden in a coffin but his presence represented) when
coming into view from their various routes to those attending the funeral
within sight of the rostra but only after the procession that included the
images of his relatives (except the deified Julius Caesar, although Romulus,
who was deified, was depicted) and prominent Romans including Pompey
the Great.[50]

Augustus was represented in various civic and military roles that com-
prised the top positions from the three traditional branches of power: army,
tribunes (for the following year), and senate. The procession evokes a military triumph that can be read as three separate triumphs that reference the
present, past, and future, to represent Augustus' conquering of all branches
of government simultaneously; thus they rival Pompey's triple triumph of

61 BCE and Augustus' own in 29 BCE. The images moved away from their seats of power to Augustus' bier where the assembled Augustuses symbolically reconstituted the various civic and military offices. Augustus, therefore, was presented as a symbol of the Roman state/empire and vice versa: the empire was embodied by Augustus.

Dio describes the clothing and roles of the images, but he does not state the chronological phase of Augustus' life that was represented: did all three Augustuses look the same (idealized as youthful, for example, in accordance with his official portraiture, which did not essentially age, despite the fact that Augustus died in old age)? From a metaphorical perspective, the images of Augustus represent a cast of corpses who animated the emperor in his various roles. The theatricalization of funerary ritual makes burial ritual and mourning theatrical acts that can be interpreted in relation to the theater with actors and audience members.[51] Despite the extensive planning, however, it is impossible to attribute a single audience response to the choreography of the procession and funeral rituals, since metaphor and symbolism, by their associative natures, cannot be predicted or necessarily shared by all onlookers.[52] A reciprocal relationship exists, therefore, between death ritual and theatrical allusion recognized by an audience which, at once, acknowledges the death of the deceased but also perpetuates a figurative living status for the dead and his deceased ancestors.[53]

Equally scripted as the entry of Augustus' corpse and multiple images into the Forum was the procession following Tiberius' eulogy to Augustus' pyre and then his cremation and depositing of his ashes into his mausoleum, which Dio describes (56.42.1–4):

> Tiberius delivered these words and afterward, the same men who carried the couch before conveyed it through the triumphal gateway, according to the senate's decree. Present and participating in the procession were the senate, the equestrians, their wives, and the praetorian guard and just about all the others who were in the city. When he was placed on the pyre in the Campus Martius, all the priests processed around it, next the equestrians, those bearing arms and the others, and soldiers from the garrison ran around it and heaped upon it all of the spoils which they had ever received from him for their valor. Then the centurions took up torches, by decree of the senate, and lit the pyre from underneath. When it burned, an eagle, released from it, flew up as though bearing his soul to heaven. After these ceremonies were completed, all the others departed but Livia stayed at that location for five days with the foremost of the equestrians, collected his bones and deposited them in his tomb.[54]

The triumph motif continues to the pyre, but the text is not explicit about the role played by the images. Did they follow the procession to the pyre? Were the images of Augustus visible to mourners and onlookers as the body of the actual Augustus was cremated? Unfortunately, Dio's narrative does not answer these questions, but the inherent theatricality of the procession continues with the prioritized ritual circumambulation around the pyre and the release of the eagle as the pyre burned as a metaphor for the apotheosis of Augustus.[55]

From a visual perspective, the traveling representations of Augustus contrasted with the stationary rotation of Caesar's image from a single location and extended the topography of the funeral (and city) into larger theater venue: the multiple images of Augustus were carried through different parts of the city, the bier was placed on the rostra, the body was cremated in the Campus Martius, and the remains were collected by Livia and conveyed to his mausoleum. The role playing by the various images of Augustus contributed in turning a funeral event into a perfectly scripted theater experience of the princeps' funeral and apotheosis. If Augustus was playing dead at his own funeral, then the populace was turned from mourners into spectators. Multiplicity of representation and venues continued with the chronology of events that lasted five days during which Livia participated each day by attending to the pyre and performing an *ossilegium* of Augustus' remains and transfering them to his mausoleum. Clearly, Augustus' funeral was magnificently scripted from the pageantry to the participation of Livia and the Claudii to the relative exclusion of Julii at the delivery of the two eulogies. Apparently all went according to plan since absent from Dio's narrative is any mention of impromptu changes or public demonstrations that characterized the events surrounding Caesar's funeral.

The narrative of Augustus' funeral provides an excellent intertext for a discussion of funerals from a theater perspective in which a funeral becomes a (figurative and representational) theater of the dead rather than a vehicle with which to reconstruct a typical aristocratic funeral or to trace the development of imperial funerary ritual.[56] I focus on the figurative impact of theatricalized elements of Roman funerals, such as the role playing by the deceased; mimes imitating the deceased; and mourners who are spectators and actors in the illusion, which blur the distinction between the living and the dead.

Polybius' description of a funeral typical of a male aristocrat in the middle Republican period (6.53.1–10) is unique since he does not give the name of a specific individual and because of his use of the generalizing term "whenever" to introduce his narrative which should be well known by his readers (6.53.1–10):

Whenever any famous man dies, he is carried in a funeral procession to the so-called rostra in the forum sometimes in an upright position, rarely prostrate. With all of the populace standing around, a son, if he is alive and happens to be present, or if not, some other relative steps up onto the rostra and speaks about the virtues and accomplishments achieved in the lifetime of the deceased. As a result, those assembled recall to mind and bring his achievements before their eyes, not only those who had taken part in these deeds, but even those who had no part, feel a sympathy not limited to those who are present but one shared in common by the populace. Next comes burial and the performance of the customary ceremonies and they place an image of the deceased in the most conspicuous part of the house, setting it in a wooden shrine. This image is a mask, a completely accurate recreation of his face, similar in appearance and features. They lovingly decorate these images and display them for public sacrifices and whenever a famous member of the family dies, they carry them to the funeral, placing them on those whom they consider to most resemble the deceased in size and posture. These men wear togas bordered by purple if the deceased was a consul or praetor, a purple toga if a censor, and embroidered with gold if he had celebrated a triumph or had achieved anything similar. They ride on chariots and carried before them are fasces, axes, and the customary things that accompany magistrates according to the dignity appropriate to each state position held in his lifetime. When they arrive at the rostra, they all sit in a row on ivory thrones. There is no finer nor ennobling spectacle for a young man who esteems fame and virtue—especially to see these images of men well known for excellence altogether as though living and breathing What spectacle would seem finer than this?[57]

The generalizing description of the funeral ceremony gives the impression that such scenes were played out without variation despite differences between deceased males in terms of personalities and place of residence. Polybius describes a tableau in which aristocratic males are stripped of any distinguishing characteristics as they, like the mime performers, assumes a generic role upon dying in a temporal and spatial vacuum but one that can be played over and over whenever someone dies and the illusion must be perpetuated again. The impression is one of the temporary repopulation of public and private space by generations of the deceased who are animated yet not quite specific to their former surroundings, but who subsume the deceased into their group even before the disposal of his remains.

Theatricalized rituals permeate the ceremony: the funeral *pompa,* or procession, which includes the wearing and carrying of masks (*imagines*), leads to a *rostra* upon a constructed platform upon which the corpse is placed.[58] The deceased is usually carried in an upright position—a posture that implies participation in events as a spectator rather than the passive focal point of a funeral and accompanied by men imitating his ancestors and riding in chariots. Since the rituals which Polybius describes took place before cremation or interment, the deceased was, in essence, a seated member of the audience among his ancestors at his own funeral.

The focus shifts from the recently deceased to his ancestors as spectators sitting in a row on ivory chairs, thereby creating a theater of the dead in the audience that mirrors the theatricalized actions of the deceased through the mime actor imitating him. This results in a concurrent or multiple layer of generations which gives the illusion of a family reunion with male ancestors, but the emphasis is on sight and not interaction with the mourners who see the ancestors seated together in a separate area. It is the spectacle of the ancestors participating in the funeral of their descendants which catches Polybius' attention and which serves a didactic purpose for their younger descendants in the audience.[59] As participants, the deceased ancestors assume the *imagines* or death masks and symbols of public office which are stored in the home and who thus reclaim their former identities and roles among the living.

When not in use for funeral ceremonies, the *imagines* were displayed in the atrium of Roman homes for occupants and visitors alike to see.[60] As with Dio's description of Augustus' funeral, sources are silent as to what happens after the funeral ceremonies. Was there a procession back to the deceased's house to deposit the deceased's mask and those of his ancestors once again in the atrium, or did the actors hand over the masks and clothing and thereby surrender their identities of the deceased and his ancestors immediately following cremation or interment? The former seems more likely, especially if the actors gathered at the deceased's home to collect their masks, but certainty is impossible.

Polybius assumes that his readers are familiar with details surrounding interment and the "customary ceremonies" which could include scenic entertainment. The restaging of a previously staged play could have topical relevance for a funeral and be ready for production within the eight days before a body was cremated—a scenario not likely for the writing and producing of a new play. Since *ludi scaenici* or scenic productions were performed at some funerals, in addition to gladiatorial combats, a stage was necessary, but it is not clear from our evidence whether the same platform that had been used to display the corpse doubled as a stage, or whether a second platform/stage was set up in sight of it.

For the funerals of nobles, these platforms were probably located in the Roman Forum, but this location is controversial since it depends on a single reference in the *Ab urbe condita* of the historian Livy, and may not be the exclusive location.[61] If the stage on which a restaged play was produced was in sight of the corpse—a configuration results which recalls the placement of temporary stages in the early Republican period directly in front of temples and thus within sight of the god or goddess being celebrated, with the temple steps doubling as theater seats.[62] Mourners and onlookers in the audience would see the deceased's ancestors sitting in a row in front of the stage, forming a symbolic barrier between the audience and the stage, between the living and the dead. Since these thrones were the symbolic seats of gods, the use of them by the deceased's dead ancestors points to a blurring of the dead with the divine for funeral games and other *ludi*. Originally reserved for gods and goddesses, the ritual of a symbolic presence at a theater became associated with mortals. According to legend, Romulus displayed a throne for his brother Remus at official functions to indicate their common rule (Servius, ad *Aen.* 1.276).

The most pivotal figure in connection with a symbolic throne, however, is Julius Caesar. A throne was reserved for Caesar for the theater among the thrones of the gods with a symbolic crown placed upon it, but it was never exhibited while he was alive, and was probably meant to be used *in absentia* as in the case of his ivory statue in the Capitoline Temple.[63] Augustus, after two unsuccessful attempts in 44 BCE after Caesar's assassination, succeeded in installing this throne in the theater.[64] Julius Caesar was also granted a *pulvinar*, a couch with divine connotations, in the orchestra of the theater.[65]

Augustus himself enjoyed honors normally reserved for the gods in the theater. Augustus was granted a curule chair (*sella curulis*) in the theater among other honors, but he never had his statue or chair carried in a procession during his lifetime.[66] Unfortunately, at the opening of the Theater of Marcellus in 11 BCE, Augustus' curule chair collapsed during dedication ceremonies (the unfinished theater was used for the *Ludi Saeculares* in 17 BCE).[67] Like Julius Caesar, Augustus was also granted a *pulvinar* for the theater, but Augustus diffused attention and deflected criticism by letting his grandchildren sit with him.[68] After Augustus, this became the official seat of the emperor and his family.

The theater throne became an important part of the Imperial ritual of the Julio-Claudians, whereby the deceased was imagined as actually present in the theater audience. After his death, a golden statue was decreed for Marcellus, together with a golden crown, and a curule chair which were to be carried into the theater at the *Ludi Romani* and placed in the midst of the presiding officials (Dio 53.30.6). A similar throne was decreed for Germanicus (Tac. *Ann.*2.83.1), Drusus (Tac. *Ann.* 4.9), Agrippina Maior (Suet. *Gaius* 15.1), and Britannicus.[69] In a variation of this ritual for dead members of the

Imperial family, Tiberius and Seianus were granted thrones for the theater *in absentia*.[70] In the later Empire, a decree was passed specifying that a golden statue of Faustina Minor was to be carried in a chair into the theater. Her image was to be present on every occasion where the emperor was a spectator, and placed in the theater seat she had occupied when alive in order to view the games, so that even in death, she might be in the company of the most influential women (Dio 72.31.2).

Further details surrounding the custom of playing dead at funerals comes from Diodorus Siculus (31.25), who describes the funeral of Lucius Aemilius Paullus in 160 BCE, giving details similar to Polybius' account of a typical aristocratic funeral with the added detail that mime actors, rather than relatives, were hired to portray the deceased's dead ancestors:[71]

> Those Romans who are distinguished by their birth and by the fame of their ancestors, when they die, are reproduced in likenesses most similar to their features and even the outline of their entire bodies, and use actors who have carefully observed them their whole lives, their movements and each peculiarity of their appearance. In the same way each of his ancestors participates in the funeral procession bearing the dress and symbols of office so that on account of these, spectators could easily discern how far each one had advanced on the *cursus honorum* and taken part in the management of the state.[72]

It is significant that Diodorus mentions that the mime actors imitate the carriage and appearance of the deceased, which suggests that these actors could earn a living as participants in funerals to supplement their stage roles. Moreover, it suggests that members of the aristocracy welcomed professional actors in their midst to portray their ancestors despite the low social standing of actors in general at Rome. This interaction must have been intimate enough for actors to observe the character traits of the deceased on more than one occasion, since Diodorus claims the mime's observation was made throughout the deceased's life. Presumably the aristocracy did not alter their behavior in fear of caricatures after death at their own funerals, and surviving family members may have welcomed it as a way to extend the life of the deceased and to lessen their grief with such a personalized and humorous imitation.

In addition to Diodorus, the biographer Suetonius also claims that it was the custom (*ut est mos*) for a mime actor to imitate the deceased in appearance and carriage, which he had observed throughout the lifetime of the deceased in order for the deceased to be a participant in his own funeral. At the funeral of the emperor Vespasian, Suetonius reports that the mime actor Favor, imitating Vespasian in "actions and words," joked about the emperor's stinginess:

> Sed in funere Favor archimimus personam eius ferens imitansque, ut est mos, facta ac dicta vivi, interrogatis palam procuratoribus, quanti funus et pompa constaret, ut audit sestertium centiens, exclamavit centum sibi sestertia darent ac se vel in Tiberim proicerent.

> But at the funeral, the arch-mime Favor, bearing his likeness and imitating his former actions and words, as is the custom, openly asked the procurators how much the funeral and procession cost. When he heard 10,000,000 sesterces, he shouted that they should give him 100,000 sesterces and throw his body into the Tiber. (*Vespasian* 19.2)

Favor assumes the identity of the deceased Vespasian and even mocks the emperor's stinginess, but the time and location of playful banter is not given. Beyond this banter, however, details surrounding funeral are not as given as they are for the funerals of Caesar and Augustus. Unfortunately, we do not know whether the mourners/audience could see Vespasian's actual corpse or bier at the same time that Favor was imitating him and playing dead during the funeral ceremony.

Imperial symbolism and theatricality mark the funeral of Pertinax. Despite being already buried, Pertinax received a second symbolic funeral and cremation by Septimius Severus on a grand scale.[73] Septimius Severus had also decreed that a golden image of Pertinax should be led to the Circus on a chariot drawn by elephants and that three golden thrones should be carried in procession into the other amphitheaters (Dio *Epitome* 75.4.1). Thus, Pertinax' image received imperial honors with divine connotations prior to his symbolic funeral and the funeral, conceived as a theatrical event, extended the metaphor of playing dead: Pertinax was symbolically present and his effigy was treated as his actual corpse and displayed before an audience even though his actual corpse was not at the ceremony (Dio *Epitome* 75.4.2–6–75.5.1–5):

> His funeral, although he was long since dead, was as follows. In the Roman Forum, a wooden platform was built near the marble rostra on which was placed a shrine, without walls but with a peristyle intricately made of ivory and gold. Inside the shrine was a bier made from similar materials, surrounded by the heads of land and sea animals adorned with purple and

gold coverlets. On top of this a wax effigy of Pertinax, dressed in triumphal
clothing, was set and a handsome youth kept the flies from it with peacock
feathers, as though he were asleep. While he was lying there, Severus with
us senators and our wives approached, dressed in mourning; the women
were seated under porticoes but the men sat out in the open. Next there
passed the images of all the ancient famous Romans, a chorus of boys and
men singing a dirge-like hymn to Pertinax. Next after these came all of
the conquered nations represented in bronze images and dressed in their
native clothing, and even the offices from the city itself: the lictors, scribes,
heralds, and other similar ones. Then came the images of other men who
had accomplished some famous task, invention or way of life. Following
these were the cavalry and armoured infantry, racehorses and the funeral
offerings all those which the emperor, we senators, our wives, select knights,
communities, and the offices of the city had sent. Next there came an altar,
gold all over, and decorated with ivory and gems from India. When these
had gone past, Severus mounted the rostra and read a eulogy of Pertinax.
We shouted many things in the middle of his speech, both praising and
lamenting Pertinax, but [shouted] the most when he ended. And finally,
when the bier was about to be moved, we all lamented and wept at the
same time. The high priests and magistrates, both those in office and those
elected for the next year, took it down from the platform and gave it to
certain knights to carry. The rest of us proceeded in front of the bier, some
beating our breasts, others playing a dirge on the flute. The emperor followed behind the others and thus did we arrive at the Campus Martius.
There a pyre resembling a tower with three stories was built decorated with
ivory, gold, and statues and on the top of it was the golden chariot which
Pertinax drove. The funeral offerings were placed inside and his bier was
set, and then Severus and the relatives of Pertinax kissed the effigy. The
emperor then ascended a platform while we, the senate, except for the
magistrates, ascended wooden stands in order to view the events safely and
conveniently at the same time. The magistrates and the knights assuming
an appearance appropriate to their position and so, too, the cavalry and
the infantry, went around the pyre, performing complex movements, both
those of peace and war. Then, finally, the consuls applied fire to the pyre
and after this was done, an eagle flew up from it. In this way was Pertinax
made immortal.[74]

The description of Pertinax's effigy further blurs the distinction between an
actual corpse and a figurative one, especially when the figurative corpse is
treated as the body of one still alive. Dio seems fascinated by the sight of the

youth who fanned the "corpse" with peacock feathers to keep the flies away as though Pertinax were actually sleeping. The dramatic illusion is further broken by the conceit of a sleeping Pertinax who is dressed in his triumphal clothing, thus adding an unlikely context for his appearance. The bier within a shrine, however, implies a divine status, like that of Julius Caesar, that competes with the illusion of his mortality. Interpretaton of the images of animal heads is problematic—did they symbolize that nature was sympathetic to his death? All living creatures must die? Or did they illustrate the geographic extent of the empire as, for example, the animal head protomes from the Forum Traianum?

The funeral procession to the Roman Forum extends the dramatic illusion of an actual funeral since the procession of conquered nations and civic representatives is actually a virtual procession made up of images. The funeral offerings that accompanied the bier included an altar with ivory and gems from India. The allusive nature of the procession that is at once an evocation of a military triumph and a religious procession adds to its theatricality and is somewhat reminiscent of the triumph which Pompey the Great restaged at the opening of his theater within the dramatic action of a tragedy.[75] Dio's first-person narrative adds to the theatricality of his description: narrator as participant and spectator of the funeral ceremony, as events unfold, who relates events to a reader who is treated like an interlocuter to whom Dio points out interesting features at the funeral. Dio is seated in the company of the emperor and other senators; therefore, his narrative also reflects a priviledged vantage point from which to watch the spectacle of Pertinax's symbolic funeral.

While Dio does not relate the words which Severus delivered in the eulogy, he does note that the audience shouted their approval several times during the speech, thus, as Dio notes, alternating between their roles as audience and mourners. Following the eulogy, both civic and religious officials, those currently in office and those elected for the following year, transferred the effigy to the knights to carry on a second procession to the Campus Martius. Severus and the company of senators and select knights accompanied the effigy to the sound of dirge-like flute playing and arrived at the site of the pyre which represents a change of venue for the visual focus of the spectacle and the spectators. The appearance of the pyre is also allusive: it resembles a tower decorated with statues and Pertinax's chariot on the top. Thus the pyre serves a visual as well as a practical purpose. After funeral offerings were deposited within the pyre, the emperor kissed the effigy of Pertinax which served as a symbolic farewell to Pertinax before the cremation of his effigy. The emperor and senators were then seated in order to view the cremation safely and conveniently; thus the cremation becomes a spectacle that was accompanied by a circumambulation around the pyre in a choreographed ceremony. The release of the eagle to symbolize the apotheosis of the already cremated Pertinax is the climax of the spectacle after which Dio's narrative changes focus so the reader does not know what happened next: how long did the ceremony last after the initial lighting of the pyre? Was there a third procession out of the Campus Martius to another location of the city? Was there a symbolic *ossilegium* and a second symbolic burial although Pertinax had been buried months before?

Thus, the theatricalized setting of Pertinax' symbolic funeral and the dual nature of the participants as mourners and spectators turned the funeral into a spectacle with various venues, choreography, and visual focal points like a theater set. The image of Pertinax and its treatment within the funeral ceremony extend the illusion of a corpse playing dead since the image of Pertinax served as a substitution for Pertinax's actual corpse, rather than a reduplication of it, whether by a mime actor or statue representation.

The theatricalized participation of the deceased who plays dead at his own funeral or the funeral of his descendant, in the case of actors dressed as ancestors, may extend to the stage itself, thus turning a theatricalized funeral performance into a theater stage performance. A modern parallel illustrates the effects on self-representation of the deceased and the role of the mourner in participating in the reanimation of the dead. Glennys Howarth has recently explored the dynamic of how the living or those dying reconstitute themselves after death through video messages recorded prior to death:

> The personal video is increasingly employed as a mechanism for leaving messages. A dying parent may leave a video recording for a child to view when they reach a certain age. The video when seen is viewed in an active rather than a passive fashion, the child responding to the visual and verbal messages left by the parent. In this way, the video is a mechanism which encourages the ongoing communion between the living and the dead, presenting as it does the voice and a visual representation of the animated body of the deceased addressing us from 'the life beyond.' Thus, by employing technology (the fruit of modernity) the dead can reconstitute themselves, bringing us animated images, representations which can convey their thoughts and messages transported to a future time: a time which they will not experience.[76]

The recording of a video parallels the commissioning of a play in which the deceased would play dead/be represented as alive in a fictive reality that would reconstitute their former identities and allow the audience to (re)familiarize themselves or communicate with the deceased. Like the deceased who would be animated whenever the video is played, the repeated imitation of the deceased at funerals would perpetuate the animated status of the deceased on multiple occasions for an ever changing audience of mourners. This "ongoing communion" between the living and the dead through (re)performance typifies Roman funerary customs from ritual to art in which the dead continued to exert their presence on the physical topography of the living through the contemplation of their images and epitaphs.

While evidence does not show conclusively that *fabulae praetextae,* or historical dramas in Roman dress celebrating the triumphal battles of famous generals, were written for performance at the funerals of the generals who commissioned these plays, it does not point to its exclusion, especially as a subsequent restaged production. The number of *praetextae* written was very small, with only three specifically commemorating the battles won by generals in the third and second centuries BCE.[77] Possible events for the original staging of *praetextae* include votive games, triumphal processions, and funerals.[78] Production of these plays at either of the first two occasions does not preclude another production at funerals. Reduplication of performance on an occasion which glorified the deceased, among his deceased ancestors and living descendants, would allude to any earlier performances of a *praetexta.* Subsequent productions of Accius' *Brutus,* which was written to celebrate the military victory of Brutus Callaicus, may be instructive. This play was reproduced several times in the late Republic and a production was intended for performance following Julius Caesar's funeral to draw a parallel between his assassins and the Brutus who expelled the Tarquins.[79] Thus a restaging could be just as effective as the original performance.

If *praetextae* were performed during the funeral *ludi* of famous generals, then the semiotic implications are fascinating: Mourners would become spectators of multiple and concurrent spectacles as the dead figuratively took to the stage as their ancestors joined them in the audience at an occasion that marked the death of someone who was represented (possibly in multiple representations: actual corpse, mime actor representing the deceased at the funeral who may/may not be the same actor who represented him on stage) as alive. The reduplication of Caesar and Augustus at their funerals with images that challenge their dead status and perpetuate their former identities illustrates the temporal blurring and reification that at once recognizes the deceased as dead and alive. The representation of the deceased, whether on stage or in the audience, also reflects audience responses to stage drama, in that the mourners/audience must accept "onstage reality" off-stage, that is, theatrical allusion extends to the audience's reality: the audience must accept actors in their midst who are portraying real individuals who are, in fact, dead. Similar to the modern effect of seeing the deceased in a video message that can be replayed and the dead be reanimated repeatedly, the sight of a deceased being animated by an actor would serve as a commemoration to some in the audience, but as an introduction to that representation of the deceased by those who did not know them in their lifetime. Thus, the past blurs with the present as the dead continue to interact with the memory or current reification process of members of the audience.

This chapter focused on the (meta)theatricality and theatricalization of death ritual, in particular the semiotics of playing dead from a narrative and dramatic perspective: death ritual as spectacle as in the case of Caesar's funeral which turned the image displayed of Caesar into an actor and the mourners into a theater audience; a character playing dead on stage, figuratively, in Seneca's *Troades,* as Astyanax hides in his father's tomb and then literally in the description of his suicide and the sacrifice of Polyxena on the tomb of Achilles to turn death ritual into a spectacle within a play; the reassembly of the dead in the *Phaedra* in which Seneca turns the funeral ritual of *ossilegium* into a dramatic act, and a cast of corpses (from the deceased, actual and representations, to the audience, figurative and actual), which turned funerals into a theater of the dead that blurs the distinction between the living and the dead with moral implications for the reading/viewing process.

In the following chapter, I explore funerary ritual as text and intertext in the epics of Vergil and Ovid through the associative reading process. The successive additions to the trope increase intertextuality between and within texts but the fictive reality created by the author to stage his funerals requires a shift in reading strategy: the reader becomes increasingly a witness rather than a participant in the ritual which ostensibly honors the disposal of a character within a narrative that distances itself from a ritual recognizable to the reader.

CHAPTER 3

Disposing the Dead

FOLLOWING the Battle of Cannae, Hannibal cremates the defeated Roman general Paullus, in Silius Italicus' *Punica* (10.560–77):

> sublimem eduxere pyram mollisque virenti
> stramine composuere toros. superaddita dona,
> funereum decus: expertis invisus et ensis
> et clipeus, terrorque modo atque insigne superbum,
> tum laceri fasces captaeque in Marte secures.
> Non coniunx native aderant, non iuncta propinquo
> sanguine turba virum, aut celsis de more feretris
> praecedens prisca exsequias decorabat imago.
> Omnibus exuviis nudo iamque Hannibal unus
> sat decoris laudator erat. Fulgentia pingui
> murice suspirans inicit velamina et auro
> intextam chlamydem ac supremo affatur honore:
> 'I, decus Ausoniae, quo fas est ire superbas
> virtute et factis animas. Tibi gloria leto
> iam parta insigni: nostros Fortuna labores
> versat adhuc casusque iubet nescire futuros.'
> Haec Libys atque repens, crepitantibus undique flammis,
> aetherias anima exsultans evasit in auras.[1]

They raised a tall pyre and built soft couches
with green grass. Gifts were piled on top,
funeral offerings: the sword hated by those who felt it

and his shield, once the cause of terror and a proud symbol,
the broken rods and axes captured in battle.
No wife nor sons were there, nor a crowd of men joined
by common blood, nor according to custom, was there
an ancient mask, preceding the tall bier, to honor the funeral.
It was bare of all spoils but Hannibal alone, as eulogizer, was
glory enough. Sighing, he placed on him a covering shining with
rich purple and a cloak woven with gold and spoke a final tribute:
"Go, glory of Ausonia, where it is right for spirits proud in courage
and deeds to go. Glory has already come to you in your
distinguished death: but Fortune directs my labors and
orders me to be ignorant of future events." So the Libyan spoke
and suddenly, as the flames crackled all around, Paullus'
soul leaping, rose up to the sky.

After a brief description of the bier and funeral offerings of weapons, the narrative emphasizes Paullus' isolation from his wife, family, and funeral rituals, such as a procession with the *imagines* of ancestors, as it focuses on Hannibal (*Hannibal unus*) who is the sole cremator, witness, eulogy deliverer (*laudator*) and mourner of Paullus' cremation.[2] A cloth shielding Paullus' corpse from the sun and a woven tunic cover the corpse as Hannibal delivers a brief eulogy. Hannibal addresses Paullus in elevated terms (*decus Ausoniae*) and speaks with modesty (*fas est*) as he expresses a commonplace that Fortune determines the fates of humans. His words are for Paullus and they reverse the dialogic direction of epitaphs addressed to passersby who are ordered to leave the gravesite after reading the inscription. The tone of the farewell is dignified and reminiscent of Ennius' Pyrrhus (*Annales,* Book 6), who treats the enemy with respect. The pyre is quickly consumed by fire and Paullus' soul ascends to the sky as the reader realizes that Paullus' corpse was not described by Silius since the narrative focus was on Hannibal.

Silius' text alludes to earlier epics, but the narrative makes it clear that Paullus is not receiving a traditional Roman funeral; therefore, it is at once similar and dissimilar to both actual funerals and literary descriptions of funerals familiar to readers. Vergil is the main intertext (cremations of Misenus and Pallas in the *Aeneid*); but Silius also alludes to pre-Vergilian (Homer; Ennius) and post-Vergilian (Ovid; Lucan; Statius) epic in his handling of the epic funeral trope, in both narrative approach and cremation details.[3] By using Vergil's description of Pallas' cremation as my starting point, which is itself the mid-point of the epic funeral trope tradition, I explore the connection between death ritual and Latin epic, in particular, death ritual as text and intertext: how Vergil and Ovid use allusions to funerary ritual to pursue various authorial agendas and how they relate to both the literary and ritual experience of the reader. I examine the correspondence between the literary and cultural intertexts in the epic to funerary practices, in particular how varying descriptions of cremations highlight the themes of Aeneas' relationship with Pallas and his mission to establish a Trojan colony in Italy. In chapter 2, I analyzed the *Troades* of Seneca, which covers similar thematic material from the point of view of funeral ritual as drama and playing dead, but here, I examine cremations as metamorphoses in the *Metamorphoses:* how Ovid uses cremation as a vehicle for transformation against his Vergilian models and within and between stories to link his Greek and Roman mythological narratives, and to anticipate the apotheosis of Julius Caesar and his own as an immortal poet. Through the associative reading process, the reader becomes a sympathetic participant in a fictive ritual, in the case of Pallas' cremation, or speechless witness to Hecuba's tragedy in the *Metamorphoses* or the apotheoses of both Julius Caesar and Ovid through funerary ritual.[4]

Cremating Pallas

In Vergil, *Aeneid* 11, Pallas, the young son of Evander, is killed in battle by the Rutulian warrior Turnus and after Evander's lamentation for his son Pallas' death, Aeneas directs Pallas' cremation:

> Haec ubi deflevit, tolli miserabile corpus
> imperat, et toto lectos ex agmine mittit
> mille viros qui supremum comitentur honorem
> intersintque patris lacrimis, solacia luctus
> exigua ingentis, misero sed debita patri.
> haud segnes alii cratis et molle feretrum
> arbuteis texunt virgis et vimine querno
> exstructosque toros obtentu frondis inumbrant.
> hic iuvenem agresti sublimem stramine ponunt:
> qualem virgineo demessum pollice florem
> seu mollis violae seu languentis hyacinthi,
> cui neque fulgor adhuc nec dum sua forma recessit,
> non iam mater alit tellus virisque ministrat.
> tum geminas vestis auroque ostroque rigentis
> extulit Aeneas, quas illi laeta laborum
> ipsa suis quondam manibus Sidonia Dido

fecerat et tenui telas discreverat auro.
harum unam iuveni supremum maestus honorem
induit arsurasque comas obnubit amictu,
multaque praeterea Laurentis praemia pugnae
aggerat et longo praedam iubet ordine duci;
addit equos et tela quibus spoliaverat hostem.
vinxerat et post terga manus, quos mitteret umbris
inferias, caeso sparsurus sanguine flammas,
indutosque iubet truncos hostilibus armis
ipsos ferre duces inimicaque nomina figi.
ducitur infelix aevo confectus Acoetes,
pectora nunc foedans pugnis, nunc unguibus ora,
sternitur et toto proiectus corpore terrae;
ducunt et Rutulo perfusos sanguine currus.
post bellator equus positis insignibus Aethon
it lacrimans guttisque umectat grandibus ora.
hastam alii galeamque ferunt, nam cetera Turnus
victor habet. tum maesta phalanx Teucrique sequuntur
Tyrrhenique omnes et versis Arcades armis.
postquam omnis longe comitum praecesserat ordo,
substitit Aeneas gemituque haec addidit alto:
'nos alias hinc ad lacrimas eadem horrida belli
fata vocant: salve aeternum mihi, maxime Palla,
aeternumque vale.' nec plura effatus ad altos
tendebat muros gressumque in castra ferebat.

After he lamented these things, he orders
the pitiable corpse to be carried and he sends
a thousand men selected from his whole army
to accompany this last honor and to share in
his father's tears, small solace for a great sorrow,
but owed to a sorrowful father. Others were
quick to weave a soft wicker bier with arbutus
shoots and oak twigs and they shade the raised
couch with a canopy of foliage.
Here they place the youth high on his rustic bed:
just as a flower plucked by the thumbnail of a young girl,
a soft violet or drooping hyacinth, that has
not yet lost its shine or its shape, although
Mother Earth no longer nourishes or gives it strength.

Then Aeneas brought out two cloaks woven with
gold and purple thread, which Sidonian Dido herself
had once made for him, the work a joy to her, and
interweaving the web with fine gold.
Grieving, he put one of these cloaks on the youth
as a final honor, and covered in a fold of it
his hair that would soon burn. Next, he collected
the considerable spoils of the Laurentine battlefield
and ordered them to be brought in a long procession;
he added the horses and weapons that he took as spoils
from the enemy. He even tied the hands behind the backs
of those hostages whom he was sending to the shades of the
dead, about to sprinkle the flames with their sacrificed blood,
and he ordered the army leaders themselves to carry tree trunks
covered with the enemy's weapons and labeled with their
hateful names. Wretched Acoetes, worn out with age,
was escorted in the procession, now beating his breast
with his fists, now his face with his nails, and collapsed
and his whole body lay stretched out on the ground;
chariots were brought sprinkled with Rutulian blood.
Next, came Aethon, Pallas' warhorse, without his gear,
crying and he drenched his face with large teardrops.
Others carried Pallas' spear and helmet, for the other things
Turnus the victor possessed. Then the mourning phalanx
of Trojans followed, and all of the Etruscans and Arcadians
with their arms reversed. After the whole procession of
Pallas' comrades had advanced some distance, Aeneas
stood and said with a deep groan: "the same grim fates
of war calls me away from here to other tears:
    Hail for ever, Great Pallas, for ever farewell."
He spoke nothing more but turned toward the high walls
of his camp and went inside. (11. 59–99)[5]

A summary of the cremation preparations, stripped of the description of Pallas' bier and the epic simile that compares him to a flower, gives the impression that Pallas receives a traditional cremation: he is laid on a bier, Aeneas covers his face with a robe once woven by Dido, as spoils including hostages who will be sacrificed are heaped onto the bier. Aeneas then orders a procession of trophies (tree trunks inscribed with name of the enemy), which is followed by Pallas' armor, horse and chariot, and a throng of mourners (with weapons reversed) away from the camp. The armor does not include the baldric among other things (*cetera*, line 91), taken by Turnus; therefore, details of the funeral foreshadow Book 12 where the sight of Pallas' baldric worn by Turnus prevents Aeneas from sparing him. After the procession departs, Aeneas says farewell to Pallas and returns to camp.

A closer look at the passage, however, with the description of the bier and the epic simile restored reveals a narrative focus that places the cremation of Pallas in a wider literary context: it alludes intratextually to the cremation preparations of Dido and the cremation of Aeneas' helmsman Misenus and intertextually to the cremation of Patroklos in Book 23 of Homer's *Iliad*. As the companion of the epic's hero, Aeneas, Pallas receives a cremation that at once alludes to earlier literary intertexts and Roman funerary ritual but with departures that situate Pallas' cremation in a bucolic setting.

In Book 4, Aeneas cuts short his relationship with Dido who commits suicide on a funeral pyre which she had ostensibly constructed to burn Aeneas' possessions and symbolically mark the end of their relationship. The pyre of piled timber on which Dido places Aeneas' bed, clothing, and most importantly a wax effigy of the hero is constructed in the courtyard of the palace.[6] Dido stabs herself after lighting the pyre and is found too late by her sister, Anna, who tries to staunch the wounds. The reader does not witness the cremation further but like the departing Aeneas, only sees the smoke from a distance.[7] Whereas Dido cremates herself with objects that she had given to Aeneas, Pallas is given as funeral honors sacrifices and armor by his fellow Arcadians and Trojan allies and farewell words from Aeneas. Significantly, Pallas is burned in a robe woven by Dido that connects the relationships of these doomed characters to Aeneas. While not an actual description of Dido's cremation, the passage is important as an intratextual link with the cremation of Pallas in Book 11 which is also connected with the cremation of Misenus in Book 6 and the mass cremations of Trojans and Latins in Book 11.

In Book 6, as the Trojan fleet nears Italy, Misenus jumps overboard under mysterious circumstances and the location of his disappearance is commemorated by being named the Cape of Misenum. Misenus is given a cremation that contains references to Roman practice:

Nec minus interea Misenum in litore Teucri
flebant et cineri ingrato suprema ferebant.
principio pinguem taedis et robore secto
ingentem struxere pyram, cui frondibus atris
intexunt latera et feralis ante cupressos

constituunt, decorantque super fulgentibus armis.
pars calidos latices et aëna undantia flammis
expediunt, corpusque lavant frigentis et unguunt.
fit gemitus. tum membra toro defleta reponunt
purpureasque super vestis, velamina nota,
coniciunt. pars ingenti subiere feretro,
triste ministerium, et subiectam more parentum
aversi tenuere facem. congesta cremantur
turea dona, dapes fuso crateres olivo.
postquam conlapsi cineres et flamma quievit,
reliquias vino et bibulam lavere favillam,
ossaque lecta cado texit Corynaeus aëno.
idem ter socios pura circumtulit unda
spargens rore levi et ramo felicis olivae,
lustravitque viros dixitque novissima verba.
at pius Aeneas ingenti mole sepulcrum
imponit suaque arma viro remumque tubamque
monte sub aërio, qui nunc Misenus ab illo
dicitur aeternumque tenet per saecula nomen.

Meanwhile, the Trojans were mourning Misenus
on the shore and paying their last respects to his
ungrateful ashes. First they built a huge pyre loaded
with pine and cut oak and into the sides they wove
dark foliage. In front of it, they set up funereal cypresses
and decorated the top with his gleaming armor.
Some prepared hot water, boiling in bronze pots over the flames,
then washed and anointed his cold body as they groaned in lament.
Next they placed his mourned body on the bier and dressed him in
purple robes, clothing familiar to all. Others undertook the sad duty
of carrying the huge bier, then looking away, applied a torch
under it in the tradition of their ancestors. The offerings, piled high,
burned: incense, ritual meal and bowls filled with olive oil.
After the ashes collapsed and the flames subsided, they
washed his remains, the thirsty ashes, with wine and
Corynaeus placed his collected bones into a bronze casket.
Three times he carried it around his comrades, sprinkling pure water
over them with the branch of a fertile olive tree,
and after he purified the men he spoke his final words.
But dutiful Aeneas placed on the huge mound, his tomb,

the warrior's armor, his oar, and horn, under that tall
peak, which is now called Mount Misenus after him
and bears his immortal name through the ages. (6.212–35)

The narrative of the cremation is more concise than Pallas' and we find
Roman elements that depict the cremation in conventional terms: a pyre is
built with pine and oak (215); surrounded by cypress trees, funereal symbols, (215–17)[8]; washing of the corpse (218–20)[9]; dressing of the corpse
(220–22); Misenus is placed on a bier (*feretrum,* 222), as onlookers light
the pyre with faces averted from the corpse (223–24)[10]; cremation with gifts,
ritual feast, and containers of olive oil (224–25); quenching of flames and
the collection of remains into an urn (*ossilegium* described at 226–28)[11];
lustration of the cremation site with the sprinkling of liquids and olive
branches[12] and the speaking of *novissima verba* / "final words" (229–30),
which according to Varro was *ire licet:* "it is time to depart."[13] Aeneas then
builds a grave mound and piles onto it Misenus' weapons, oar, and trumpet
(232–34). The narrative follows the ceremony from mourning to burial,
including the collecting of Misenus' ashes which goes beyond the ceremony
that is described for Pallas. Aeneas will soon see Misenus in the Underworld,
which adds an unexpected finality to the funeral rituals since it is due to
the funeral which he receives that Misenus is allowed to enter Hades. Vergil
connects the cremation with the etymological origins of the name of Cape
Misenum.

The narrative of Misenus' cremation, while seemingly straightforward in
its evocation of Roman funeral ritual, is interesting for the narrative emphasis that it receives, in particular, for the description of the cutting of wood
for his pyre that introduces the cremation narrative:

itur in antiquam silvam, stabula alta ferarum;
procumbunt piceae, sonat icta securibus ilex
fraxineaeque trabes cuneis et fissile robur
scinditur, advoluunt ingentis montibus ornos.

They go into the ancient forest, the deep shelter of wild beasts;
the pine comes down, the ilex struck by the axe resounds,
ash beams and the oak are split with wedges,
and they roll giant ashes from the mountain. (6.179–82)

This passage is part of an epic trope discussed above from Homer for the
cremation of Patroklos[14] to Ennius for the mass cremation following the

Battle of Heraclea.[15] Vergil varies the list of trees and active and passive verbs of cutting and falling, but its relationship to the earlier texts is clear. Since Misenus is a relatively minor character in the epic, it is odd that the intertextual allusion to the trope is not used for Pallas instead, who occupies an important narrative role like Patroklos in the *Iliad,* or even for the mass cremation of Trojan and Latin dead in Book 11, the narrative of which resembles the context of mass cremations in Ennius' *Annales. Aeneid* 11.135–38 is preceded by a description of wood gathering for the construction of a pyre, but its formulation is not as tightly alligned with the Homeric and Ennian passages:

> fero sonat alta bipenni
> fraxinus, evertunt actas ad sidera pinus,
> robora nec cuneis et olentem scindere cedrum
> nec plaustris cessant vectare gementibus ornos.

> The tall ash resounds from the two-bladed axe,
> pines aiming for the sky are overturned, nor did they
> rest from cutting the oak and scented cedar with wedges
> nor carrying mountain ash tress on groaning carts.

The absence of the trope in connection with Pallas' cremation leaves Pallas without an epic intertext for the construction of his pyre, but Vergil fills the intertextual void with a cremation that is grounded in a bucolic rather than an epic landscape. Before turning to the bucolic features and evocations of Pallas' cremation, however, a closer look at the trope of cremations will illustrate the uniqueness of his cremation.

In Homer's *Iliad,* Patroklos, as the companion of Achilles, receives a special funeral that occupies the whole of Book 23. Homer describes the anointing of Patroklos' body (18.343 ff.); lamentation (18.354–55 and 23.12ff.); the cutting of trees to make a pyre (23.114 ff.); the covering of his corpse with shorn hair (23.135–36 and when Achilles cuts a lock of his own hair); the gift of jars of honey and oil (23.170–71); the sacrifice of horses, dogs, and captured Trojans on the pyre (23.171 ff.); the lighting of the pyre which does not take the first time (23.192); the second successful attempt at night to light the pyre after Achilles prays for favorable winds to fan the flames (23.212 ff.); the cremation (23.217–18); the quenching of flames with wine (23.250 ff.); the collecting of bone fragments and their placement in an urn (23.252 ff.); the construction of a grave mound at the site of the cremation (23.255 ff.); and funeral games (23.262 ff.). In many ways the cremation of Patroklos (and that of Hector at the epic's end) prefigures the funeral honors that await Achilles since his death occurs outside the narrative of the *Iliad.* It also interrupts the narrative of the death of Hector, who is killed by Achilles in Book 22 but does not receive his own cremation, described in the barest of terms, until the end of Book 24.[16]

Perhaps because of the close relationship between Aeneas and Pallas, Vergil raises the expectation that the cremations of Patroklos and Pallas would be similar. Both cremations receive a narrative emphasis that breaks the dramatic action of the war in the second to last books of both epics and the details of the gifts and sacrifices, while differing in particulars, highlight the important social status of the deceased and their relation to their heroic counterparts. But there are important differences that become apparent when other literary intertexts and the mass cremation of Trojans and Latins that occurs later in Book 11 and which includes details closer to the cremation of Misenus in Book 6 are considered. Pallas appears to receive a plausible cremation, but Vergil alters aspects of the Roman custom and departs from his Homeric model in favor of bucolic and lyric intertexts to emphasize the close relationship between Aeneas and Pallas without stating the nature of their relationship overtly. Pallas' cremation emerges as a metaphor for this key relationship in the poem.

Unlike the pyres of Misenus and Patroklos, Pallas is placed on a bier composed of tender shoots and twigs that resembles a rustic bed (11.64–71). The description of Pallas' cremation is described in tender terms and takes place amidst a pastoral setting, and here we are aided in our interpretation of the passage by Servius, the ancient commentator on Vergil's *Aeneid.* Looking first at Pallas' bier, the word *feretrum* is a Greek word, perhaps emphasizing Pallas' Arcadian ancestry, which Servius contrasts with the Latin *capulus.*[17] The *feretrum* is soft (*molle*) and composed of arbutus twigs and Pallas lies on a *torus,* which can refer to a couch or bed, made of shoots of oak saplings that is described as a rustic bed (*agresti . . . stramine*). It is significant that the word *stramen* does not seem to have been used before Vergil to denote a bier and is used only here.[18] Absent are trees specifically associated with death ritual, such as cypress trees that were present in the description of Misenus' cremation (6. 215).

Technical terms to describe the pyre (*pyras; rogos; busta*) and traditional elements of a Roman cremation are absent, but are used earlier in description of Misenus' cremation and again later in the description of the mass cremations of Trojan and Latin dead.[19] In his description of Pallas' bier, Vergil emphasizes young shoots as a metaphor, perhaps, of the young Pallas and his untimely death, but they are hardly practical: young shoots or sprigs would not burn as effectively as mature or dried wood, and it would take too many over a long period of time to burn since even with mature wood, cremations took several hours to days.[20] The description of the pyre does not mention nor does it preclude the possibility that the young shoots would be supplemented by mature wood, but Vergil gives the impression that the pyre could burn and therefore would emerge discordant with nature: nature would grudgingly acquiesce in the burning of the twigs for the cremation but only with great effort over a long period of time.

The description of Pallas' still handsome corpse amidst the pastoral setting contributes to an underlying erotic tone.[21] Servius, for example, describes the setting of Pallas' bier as a "room" due to the interweaving of branches that shades his couch.[22] The unexpressed purpose may be to protect the corpse from the sun, but the bower-like structure under which Pallas lies contributes to the pastoral setting and is reminiscent of the overhanging trees under which shepherds in Vergil's *Eclogues* gather and exchange verse.[23] An erotic tone is further encouraged by the simile that compares the dead youth to a flower plucked by a young girl (68–71), a violet or hyacinth, which has lyric antecedents in the poetry of Sappho and Catullus (11.21–24; 62.39–44) where the rejected poet compares his love to a flower in a field which a plough has unwittingly cut (the simile is used intratextually by Vergil of the dying Euryalus at *Aeneid* 9.433–37).[24] Servius links the hyacinth in the simile to Eclogue 3.62–63 where Menalcas claims Apollo loves him and that his gifts, the laurel and hyacinth, are always with him, thus connecting Apollo's love for him with Apollo's love for Daphne and Hyacinthus.[25] Does Servius, in turn, detect an amorous connection between Aeneas and Pallas? Like Vergil, Servius does not say, although the bucolic and lyric intertexts encourage the connection.

While details of the narrative allude to features of bucolic poetry, an allusion to a specific funeral in Bucolic poetry is difficult due to conventions of the genre in which death does not intrude upon the idyllic landscape of Arcadia. In Idyll 7 of Theocritus, the character Simichidas (meeting Lycidas) is never able to see a tomb just off in the distance, whereas Vergil in Eclogue 9, in imitation of this passage, allows Moeris (meeting Lycidas) to see a tomb in the distance.[26] Vergil gives his characters and readers a view of death, but he goes further than his Theocritean model in Eclogue 5 by introducing death and death ritual, more specifically the death of Daphnis, to the genre of bucolic poetry.[27] In Eclogue 5, the shepherd Mopsus points out a cave to Menalcas that is bucolic in appearance with wild vines growing within, but which emerges as a metaphorical tomb as the shepherds sing about the death of Daphnis and his apotheosis (*aspice, ut antrum / silvestris raris sparsit labrusca racemis,* 6–7).[28] Allusion to death ritual intrudes upon the narrative as Daphnis himself has left directions for his own funeral: he orders leaves to be sprinkled on the ground, shade to cover fountains, and a tomb containing an epitaph (*carmen,* 42) that he composed himself:

> spargite humum foliis, inducite fontibus umbras,
> pastores (mandat fieri sibi talia Daphnis),
> et tumulum facite, et tumulo superaddite carmen:
> 'Daphnis ego in silvis, hinc usque ad sidera notus,
> formosi pecoris custos, formosior ipse.'

> Sprinkle the ground with leaves, draw shade over the fountains,
> shepherds (Daphnis orders such things be done for himself),
> and make a mound, and add this epitaph to his tomb:
> *"I was Daphnis in the woods, famous here and to the stars,*
> *the guardian of beautiful cattle, but I was more beautiful."* (40–44)

The landscape, affected by his death, has exchanged violets and hyacinth for prickly flowers.[29] The narrative makes no mention of his cremation but the omission keeps Daphnis timeless: the actual time in the narrative in which he is dead is brief since he "lives again" almost immediately in heaven (56–57) as a golden age returns to world of the shepherds.[30]

Somewhat overshadowed by the pastoral setting and the allusive referents of Vergil's narrative of Pallas' cremation is Pallas' actual corpse. Like bucolic shepherds who only get a glimpse of tombs from a distance, it is difficult for the reader to distinguish Pallas from the landscape setting. The reader is not a spectator to the cremation as he or she is in the cremation of Misenus in Book 6 and the mass cremations of Trojans and Latins in Book 11.[31] Since Aeneas follows the funeral cortege for a short distance before turning back to his camp, he does not witness the cremation either. Rather, before Aeneas loses sight of Pallas, he utters farewell words (11.96–98). The model for this speech is *Iliad* 23.179–83: Achilles' farewell to Patroklos which is full of expressions of revenge that Vergil removes, but the wording at the beginning of the speech comes from *Aen.* 3.493–94: Aeneas' farewell to Andromache, the widow of Hector, whom he encounters on his voyage to Italy: *nos alia ex aliis in fata vocamur.* The wording at the speech's close echoes Catullus' farewell to his brother in a poem that commemorates his visit to his grave in Asia which he will never see again: 101.10: *in perpetuum . . . ave atque vale.* Lost in the sentimentality is the fact that Aeneas is not speaking these words close to Pallas' corpse, but rather utters them as the cortege is some distance away. The words do provide a sort of epitaph that gives Aeneas and the reader closure to the cremation. Aeneas' impromptu epitaph, however, spoken at a distance from the site of Pallas' pyre and furthermore not recorded on Pallas' grave marker, must remain elusive since it is fixed in neither time nor place. We follow Aeneas as the epic hero, and we lose sight of Pallas on his bier since the collection of his ashes and his burial are not explicitly stated.[32] The diachronic narrative, therefore, that allows the cremation to take place while Aeneas returns to camp and away from the eyes of the reader, keeps Pallas in his flower-like, ever youthful state in a bucolic setting.

Bucolic echoes of the narrative of Pallas' cremation are more marked when one compares it intratextually to the mass cremations of Trojans and Latins following the cremation of Pallas which, like the cremation of Misenus, more closely follow literary intertexts and Roman funerary ritual. The narratives of the cremations appear successively after wood is cut for the pyre:

Aurora interea miseris mortalibus almam
extulerat lucem referens opera atque labores:
iam pater Aeneas, iam curvo in litore Tarchon
constituere pyras. huc corpora quisque suorum
more tulere patrum, subiectisque ignibus atris
conditur in tenebras altum caligine caelum.
ter circum accensos cincti fulgentibus armis
decurrere rogos, ter maestum funeris ignem
lustravere in equis ululatusque ore dedere.
spargitur et tellus lacrimis, sparguntur et arma,
it caelo clamorque virum clangorque tubarum.
hic alii spolia occisis derepta Latinis
coniciunt igni, galeas ensisque decoros
frenaque ferventisque rotas; pars munera nota,
ipsorum clipeos et non felicia tela.
multa boum circa mactantur corpora Morti,
saetigerosque sues raptasque ex omnibus agris
in flammam iugulant pecudes. tum litore toto
ardentis spectant socios semustaque servant
busta, neque avelli possunt, nox umida donec
invertit caelum stellis ardentibus aptum.

Nec minus et miseri diversa in parte Latini
innumeras struxere pyras, et corpora partim
multa virum terrae infodiunt, avectaque partim
finitimos tollunt in agros urbique remittunt.

cetera confusaeque ingentem caedis acervum
nec numero nec honore cremant; tunc undique vasti
certatim crebris conlucent ignibus agri.
tertia lux gelidam caelo dimoverat umbram:
maerentes altum cinerem et confusa ruebant
ossa focis tepidoque onerabant aggere terrae.
iam vero in tectis, praedivitis urbe Latini,
praecipuus fragor et longi pars maxima luctus.
hic matres miseraeque nurus, hic cara sororum
pectora maerentum puerique parentibus orbi
dirum exsecrantur bellum Turnique hymenaeos;
ipsum armis ipsumque iubent decernere ferro,
qui regnum Italiae et primos sibi poscat honores.
ingravat haec saevus Drances solumque vocari
testatur, solum posci in certamina Turnum.
multa simul contra variis sententia dictis
pro Turno, et magnum reginae nomen obrumbrat,
multa virum meritis sustentat fama tropaeis.

Meanwhile, Aurora had lifted her nurturing light
for miserable mortals, restoring light for their labor and toil:
Both father Aeneas and Tarchon built pyres along the
curving shore. Here, each carried the corpses in the
tradition of their own ancestors, and once the black torches
were applied to the fires, the sky was buried deep in smoke
and shadows. Three times they ran around the burning pyres
in gleaming armor, three times they purified the mournful fire
of the funeral on horseback with the wail of lamentation on their lips.
The earth was sprinkled by their tears, even their armor,
as the clamor of men and the sound of trumpets went up to heaven.
Here some toss the spoils stripped from dead Latins onto the fire,
helmets, ornamental swords, bridles and wheels still warm;
while others tossed items familiar to the dead as offerings: their own
shields and unlucky spear. All around, many oxen were sacrificed
to the god of Death and bristly boars and herds taken from all of
the fields were slaughtered over the fire. Along the whole shore
they watched their comrades' cremations and tended to the burning
pyres, nor could they be drawn away until the humid night
returned a sky adorned with burning stars.

    On another part of the shore, the grieving Latins also
built countless pyres, some men's bodies they buried in the earth,

some they picked up and carried to the field's borders or
returned them to the city. They cremated the others uncounted
and unhonored, a massive heap of entangled bodies; then the
broad fields vied with each other as they glowed from the crowding
      flames.
When the third day had removed the cool darkness from the sky,
the mourners collapsed the piled ash and the bones mixed in with
the pyre which they weighed down with a warm mound of earth.
Then within the homes in the city of wealthy Latinus, was the clamor
distinct, the greatest concentration of a common grief.
Here mothers and wretched daughters-in-law, here the
tender affection of grieving sisters and children now
without fathers cursed the fatal war and Turnus' marriage
and demanded that he alone, with his armor and sword,
should settle the war since he was seeking the kingdom
of Italy and the highest honors for himself.
The cruel Drances aggravated things by claiming
Turnus alone was singled out, that Turnus alone was
being demanded to fight. At the same time, though,
many contrary views and arguments were expressed in
favor of Turnus—the great name of the queen gave him
protection and the great fame he enjoyed, earned from his spoils.
      (11.182–224)

Turning first to the description of the Trojan cremation, Vergil signals
pathetic fallacy from the start by using the verb *extulerat,* from *effero/ecfero,*
a verb associated with the carrying out of the dead, to describe the arrival of
day and at the end with the appearance of burning stars at night.[33] Whereas
the time of day was not specified in the cremations of Misenus and Pallas,
the mass cremation of Trojans takes place at dawn. This contrasts with the
mass cremations, in Ennius' *Annales,* following the Battle of Heraclea in
which Pyrrhus cremates the Roman dead with his own.[34] Ennius places
the cremation at night for dramatic effect in imitation of the cremation of
Patroklos in the *Iliad,* whose pyre did not light successfully in the daytime
(24.785ff.), but did burn during the second attempt at night. Vergil's cremation of the Trojans takes place at dawn and ends at nightfall, but the smoke
from the flames create an artificial night.[35]
    In contrast to the description of Pallas' cremation, the passage contains
technical language for cremations. Servius remarks that words reflecting
the three stages of cremation are given: *pyras* (185) signifies the stack of
wood that comprises the pyre; *rogos* (189) refers to the pyre once it has

begun to burn; and *busta* (201) the burned-out pyre.[36] Further references to funeral rituals echo Misenus' cremation and include a *lustratio*—a procession around the pyre (188–90); symbolic purification of the cremation site with the tears of onlookers (191); dedication of spoils; and animal sacrifices to Morta (197) the Roman goddess of death. The narrative emphasis is on the performance of the mass cremation and the observance of Roman custom. Friend cremates friend and caringly tends to the flame throughout the day.

The cremation of Trojans serves as a prelude to the cremation of Latins as descriptions of death ritual carry over and connect the disposal of the dead by the two camps. A separate but shared narrative is fitting since these two peoples will eventually, that is historically, unite and become the forefathers of the future Roman race. The focus of the Latin cremation is on the collection of the remains and the relation of the dead to the living. Although the narrative implies a sequential order of events, it is not clear whether the Latin cremation is actually contemporaneous with the Trojan cremations. After some bodies are removed from the battlefield, the remaining corpses are heaped up indiscriminately together (*confusaeque ingentem caedis acervum*, 207), and given a mass cremation, significantly without any funeral honors (*nec honore cremant*, 208).[37] We are given no explanation why these men were not claimed for a private burial or cremation earlier or why they must suffer an anonymous funeral. The bones are collected and buried after three days and again the emphasis is on anonymity of the deceased and the confusion of body parts.[38] Mourning takes place in homes away from the pyres, in particular the town of King Latinus. The emphasis is on the familial relationships between the mourners and the deceased, but nowhere does the text explicitly state that they mourn for any of the soldiers who received a mass cremation (11.215–19).

The mourners use the occasion of their grief to express their anger against Turnus and implicitly make the connection between the deaths of their loved ones and his political aims to obtain Lavinia in marriage, the daughter of King Latinus, who is now promised to Aeneas, in order to secure an alliance between Rutulians and Latins. The mourners' call for a duel between Turnus and Aeneas over the hand of Lavinia makes the reader aware for the first time in the narrative of the mass cremations of Latins that Turnus is not present as was Aeneas at the cremations of Misenus, Pallas, and the Trojan dead. The nameless Latin dead have been abandoned for a second time, the first time on the battlefield unclaimed by any of the living, but this time by their leader.[39]

Thus, Vergil presents his readers with two cremation narrative models based on epic and bucolic intertexts. The cremation of Pallas alludes at once to these earlier intertexts and to Roman funerary ritual. Points of departure, however, highlight the unique funeral given to Pallas in which bucolic and lyric intertexts evoke a pastoral setting. Erotic elements offer variations of Roman funerary practices that distinguish Pallas' cremation from those of Misenus and the mass cremations of Trojan and Latin dead which more closely follow epic precedents and Roman ritual. Unlike the *Iliad* which ends with the funeral of Hector and the imminent death of Achilles, the poem does not end with the funeral of Turnus that would provide narrative closure to both character and epic and thus avoid turning the poem into an episode of Aeneas' epic cycle with a fixed ending. Lack of closure, however, reflects the future of Aeneas' fictional reality beyond Vergil's text: Evander's bucolic Arcadia has vanished with the death of Pallas and Aeneas' young bride must bury her mother Amata and her former fiancé Turnus as Aeneas begins to integrate his Trojans with Latins. The reader must anticipate the hardships that Aeneas will face, but without the sense of closure that accompanies burial and funeral ritual that put the past into context and provide hope for the future.

Ovid: Cremations as Metamorphoses

Ovid's *Metamorphoses* is filled throughout with references to Roman death ritual from funerals, cremations, graves, to epitaphs. From a death ritual perspective, cremations provide closure, but Ovid, as poet, asserts narrative control through his manipulation of death and death ritual and uses cremations to link stories and to continue the narrative flow, often functioning as vehicles for further metamorphoses. Apollo, for example, after performing Coronis' cremation rites, rescues their son as she burns on her pyre (2.619–30); thus cremation is a source of life (and further narrative material). The cremation of Hercules (9.229–72), in which he constructs his own pyre, is used as a vehicle for further metamorphosis and his deification: Jupiter rescues the divine part of Hercules as his human part is cremated and remains on earth, in a foreshadowing of Julius Caesar's cremation and deification in Book 15. A variation on the theme is given in the description of Narcissus' cremation: just before his pyre is lit, his body has been replaced by a flower (3.508–10), therefore metamorphoses prior to cremation rather than as a consequence of it. In a few stories, however, cremations provide narrative detail and closure. Pyramus and Thisbe are cremated and their remains are placed in the same urn (4.166); Niobe's sons are placed on a bier and mourned by her daughters before they too are slain (6.288–89); the cremation of Aigina plague victims (7.606–13) is used to show the worst side of humanity as plague survivors ignore decency and death ritual customs; and Chione's father tries to reach her body several times as she burns on her pyre until he is turned into a hawk (11.332–45).

The greatest number of references to cremations, however, comes in Book 13 following the destruction of Troy. Thematically, the narrative of Troy's fall divides the Greek myths from the Roman myths and legends, as the burned Troy is resurrected in Italy, and introduces Ovid's mini-*Aeneid* followed by the teleological focus of the epic, the metamorphosis of Julius Caesar. I would like to focus on the narrative of Hecuba's sorrows which Ovid presents as a tragedy within his epic.

Ovid's Hecuba

The narrative of Hecuba's sorrows resembles a tragedy in format and theme as the epic reader becomes a tragedy spectator.[40] The Trojan women are on shore following the destruction of Troy and waiting to be conveyed to their new masters. Following the death of Astyanax, Hecuba is faced with the further tragedies of the slaughter of Polyxena on Achilles' tomb and the discovery of Polydorus' corpse. Her tragedy takes place on the shores of Troy and the shores of Thessaly. Ovid's linking of the two events in his narrative anticipates Seneca's linking of the death of Astyanax and the sacrifice of Polyxena in his *Troades*. Ovid centers his double tragedy around funeral ritual/cremation; however, unlike metamorphoses that result from cremation, it is Hecuba who undergoes a physical transformation at the height of her anger and despair.

The reader first encounters Hecuba in Troy among the tombs of her children and clinging to Hector's grave as she is pried away to be taken to Ithaca as Ulysses' slave:

> in mediis Hecabe natorum inventa sepulcris:
> prensantem tumulos atque ossibus oscula dantem
> Dulichiae traxere manus, tamen unius hausit
> inque sinu cineres secum tulit Hectoris haustos;
> Hectoris in tumulo canum de vertice crinem,
> inferias inopes, crinem lacrimas reliquit. . . .

> Hecuba was found among the tombs of her sons:
> The hands of the Dulichian dragged her away
> as she was clinging to their tombs and giving

kisses to their bones, and in her lap she carried
off the gathered ashes of Hector;
on the top of Hector's tomb she left a lock of her white hair,
poor offering for the dead, a lock and tears. (13.423–29)

The scene arouses pathos as Hecuba kisses the bones of her children as a farewell gesture (of her departure from Troy, unlike their funeral which was her farewell gesture to their deaths). But if they were cremated before burial, the reader wonders how she can kiss their bones (just fingers from the *ossilegium* and removed from cremation urns implied?). Hecuba carrying off Hector's ashes and his urn becomes a symbol of her futility to save her children and her future inability to pay her respects at their tombs. The physical disconnect between place of burial and place of funeral ritual has already begun: Hecuba leaves a lock of her hair as a funeral offering to Hector on his tomb, but since she is carrying his ashes, he is no longer buried there. Is Hector's tomb, which is a symbol for him, also a symbol of the fallen Troy for Hecuba which she will never see again? If so, what should the reader make of her removal of Hector's ashes from his tomb so that she can bring them to Ithaca as a constant reminder of Troy's fall and the death of her children? When Hecuba turns into a dog, the text does not say what happens to Hector's ashes; but if they were re-buried in Thessaly, then Hector would have two tombs, one in Troy and one in Thessaly, which would, presumably, also house the tombs of Polyxena and Polydorus.

The scene quickly shifts to the shore of Thessaly where Hecuba and the Trojan women face the double tragedies of the sacrifice of Polyxena and the discovery of Polydorus' corpse which is washed on shore at the very moment that Hecuba approaches the sea to fill an urn with water to wash Polyxena's corpse. The horrors of Troy's destruction have accompanied Hecuba to another shore, but the narrative of Hecuba's grief is tragicomic in the unbelievable and consecutive disasters that she meets. Hecuba, therefore, emerges as the thematic link to the double tragedy, as both the recipient and audience of the horrors she experiences, leaving the reader almost breathless as the spectators of her improbably swift suffering.

The narrative of Polyxena's sacrifice is the main thematic focus of Hecuba's sorrows. Almost as soon as the ghost of Achilles appears to demand the sacrifice of Polyxena on his grave (13.441–48), she is torn from Hecuba's arms, in a gesture recalling Hecuba's embrace of her children's tombs and sacrificed by Achilles' son Neoptolemus: . . . *fortis et infelix et plus quam femina virgo / ducitur ad tumulum diroque fit hostia busto. /* " . . . brave, doomed and more than a woman, the virgin is led to his grave and becomes a sacrifice over the hated tomb," 13.451–52. Ovid refers to Achilles' grave as *tumulus* and *bustum,* but the terms are not synonymous, they are sequential: remains of a pyre (*bustum*) would have been covered by piled earth (*tumulus*). Polyxena faces death bravely (and in a masculine way); she also gives a final speech to her murderers in which she wishes that Hecuba not learn of her death and asks the Greeks to respect her social status and not to abuse her corpse, but to return it to her mother for burial (13.457–73). Neoptolemus and an audience of onlookers weep as, even in death, Polyxena protects her modesty: *tunc quoque cura fuit partes velare tegendas, / cum caderet, castique decus servare pudoris.* (even then, while she was falling, she cared to cover her body and to protect the honor of her chaste modesty, 13.479–80). The enjambment of *cum caderet* imitates the falling of Polyxena's corpse.

Trojan women collect Polyxena's body and mourn for her, as the latest victim of Priam's doomed family, and they reflect on Hecuba's changed fortunes as the recent queen of Troy and the former mother of many children. Hecuba embraces her daughter's corpse and pours tears into her daughter's wounds: . . . *huic quoque dat lacrimas: lacrimas in vulnera fundit /* "to her she gives even tears: she pours her tears into her wounds," 13.490. A scene of pathos takes on a grotesque and absurd tone by this detail of tears pouring into Polyxena's wounds since it focuses the reader's attention onto and into the holes in her body (the text earlier, however, only specified a single stab wound to the chest at 13.476), rather than the grief of a mother embracing her dead child. Polyxena's wound is also the focus of Hecuba's address to her daughter's corpse that links mother to her daughter's wound and killer. Hecuba uses language that turns her lament into an impromptu epitaph for her daughter and for Troy, which she starts and then interrupts:

> nata, tuae—quid enim superest?—dolor ultime matris,
> nata, iaces, videoque tuum, mea vulnera, vulnus:
> en, ne perdiderim quemquam sine caede meorum,
> tu quoque vulnus habes; at te, quia femina, rebar
> a ferro tutam: cecidisti et femina ferro,
> totque tuos idem fratres, te perdidit idem,
> exitium Troiae nostrique orbator, Achilles;
> at postquam cecidit Paridis Phoebique sagittis,
> nunc certe, dixi, non est metuendus Achilles:
> nunc quoque mi metuendus erat; cinis ipse sepulti
> in genus hoc saevit, tumulo quoque sensimus hostem:
> Aeacidae fecunda fui! iacet Ilion ingens,
> eventuque gravi finita est publica clades,
> sed finita tamen; soli mihi Pergama restant.

Daughter,—what else do I have?—a final misery for your mother,
daughter, you lie dead and I see your wound, my wound:
so that I would not lose any of my children without slaughter,
you, too, have a wound; but I thought you would be safe from
the sword, being a woman: but you have died by the sword even
as a woman, and that same Achilles, the ruin of Troy and depriver of my
     childen,
killed so many of your brothers, has killed even you; but after he fell
from the arrows of Paris and Phoebus, "Now, for certain," I said, "Achilles
     is
no longer to be feared." Even now, though, I should have feared him;
his ashes in his grave rage against our race, even in his tomb we felt he
was our enemy: I was fertile for the descendants of Aeacus!
Great Troy lies dead, the public disaster was ended by a tragic outcome,
and even though it was ended, for me alone Pergamum still stands.
          (13.494–507)

Hecuba self-identifies with the dead Polyxena as mother and fellow victim
of Achilles and his son. Her epitaph for Polyxena becomes an impromptu
epitaph for herself as she mockingly lists her main life's accomplishment
as having supplied children for Achilles and his son to murder: *Aeacidae
fecunda fui!* By referring to them as descendants of Aeacus, Hecuba frames
the loss of her own family within the context of a genealogical animosity.
Hecuba also gives an epitaph for Troy: *iacet Ilion ingens,* and thus she links
herself to daughter and fallen city. When Hecuba imagines Penelope pointing her out as her slave, the deictic also imitates the language of epitaphs as
though Hecuba sees her fate as Ulysses' slave synonymous with her death:
'haec Hectoris illa est / clara parens, haec est' dicet 'Priami coniunx' / "'here she
is, that famous mother of Hector,' she will say, 'here is the wife of Priam,'"
13.512–13.
     It is only in Hecuba's lament that she connects the sacrifice of Polyxena
with her marriage to Achilles that turns her funeral into her wedding and
her burial into her wedding gift:

at, puto, funeribus dotabere, regia virgo,
condeturque tuum monumentis corpus avitis!
non haec est fortuna domus: tibi munera matris
contingent fletus peregrinaeque haustus harenae!

but, I think, you will be given a funeral as your dowry, royal virgin,

and your body laid to rest in your ancestors' tomb!
this is not our house's fortune: the tears of your mother
will reach you as your gift seeped down by foreign sand! (13.523–26)

The reference to the sand on the shore connects almost immediately with
Hecuba's wish to wash her daughter's corpse. As she approaches the water's
edge, however, she sees the corpse of her son Polydorus and is struck dumb
with grief (13.540–44):

[. . .] duroque simillima saxo
torpet et adversa figit modo lumina terra,
interdum torvos sustollit ad aethera vultus,
nunc positi spectat vultum, nunc vulnera nati,
vulnera praecipue, seque armat et instruit ira.

[. . .] she stood like a hard rock
and held her eyes fixed to the ground,
meanwhile, she raised her grim face to the sky,
now looking at the face of the corpse, now the
wounds of her son, especially his wounds, she
steeled herself and her anger mounted.

Again, wounds are the focus of her and the reader's gaze. Hecuba is compared to a rock in her grief and recalls Niobe who was turned to stone
following the deaths of her children.[41] Just as Niobe becomes a tombstone
to her children and husband, so too, does Hecuba resemble a tombstone
as she marks the place of her son's death. Grief over Polydorus' death turns
into revenge as she plots the death of his murderer, Polymestor. Her revenge
is a digression that interrupts her funeral of Polyxena and which postpones
her funeral of Polydorus since she is turned into a dog before either can be
completed (13.567–71). Therefore, we witness her grief as metamorphosis
as Hecuba changes from mother to childless widow to stone to a dog.

Ovid uses the grief of Hecuba over the loss of her children to connect the
story of Aurora's grieving for her son Memnon (13.576–622). Two mothers, connected to Troy by marriage, are further connected by loss and ritual
mourning and yet they mourn differently: whereas Hecuba and the reader
gazed on the corpses of Polyxena and Polydorus, Aurora is not able to look
at her son's corpse lying on the pyre (*at non inpositos supremis ignibus artus /
sustinuit spectare parens, sed crine soluto / . . . /* "but his mother was not able
to look at his limbs placed on the pyre, but with loosened hair . . . ," 13.583).
Like Thetis, who mourned the death of Patroklos and the impending death

of Achilles by wearing a black veil (*Iliad* 24), thus bridging or, alternately, even separating further, the world of immortals and immortals, Aurora, in ritual mourning for Memnon, loosens her hair which she keeps unbound as she asks Jupiter to honor her son (13.584 ff.). Jupiter grants her request and gives a portent once Memnon's body begins to burn on the pyre: the smoke that rises takes on the appearance of birds which fight each other until their ashen bodies collapse back onto the pyre as a funeral offering to Memnon (*inferiaeque cadunt cineri cognata sepulto / corpora seque viro forti meminere creatas /* "their bodies related to the buried ashes fell as a funeral offering and they remembered that they themselves sprang from that brave man," 13.615–16). The birds reappear each year to mark the death of their parent Memnon. Therefore, cremation as metamorphosis keeps Ovid's narrative flowing.

Aurora's connection to the house of Priam, through Tithonus, provides a genealogical link to the fall of Troy and Aeneas' arrival in Italy. Aurora's mourning for Memnon further connects the numerous references to cremation that connect the fall of the Troy with the rise of Rome and, ultimately, the comet symbolizing Julius Caesar's deification. Ovid emphasizes the theme of regeneration through cremation and allusions to rebirth after civil war. On his way to Italy, Aeneas visits Anius, priest of Apollo, on the island of Delos. Anius gives Aeneas a cup on which is depicted Thebes and various funeral scenes that followed the civil war between Polynices and Eteocles, including the death and disposal of Orion's daughters (13.685–99):

urbs erat, et septem posses ostendere portas:
hae pro nomine erant, et quae foret illa, docebant;
ante urbem exequiae tumulique ignesque rogique
effusaeque comas et apertae pectora matres
significant luctum; nymphae quoque flere videntur
siccatosque queri fontes: sine frondibus arbor
nuda riget, rodunt arentia saxa capellae.
ecce non femineum iugulo dare vulnus aperto,
illac demisso per fortia pectora telo
pro populo cecidisse suo pulchrisque per urbem
funeribus ferri celebrique in parte cremari.
tum de virginea geminos exire favilla,
ne genus intereat, iuvenes, quos fama Coronas
nominat, et cineri materno ducere pompam.

There was a city, and you could see seven gates:
this is where the city's name came from, and told which one it was;

in front of the city were funerals, graves, fires, pyres, and
mothers with disheveled hair and breasts bared for beating
that signified grief; nymphs seemed to cry and lament their
dried-up pools; a tree stood naked without leaves, goats
chewed on the parched rocks. See Orion's daughters, revealing
masculine wounds to their bared throats and a sword sent through
their brave chests, who died for the sake of their own people,
carried in beautiful processions throughout the city
and cremated before a large crowd.
Then so that their line would not perish, from
the virgin ashes arise two young men whom fame
calls the Coronae, who lead the procession for their
maternal ashes.

The cup focuses on the aftermath of civil war and contrasts its effect on urban and rural life: goats out to pasture are unaffected by human drama. The number of tombs and pyres are not specified, but the narrative focus is on the daughters of Orion who give birth through cremation to two men named the Coronae who immediately assist in the cremation rites of their mothers. While there are echoes of fallen Troy, also important is the theme of regeneration through metamorphosis that foreshadows the rebirth of Rome following the apotheosis of Caesar and the principate of Augustus. The participation of Nymphs in the funeral rituals foreshadows Venus' mourning for Caesar. Aeneas exchanges gifts for the cup; Ovid gives no indications, however, that he interprets the cup's images in relation to his own experiences or anticipated future.

The wanderings of Aeneas continue in Book 13 and extend into Book 14 as he approaches Latium. At Caieta, named after Aeneas' nurse, Aeneas encounters Achaemenides who recounts Ulysses' adventure with the Cyclops and Macareus who describes the evils of Circe. After these extended stories, the narrative suddenly shifts to the funeral urn of Caieta. Her death and cremation presumably occurred after Aeneas' arrival, but at no time during the speeches of Achaemenides and Macareus were they described. Caieta is given an epitaph on her tomb (14.441–44):

> [. . .] urnaque Aeneia nutrix
> condita marmorea tumulo breve carmen habebat
> HIC ME CAIETAM NOTAE PIETATIS ALUMNUS
> EREPTAM ARGOLICO QUO DEBUIT IGNE CREMAVIT

> [. . .] and Aeneas' nurse, placed in a

marble urn, had this brief epitaph on her tomb:
HERE HE WHOM I NURSED, FAMOUS FOR HIS PIETY, PROPERLY
    CREMATED
ME, CAIETA, WHO WAS SNATCHED FROM GREEK FIRE.

The epitaph emphasizes the moral virtues of Aeneas (famous for piety before her death for which his pious execution of her funeral rituals is yet another example and also noted), rather than the virtues of the deceased. Aeneas receives mention in the nominative case as Caieta refers to herself in the accusative case, thus showing deference to her ward even in death. The irony of her survival from Greek fire only to be consumed by the fire of her cremation is emphasized through the side-by-side placement of *igne* and *cremavit*. Following the quotation of the epitaph, no further mention is made of Caieta and the Trojans leave and quickly arrive in Latium, where Aeneas is given Latinus' daughter Lavinia in marriage and must fight the rejected Turnus.[42] In Vergil's *Aeneid*, Anchises dies under mysterious circumstances and his remains are later buried in Sicily.[43] Ovid makes no reference to Anchises' death, and Caieta's death and burial seem to serve as a substitution. Aeneas arrives in Latium without his father and Nurse in the *Metamorphoses* and thus emerges as a hero outside of their protective shadows.

    Caieta's cremation is followed by the cremation of Iphis, who hanged himself after being rejected by Anaxarete. Iphis' mother embraces the body of her son in a gesture reminiscent of Hecuba's embrace of Polyxena's corpse. The emphasis on the dual roles of deceased father and mother which Iphis' mother must play at his funeral draws attention to her solitude (14.743–47):

accipit illa sinu conplexaque frigida nati
membra sui postquam miserorum verba parentum
edidit et matrum miserarum facta peregit,
funera ducebat mediam lacrimosa per urbem
luridaque arsuro portabat membra feretro.

She took her son into her arms and embraced his
cold limbs and, after she spoke the words which wretched fathers say
and carried out the deeds which wretched mothers do,
tearful, she led the funeral throughout the city
and carried his pale limbs on a bier that would soon burn.

Iphis' bier is carried past Anaxarete's house and when she sees him lying dead, she turns to stone. The same sentence that informs the reader that the statue of the transformed Anaxarete is displayed on the island of Salamis also makes reference to a temple in honor of Venus: *neve ea ficta putes, dominae sub imagine signum / servat adhuc Salamis, Veneris quoque nomine templum / Prospicientis habet.* / "so that you do not think that this story is fiction, even now Salamis preserves a statue in the form of the mistress, and has a temple by the name of Venus Gazing," 14. 759–61. The emphatic, and somewhat forced, connection between the statue of Anaxarete and the temple of Venus links the goddess to a story of unrequited love, but the association also connects the goddess to Iphis' mother as the narrative anticipates, again, Venus' own grief over the death of Caesar. The cremation of Iphis is the last one described in the *Metamorphoses;* yet it, with others, provides an intra-textual link with mourning over Caesar's death and the comet that signals his apotheosis.[44]

Julius Caesar's Apotheosis as Cremation

The apotheosis of Julius Caesar is the teleological focus of the poem, but it is not the final metamorphosis which Ovid reserves for himself. Ovid focuses on the assassination of Caesar and the roles played by Venus and Augustus in securing his apotheosis, but not his funeral and cremation. Considering the preceding number and detailed descriptions of cremations that led to further metamorphoses, a reader might expect a description of Caesar's cremation on the model of Hercules' cremation in Book 9 (229–72) since it, too, served as a vehicle for his apotheosis. Ovid also deemphasizes the apotheosis of Romulus, the only historical Roman deified before Julius Caesar, and makes no connection between Romulus' apotheosis and Caesar's.[45] Caesar had assimilated himself with Romulus, but an association with Romulus was also cultivated by Augustus and this may explain Ovid's reluctance to make explicit any connection between Romulus and Caesar, despite elements discussed in chapter 2 for reading Caesar's funeral as apotheosis through funerary ritual.[46] Ovid also downplays historical details of Caesar's funeral with the result that the comet that signals Caesar's apotheosis in the *Metamorphoses* serves as both an apotheosis symbol and a substitution for a description of his actual cremation in order to signal Augustus' own metamorphosis into the son of a god. Ovid also uses the narrative of Caesar's apotheosis to emphasize his own role in immortalizing both Caesar and Augustus in the poem.

The narrative of Caesar's apotheosis is preceded by the introduction of Aesculapius' cult to Rome (15.622–44). Ovid contrasts Aesculapius' arrival at Rome, as a foreign god in snake form, with Caesar's divinity in the city of Rome (15.745–51):

Hic tamen accessit delubris advena nostris:
Caesar in urbe sua deus est; quem Marte togaque
praecipium non bella magis finita triumphis
resque domi gestae properataque gloria rerum
in sidus vertere novum stellamque comantem,
quam sua progenies; neque enim de Caesaris actis
ullam maius opus, quam quod pater exstitit huius [. . .]

He, however, arrived at our shrines as a foreigner.
Caesar is a god in his own city; he, conspicuous in war and peace,
was changed into a new heavenly body, a flaming star, not so
much for wars that ended in triumphs or the accomplishment of civic
deeds or his hastened glory as much as his own offspring; for
there is no greater achievement from Caesar's deeds, than that
he became the father of him [. . .]

The deification of Caesar is stated explicitly before his apotheosis is described
in the narrative, as is the role played by Augustus in furthering the deification along. Caesar's metamorphosis into a star and comet (*in sidus vertere
novum stellamque comantem*) is listed among other *res gestae* and furthermore
it ensured that Augustus would be born the son of a god: *ne foret hic igitur
mortali semine cretus, / ille deus faciendus erat [. . .] /* "so that he would not
be created, therefore, from mortal seed, Caesar needed to be made into a
god [. . .]," 15. 760–61.

Caesar's assassination is then seen from a god's eye view on Olympus:
Venus asks other gods to intervene; however, they cannot contradict rules
of fate that separate mortals from immortals. Portents of light and darkness
foreshadow the murder of Caesar which serves to contrast with the eventual
fire of his comet (15.785–90):

[. . .]; solis quoque tristis imago
lurida sollicitis praebebat lumina terris;
saepe faces visae mediis ardere sub astris,
saepe inter nimbos guttae cecidere cruentae;
caerulus et vultum ferrugine Lucifer atra
sparsus erat, sparsi lunares sanguine currus.

[. . .] also the sad face of the sun
shone a pale light over lands filled with apprehension;
often torches seemed to burn under the stars,
often drops of blood to fall from the clouds;

and the Morning Star was bluish and his face
covered with a metallic darkness, and the Moon's
chariot seemed stained with blood.

Among other signs of heavenly despair are funereal imagery: the sun's face is
compared to an ancestor mask (*imago*), and the facial discoloring of Lucifer,
the morning star, evokes a diseased and deathlike appearance; therefore gods
associated with light go into mourning before the actual murder. The assassination occurs in the narrative gap between the mention of weapons used
to kill Caesar and Venus' mourning (15.799–806):

> non tamen insidias venturaque vincere fata
> praemonitus potuere deum, strictique feruntur
> in templum gladii: neque enim locus ullus in urbe
> ad facinus diramque placet nisi curia caedem.
> tum vero Cytherea manu percussit utraque
> pectus et Aeneaden molitur condere nube,
> qua prius infesto Paris est eruptus Atridae,
> et Diomedeos Aeneas fugerat enses.

> Nonetheless, the warnings of the gods were
> unable to overcome plots and the coming fates.
> Drawn swords are carried into the sacred curia:
> for no other place in the city than the curia would
> suit the crime and ill-omened murder.
> Then truly did Cytherea strike her breast with
> both hands and tried to hide her Aenean offspring in a
> cloud—the one in which she had rescued Paris from the
> dangerous son of Atreus and in which Aeneas
> had eluded Diomedes' sword.

Ovid initially designates the place of murder as *templum* (801) and then as
curia (802), to emphasize Caesar's divine status and the religious sacrilege
of his assassination (*pontifex maximus*). The sequence and shift in designa-
tion from temple to curia also highlights the criminality of the act from
a human and civic perspective. Venus beats her breasts in mourning, in a
gesture reminiscent of Aurora's mourning for Memnon in Book 13, but
Jupiter predicts Caesar's imminent deification through her agency and the
agency of Caesar's (adopted) son Augustus (15.818–819).[47] Jupiter then
prophesies Augustus' struggles against Caesar's murderers and Antony and

Cleopatra as well as his civic reforms, and instructs Venus to assist in Caesar'
apotheosis:

'hanc animam interea caeso de corpore raptam
fac iubar, ut semper Captolia nostra forumque
divus ab excelsa prospectet Iulius aede!'

"Meanwhile, make his soul, snatched from his murdered
body, into a star, so that as the divine Julius he will always
gaze over our Capitol and forum from his lofty temple!" (15. 840–42)

Venus immediately releases Caesar's comet unseen in the senate house (but
Ovid knows of her role; therefore, he narrates from a privileged position).
From a narrative perspective, the speed with which Caesar's apotheosis occurs
is almost as quick as the narrative of his murder. Venus' unseen participation
allows Ovid (and other contemporaries) to postulate divine intervention in
Caesar's apotheosis, although, according to Suetonius, divine honors were
voted for Caesar by senators (*Divus Iulius,* 84.2).[48]

Ovid is more concerned with the apotheosis of Caesar than with the
historical details of his funeral and the disposal of his remains.[49] In fact,
Ovid's narrative glosses over and modifies actual events of Caesar's apotheosis and funeral, but according to the ancient sources discussed in chapter 2,
details surrounding Caesar's funeral were unusual. Ovid's narrative does not
compete with the theatricality of Caesar's funeral, but rather, it poeticizes
Caesar's metamorphosis and apotheosis by means of Venus' release of the
comet. The narrative of Caesar's altered form and divine status, however,
does reflect a change that had already taken place in Caesar's portraits. Following the appearance of the comet that signaled Caesar's apotheosis, a star
was added to the heads of his portraits:

Periit sexto et quinquagensimo aetatis anno atque in deorum numerum
relatus est, non ore modo decernentium sed et persuasione volgi. Siquidem
ludis, quos primos consecrato ei heres Augustus edebat, stella crinita per
septem continuos dies fulsit exoriens circa undecimam horam, creditumque
est animam esse Caesaris in caelum recepti; et hac de causa simulacro eius
in vertice additur stella.[50]

He died in his fifty-sixth year and was registered among the number of gods,
not only by formal decree but by popular conviction. At the games which
his heir Augustus first gave in honor of his apotheosis, a comet shone for

seven straight days, rising around the eleventh hour, and was believed to be
the soul of Caesar received into heaven; for this reason a star is added on
top of the head of his statue. (Suetonius, *Divus Iulius,* 88)

Suetonius links the changes in portraits in the same paragraph as Caesar's
death notice and the appearance of the comet that was linked to his apotheosis. To Romans unfamiliar with the symbolism of the star on Caesar's
portraits, Ovid's text would serve an aitiological function. Suetonius' passage
lends itself to an iconic or visual reading: the narrative placement of Augustus' name between Caesar's death, and his apotheosis reflects the central
role played by Augustus in exploiting the comet as a symbol of Caesar's
deification.

If Caesar became a god, then Augustus became the son of a god (Ovid,
Met. 15. 745–51, quoted above, actually reverses the priority of Caesar's
apotheosis: he became a god in order for Augustus to become the son of a
god). Just as Caesar's portraits reflected his divine status, Augustus' portraits
also underwent a similar metamorphosis. Statues, such as the portrait of
Augustus Primaporta, exploit the emperor's divine links to Venus, through
Caesar, to suggest that Augustus, as the son of a god, is himself a living god
on earth. Portraits that depict the emperor as perennially young further suggest the ongoing process of apotheosis during his lifetime.[51]

Ovid uses the narrative of Julius Caesar's assassination and apotheosis to
link the final lines of the poem to a final metamorphosis: the future apotheosis of himself through his poetry (15.871–79):

> Iamque opus exegi, quod nec Iovis ira nec ignis
> nec poterit ferrum nec edax abolere vetustas.
> cum volet, illa dies, quae nil nisi corporis huius
> ius habet, incerti spatium mihi finiat aevi:
> parte tamen meliore mei super alta perennis
> astra ferar, nomenque erit indelebile nostrum,
> quaque patet domitis Romana potentia terris,
> ore legar populi, perque omnia saecula fama,
> siquid habent veri vatum praesagia, vivam.

> I completed a work, which neither the anger of Jove
> nor fire, nor sword, nor devouring time will be able to destroy.
> When it will, let that day, which has control only of this body,
> end the span of my uncertain years: nevertheless, in the
> better part of myself, I will be carried, immortal, above the lofty stars,

and my name will be everlasting. Wherever Roman power
covers the conquered world, I will be spoken on the lips of men,
throughout all the centuries, if the predictions of poets are true,
and in fame live on.

The framing of poetic achievement in architectural terms evokes Horace's
declaration of immortality at Ode 3.30 (*exegi monumentum*), but other
intertexts that emphasize the flight of the poet to survey the extent of his
fame include Theognis, Ennius, Vergil, and Horace (*Ode* 2.20).[52] The listing
of the wrath of Jove as a possible factor in diminishing the immortality of
Ovid's poem, however, is unique. The reference to Jupiter's anger follows
Jupiter's prophecy to Venus that includes Augustus' future political achievements, among which is the deification of Julius Caesar. Multiple meanings
to the reference to Jupiter are possible, including a thematic one: Ovid
connects the narrative of Julius Caesar's apotheosis, through the reference
to Jupiter, to his own metamorphosis into an immortal poet. Through fire
imagery, Ovid transfers the image of the potential burning of his poem to
the future cremation of his own body. Flames, however, will destroy neither
poem nor poet. Thus, Ovid anticipates and actualizes, through his verse, his
own cremation and apotheosis which will take him beyond the imperium of
Caesars and the limits of the stars.

Ovid's *sphragis* expresses his own poetic success through a celestial boundary without end (*supra astra*) that extends beyond the terrestrial imperium
destined for Augustus (across the earth and *extra sidera*) outlined in Vergil's
Aeneid (6.791–97):

> hic vir, hic est, tibi quem promitti saepius audis,
> Augustus Caesar, divi genus, aurea condet
> saecula qui rursus Latio regnata per arva
> Saturno quondam, super et Garamantas et Indos
> proferet imperium; iacet extra sidera tellus,
> extra anni solisque vias, ubi caelifer Atlas
> axem umero torquet stellis ardentibus aptum.[53]

> Here is the man, here he is, whom you often hear is promised to you,
> Augustus Caesar, son of a god, who will found a golden age again
> over the fields of Latium once ruled by Saturn and extend the
> empire beyond the Garamantes and Indians; beyond the stars
> lies a land, beyond the annual path of the sun, where Atlas the
> skybearer, on his shoulder, turns the axis adorned with burning stars.

Here, Anchises points out the future Augustus to Aeneas, both of whom will conquer geography and time to achieve immortality. Anchises uses the language of epitaphs to describe Augustus and the limits of his imperium (*hic vir, hic est . . . iacet*) and the allusion to funeral ritual plays on the conceit that future Roman heroes who are not yet born are already in Elysium in the Underworld, but the epitaph commemorates only Augustus and his achievements. From a narrative perspective, Vergil's allusion to funeral ritual in introducing the future princeps to his readers and in describing the boundaries of Augustus' imperium provides closure and nonclosure: descriptions of death or a funeral give authorial control to a poet and Vergil, as epitaph writer, limits Augustus' fame by marking the passing of its existence before its boundaries are actually demarcated.

From a semiotic perspective, however, Vergil's epitaph does not mark the physical location of Augustus, who is not in Elysium (at time of composition), despite Anchises' pointing gesture, and since the future deification of Augustus is anticipated in the text, Augustus will be (however temporary until his reincarnation/birth into the real world) in Elysium and not Tartarus, implying that a favorable judgment has already been passed on him. Vergil's epitaph, which should mark death, actually allows Augustus to cheat death and make his imperium his final resting place and achievement for fame. The reading process actualizes what is a temporal conceit in the poem (the future fame of Augustus) since it is Vergil's text that immortalizes both emperor and poet.

Ovid evokes the Vergilian formulation of using death ritual to anticipate the future fame of Augustus which he connects with the deification of Julius Caesar, but it is also tied to and surpassed by his own fame as a poet. The architects of metamorphosis and immortality are themselves transformed and immortalized. Ovid's *sphragis* becomes a figurative epitaph that represents a teleology of the poet's life and literary work that both marks and does not mark a limitless and timeless final resting place for his poetry.

In his exile, however, Ovid wrote an epitaph in the *Tristia* (3.3.73–76) for himself that wittingly plays on the epitaphic tradition as it refocuses the claim of immortality through his poetry to a declaration of his mortality through his poetry:

HIC EGO QUI IACEO TENERORUM LUSOR AMORUM
   INGENIO PERII NASO POETA MEO
AT TIBI QUI TRANSIS NE SIT GRAVE QUISQUIS AMASTI
   DICERE NASONIS MOLLITER OSSA CUBENT[54]

HERE I LIE, HE WHO WAS THE PLAYER OF TENDER LOVES
    BY MY TALENT, I, THE POET NASO DIED
BUT YOU, WHOEVER YOU ARE WHO HAVE LOVED, AS YOU WALK
    BY, PLEASE
SAY, "MAY THE BONES OF NASO LIE LIGHTLY."

The epitaph qualifies and undercuts the *sphragis* and its placement in the *Tristia* literally marks Ovid's life and career as a poet even though he considers the poems themselves as a greater monument (*monimenta* 3.3.78) than his epitaph.[55] Ovid's actual burial at Tomis, rather than Rome, further demarcates the boundary of Augustus' empire beyond which his earlier poetry soared.

An examination of the intertextuality of the funeral trope between and within the epic texts of Vergil and Ovid reveals authorial agendas, in which descriptions and allusions to funerals become less familiar to the experience of the reader. The fictive reality created by these narratives contributes to the participatory reading experience: pathos is aroused in Vergil's description of Pallas' funeral through allusion to bucolic poetry, whereas the "tragedy" of Hecuba in the *Metamorphoses* distances the reader from a text that seems designed to shock through paradox and grotesque positioning—a pattern that continues in the epics of Lucan and Statius which forms the focus of chapter 4. Ovid's use of funerary ritual to frame the climax of the poem, however, reveals a different agenda: to displace the apotheosis of Julius Caesar as the teleological focus of the poem with his own apotheosis as an immortal poet.

CHAPTER 4

Disposing the Dead?

Barlow Bonsall cook @ 1700–1800 for 2 to 3 hours

So READS the text of a tattoo, inside a yellow and orange flame, of Army veteran and cancer survivor Russell Parsons.[1] "It's a recipe," the 67-year-old widower from Hurricane, West Virginia said. "It's a recipe for cremation." Barlow Bonsall, the addressee of the tattoo, is the name of the Funeral Home and Crematorium that will carry out the cremation. In a variation of a will or epitaph designed to identify the deceased or the location of their remains, the unique tattoo ensures that Parsons's corpse itself will communicate directions for a proper disposal to the crematorium staff. No mention is made of what will happen to his remains after his cremation, rather the words describe the process of cremation that will perish during the cremation process. Since Parsons refers to the tattoo as a "recipe" rather than "directions" for a cremation, the tattoo alludes to recipes found in a cookbook: Parsons humorously self-identifies his future corpse as a meal that will be prepared by a cremating chef. Parsons's tattoo is now a symbol of his mortality that allows the living to interpret and even commemorate his future death and disposal.

With the exception of Parsons's tattoo, the bodies of corpses themselves do not normally communicate with those in charge of their disposal. The tattoo, however, is instructive of the interpretative challenge posed by descriptions of cremations in Latin epic. Corpses and their disposal both in the reader's experience and within a narrative can be read figuratively. Chapter 3 examined the descriptions of cremation in Vergil and Ovid as elements of a narrative strategy that turns the associative reading experience into a participatory act: Vergil aroused pathos through allusions to pastoral poetry in the cremation of Pallas, whereas Ovid's absurd treatment of Hecuba's grief in locating the discovery of her dead son Polydorus at the same time as she prepares to wash her daughter's corpse subverted the solemnity of funeral ritual into bathos. The displacement of Julius Caesar's cremation allowed Ovid to make himself the teleological focus of the poem and to express his poetic immortality through allusion to death ritual.

In this chapter, I look at how the reader's participatory reading experience is further manipulated by authorial agendas that make narratives of funeral rituals even more disturbing and bizarre. Lucan takes Ovid's cue and exploits the potential inherent in the historical details surrounding Pompey's death and cremation to turn the reader into a voyeuristic audience of a grotesque spectacle. In the *Thebaid*, Statius also engages the reader's familiarity with the topos of cremation to turn it into an intertextual exercise that has little in common with either the ritual itself or epic intertexts. The descriptions of the dual cremations of Opheltes and the serpent, the cremations of Eteocles and Polynices, and the abandoned description of Creon's funeral and cremation challenge the reader's familiarity with funerary ritual and previous literary intertexts in a disassociative narrative designed to repel and confuse.

Cremating Pompey in Lucan's *Bellum Civile*

At *Bellum Civile* 8.692–700, Lucan contrasts the tomb of Alexander the Great and the funeral monuments of the Ptolemies (pyramids and mausolea) with Pompey's unburied corpse:

> litora Pompeium feriunt, truncusque vadosis
> huc illuc iactatur aquis. adeone molesta
> totum cura fuit socero servare cadaver?[2]

> The shores beat against Pompey, his headless corpse
> is tossed, here and there, by the shallow waters.
> Was it too much trouble to keep the corpse whole
> for his father-in-law? (8.698–700)

The restful slumber of Alexander and the Ptolemies focuses by contrast on the abuse suffered by Pompey's corpse. Lucan elicits pathos with his description of Pompey's headless body (*truncus*) being tossed about (*huc illuc*) by the waves. Pathos, however, turns to voyeuristic fascination when Lucan focuses on the corpse on the beach:

pulsatur harenis,
carpitur in scopulis hausto per vulnera fluctu,
ludibrium pelagi, nullaque manente figura
una nota est Magno capitis iactura revulsi.

He is beaten by the sands,
he is torn on the rocks as water is drawn in through
his wounds, he is the plaything of waves, with no
distinguishing feature remaining, the loss of his
decapitated head makes him recognizable as Magnus. (8.708–11)

Pompey is now described as the plaything of waves (*ludibrium*) as water fills
and flows in and out of his body cavity and foreshadows Cordus' lament
over the corpse when his tears fill every wound (8.727) and echo Ovid,
Met. 13.490 where Hecuba's tears fill the wounds of Polyxena's corpse: *huic
quoque dat lacrimas; lacrimas in vulnera fundit.*[3] Ironically, it is because the
corpse has no head that it is identifiable as Pompey's.[4] How should the
reader interpret this passage which at once arouses sympathy, disgust, and
even humor?[5]

The passage also parallels the well-known passage of *Aeneid* 2. 557–58,
where the headless corpse of Priam evokes the death of Pompey.[6] Vergil's
readers, like Aeneas, lose sight of Priam's corpse before it receives burial.[7] In
Lucan, however, Book 8 focuses on the murder, decapitation, and burial of
Pompey's corpse. Whereas Vergil elicits pathos in his allusion to Pompey's
death, Lucan, like Ovid, undercuts his narrative with the grotesque and
absurd.[8] The narrative of Pompey's decapitation and treatment of his corpse,
through allusion to Roman burial ritual, places the reader in the alternating
roles of reader/spectator and participant who is drawn to the repulsive details
of Pompey's extended death and burial.[9]

Text as Corpse

Lucan's narrative reflects the treatment of Pompey's mutilated corpse. The
description of Pompey's death and burial extends over Books 7, 8, and
9 and provides thematic unity even while structurally severing the narrative of his unnaturally prolonged death.[10] Book 9, furthermore, opens and
closes with Pompey's death.[11] Like the decapitation of Pompey, the narrative
of the decapitation is, itself, divided into two parts: the actual decapitation (8.663–87) and the preservation of his head (8.688–91). Narrative

interruptions, from Pompey's purported final thoughts (8.622 ff.) to his wife Cornelia's lament (8.639 ff.), delay the anticipated description of his decapitation and reflect Pompey's prolonged death. The historical Pompey has become a rhetorical persona whose death can be manipulated to suit narrative purposes.[12]

Lucan's narrative focus further reflects his manipulation of details surrounding the death and burial of Pompey. The encounters between Pompey and his killer Achillas and his beheader Septimius evoke a gladiatorial combat that turns the amphitheater into a metaphor for civil war.[13] The narrative of the decapitation, furthermore, elicits a voyeuristic response that turns the reader into what Matthew Leigh describes as an amphitheatrical audience.[14] The narrative encourages a disengaged emotional response to Pompey's decapitation, which contrasts with a narrative voice that reserves its sympathy for the poetic outbursts that frame descriptions of Pompey's murder and mutilation. In other words, the narrator interprets the mutilation of Pompey's corpse as a moral act while the narrative of the mutilation treats it as a physical one, causing the reader to alternate between feelings of sympathy and disengaged curiosity.[15] From an aesthetic perspective, the abuse of Pompey's corpse can also be read as a *damnatio memoriae* and a similar viewer response results from a narrative process whereby Pompey's corpse substitutes for the mutilation of his statue contemporaneously with his murder.[16]

Lucan anticipates the decapitation by concentrating the reader/audience's attention on Pompey's head, with the narrative equivalent of a zoom lens: at 8.613 ff.: after Pompey sees Septimius with knives, he covers his head and remains silent with eyes closed and imagines that it is Caesar rather than Achillas who murders him.[17] The effect of this narrative focus is that the reader "sees" the scene more clearly than Pompey himself (613–17):[18]

> ut vidit comminus ensis,
> involvit vultus atque indignatus apertum
> Fortunae praebere caput; tum lumina pressit
> continuitque animam, ne quas effundere voces
> vellet et aeternam fletu corrumpere famam.

> When he saw the sword nearby,
> he covered his face and head, scorning to offer
> it bare to Fortune; then he sealed his eyes and
> held his breath in case he would pour out his feelings
> and ruin his immortal fame with tears.

Pompey is dead to the narrative of his murder in the text before the description of his actual death. It is only when Septimius slits the fabric of his head covering to decapitate Pompey (669), that he "faces" his murderers. Ironically, Pompey is a metaphorical corpse before his actual death. The paradox continues after his death and is reversed: his head is seemingly alive while impaled. From this point, Pompey is reduced to a head with a soon-to-be-severed body.[19]

Text with a Corpse

The description of Pompey's murder is unexpectedly brief:

> sed, postquam mucrone latus funestus Achillas
> perfodit, nullo gemitu consensit ad ictum
> respexitque nefas, servatque immobile corpus [. . .]

> But after the deadly Achillas dug into his side with his sword,
> with no groan did he acknowledge the blow and heed the crime,
> but kept his body motionless [. . .] (618–20)

Lucan devotes more space to dying, decapitation, and poetic outburts. The quickness of Achillas' actions contrasts with Pompey's slow death. Lucan does not state explicitly that both Achillas and Septimius were present during Pompey's murder and mutilation. Rather Achillas seems to be present for the stabbing while Septimius performs the decapitation.[20] The focus in each event, therefore, is on just two combantants, killer and victim, emphasizing the reader's role as amphitheater audience.

The narrative interruptions following Pompey's murder make it easy to overlook the fact that Pompey is still alive, both when Lucan attributes final thoughts to him (8.622 ff),[21] and during Cornelia's outburst before leaving her dying husband before the decapitation (8.639–62). Therefore, narrative interruptions that delay the actual moment of Pompey's death reflect his prolonged agony.[22] The prolonged process of the decapitation (*diu,* 323) mirrors, in turn, the prolonged narrative of Pompey's death.[23]

The description of Pompey's decapitation focuses on the process of the act and Septimius' difficulty in cutting the head from the body:

> At, Magni cum terga sonent et pectora ferro,
> permansisse decus sacrae venerabile formae

placatamque deis faciem, nil ultima mortis
ex habitu vultuque viri mutasse fatentur
qui lacerum videre caput. nam saevus in ipso
Septimius sceleris maius scelus invenit actu,
ac retegit sacros scisso velamine vultus
semianimis Magni spirantiaque occupat ora
collaque in obliquo ponit languentia transtro.
tunc nervos venasque secat nodosaque frangit
ossa diu: nondum artis erat caput ense rotare.
at, postquam trunco cervix abscisa recessit,
vindicat hoc Pharius, dextra gestare, satelles.
degener atque operae miles Romane secundae,
Pompei diro sacrum caput ense recidis,
ut non ipse feras?

But, while the back and chest of Magnus resonated with the sword,
the august beauty of his sacred features remained and his expression
was at peace with the gods, and those who saw the severed head
claimed that death did not change his appearance and his face.
In the very act of committing a crime, cruel Septimius discovered
a greater one. By tearing the covering, he laid bare the sacred features
of the half-alive Magnus, grabbed the still breathing head and
laid the drooping neck across a bench. Then, for a long time, he cut
the muscles, the veins, and the knotty bones: not yet was it an art to
make heads roll with the sword. But, after the severed neck was
separated from his torso, the subordinate Pharius claimed the right
to carry it in his right hand. You degenerate and a Roman soldier of
an inferior deed, do you sever the sacred head of Pompey with your
polluted sword, in order not to carry it yourself? (8.663–78)

At several points, Lucan includes details that further prolong the narrative
by causing the reader to question the accuracy of the account: *fatentur* (line
666), for example, undercuts the narrator's credibility as an eyewitness and
describes the state of the head at a later time and not at the time of its
removal.[24] In addition, the detail on the type of weapon used reads more
like a footnote to Lucan's contemporary readers who might wonder why
Pompey's head is cut off with an axe, rather than the sword, which was not
yet in current use. The focus on details surrounding the severing of specific
body parts makes it easy to get lost in the gore and to forget the larger focus
that it is Pompey's head being severed rather than the head of a sacrificial

animal. The description of Pompey's decapitation is so graphic that one can almost hear it.

It is significant that the actual moment of death is not given. In fact, Pompey is described as half-alive (*semianimis,* 670), so not only did Achillas not kill him, Pompey is still alive when Septimius beheads him and even, seemingly, when he is impaled. To make the status of Pompey more confusing, the narrator claims that those who saw Pompey's head noticed no change in his features (665 ff.), before Septimius slit the fabric and actually exposed the head (669). It is the realization of this constantly suffering Pompey, strangely never quite dead or alive, which makes the narrative more disturbing.[25] The description of Pompey as *semianimis* provides a flashback to the beginning of Book 8 when Cornelia faints while Pompey visits her on Lesbos: *semianimem . . . eram* (8.66). The additional irony that Pompey exiting Italy boasted of "beheading" Crassus (2.546–47) is not lost on the reader.[26]

The manipulation of scenery and narrative focus also affect the reader's response to Pompey's decapitation.[27] The scene evokes the gladiatorial aspect of the famous duel between Manlius Torquatus and the Gaul. Livy (7.10.6), and Claudius Quadrigarius before him, focus more on the provocation and combat, before an audience of Romans and Gauls, than the actual decapitation of the fallen Gaul.[28] Evocations of Aeneas' duel with Turnus are also present in the narrative of Pompey's decapitation.[29] Unlike Vergil, however, who gives a panoramic view of Turnus' death with the hero himself the object of a sympathetic collective groan, Lucan gives a close-up and even magnified view.[30] In Lucan's narrative, Pompey and the reader hear only the surf and its waves that will continue to ebb and flow after Pompey's death. The sound and rhythmic movement of the sea contrast with Pompey's separation and imminent departure from nature, and they seem to mock rather than comfort him in his silence and expectation of death. By alluding to these earlier combats, Lucan identifies Pompey with anti-heroes, but while the allusions encourage us to cheer on the one doing the slaying, the narrative encourages us, as with the death of Turnus and Hector before him, to sympathize with Pompey the slain.

The description of Pompey's decapitation also contains allusions to funeral rituals. These allusions serve as cultural markers to arouse sympathy and pity through the evocation of rituals known to the reader, but shock when the reader's experience is not reflected in the text. Since Pompey dies alone, pathos is aroused since no one can catch his last breath with a kiss.[31] By alluding to Pompey's head in terms reserved for *imagines: sacros . . . voltus* (8.669) before the actual decapitation and *sacrum caput* (8.677) thereafter,

Lucan recalls ancestor masks which, as discussed above, were stored in the atrium of a Roman house and either carried during a funeral *pompa* or worn by an actor who would imitate the deceased.[32] Pompey's head stands, by synecdoche, for Rome: Lucan claims that the head was one which Rome was once proud to wear (*hac facie, Fortunam tibi Romana, placebas* (8.686), thus identifying Rome with a mime wearing the mask of a deceased person, perhaps at the funeral of the Republic itself.

Even more disturbing than the comparison of Pompey's head to an *imago* is the fact that the reader is still not entirely sure that Pompey is dead, since his head is impaled while seemingly still alive:

> impius ut Magnum nosset puer, illa verenda
> regibus hirta coma et generosa fronte decora
> caesaries comprensa manu est, Pharioque veruto,
> dum vivunt vultus atque os in murmura pulsant
> singultus animae, dum lumina nuda rigescunt,
> suffixum caput est [. . .]

> So that the impious boy would recognize Magnus,
> that thick hair revered by kings and the curls handsome
> on his noble brow were grabbed with his hand, and on
> a Pharian spear, while the face was living and gasps
> of breath forced the mouth to murmur, while the
> unclosed eyes became stiff, his head was fixed. . . . (8.679–84)

The narrative focus remains Pompey's head. *Vivunt vultus* (682) echoes the description of Pompey as *semianimis* during the decapitation and reminds us of his prolonged death. The emphasis on the still living features of the dying Pompey recalls Sallust's description of the dying Catiline (*Cat.* 61.4, cited in chapter 1). As with Lucan's Pompey, Sallust focuses on Catiline's face. Catiline's lifelike features in death, like those of Pompey, are described in terms similar to those of an *imago*.[33] Sallust emphasizes the isolation of Catiline's cadaver since it is separated from his own men and is now among the enemy, but also the unnaturalness of Catiline's prolonged life after death. Lucan's allusion to this passage provides another example of how the narrative encourages the reader to view Pompey in antiheroic terms as it also arouses sympathy for him.

The second part of the narrative that focuses on the decapitation concerns the preservation of Pompey's head as proof of death. The description of the head's preservation by embalming is graphic, like its severing, which focuses on the liquids pouring out of the head rather than on the head itself:

> nec satis infando fuit hoc vidisse tyranno:
> vult sceleris superesse fidem. tunc arte nefanda
> summota est capiti tabes, raptoque cerebro
> assiccata cutis, putrisque effluxit ab alto
> umor, et infuso facies solidata veneno est.

> Nor was this enough for the unnatural tyrant to look at:
> he wants a proof of his crime to survive. Then by the
> impious art, the fluid is drawn from the head, the brain
> removed, and the skin dried. Putrid fluid poured out from
> deep within and his features stiffened when a potion was poured in.
>   (8.687–91)

Lucan refers to embalming as *arte nefanda* (688), which are related to the arts of Erictho and thus designated as morally suspect. The graphic description suggests that embalming was a procedure outside of Roman funerary custom, thus further alienating the reader as mourner. Descriptions of Poppaea's embalming also treat the procedure as foreign rather than a customary form of corpse treatment.[34] The embalming of Pompey's head recalls Lucan's narrative of the beheading (8.665 ff.), while Pompey was seemingly still alive, where Pompey's facial features are described as fixed in death. The embalming seems unnecessary in a narrative that repeatedly emphasizes the lingering life of Pompey and his head, thus making the graphic description of the embalming seem like an additional outrage to Pompey's corpse. The textual emendation of *placatam* for *irratam* to describe the head (665) alters the scene dramatically: a preserved expression of anger would serve as condemnation for the treatment of his corpse while a peaceful expression would imply Pompey's acceptance of his fate, perhaps to the chagrin of Septimius and Caesar.[35] It is significant that the features of Pompey's head later change—exactly how is not stated—when the head is brought to Caesar as proof of Pompey's death (Book 10), providing yet another instance of how Lucan keeps Pompey and his remains seemingly alive beyond the narrative of his death.

Lucan describes the cremation of Pompey's corpse in terms which evoke a pauper burial.[36] In an extended narrative composed of numerous prayers, the quaestor Cordus retrieves Pompey's corpse and prays to Fortune to grant Pompey a meager funeral.[37] Cordus laments that his burial of Pompey is inexpensive: *non pretiosa . . . sepulchra* (8.729), with no funeral procession, no funeral oration in the forum, and no military tributes (8.731–35). In other words, Pompey "the Great" is to receive a pauper's burial: *vilem plebei funeris arcam* (8.736). The paltry cremation materials contrast with the tree-felling passages of Ennius and Vergil, adding to the anti-heroic tone of the passage:[38]

> non pretiosa petit cumulato ture sepulchra
> Pompeius, Fortuna, tuus, non pinguis ad astra
> ut ferat e membris Eoos fumus odores,
> ut Romana suum gestent pia colla parentem,
> praeferat ut veteres feralis pompa triumphos,
> ut resonent tristi cantu fora, totus ut ignes
> proiectis maerens exercitus ambiat armis.
> da vilem Magno plebei funeris arcam
> quae lacerum corpus siccos effundat in ignes;
> robora non desint misero nec sordidus ustor

> Your Pompey, Fortune, does not seek a precious pyre with incense
> heaped up, nor that the thick smoke should carry eastern scents
> from his body to the stars, nor that dutiful Roman necks should bear
> their parent, nor that his funeral procession should display his triumphs
> of old, nor that the Fora should echo with sorrowful song, nor that the
> whole army in mourning should lay down their arms and walk around
> the flames. Give to Magnus the cheap coffin of a plebeian funeral
> which will pour out the mutilated body onto the thirsty flames;
> but do not let the miserable one lack timber or a cheap corpse-burner.
> (8.729–38)

Cordus proceeds to give Pompey's headless corpse a partial cremation by stealing the burning embers from someone else's bier:[39]

> Sic fatus parvos iuvenis procul aspicit ignes
> corpus vile suis nullo custode cremantis.
> inde rapit flammas semustaque robora membris
> subducit. 'quaecumque es,' ait 'neglecta nec ulli
> cara tuo sed Pompeio felicior umbra,
> quod iam compositum violat manus hospita bustum,
> da veniam: si quid sensus post fata relictum est,
> cedis et ipsa rogo paterisque haec damna sepulchri,

teque pudet sparsis Pompei manibus uri.'
sic fatus plenusque sinus ardente favilla
pervolat ad truncum, qui fluctu paene relatus
litore pendebat. summas dimovit harenas
et collecta procul lacerae fragmenta carinae
exigua trepidus posuit scrobe. nobile corpus
robora nulla premunt, nulla strue membra recumbunt:
admotus Magnum, non subditus, accipit ignis.

Thus having spoken, the youth saw small fires in the distance,
with no guard, cremating a body worthless to its family.
Next, he seized fire and half-burnt timbers from under the limbs.
"Whoever you are," he said, "abandoned shade and dear to none of
yours but luckier than Pompey, forgive that a stranger's hand
violates your assembled pyre: if there is any feeling left after death,
give over these things from your pyre and these losses from your grave
and feel shame that you were burning while the shades of Pompey lie
        scattered."
Thus he spoke and with his cloak full of burning ashes,
flew to the torso which, almost carried off by the waves,
was hanging on the shore's edge. He moved aside the topmost sand
and shaking, placed into the shallow pit the fragments of a broken boat
found at a distance. No timbers press against his noble body,
no limbs lie on a pile: a fire placed beside, rather than beneath, burns
        Magnus. (8.743–58)

Pompey's pauper burial is all the more shocking because of the narrative that
barely makes the pauper burial happen: while Cordus was stealing wood
from someone else's pyre, which may be contaminated with his ashes, a
wave almost carried away his torso;[40] the pyre is not constructed of wood;
the cremation pit is barely drawn into the sand; and the fire that should be
burning below the corpse actually burns beside it.

The narrative calls attention to Cordus' gathering of wood and his preparation of the pyre in a way that evokes *Metamorphoses* 8.640–45 when
Philemon and Baucis entertain the gods, in particular, Baucis' preparation
of a fire with which to cook the meal.[41] By connecting Pompey's pyre with
Baucis' hearth, Lucan presents Pompey as the victim of fate who is offered
to the gods as reproach for the inhumane treatment suffered by his corpse.
The cannibalistic implications are reminiscent of Seneca, *Thyestes* 760 ff.,
where Atreus cuts off the limbs of Thyestes' sons and boils their body parts.
The actual description of the cremation is brief compared to the narrative

of its preparation, but the reference to Magnus personifies Pompey's corpse in an unsettling way:

excitat invalidas admoto fomite flammas.
carpitur et lentum Magnus destillat in ignem
tabe fovens bustum.

He rouses the weak flames by adding fuel.
Magnus is reduced and drips into the slow fire,
feeding the pyre with his melting flesh. (8.776–78)

The setting sun interrupts the order of Pompey's cremation (*ordine rupto / funeris,* 779–80), and coincides with the glowing of the ashes as Cordus gathers the bones for burial.

The cremation, however, is not complete as sinews and marrow cling to the bones:

semusta rapit resolutaque nondum
ossa satis nervis et inustis plena medullis
aequorea restinguit aqua congestaque in unum
parva clausit humo.[42]

He seized the half-burnt bones, not sufficiently
separated from the muscles and full of burned marrow,
extinguished them with sea water, piled them up
and covered them with a bit of earth. (8.786–89)

Reflecting the simple burial, few words are devoted to its narrative. Pothinus gives further details about the small mound's appearance when he points it out in Book 10:

aspice litus,
spem nostri sceleris; pollutos consule fluctus
quid liceat nobis, tumulumque e pulvere parvo
aspice Pompei non omnia membra tegentem.

Look at the shore,
the pledge of our crime; consult the polluted waves
about what we can do, and look at the grave made from meager
dust, not covering all of Pompey's limbs. (10.378–81)

The description of the grave can be interpreted two ways: that it was insufficient to cover all of Pompey's remains and barely in compliance with burial ritual or that the insufficient burial did not contain all of Pompey's remains since it does not contain his head (*non omnia membra,* 381). The reminder that Pompey is not all there suggests that his corpse has no identity like the corpse whose embers Cordus stole.

The narrative of Pompey's cremation extends to Book 9 with the apotheosis of Pompey's soul, lamentation for his death, and Cornelia's substitute cremation of Pompey's clothing. Pompey's soul rises from his ashes and laughs at the abuse inflicted on his corpse as he flies over the battlefields of Pharsalus (9.1–18):

> At non in Pharia manes iacuere favilla
> nec cinis exiguus tantam compescuit umbram:
> prosiluit busto semustaque membra relinquens
> degeneremque rogum sequitur convexa Tonantis.
> qua niger astriferis conectitur axibus aer
> quodque patet terras inter lunaeque meatus,
> semidei manes habitant, quos ignea virtus
> innocuos vita patientes aetheris imi
> fecit et aeternos animam collegit in orbes.
> non illuc auro positi nec ture sepulti
> perveniunt. illic postquam se lumine vero
> implevit, stellasque vagas miratus et astra
> fixa polis, vidit quanta sub nocte iaceret
> nostra dies risitque sui ludibria trunci.
> hinc super Emathiae campos et signa cruenti
> Caesaris ac sparsas volitavit in aequore classes,
> et scelerum vindex in sancto pectore Bruti
> sedit et invicti posuit se mente Catonis.
>
> But his spirit did not lie among the Pharian embers
> nor did the meager ash confine such a shade:
> it leapt up from his grave and leaving his half-burnt limbs
> and the unworthy pyre, heads for the Thunderer's vault.
> Where the dark air is connected to the star-bearing heavens
> in the regions between the earth and the paths of the moon,
> semidivine shades live, those whom innocent in life, their
> fiery virtue has made able to endure the lower aether and
> has gathered their spirits among the eternal spheres.
> Not there do people laid in gold or buried with incense

come. There, after Pompey's spirit filled itself with true light,
and having marveled at the wandering planets and the stars
fixed to the heavens, it saw how much our daylight lies under
the night and it laughed at the insults to his torso.
From here, it flew above the Emathian fields, the standards
of Caesar and the fleet arrayed in the sea and as an avenger
of crime, it settled in the sacred breast of Brutus and positioned
itself in the mind of invincible Cato.

Pompey's apotheosis takes place much faster than the narrative of his lingering death and abuse of his corpse and Pompey's soul takes on a vigor
that contrasts with his former passivity. A temporal adjustment is needed
since his corpse was abused before its cremation. The reader, therefore,
must now imagine that Pompey's soul (even prior to his cremation) was
witnessing events from Book 8, like his murder and abuse of his corpse,
with the reader unaware of his soul's presence. From a semiotic perspective,
Pompey was an audience to his own audience of events on earth, watching
himself watching events of his murder unfold, watching his corpse being
decapitated and abused (now referred to as a spectacle: *ludibria*), watching
Cordus' hasty funeral and the cremation of his remains from which his
soul arose. Pompey continues to be both dead and alive and his remains
both separated, while his head awaits cremation, and reconstituted as his
soul soars over the earth as a witness and audience of events, past and current. Thus, Pompey emerges as a self-representational character, changing
his role from character to author, as he provides closure to the narrative
of his death and disposal denied to him by Lucan. The description of his
apotheosis becomes his own *sphragis* on Lucan's text: Pompey has achieved
immortality as both a character and author. Like Horace in *Ode* 2.20 where
the poet soars as a swan making Augustus' empire the boundaries of his,
the poet's, fame, Pompey surveys the geographic and poetic boundaries of
his own renown.

Despite his apotheosis and self-asserted self-representation in the text,
Lucan regains authorial control as the text returns to Pompey's corpse and
his second (symbolic) cremation. In a gesture reminiscent of Dido in *Aeneid*,
Book 4. 642 ff., Cornelia burns clothing (*Iliacas vestis*, 648) and other items
belonging to Pompey, but absent is any allusion to the effigy of Aeneas which
Dido had placed on her pyre:

sed magis, ut visa est lacrimis exhausta, solutas
in vultus effusa comas, Cornelia puppe
egrediens, rursus geminato verbere plangunt.

ut primum in sociae pervenit litora terrae,
collegit vestes miserique insignia Magni
armaque et impressas auro, quas gesserat olim
exuvias pictasque togas, velamina summo
ter conspecta Iovi, funestoque intulit igni.
ille fuit miserae Magni cinis. . . .

But all the more do they wail and redouble the
strikes against their breasts when they see
Cornelia leaving her ship, worn out by tears and
disheveled, hair loosened across her face.
When at first she arrived on the shores of allied land,
she collected the clothes and insignia of wretched Magnus,
his weapons and armor, impressed with gold, which he
once had worn and his embroidered togas, garments seen
three times by highest Jove, and she placed them on the
funeral fire. To the pitiable woman, that was the
ash of Magnus. (9.171–79)

Cornelia does not perform an actual cremation, but rather a substitute cremation since Pompey's trunk has already been burned. But by including a second cremation of Pompey, Lucan makes the reader mourn again. The prolonged and repetitive treatment of the corpse reflects the prolonged narrative of his decapitation and lingering death (or rather the lingering life attributed to his head).

While Cornelia is performing her substitute cremation, Pompey's head is apparently en route to Caesar who has arrived in Egypt. When Pompey's head is brought to Caesar, he first treats Pompey as a foe and then as a kinsman as he sheds crocodile tears (9.1064–1104). When Pompey's head is revealed, the face has been changed in death and its features both attract and repel Caesar's gaze:

> Sic fatus opertum
> detexit tenuitque caput. iam languida morte
> effigies habitum noti mutaverat oris.
> non primo Caesar damnavit munera visu
> avertitque oculos; vultus dum crederet, haesit;

> Thus he spoke and uncovered and
> held up his head. Already, the head, languid
> in death, had changed the appearance of his familiar

features. At first, Caesar did not condemn the gift
nor turn his eyes from the sight; he stared until
he believed it was his face. (9.1032–36)

The ability of Pompey's face to change features again suggests that he is still
not dead and that he is playing dead like the dying Catiline in Sallust. In
this case, however, the moral consequence of the ambiguity falls on Caesar,
rather than Pompey, whose head reminds the reader (and Caesar in the text)
of Pompey's brutal murder and decapitation. The staging of the scene also
reinforces Caesar's guilt: Pompey's head becomes the narrative focus as we
watch Caesar looking at Pompey's head as he scrutinizes the features for a
long time. Surprisingly, Lucan does not tell us whether Pompey was looking
back at Caesar since the text does not make explicit whether or not Pompey's
eyes are shut. Caesar's reluctance to look at Pompey's head when it is shown
to him reflects a merging or fusion of the amphitheatrical audience between
reader and epic character. Should the reader continue to follow Caesar as he
looks away from the head or should the reader keep looking at Pompey? The
reader, therefore, remains voyeuristically involved in the narrative.

Caesar immediately plans a proper burial for Pompey's head which is to
be interred with the ashes of his cremated remains:

> vos condite busto
> tanti colla ducis, sed non ut crimina solum
> vestra tegat tellus: iusto date tura sepulchro
> et placate caput cineresque in litore fusos
> colligite atque unam sparsis date manibus urnam.
> sentiat adventum soceri vocesque querentis
> audiat umbra pias.

> Bury the head of so
> great a leader in a grave, but not only so that the
> earth can conceal your crimes: offer incense on a
> proper grave and revere the head and after you have
> collected all of his ashes spread along the shore,
> place the scattered shades into a single urn. Let his
> shade sense the arrival of his father-in-law and let it hear
> his pious complaints. (9.1089–95)

Caesar's call to reassemble Pompey's corpse also functions at the symbolic
level: now that Caesar has confirmed the identity of the head and acknowl-
edged the death of Pompey, he proposes to transfer Pompey's identity onto

his remains. By giving directions to collect the ashes of Pompey's trunk (*cineresque in litore fusos / colligite,* 1092–93), Caesar ignores Cordus' earlier pauper burial of Pompey's remains and suggests that he alone would be providing a proper burial. Caesar's proposal also represents a variation of the Roman burial ritual of *ossilegium* whereby a severed body part, normally a finger, was placed in an urn with the cremated remains, discussed in chapter 2 in connection with Theseus' gathering of Hippolytus' remains.[43] Since Caesar does not suggest cremating the head, the reader is left with the image of Pompey's head sitting in an urn. In fact, Lucan does not tell us whether Caesar's plans for a burial were carried out, so Pompey's corpse remains unassembled in the poem. As with Cornelia's substitute cremation, Caesar's planned burial of all of Pompey's remains further prolongs the reader's mourning process as Lucan, again, denies both characters and reader any closure to Pompey's death and burial.

Corpse with a Text

When Cordus provides Pompey's remains with a pauper burial, he marks the spot with a stone (8.789–93):

> tunc, ne levis aura retectos
> auferret cineres, saxo compressit harenam,
> nautaque ne bustum religato fune moveret
> inscripsit sacrum semusto stipite nomen:
> 'hic situs est Magnus.'

> Then, so that a gentle breeze
> would not uncover and carry off the ashes,
> he weighed the sand down with a rock, and
> to prevent a sailor from disturbing the grave
> with a mooring rope, he wrote his sacred name
> with a half-burnt stick: "*Here lies Magnus.*"

The epitaph which Pompey receives hardly befits his enormous fame and the one word *Magnus* must suffice to identify the remains of this great Roman. Unlike Priam's corpse in *Aeneid,* 2.558 which is described as nameless (*sine nomine corpus*), Pompey's corpse is identified by the epitaph, but there is an irony in referring to him by his cognomen alone that goes beyond referring to someone as a great person whose name actually was "great." On the one hand the reference is flattering: this person is so great that everyone knows his actual name; but it is also unflattering. If this person is so great, why is he buried in such a simple way in such a strange location?

There is a sense of urgency connected with the burial: Cordus writes Pompey's name onto a rock with a charred stick (*semusto stipite*, 792); therefore, the inscription is a highly perishable and time-sensitive grave marker, especially considering its proximity to water. In addition, the posting of an epitaph identifying the remains as those of Pompey recalls the description of the impaling of his head (*suffixum caput est*, 684). Since the epitaph is only for Pompey's trunk, however, both the epitaph and the allusion to his impaling serve as substitutes for his head while simultaneously calling greater attention to its absence.

The epitaph *Hic situs est Magnus* (8.793) serves as both grave marker and text marker: *hic* (793) is locative and indicates that the corpse is no longer rolling in the surf. But where exactly is *hic*? Unlike burials along the Via Appia in Rome, for example, Pompey's tomb lies somewhere along the shore in a foreign land. Lucan tells us that the corpse is buried *hic*, but we know that the head is en route to Caesar as Cordus performs his pauper burial and that, at least in the poem, Pompey's head is not reassembled to his trunk. Therefore, the epitaph misrepresents the truth about its location and its contents and the ambiguity further prolongs the abuse suffered by Pompey's still improperly buried corpse.

In a final description of Pompey's tomb (8.816–22), Lucan notes that no description of Pompey's life appears, other than his name which used to adorn temples and arches.[44] The epitaph simply informs the passerby or reader that Pompey's remains were located at the spot marked by the epitaph without giving any further information about his identity or life accomplishments. The narrator's lament of the lack of biographical details serves as substitution for information normally contained in an epitaph. Lucan, therefore, severs a traditional epitaph, by separating references to Pompey's name from his accomplishments as an allusion to the actual severing of his head.

Cordus as epitaph writer parallels Lucan as narrator.[45] Both authors mark the death of Pompey but since Cordus writes a highly perishable inscription, like Parsons's cremation tattoo intended to burn with his body, it is Lucan's verse that will immortalize Pompey:

> haec et apud seras gentes populosque nepotum,
> sive sua tantum venient in saecula fama
> sive aliquid magnis nostri quoque cura laboris
> nominibus prodesse potest, cum bella legentur,

spesque metusque simul perituraque vota movebunt,
attonitique omnes veluti venientia fata,
non transmissa, legent et adhuc tibi, Magne, favebunt.

Even among later peoples and the descendants of grandsons,
these events, whether by their own fame they survive into the future
or whether the care of my labor can be useful to great names, will
instill hope and fear and, at the same time, doomed prayers when battles
are read, and all will be amazed when they read about events, as
    forthcoming
rather than in the past, Magnus, and they will still be favorable to you.
    (7.207–13)

Lucan's readers will read Pompey as they read his poem. Therefore, the poet's
conceit and his future success are tied to his narrative of Pompey. The poet's
immortality is also related to Pompey's catasterism in Book 10: Pompey is
immortalized in a poem that seeks immortality through a narrative of his
death and burial.

The poet's allusion to death ritual and poetic (self) referencing, however,
does not end in Book 10. Tacitus' description of Lucan's own death provides
an epilogue to the *Bellum Civile* in which Lucan continues to engage his
amphitheatrical audience:

> Exim Annaei Lucani caedem imperat. is profluente sanguine ubi frigescere
> pedes manusque et paulatim ab extremis cedere spiritum fervido adhuc
> et compote mentis pectore intelligit, recordatus carmen a se compositum
> quo vulneratum militem per eius modi mortis imaginem obisse tradiderat,
> versus ipsos rettulit eaque illi suprema vox fuit.[46]

> Next he [Nero] ordered the death of Annaeus Lucanus. When he felt that
> the loss of blood was beginning to turn his feet and hands cold and his life
> gradually leaving his extremities, although there was still heat in his heart
> and a presence of mind, he remembered a poem, written by himself, that
> told how a wounded soldier died in a way similar to his own death and
> recited them and these were his very last words. (*Annales*, 15.70.1)

According to Tacitus, Lucan cites his own verses with his dying breath in a
narrative that seems to satirize the unnaturally prolonged death of Pompey
(*paulatim*). We are not told whether Lucan quoted from his *Bellum Civile*,
only that he quoted lines from a *carmen* which he had given to one of his

literary characters—a dying soldier. Suetonius, however, does not mention the recitation of lines, only that Lucan wrote directions for the editing of his poetry.[47] In Tacitus' more dramatic version, Lucan rhetoricizes his own death by assuming a fictional identity as a response to his forced suicide. Fiction and reality blend when both actor and character die simultaneously, but reality reasserts itself with the poet's final breath since the corpse, stripped of its fictional identity, belongs to the poet Lucan. In framing his death in either literary or dramatic terms, Lucan (through Tacitus' narrative) also turns his witnesses into readers/audience members to create a theater of death that reverses the role played by his epic readers. Lucan's epic readers now mourn the death of the poet, as the poet, metaphorically, becomes his poem.

Lucan's narrative of Pompey's death and burial, therefore, confounds the reader's role as mourner. The narrative elicits pathos for the grotesque treatment of Pompey's corpse and its allusion to Roman funerary ritual, but it also exasperates the reader when it frustrates the reader's experience of those rituals to produce the double outrage that results from imagining Pompey's death and reading Lucan's account of it. Pompey's lingering death, the lifelike appearance and behavior of his corpse, and the repeated funerary rituals imagined or performed on his remains deny closure to both Lucan's characters and his reader/audience.

The Cremation of Opheltes in Statius' *Thebaid*

The *Thebaid* contains two major cremation episodes in Books 6 and 12: Book 6 describes the cremation of the infant Opheltes, the son of Eurydice and Lycurgus of Thebes, and a second pyre to expiate the death of the serpent that killed Opheltes; Book 12 contains the cremation and burial of Theban dead, including the cremations of Polynices and Eteocles. Statius' narrative of funerary ritual is complex in its intertextuality with the descriptions of cremations and burials found in preceding epics. A reader familiar with Ovid's manipulation of Hecuba's grief and Lucan's maltreatment of Pompey's corpse could expect the grotesque elements to rise exponentially, but Statius takes his narrative in another direction. The fictive reality of the *Thebaid* does not allude to actual funerary ritual familiar to his readers, but rather to literary descriptions of cremations and burials found in Vergil, Ovid, and Lucan.[48] Like Ovid, Statius uses funerary ritual to comment on the writing process and his role as poet.

In Book 6, Statius alludes to the cremation of Pallas in his description of Opheltes' cremation and to the cremation of Misenus in his description of the pyre dedicated to the serpent. But he adds grotesque and absurd elements found in the *Metamorphoses,* the *Bellum Civile,* and Senecan drama to his Vergilian intertexts to create an original description of Opheltes' funeral and cremation.[49] The addition of new intertexts, such as Catullus and Seneca, signals Statius' intent to engage the reader's recognition of elements from the epic trope of cremations, but also to engage the reader in a complex narrative strategy: the text constantly varies its thematic focus and questions its own emphasis on various episodes, such as the excessive ceremony and intertextual details that accompany Opheltes' cremation.

The narrative of Opheltes' cremation is unique. The child was in the care of Hypsipyle of Lemnos, who arrived in Thebes as a fugitive for sparing her father when the island's women were slaughtering all male inhabitants, but was killed by a serpent while Hypsipyle, forgetful of him, was narrating the details surrounding events on Lemnos.[50] The description of the sleeping child foreshadows his death and burial:

> ille graves oculos languentiaque ora comanti
> mergit humo fessusque diu puerilibus actis
> labitur in somnos, prensa manus haeret in herba.[51]

> He buries his heavy eyes and drooping head into
> the leafy soil and, tired from too much child's play,
> he sinks to sleep and his hand holds grass tightly clutched. (5.502–4)

After the serpent is killed, Hypsipyle discovers the mangled corpse of Opheltes, which evokes the corpse of Hippolytus in Ovid's *Metamorphoses* (15.529: *unumque erat omnia vulnus*), Seneca's *Phaedra* (1265–66: *hoc quid est forma carens / et turpe, multo vulnere abrumptum undique?*), and the corpse of Astyanax in Seneca's *Troades* (1116–17: *iacet / deforme corpus*):

> non ora loco, non pectora restant,
> rapta cutis, tenuia ossa patent nexusque madentes
> sanguinis imbre novi, totumque in vulnere corpus.

> No face or chest were left in place,
> skin torn away, thin bones lay bare and sinews
> are soaked in fresh currents of blood—the whole
> body is one wound. (5.596–98)

The placement of Opheltes' corpse among so many intertexts illustrates the complexity of Statius' narrative and raises the expectation that the cremation and burial of the infant's corpse will also be linked with these same intertexts.

Many details of Opheltes' cremation, however, depart from these initial intertexts to allude to the cremation of Pallas in the *Aeneid*. What makes his cremation even more unusual than the fact that an infant receives a funeral worthy of a warrior, is that it is accompanied by a second and contemporaneous cremation designed to expiate any evil resulting from the killing of the serpent rather than to cremate an actual corpse. Variation on a theme is accompanied by reduplication of that variation. The allusion to intertexts followed by reader frustration at having been misled by expectations of familiarity when the narrative diverges from the trope is part of Statius' narrative strategy and allows him, at once, to allude to and to vary the epic trope of funerals.

The cremation of Opheltes is the narrative focus of Book 6 and he is honored with a cremation worthy of a seasoned warrior:

Tristibus interea ramis teneraque cupresso
damnatus flammae torus et puerile feretrum
texitur: ima virent agresti stramina cultu;
proxima gramineis operosior area sertis,
et picturatus morituris floribus agger;
tertius adsurgens Arabum strue tollitur ordo
Eoas complexus opes incanaque glebis
tura et ab antiquo durantia cinnama Belo.
summa crepant auro, Tyrioque attolitur ostro
molle supercilium, teretes hoc undique gemmae
irradiant, medio Linus intertextus acantho
letiferique canes: opus admirabile semper
oderat atque oculos flectebat ab omine mater.
arma etiam et veterum exuvias circumdat avorum
gloria mixta malis adflictaeque ambitus aulae,
ceu grande exsequiis onus atque immensa ferantur
membra rogo, sed cassa tamen serilisque dolentes
fama iuvat, parvique augescunt funere manes.
inde ingens lacrimis honor et miseranda voluptas,
muneraque in cineres annis graviora feruntur;
namque illi et pharetras brevioraque tela dicaret
festinus voti pater insontesque sagittas;
iam tunc et nota stabuli de gente probatos
in nomen pascebat equos cinctusque sonantes
armaque maiores exspectatura lacertos.

[†spes avidi quas non in nomen credula vestes†
urgebat studio cultusque insignia regni
purpureos sceptrumque minus, cuncta ignibus atris
damnat atrox suaque ipse parens gestamina ferri,
si damnis rabidum queat exsaturare dolorem.]

Meanwhile, the bier condemned to burn and the child-sized litter
are woven with gloomy branches and tender cypress;
the lowest part of the bier is lush with rustic greens;
the area closest is more ornate with woven grass,
and the pile is decorated with flowers about to die;
the third level rises piled with Arabian spices encircled by
Eastern riches and clumps of white incense and cinnamon
from the time of Belus. The top rustles with gold and a
soft covering made with Tyrian purple is raised high;
here and there polished gems sparkle within the acanthus
border, Linus is woven and the hounds that brought him death:
his mother always hated this admirable work and always
turned her eyes away from the omen. Even weapons and the
armor of ancient ancestors are spread around the pyre,
the glory of the distressed house mixed with its misfortunes,
just as though the procession were carrying a heavy burden and
huge limbs to the pyre; yet even his empty and immature fame
is a comfort to the mourners and Opheltes' tiny shade is magnified
by the funeral. Then comes the great honor of tears, a pitiable
delight as gifts greater than his years are carried to the pyre;
For his father, hasty in his vow, had set apart for his son
quivers, small spears and innocent arrows; he was even rearing
in his name excellent horses from the famous herd of his stable,
clanging belts and armor more suited to fuller shoulders.
[†Empty hopes: what cloaks in his name, hopeful,†
in her zeal, did she not hasten, the emblems of royal ritual,
purple robes and a miniature scepter? All his fierce father himself
condemns to the black flames and even his own insignia to be
brought out if only to satiate his rabid grief by their loss.] (6.54–83)

Many details of Opheltes' bier (*torus . . . feretrum*, 6.55) allude to the cremations of Pallas and Misenus, but Statius goes beyond his Vergilian intertexts to make the infant's funeral at once exotic and excessive. The bier is childlike in size and is composed of gloomy branches and cypress shoots. While cypress trees surrounded the pyre of Misenus (*Aen.* 6.216–17), here cypress trees comprise the actual bier—funereal symbol has become a funeral accessory. The bier rests on top of four layers that are unique and prioritized: the higher the layer, the more expensive the offering.[52] The prioritized objects also reflect a metaphorical transition: from bucolic innocence to civilized materialism with Opheltes' body closest to most expensive items. From a sensory perpective, there is a transition from smell (cypress to incense/spices) to sight (jewels).

The bottom two layers evoke bucolic imagery and are reminiscent of Pallas' cremation: the tender shoots reflect the age of the deceased but, like the tender shoots of Pallas' pyre, they are impractical from a cremation point of view. Pallas was placed on top of a rustic bier (*hic iuvenem agresti sublimem stramine ponunt,* 11.67) but rustic greens comprise the lowest level of Opheltes' bier: *ima virent agresti stramina cultu* (6.56). Shared language connects the two biers but Opheltes' corpse does not share the same proximity with rustic foliage as did Pallas. Statius further changes the bucolic imagery of Pallas' cremation: whereas Pallas was compared to a cut flower (*Aen.* 11. 68–71) to emphasize his youth, flowers that are soon to die decorate the second layer together with grassy wreaths. As with the cypress trees, funereal symbol has become a funeral accessory.

The third layer of Opheltes' bier is composed of incense and exotic spices that separate the bucolic layers from the fourth layer, a canopy of Tyrian purple (6.62–63) which is decorated with gold and jewels. Prior to his lighting of the pyre, Lycurgus places locks of his cut hair over Opheltes' face so presumably Opheltes' body lay on top of layer 3 but below layer 4, therefore among the most valuable of the objects. The description of the canopy is unique in its intertextuality: the reference to Tyrian purple evokes Dido's cloak which was placed on Pallas' corpse (*Aen.* 11.74–75). It is only with the description of this fourth layer that the reader realizes that Statius has deconstructed Dido's cloak for the third and fourth layers of Opheltes' pyre. The canopy is decorated with a representation of Linus and the hounds who killed him (6.64–66). Allusion to Linus connects Eurydice with a mythological intertext of a youth killed by animals, but the narrative also makes it clear that this is not the first time that she has seen the canopy since it was hateful to her even before Opheltes' cremation and she interpreted the myth depicted on it as a bad omen for her own child. The canopy has served its intertextual purpose and now burns with her child.

Statius contrasts the size and age of Opheltes with the excessive honors of his cremation. Mourners add the armor of the infant's ancestors onto the bier (now described as *rogus* at 6.70) to make it bigger and heavier (6.67–70), which also seem to make Opheltes' shade increase in size (6.71). Lines 79–83 are marked as spurious in some editions, but as they now stand, Opheltes' father increases the number of items placed on the pyre that contrast with the age and military experience of the boy. Mourners become actors as they treat the infant's corpse as though he were an adult deserving of the military honors of his ancestors. Transferring future accomplishments prospectively (hypothetically) onto the child gives real meaning to their role-playing gestures in the present. Just as the bier is suddenly referred to as a pyre, Opheltes is also transformed by the mourners' gestures and his tiny body seems to grow in stature (*parvi augescunt funere manes*). Even the funeral offerings contrast with the youth of Opheltes (*muneraque in cineres annis graviora feruntur,* 6.73). The irony or asymmetry of the excessive funeral for the dead Opheltes extends to the narrative itself: why devote so much attention to an infant's cremation? Does the excessive treatment signal the narrative's recognition of its inappropriateness? The reader must interpret the scene from these two juxtaposed narratives: the actual cremation of an infant which should arouse sympathy and the hyperbolic treatment of that cremation which could alienate another or the same reader.

Just as the reader's attention is focused on Opheltes' pyre and the piling of offerings, the narrative shifts to a second pyre located *parte alia* to expiate the killing of the serpent (6.84).[53] The two pyres evoke the narrative shift in the description of the two pyres built for the mass cremations of Trojans and Latins in the *Aeneid: diversa in parte* (11.203), which turns the reader's attention to the Latin pyre after the description of the Trojan pyre. In both epics, the reader's focus is prioritized: the pyre of Opheltes is thematically more important than the expiatory pyre as is the Trojan pyre over their Latin opponents. Ironically, Statius further distinguishes the two pyres by describing how similar they are:

> Iamque pari cumulo geminas, hanc tristibus umbris
> ast illam superis, aequus labor auxerat aras,
> cum signum luctus cornu grave mugit adunco
> tibia, cui teneros suetum producere manes
> lege Phrygum maesta. Pelopem monstrasse ferebant
> exsequiale sacrum carmenque minoribus umbris
> utile, quo geminis Niobe consumpta pharetris
> squalida bissenas Sipylon deduxerat urnas.

> Already equal labor had built twin altars of similar
> height, one to the gloomy shades, the other to the
> gods above, when the lamentation from the curved
> horn gave the sad signal, at which it was the custom

according to the mourning ritual of Phrygians to
carry out the young dead. They say that Pelops taught
this funeral rite and chant used for the youthful dead,
by which Niobe, consumed by the twin quivers,
in mourning brought out twelve urns to Sipylus. (6.118–25)

Thematically, the two pyres evoke those two pyres constructed for the mass cremations of Trojans and Latins in the *Aeneid,* but the description also serves an aitiological purpose: the music was originated by Pelops for the funeral at which Niobe cremated her twelve children. Niobe was punished for boasting about her fertility, but her punishment was also visited upon her innocent children and so, too, is the infant Opheltes punished for civic strife for which he is not responsible.

The two pyres compete for the reader's attention: the pyres are identical and yet prioritized; one is for a specific person, the other for the slain serpent; one is dedicated to the shades below and the other to the gods above. Numerous digressions and references to the second pyre also divert the reader's attention from Opheltes' pyre. Statius now refers to the pyres as altars (6.119), but they are clearly constructed as pyres so their twofold purpose reveals another detail of their appearance and function. The reader must also refocus her narrative gaze and look left or right to imagine the second pyre and then down and up for the dedicatees of the pyres. Since Opheltes' pyre is the thematic focus, the reader's attention returns to it but only after the multisensory diversion occasioned by the second pyre. From an aural point of view: the funereal pipes and *carmen* add another sensory detail to the scene; however, Statius does not record the words of the *carmen* for his readers, and so his own narrative alludes to and also substitutes for the *carmen.*

The narrative of the army's cutting of trees for the second funeral pyre is excessive in its emphasis and intertextuality of the epic trope of tree felling for the construction of a pyre (6.90–117):

sternitur extemplo veteres incaedua ferro
silva comas, largae qua non opulentior umbrae
Argolicos inter saltusque educta Lycaeos
extulerat super astra caput: stat sacra senectae
numine, nec solos hominum transgressa veterno
fertur avos, Nymphas etiam mutasse superstes
Faunorumque greges. aderat miserabile luco
exscidium: fugere ferae, nidosque tepentes

absiliunt (metus urget) aves; cadit ardua fagus,
Chaoniumque nemus brumaque illaesa cupressus,
procumbunt piceae, flammis alimenta supremis,
ornique iliceaque trabes metuendaque suco
taxus et infandos belli potura cruores
fraxinus atque situ non expugnabile robur.
hinc audax abies et odoro vulnere pinus
scinditur, acclinant intonsa cacumina terrae
alnus amica fretis nec inhospita vitibus ulmus.
dat gemitum tellus: non sic eversa feruntur
Ismara cum fracto Boreas caput extulit antro,
non grassante Noto citius nocturna peregit
flamma nemus. linquunt flentes dilecta locorum,
ostia cana, Pales Silvanusque arbiter umbrae
semideumque pecus, migrantibus aggemit illis
silva, nec amplexae dimittunt robora Nymphae.
ut cum possessas avidis victoribus arces
dux raptare dedit, vix signa audita, nec urbem
invenias; ducunt sternuntque abiguntque feruntque
immodici, minor ille fragor quo bella gerebant.

Immediately, a wood, never before deprived of its ancient branches,
is felled by an axe, none more opulent than which in the deep shade,
between the glades of Argos and Lycaeus, raised its top above the
stars. It stands hallowed by the sanctity of old age; not only is it said
to go back in years before the ancestors of men but also to have outlived
the succession of Nymphs and flocks of Fauns. In that wood came
          pitiable
destruction: beasts flee, birds in their terror leap out of warm nests, the
lofty beech falls, the Chaonian groves and the cypress unharmed in
winter, pine trees lie on the ground, nourishment for cremation fires,
ash trees, timbers of ilex, the yew feared for its sap, mountain ashes soon
to drink the horrific blood of battle, and the oak invincible in its place.
Then the bold fir and the pine with its scented wound is cut; the alder,
          friend
to the seas, bends untrimmed tops toward the ground, and the elm ever
welcoming to the vine. The Earth groans: not so are the Ismaran woods
carried away uprooted when Boreas freed from his cave raises his head,
no swifter does a nighttime blaze consume a forest when Notus
          approaches.

Weeping, they leave their choice lairs, ancient homes, Pales and Silvanus,
ruler of the shade, and the semidivine flock and at their departure, the
    wood
sobs and embracing Nymphs hold tight to their oaks. Just as when a
    general
hands over to the greedy victors captured citadels to plunder, the signal is
barely heard, nor after would you find a city: greedily, they carry off,
    overturn,
haul away, and plunder, the sound of battle waged was not as loud.

Statius goes beyond his epic intertexts of Homer, Ennius, and Vergil in the
variety and sensory descriptions of the trees as he focuses on the effect of
the destruction caused to the forest and its inhabitants by the removal of
the trees. The woodland gods lament the destruction of the forest but not
the death of Opheltes (*aderat miserabile luco / exscidium*) and their mourning
for the lost trees competes with humans' mourning for Opheltes. However
beloved the trees to the woodland gods, the trees are cut and nature is
marred; therefore, human grief is prioritized as more important than the
preservation of such a hallowed and nurturing setting, thus calling attention
to the incongruous mourning ritual for the dead child. The metaphor of the
captured town further reminds readers that Opheltes is an infant and not a
military hero and perhaps undeserving of such excessive grief.

The focus of the wood gathering, although connected with the death of
Opheltes, is properly for the dead serpent, and the narrative is more elaborate than the description of the wood gathered for his pyre. Since the reader
encounters the pyre of Opheltes first, there is a certain narrative tension over
whether Statius will allude to the trope. This prioritizing of the narratives
recalls Vergil's use of his Homeric and Ennian intertexts of tree felling for the
pyre of Misenus rather than that of Pallas. Once both pyres are constructed,
however, the prioritizing of the tropes reveals that Statius' allusions to Vergil
are chiastic: he first alludes to the bier of Pallas, which occurs in *Aeneid* Book
12, after the description of Misenus' pyre, in connection with the bier of
Opheltes. He then proceeds to the construction of the serpent's pyre, thus
alluding to the construction of Misenus' pyre which the reader encounters
first in *Aeneid* Book 6. The complex relationship of the intertextuality of the
descriptions begins to resemble the complexity of the intertextuality of the
pyres themselves.

After the digression to the forest, the narrative returns to Opheltes' bier
as Greek leaders bring gifts and offerings for burning (6.126 ff). It is only
after a second lengthy interval (*longo post tempore*, 6.128) that Opheltes'

body is carried on his bier (*torus*) to his pyre accompanied by his parents, but the text is vague as to the distance between the bier and the pyre. The reference to the transfer of Opheltes' corpse occurs so briefly that his body gets lost in the crowd of mourners. Visualizing the scene, however, would restore Opheltes not among the crowd, but rather above it—on top of the many layers of his bier carried on the shoulders of young men with the canopy rising even higher.

The lamentation of Opheltes' mother, Eurydice (6.135–85), alludes to speeches by Evander and Aeneas lamenting the death of Pallas.[54] Statius also uses the trope of a parent lamenting the loss of a child to double as a call for revenge. Following Eurydice's lament, the narrative focus returns to the pyre as her husband, Lycurgus, throws his scepter on it (6.193) and covers Opheltes' face with his cut hair (6.194–96). Lycurgus then sets fire to the pyre by lighting the bottom timber first: *iam face subiecta primis in frondibus ignis / exclamat; labor insanos arcere parentes* / "already the torch is applied and the fire crackles among the lowest branches; it was hard to keep his stricken parents away," 6.202–3. The emphasis is on lighting the lower flames first in order for the pyre to catch fire sufficiently. Denying access to the grieving parents who approach the burning pyre of their child adds a further touch of pathos to the scene as fire, which is a symbol of purification, also becomes a symbol of demarcation that separates the living from the dead.

Statius describes the cremation in-progress, but the description of the melting and burning sacrificial offerings substitutes for a description of Opheltes' burning flesh (6.204–12):

> Stant iussi Danaum atque obtentis eminus armis
> prospectu visus interclusere nefasto.
> ditantur flammae; non umquam opulentior illis
> ante cinis: crepitant gemmae, atque immane liquescit
> argentum, et pictis exsudat vestibus aurum;
> nec non Assyriis pinguescunt robora sucis,
> pallentique croco strident ardentia mella,
> spumantesque mero paterae verguntur et atri
> sanguinis et rapto gratissima cymbia lactis.

> The Danaans, ordered, stand and, with their armor
> positioned, they block their view at some distance from the
> horrific sight. The flames are enriched, never was there
> a more lavish fire before turning to ashes: gems crackle, a huge

amount of silver melts, and gold oozes from the embroidered
cloaks; the timber is fattened with Assyrian fluids, and burning
honey hisses with the pale crocus, plates spewing wine are
overturned and cups of black blood and milk most pleasant
to the one taken away.

No mention is made of Opheltes' burning corpse and Statius shields the reader from his cremation, as do his characters who use their armor to avert their gazes from the pyre. The description of the burning pyre is unique: although the timbers at the bottom of the pyre were set on fire first, the pyre burns from top to bottom and the order in which the offerings burn is prioritized as though the flames respect the narrative layering of the offerings. As the pyre burns each layer, the narrative order of the cremation reverses the earlier order of the piling as the most expensive objects on top of the pyre, which were placed last, burn first and the least expensive objects, which were placed first, burn last.

Although the reader does not see Opheltes' corpse burn on the pyre, Statius uses an allusion to Seneca's *Thyestes* to draw a grotesque parallel between the burning corpse of Opheltes and Atreus' boiling of his nephew's flesh:

haec veribus haerent viscera et lentis data
stillant caminis, illa flammatus latex
candente aeno iactat.
        Impositas dapes
transiluit ignis inque trepidantes focos
bis ter regestus et pati iussus moram
invitus ardet. strident in veribus iecur;
nec facile dicam corpora an flammae magis
gemuere.[55]

The innards are stuck on spits and drip above a slow
fire, boiling water in a heated pot tosses the other parts.
The fire leaps around the feast placed over it but is
thrown back onto the blazing hearth over and over again,
and ordered to endure it, unwillingly burns. Liver hisses
on the spits; not easily could I say whether the bodies
or the flames groaned more. (765–72)

Like Seneca, Statius' narrative of the cremation emphasizes the melting, flowing, sputtering, and hissing of the offertory objects, in particular, his allusion to the detail of hissing spits of liver: *strident in veribus iecur* (770), by using the same verb to describe the burning of offerings (6.210). The personification of the burning offerings substitutes for a description of the burning Opheltes, but it also dehumanizes the boy who burns among disturbing literary intertexts. The intertextual reference to Atreus is furthermore unsettling when one recalls that Opheltes is an infant who died an untimely death is compared to Thyestes' sons (three in Seneca's play) and unexpected considering the multiple references/allusions to Vergil's *Aeneid* and the death of Pallas.

The ceremony moves from the center of the pyre to its perimeter: Lycurgus leads seven squadrons around the pyre with their shields reversed, with their circular motion from the left hand side being emphasized (6.214 ff).[56] They circle the pyre seven times as the clashing of weapons alternates with the wailing of women. Statius then redirects the focus away from Opheltes' pyre to another pyre on which animals are offered, although it is not clear whether he is referring to a fire next to Opheltes' pyre or the serpent's pyre, which is burning contemporaneously, before returning to the final offerings made to Opheltes: *semianimas alter pecudes spirantiaque ignis / accipit armenta* (6.220–21). The prophet orders the mourners to change directions, and they now encircle the pyre from the right hand side (6.221ff) as they throw armor onto the flames. Opheltes' pyre burns completely and is watered down (6.234–37):

> Finis erat, lassusque putres iam Mulciber ibat
> in cineres; instant flammis multoque soporant
> imbre rogum, posito donec cum sole labores
> exhausti; seris vix cessit cura tenebris.

> This was the end and tired Mulciber was already
> consumed among the decaying ashes; they approached
> the flames and soaked the pyre with much water,
> until their labor ended with the setting of the sun;
> scarcely did their care yield to the late shadows.

The text announces that this was the end of the cremation, but the narrative omits details of the gathering of Opheltes' cremated remains which could have provided further intertextuality with texts discussed in chapter 2, such as Seneca's *Phaedra,* that include a performative description of the ritual *ossilegium.* Hypsipyle's earlier gathering of Opheltes' mangled flesh (605–6), rather, anticipates and serves as a substitution for the actual gathering of his cremated remains.

After nine days have passed, the cremation site has undergone a change and the focus is now a marble temple built over the pyre to house Opheltes' ashes (6.242–48):

> stat saxea moles,
> templum ingens cineri, rerumque effictus in illa
> ordo docet casus: fessis hic flumina monstrat
> Hypsipyle Danais, hic reptat flebilis infans,
> hic iacet, extremum tumuli circum asperat orbem
> squameus: exspectes morientis ab ore cruenta
> sibila, marmorea sic volvitur anguis in hasta.

> A marble heap stands,
> a huge temple to his ashes, with a sculpted frieze that
> tells of his misfortunes: here Hypsipyle points out the
> river to the tired Danai, here crawls the weeping baby,
> here he lies, the scaly serpent ravages the furthest area of the
> mound: you would expect hissing from the bloody mouth
> of the dying serpent, thus does it coil around the marble spear.

The temple contains a frieze with a narrative cycle that describes the two causes of Opheltes' death: Hypsipyle and the serpent. Select scenes are depicted on the temple (unless the narrative only focuses on select scenes): the unattended Opheltes (killed while Hypsipyle was recounting the details of Lemnian slaughter and her sham cremation of her father), the dead child, the retreating serpent, and his death in progress. The actual death of Opheltes is not shown. *hic iacet* (6.246) gives an epitaph to the dead Opheltes which is not otherwise explicitly described as part of the temple or frieze detail.

The narrative frieze changes appearance as it recounts details surrounding the deaths of Opheltes and the serpent and reflects the shifting appearance of the site into a temple which represents a second metamorphosis of the site as it changes from pyre to altar and then to a temple following Opheltes' cremation. The changing appearance and function of the site are appropriate since they reflect the various metamorphoses of Opheltes: a dead infant who is cremated as an adult warrior reduced to ashes and commemorated with a temple. The funeral games that follow the cremation are also transformative as the landscape provides a theatrical backdrop to the games in much the same way that nature provided a theater for the deaths of Astyanax and Polyxena in Seneca's *Troades*.

Thus, Statius' approach to intertexts in Book 6 is complex as he at once alludes to or sets up an expectation of an allusion to the epics of Vergil, Ovid, and Lucan and other intertexts such as Seneca's *Phaedra* and *Thyestes*. He also diverges from them to create an original description of Opheltes' cremation. The result is a text in which the infant Opheltes is transformed and overshadowed by the narrative of his own cremation and the competing and reduplicating narrative of the symbolic cremation dedicated to the serpent. The reader loses sight of Opheltes almost as soon as his body is laid on top of his unique and intertextual bier. The narrative further distances the reader from Opheltes' corpse and cremation by questioning its own epic treatment of the cremation and thus leaving the reader an univited guest at a funeral that assaults the reader's sense of propriety and familiarity with the trope of epic funerals.

Corpses in Search of a Cremation

The first half of Book 12 (lines 1–463) revolves around the cremation and burial of Theban dead from which the devotion of Argia, daughter of Inachus, and of Antigone to cremating Polynices becomes a central issue, especially, in light of Creon's ban against cremating the Argive dead.[57] The women are affected by the war, but they can only enter the battlefield following the battle to look for the corpse of Polynices. They find his corpse by different routes, and out of varying motivations give his corpse a cremation but inadvertently on the same pyre that is consuming Eteocles' corpse. Their piety contrasts with the actions of Hypsipyle in Book 5, in particular, her sham cremation for her father, but their rivalry following the discovery of their cremation of Polynices echoes the brothers' enmity toward each other.[58] The episode is a turning point as Theseus kills Creon in the book's second half; but like the rivalry between Argia and Antigone, the killing of Creon is the just the latest perpetuation of more rivalry and bloodshed. After a series of endings, Statius claims in a *sphragis* that he is unable to describe the countless funerals that followed and wishes an immortal fame for his poem that will respect the primacy of the *Aeneid*. Statius, however, continues to allude to both death ritual and Vergil, thus negating his claim that he is not capable of further intertextuality.

Burial of the dead is both a moral and narrative imperative as the epic continues to use allusions to death ritual and epic intertexts to inform and challenge the narrative and the reader.[59] Statius goes beyond his Vergilian intertext in a number of ways: by imitating the narrative excesses and grotesque and absurd elements from Ovid and Lucan to describe the roles played by Argia and Antigone to bury Polynices, the description of the joint cremation of Polynices and Eteocles, and by alluding to the ending of the *Aeneid* at line 781 but then extending his own narrative and his intertextuality with the *Aeneid* further. The various endings of the *Thebaid*, both before line 781 and the narrative beyond, are informed by death ritual: as a comment/appendix to the death of Turnus in the *Aeneid*; intertextuality, however abbreviated, with the epic trope of funerals and cremations negates the conceit of Statius' *sphragis* that he is not up to the challenge of describing funerals or engaging previous texts. The *sphragis* itself connects both poet and poem to Vergil as poet and funereal symbol, thus further extending intertextuality with Vergil and literary allusions to death ritual. Statius, therefore, goes beyond his Vergilian intertext; but his professed inability to engage further the epic trope of funerals and cremation points to a narrative in which the trope, reduced to brief allusions and finally abandoned by the poet, is actually in search of a narrative.

The *Thebaid* reaches a melodramatic climax in Book 12 following the battle between Eteocles and Polynices. In the aftermath of battle, fallen soldiers and body parts are collected by survivors (12.22–37):

Itur in exsanguem populum bellique iacentis
reliquias, qua quemque dolor luctusque, cruenti,
exagere, duces; hi tela, hi corpora, at illi
caesorum tantum ora vident alienaque iuxta
pectora; pars currus deflent viduisque loquuntur,
hoc solum quia restat, equis; pars oscula figunt
vulneribus magnis et de virtute querentur.
frigida digeritur strages: patuere recisae
cum capulis hastisque manus mediisque sagittae
luminibus stantes; multis vestigia caedis
nulla: ruunt planctu pendente et ubique parato.
at circum informes truncos miserabile surgit
certamen, qui iusta ferant, qui funera ducant.
saepe etiam hostiles (lusit Fortuna parumper)
decepti flevere viros; nec certa facultas
noscere quem miseri vitent calcentve cruorem.

They go among the bloodless masses and the remains
of those fallen in war, bloody guides lead them where
there is pain and grief; some see weapons, some see bodies
but others see the faces of those cut down near someone

else's torso; some lament chariots and speak to widowed
horses—because his alone is left them; others plant kisses
on deep wounds and express grief over their virtue.
the cold heap is sorted through: severed hands are visible
still holding lances and swords and arrows stuck in the
middle of eyes; to many, there are no traces of their dead:
they rush around everywhere on the verge and ready to wail.
But around the shapeless corpses a pitiful struggle arises over
who will perform the rites, and who will attend to the funerals.
often, deceived (Fortune toyed with them for a little while)
they wept for the enemy; nor was there a clear way for the
grievers to know what gore to avoid and what to step on.

As the reader surveys the bloody aftermath of the battle, grotesque and
absurd narrative features of Ovid and Lucan emerge and the scene is at once
horrifying and humorous: body parts are intermingled, mourners address
chariots and animals as substitutions for lost loved ones, and severed hands
still hold swords and arrows stand on end sticking out of the skulls of
corpses.[60] Fortune takes part in the role of a joker and narrator/dramaturge
as she directs the action of the characters for her own pleasure. The reader
becomes a secondary audience to Fortune's primary audience of the events
that she directs. The search for loved ones continues and leads to the mis-
taken identity of corpses as the searchers themselves become attracted to
their own misery: *amant miseri lamenta malisque fruuntur* (12.45).

On the third day following the battle, Statius describes the mass cremation of the Theban forces (12.50–59):

> Tertius Aurorae pugnabat Lucifer, et iam
> montibus orbatis, lucorum gloria, magnae
> Teumesi venere trabes et amica Cithaeron
> silva rogis; ardent excisae viscera gentis
> molibus extructis: supremo munere gaudent
> Ogygii manes; queritur miserabile Graium
> nuda cohors vetitumque gemens circumvolat ignem.
> accipit et saevi manes Eteoclis iniquos
> haudquaquam regalis honos; Argivus haberi
> frater iussus adhuc atque exsule pellitur umbra.

For the third time, the Morning Star was struggling
with Aurora, and already the mountains were stripped,
the glory of forests, the great timbers of Teumesus

arrived and the Cithaeron wood a friend to pyres;
they burn the inner parts of the cut-down race on
built-up heaps: the Ogygian shades delight in this
final tribute; but an unburied troop of Greeks lament
and, groaning, fly around the forbidden fires.
Hardly does a royal honor receive the hostile shade of
cruel Eteocles; his brother, ordered to be considered
an Argive still, is driven away, an exiled shade.

Such a cursory description of tree cutting and the burning of corpses on the pyre seems designed to elude the notice of Creon and, in the process, it barely informs the reader expecting an allusion to the mass cremations of Trojans and Latins in the *Aeneid.* Even Eteocles is cremated with less ceremony than the infant Opheltes (*haudquaquam regalis,* 12.58), but the text does not explicitly state where his cremation takes place: *accipit et* is vague and it is not clear whether he is being cremated on the same pyre as the other soldiers or on his own. Statius' description of the unburied dead lingering around the pyre adds a visual variation on the cremation theme as the living mix with the dead who either mourn the buried dead with the living or, unseen by the living, lament their own uncremated condition by threatening the ritual purity of those of the others.[61] Although in another camp, physically and figuratively, Polynices remains uncremated, thus the brothers are narratively linked in anticipation of their joint cremation.

An exception to the mass cremation is Menoecus, son of Creon, who did not want him to share a plebeian pyre (12.60–70):

At non plebeio fumare Menoecea busto
rex genitor Thebaeque sinunt, nec robora vilem
struxerunt de more rogum, sed bellicus agger
curribus et clipeis Graiorumque omnibus armis
sternitur; hostiles super ipse, ut victor, acervos
pacifera lauro crinem vittisque decorus
accubat: haud aliter quam cum poscentibus astris
laetus in accensa iacuit Tirynthius Oeta.
spirantes super inferias, captiva Pelasgum
corpora frenatosque, pater, solacia forti
bellorum, mactabat equos [. . .]

But the king his father and Thebes forbid Menoecus
to burn on a plebeian pyre, they do not pile oak timbers
in the manner of a common pyre, but a warlike heap is built

with chariots and all the weapons of the Greeks; and he himself,
like a victor, lies on top of the heap of enemy armor, his hair
ornamented with a laurel wreath and fillets: not otherwise did
Tirynthius lie happy on burning Oeta at the request of the stars.
His father sacrificed even living victims, the captive bodies of
Pelasgians and the bridled horses of warriors as a solace for
his bravery [. . .]

Menoecus' cremation is an abbreviated allusion to the trope and Creon
calls attention to its uniqueness in the text by refusing to give his son a
common pyre (*vilem rogum*), but rather opting to give him a warlike pyre
(*bellicus agger*) with armor offerings and human sacrifices. Menoecus wears
laurel around his head which represents a shift in Statius' narrative focus
since Book 6 where Opheltes lay on top of symbolic greenery, but it also
alludes to the appearance of a sacrificial animal which reminds the reader of
Menoecus' suicide to effect a peace between the warring factions. It is ironic
that Creon sacrifices captive warriors to his son who was himself a sacrificial
victim for those same warriors.

On his pyre, Menoecus is compared to Hercules (*Tirynthius*), the first
of three successive metaphors that connect funeral ritual of a character with
a mythological referent; thus the metaphor distinguishes him from other
cremated heroes. Despite Creon's insistence that his son's pyre not be like
the one burning the anonymous soldiers and varying details, the two pyres
compete with each other and again we have reduplication of pyres, just as in
Book 6, that burn at the same time. After Creon's lamentation (12.72–104),
he is carried back to the palace and both he and the reader do not see
Menoecus' pyre again. Nor are there any explicit directions or a description
of the quenching of the pyre or the collection of his remains.

As Menoecus' corpse burns, the narrative turns elsewhere to return the
focus onto the women of Thebes, including Argia. After communal mourning (12.105 ff), chthonic goddesses (Hecate, Ceres, and Saturnia) provide
assistance to the women as they lead them through the battlefield and camps
and Iris preserves the bodies of the leaders in a fresh state for cremation
(12.138–40). In Argia's mind, Polynices demands cremation: *sed nulla animo
versatur imago / crebrior Aonii quam quae de sanguine campi / nuda venit pos-
citque rogos /* "but no other image is turned in her mind / more often than
the one which comes from the blood of the Aonian battlefield unburied and
seeks a pyre," 12.191–93. She is so preoccupied with his burial that she is
in love with death and the dead: *funus amat* (12.195). Argia resolves to give
her dead husband a proper burial (12.256 ff) and looks for his corpse. Her

search becomes a metaliterary metaphor of the epic trope of funerals looking for a narrative.

When Argia finds Polynices, the narrative becomes a series of recognition scenes: Argia recognizes her husband's corpse through recognition of his cloak (12.312 ff). Antigone, who was also looking for Polynices in order to cremate his corpse, chances upon Argia and the two women meet for the first time and recognize each other's claims to his corpse as wife and sister. They drag Polynices' body to the river to wash it, in a scene reminiscent of Hecuba's action in Ovid's *Metamorphoses* when she sought water to wash Polyxena's corpse (13.533 ff). Statius compares the washing of his corpse with a second mythological allusion to funeral ritual: Phaëthon's corpse being washed by his sisters and then cremated and buried (12.409–28):

Haud procul Ismeni monstrabant murmura ripas,
qua turbatus adhuc et sanguine decolor ibat.
huc laceros artus socio conanime portant
invalidae, iungitque comes non fortior ulnas.
sic Hyperionium tepido Phaëthonta sorores
fumantem lavere Pado; vixdum ille sepulcro
conditus, et flentes stabant ad flumina silvae.
ut sanies purgata vado membrisque reversus
mortis honos, ignem miserae post ultima quaerunt
oscula; sed gelidae circum exanimesque favillae
putribus in foveis, atque omnia busta quiescunt.
stabat adhuc, seu forte, rogus seu numine divum,
cui torrere datum saevos Eteocleos artus,
sive locum monstris iterum Fortuna parabat,
seu dissensuros servaverat Eumenis ignes.
hic tenuem nigris etiamnum advivere lucem
roboribus pariter cupidae videre, simulque
flebile gavisae; nec adhuc quae busta repertum,
sed placidus quicumque rogant mitisque supremi
admittat cineris consortem et misceat umbras.

Nearby, a roar signaled the banks of the Ismenos river
where it flowed thick and dark with blood. Here,
weak and in like purpose, they carry his wounded limbs,
and their companion, no more strong, adds his arms to the task.
So did his sisters wash smoldering Phaëthon, son of Hyperion,
in the warm Padus; scarcely had he been buried when a weeping

forest stood along the riverbank. When the filth had been washed
in the water and beauty had returned to his dead limbs, the wretched
women gave final kisses and searched for a fire. But the embers
were cold and dead in the decaying pits and all of the pyres lay still.
There was a pyre still standing, whether by chance or by the will of
the gods, on which the limbs of fierce Eteocles had been placed for
cremation, whether Fortune had again prepared a place for portents
or the Furies had saved it for dissenting flames. Here, both eager,
they saw a tender flame to glow and joyfully wept at the same time.
they still did not know whose pyre had been found but they asked,
whoever it was, that he be favorable and gracious and allow
a companion of his final ashes and mix their shades.

The allusion to the funeral of Phaëthon, while it connects the women to a
mythological exemplum of devotion, also connects the fire of the sun that
burned Phaëthon with the fire of a pyre that will burn Polynices' corpse.
The women inadvertently place Polynices onto Eteocles' pyre (the text
questions divine motivations or meddling Fortune who may be still toying
with humans for her own pleasure in effecting the coincidence). Thus, the
women's act of piety is also contrary to Creon's edict in the text and to the
Roman funerary practices of Statius' readers which forbade the interference
with a cremation in progress.

Both brothers' corpses burn on the same pyre and are therefore reunited
in death, but Eteocles sends forth a menacing flame as an indication that
their feud endures even after death (12.429–36):

> Ecce iterum fratres! primos ut contigit artus
> ignis edax, tremuere rogi et novus advena busto
> pellitur; exundant diviso vertice flammae
> alternosque apices abrupta luce coruscant.
> pallidus Eumenidum veluti commiserit ignes
> Orcus, uterque minax globus et conatur uterque
> longius; ipsae etiam commoto pondere paulum
> secessere trabes.

> Look, once again, on the brothers! As soon as
> the greedy fire touched his limbs, the timber shook and
> the new arrival was expelled from the pyre; flames flowed
> up with a double head and flashed alternating tips in the
> broken light. Just as though pale Orcus had mixed the

fires of the Furies, and each mass threatened and tried to
burn longer than any other; the timbers themselves even
moved a little from the shifted weight.

Ecce functions as a stage direction to the reader to focus on the warring
flames and to participate in the cremation of the brothers.[62] A third mythological allusion to death ritual compares the animated activities of the pyre
to the fire of the Furies and further extends the fire metaphor of the previous two mythological allusions. Belatedly, the women realize that they have
placed Polynices onto Eteocles' pyre (12.436–46) and they are captured and
brought before Creon for disobeying his burial edict.[63]

The women vie with each other for responsibility for the cremation of
Polynices; their rivalry echoes the feud between the brothers and the pyre
portent, which is itself echoed in the rebellion of their ashes and the pyre
that is consuming their corpses (12.447–63):

> Vix ea, cum subitus campos tremor altaque tecta
> impulit adiuvatque rogi discordis hiatus,
> et vigilum turbata quies, quibus ipse malorum
> fingebat simulacra Sopor: ruit ilicet omnem
> prospectum lustrans armata indagine miles.
> illos instantes senior timet unus; at ipsae
> ante rogum saevique palam sprevisse Creontis
> imperia et furtum claro plangore fatentur
> securae, quippe omne vident fluxisse cadaver.
> ambitur saeva de morte animosque leti
> spes furit: haec fratris rapuisse, haec coniugis artus
> contendunt vicibusque probant: 'ego corpus,' 'ego ignes,'
> 'me pietas,' 'me duxit amor.' deposcere saeva
> supplicia et dextras iuvat insertare catenis.
> nusquam illa alternis modo quae reverentia verbis,
> iram odiumque putes; tantus discordat utrimque
> clamor, et ad regem qui depredere trahuntur.

Scarcely had she finished speaking when suddenly,
a sudden tremor shook the fields and tall roofs, and widened
the gap of the warring pyre. It even disturbed the sleep of the
watchmen, for whom Sleep himself was crafting images of evils:
Immediately, soldiers rushed out, in armed circle formation,
covering over the whole area. The old man alone feared their arrival;

but the women, before the pyre, openly confess that they scorned
the edicts of savage Creon and, without caring what happens, admit the
   crime with
loud wailing, after seeing that the whole cadaver had burned. They
plead for a savage end and hope fires thoughts of death: they compete
in claims of theft, this one that she took the limbs of her brother, the
   other
those of her husband and, in turn, offer proof: "I snatched the body,"
"I, the fire," "I acted out of piety," "I out of love." It gives them joy to ask
for a savage punishment and to place their arms in chains.
No more is there the reverence that was recently in the words of each,
you would think it rage and hatred; such a great dissension divided
each side, and they even dragged those who had seized them.

The scene of rivalry between the women also competes with the narrative: their claims of responsibility serve to deconstruct and reverse the narrative of the cremation and reverse the order of narrative events in Book 12: body, fire, piety, and love of their competing claims reverses the narrative order of these themes (love; piety; cremation fire; body) and reduces the plot of the first half of Book 12 to just four words. The chiasmus reflects the intertextuality of the pyre and the entwined limbs of the brothers on the pyre as it prioritizes the actions and responsibility from a grammatical perspective (nominative *ego* vs. accusative *me*): the women each emphasize the active roles they played in finding and cremating the body, but express their roles in being led passively by piety and love. The active and passive roles also contrast action with motivation and the morality of their actions. Thus the rivalry between Antigone and Argia surpasses the competing claims of Antigone and Ismene in Sophocles' *Antigone*.

The narrative then shifts from the rivalry between two women to the collective actions of matrons who appeal to Theseus for aid in burying their dead. Creon refuses Theseus' request to bury the Argive dead and the tyrant who had planned to kill Argia and Antigone (12.677ff) is himself killed over the issue of burial. The contest between Creon and Theseus at the epic's end parallels the duel between Aeneas and Turnus at the ending of the *Aeneid*.[64] Theseus' words over the dying Creon ("Go, make funereal offerings," 12.779–81), which make his clemency explicit, contrast with Creon's edict that banned burial of the Argive dead (12.779–81):

'iamne dare exstinctis iustos,' ait, 'hostibus ignes,
iam victos operire placet? vade atra datura
supplicia, extremique tamen secure sepulcri.'

"Now is it pleasing to grant just fires to the dead enemy," he said,
"and to bury the conquered? Go, you who will soon receive your deadly
    punishment,
at least are assured of a final grave."

Theseus' promise of a burial, however, contrasts with Aeneas' final words
to Turnus which transfer the responsibility of his killing of him to Pallas.
Despite Turnus' request that his body be returned to his father for burial, the
Aeneid does not describe Turnus' funeral, as Homer does for Hector in order
to provide closure to the Trojans and to anticipate the funeral of Achilles.
Ending an epic with a funeral also provides closure to the epic narrative,
as both mourners in the text and readers of the text have no knowledge of
events that will take place the day after the funeral, and thus an epic that
provides closure also provides an opportunity for every reader to imagine
their own continuation of the story.

Since Theseus has promised Creon burial and the narrative of the *Thebaid* continues beyond his death, Statius raises the expectation that he will
include a description of Creon's funeral/cremation or the cremation of the
dead soldiers, but he uses the final lines to close his epic with a *sphragis* that
states his inability to describe funerals (12.797–819):

Non ego, centena si quis mea pectora laxet
voce deus, tot busta simul vulgique ducumque,
tot pariter gemitus dignis conatibus aequem:
turbine quo sese caris instraverit audax
ignibus Evadne fulmenque in pectore magno
quaesierit; quo more iacens super oscula saevi
corporis infelix excuset Tydea coniunx;
ut saevos narret vigiles Argia sorori;
Arcada quo planctu genetrix Erymanthia clamet,
Arcada, consumpto servantem sanguine vultus,
Arcada, quem geminae pariter flevere cohortes.
vix novus ista furor veniensque implesset Apollo,
et mea iam longo meruit ratis aequore portum.

    Durabisne procul dominoque legere superstes,
o mihi bissenos multum vigilata per annos
Thebai? iam certe praesens tibi Fama benignum
stravit iter coepitque novam monstrare futuris.
iam te magnanimus dignatur noscere Caesar,
Itala iam studio discit memoratque iuventus.
vive, precor; nec tu divinam Aeneida tempta,

sed longe sequere et vestigia semper adora.
mox, tibi si quis adhuc praetendit nubila livor,
occidet, et meriti post me referentur honores.

I could not, even if some god released a hundred voices
in my heart, [recount] so many cremations of plebeians and leaders,
or as many lamentations equal to a worthy effort:
with what wildness the bold Evadne surrounded herself with
the cremations of loved ones and sought a thunderbolt in her
heroic breast; how the wretched wife, as she lay, made excuses
above the mouth of Tydeus' fierce body; how Argia describes the
cruel watchmen to her sister, with what wailing, the
Erymanthian mother laments the Arcadian, the Arcadian who
preserves his beauty even with the loss of his blood, the Arcadian
whom both armies lament equally. Hardly would new passion or
Apollo's arrival fill out my narrative and my ship, already in
deep waters, has deserved a harbor.
    Will you last a long time outliving your master and be read,
O my *Thebaid*, cause of much sleeplessness for me for twelve years?
Even now, no doubt, present Fame has paved a favorable road for you
and has begun to point you out, although young, to future ages.
Already, magnanimous Caesar thinks it worthy to know you,
and already, the Italian youth zealously learns and memorizes you.
Live on, I pray: nor rival the divine *Aeneid*, but follow at a distance and
always revere its footsteps. Soon, if any envy now clouds you over,
it will dissipate and after my death, deserved honors will be paid.

The reader has been duped by the shift in Statius' narrative strategy and
may be further unsatisfied with his allusion to the literary topos of a poet's
inability to voice his thoughts to explain the omission of a description of
Creon's funeral, in particular to Vergil, *Georgics* 2.42–44 (*non ego cuncta
meis amplecti versibus opto, / non, mihi si linguae centum sint oraque centum,
/ ferrea vox*).[65] Statius even omits a verb of speaking when listing topics
connected to the funerals and subsequent events to emphasize his inability
to continue with the narrative. The repetition of *Arcada* (lines 805–7) even
raises the hope that he will engage the bucolic intertexts of Pallas' funeral
in the *Aeneid* or even the death of Daphnis in *Eclogue* 5 in addition to the
earlier intratexts of Opheltes' funeral, the mirror cremation of the serpent,
and the joint cremation of Eteocles and Polynices. Statius, however, is more
than able to describe funerals and to continue his narrative. It does not take

much for the reader to see through the affectation and gesture of humility. Thus, at the poem's end, corpses are in search of a cremation and the reader is in search of a narrator who will describe them.

The narrative does continue, however, as Statius gives alternate endings to the poem within his *sphragis,* but he makes himself and his relation to previous poems the teleological focus of the epic.[66] Statius surrenders some of his authorial control by replacing the narrative finality that accompanies a description of a character's funeral with a hope that this poem will last long beyond his death. The hope is expressed in terms more tentative than Horace's declaration comparing his poetry with a monument (*Odes* 3.30) that rivals the achievements of pharoahs and emperors; it is deferential to the primacy of Vergil's *Aeneid* (*vestigia semper adora*).[67] Thus Statius transfers an expression of immortality from himself, unlike his epic and lyric precursors, to the *Thebaid* itself. The analogy to a poetic monument is apt since Statius' *sphragis,* like Ovid's in the *Metamorphoses,* serves as a figurative epitaph which becomes a virtual tombstone and perpetuation of the poet's identity through his poetry. Moreover, reading the poem will be synonymous with paying tribute to the dead poet. Funeral ritual, therefore, is co-opted into a literary work and yet another form of closure to a professed open-ended epic, which further connects the *Thebaid* to the *Aeneid.*

Elsewhere, Statius makes the connection between himself and Vergil through funerary ritual explicit. In his *Silvae,* Statius situates himself (and his poetry) near Vergil's tomb (4.4.51–55):[68]

> en egomet somnum et geniale secutus
> litus ubi Ausonio se condidit hospita portu
> Parthenope tenues ignavo pollice chordas
> pulso, Maroneique sedens in margine templi
> sumo animum et magni tumulis accanto magistri.

> I myself, in pursuit of sleep and the hospitable shore
> where the stranger Parthenope settled herself in an Ausonian
> port, pluck the slender strings with an unworthy thumb, and
> sitting on the edge of Vergil's tomb I take heart and sing
> on the grave of the great master.

The passage serves as Statius' postscript to Vergil's text: *accanto* plays on *cano,* the first verb of the *Aeneid* and attributes to Vergil the same nurturing role given to him by Parthenope (*Georg.* 4. 564), Naples, in inspiring Statius' own poetic endeavors (*magistri*).

Statius also derives poetic inspiration from the tomb itself. But the tomb is more than a symbol of literary inspiration in an idyllic setting, it is also a source of literary competion: Statius omits any reference to Vergil's own words which Suetonius (*Vita* 36) records as Vergil's own epitaph:

> Mantua me genuit, Calabri rapuere, tenet nunc
> Parthenope; cecini pascua rura duces.[69]

> Mantua gave me birth, Calabria death, now
> Parthenope holds me; I sang of pastures, the country, and leaders.

Vergil does not include his own name in his epitaph, rather he lists locations that mark phases of his biological life (birth, death, burial). This marks a break with the epitaphs of his literary precursors Naevius, Ennius, Plautus, and Pacuvius.[70] In the second colon, in which he lists the subjects of his major poetic works in order of publication. the verb *cecini* serves as a bridge between the biology and bibliography of his life. Statius, while acknowledging his poetic debt to Vergil, controls the description of the idyllic setting that serves as inspiration to his own poetry and suppresses Vergil's final words in favor of his own voice.

As a source of inspiration and intertextuality, Vergil's tomb functions as a symbol of literary power that allows Statius to engage in the same self-fashioning as Augustus, who visited the tomb of Alexander the Great in Alexandria (Suetonius, *Aug.* 18):

> Per idem tempus conditorium et corpus Magni Alexandri, cum prolatum e penetrali subiecisset oculis, corona aurea imposita ac floribus aspersis veneratus est consultusque, num et Ptolemaeum inspicere vellet, regem se voluisse ait videre, non mortuos.

> Around this time, when the tomb and body of Alexander the Great had been brought out from its shrine and placed before his eyes, he venerated it by placing a gold crown on it and strewing flowers. When he was asked whether he wished to see the tomb of the Ptolemies, he replied that he wished to see a king, not corpses.

The quote attributed to Augustus makes the political message clear: he came to the tomb of Alexander to pay tribute to him alone. As a symbol, Alexander's corpse could confer universal power and legitimacy to his Roman imitators; therefore, Augustus' first act after visiting the tomb was to reduce

Egypt to a province. The legendary conqueror has himself been surpassed and his own tomb in the city that he founded has been conquered by this latter-day Alexander. An act of commemoration at Alexander's tomb becomes competition through political manipulation of death ritual.[71] By alluding to tomb visits as acts of commemoration and political competition, Statius uses Vergil's tomb as a metapoetic statement that his poetry rivals and surpasses the poems of his mentor, and in turn adds a political resonance by equating his own literary accomplishments with the empire of his imperial patron, as Horace had done in *Odes* 3.30.

Statius' manipulation of funeral ritual as a metapoetic statement of his literary success in the *Silvae* is also apparent at the end of the *Thebaid*. Statius simultaneously expresses an inability to extend his narrative and further engage the trope of funerals and cremations as he inserts himself into the poem's ending through a *sphragis* that serves as an ending and a beginning to the epic, thus allowing the poet to become the teleological focus of the poem. By informing his readers of what is not there (yet another description of a funeral), Statius prioritizes his narrative agenda. Like his expression of poetic debt and rivalry to Vergil through death ritual in the *Silvae*, the *sphragis* is both a wish for poetic immortality and an expression of conquest over his poetic and imperial patrons.

This chapter focused on the evolution of the funeral trope from the epics of Vergil and Ovid to those of Lucan and Statius and how the participatory reading experience is further manipulated by authorial agendas. Successive treatments of the epic trope of funerals and cremations further challenge the reader's (and character's) experience with those rituals and their knowledge of the trope. By treating Pompey's corpse as a plaything and turning the reader into a voyeuristic audience, Lucan turns Pompey's cremation and burial into a grotesque spectacle. Any sympathy aroused for Pompey comes despite the narrative. Statius also manipulates death ritual to serve his authorial agenda. The dual cremations of Opheltes and the serpent, the cremations of Eteocles and Polynices, and the abandoned description of Creon's funeral and cremation have little in common with either funerary ritual or previous intertexts and encourage a disassociative reading experience.

In the following chapter, I focus on death ritual as visual referent in order to consider epitaphs, both actual and literary, from a figurative perspective and the author/reader dynamic that animates the deceased. Self representation of the dead competes with the authorial voice of narratives as the dead take control of their own authorial agenda and future commemoration.

CHAPTER 5

Animating the Dead

Tunc uno quoque hinc inde instante ut quam primum se impendentibus contu-
meliis eriperet, scrobem coram fieri imperavit dimensus ad corporis sui modulum,
componique simul, si qua invenirentur, frusta marmoris et aquam simul ac ligna
conferri curando mox cadaveri, flens ad singula atque identidem dictitans: "Qualis
artifex pereo!"[1]

Then with each of his companions urging him to free himself as soon as possible
from the looming abuses, he ordered them to dig a pit, the size of his own body
in dimension, and to gather at the same time pieces of marble, if any could be
found, and for water and wood to be brought for the imminent preparation of
his body, weeping at each step and saying over and over, "What an artist I die!"
(Suetonius, *Nero* 49.1)

IN THIS famous passage, Suetonius describes Nero's directions for
his grave just prior to his suicide, but the pathos of the scene is undercut
by details surrounding his directions and the infamous quote which Nero
dictates. Nero's insistence that the length of the grave equal his actual height
signals his fear of being beheaded as soon as he is dead and perhaps his
realization that there would be no time to start and complete a cremation of
his remains.[2] Calls for water and fire in order to cleanse his corpse prior to
burial might seem unnecessary given the haste needed to bury his body to
avoid defilement. That the fire is intended to heat the water rather than to
cremate Nero's corpse seems likely in light of his directions that the length
of the grave match his exact height. The pieces of marble reflect Nero's vanity to have elements of common memorial materials, but they would call
attention to his tomb in a way that soil and stones would not. Suetonius'
narrative makes clear that time is of the essence for Nero to commit suicide
and have his remains buried in this impromptu grave.

The infamous quote, in which Nero sums up his life's main accomplishment and often read as a statement of his egomaniacal self-delusion,
might also be read as Nero's dictation of his own epitaph. The first-person

narrative is common on graves to (self) identify the deceased and their accomplishments, but the third-person narrative normally marks the location of the remains (*iacet*). The present tense of *pereo* signifies the act of dying rather than lying and would repeat Nero's final words each time they are read and thereby promote the conceit that Nero is not actually dead (and buried). There is a further conceit, on Nero's part, that passersby would know that the epitaph marked the location of his grave even without his proper name specified. Even in this somewhat anonymous state, marking the location of his corpse with such an epitaph would serve to betray the location of his corpse more than to eulogize the life accomplishments of the grave occupant.

Suetonius (*Nero* 50) provides further details surrounding Nero's actual burial:

Funeratus est impensa ducentorum milium, stragulis albis auro intextis, quibus usus Kal. Ian. fuerat. Reliquas Egloge et Alexandria nutrices cum Acte concubina gentili Domitiorum monimento condiderunt, quod prospicitur e campo Martio impositum colli Hortulorum. In eo monimento solium porphyretici marmoris, superstante Lunensi ara, circumsaeptum est lapide Thasio.

He was buried at a cost of two hundred thousand sesterces and laid out in white robes woven with gold which he had worn on the Kalends in January. His nurses Egloge and Alexandria, with his mistress Acte, placed his remains in the family tomb of the Domitii which is located on the hill of the Gardens and visible from the Campus Martius. In the tomb, his sarcophagus of porphyry, with an altar of luna marble above it, was enclosed by Thasian stone.

The details are remarkable for a former emperor. No eulogy is specified: Nero is buried by social inferiors and he is laid to rest in the tomb of the Domitii rather than Augustus' mausoleum. Despite the irony of his burial in the tomb, considering the offense he took at being called Domitius by Britannicus (Suet. *Nero* 7), the burial complies with Nero's wish to change his name and identity from a Julio-Claudian back to Domitius to give up Imperial power and become a private citizen (Suet. *Nero* 51.1). Only the details of the porphyry sarchophagus and its setting seem appropriate to his former position. The site was later considered haunted (like the Lamian Gardens which were believed haunted by Caligula's spirit) and was located at the current site of the church of S. Maria del Popolo.

Thus, Suetonius' allusion to funerary ritual provides his readers with a cultural intertext against which to read Nero's final moments. Nero imagines himself dead, cleansed, buried, and (self) represented by an epitaph while he is still alive, as he reifies his own funeral and burial as a physical and figurative experience, but the narrative also elicits questions concerning the rituals and Nero's role in directing his own funeral and burial as a living corpse. Like Nero sightings all over the Empire following his death, the presence of Nero haunted the Via Flaminia and extended his (self) representation in a way more memorable than an epitaph.

In this chapter, I examine the animation of the dead through select epitaphs from a narrative and semiotic perspective, rather than as evidence for historical, sociological, or anthropological reconstructions. I make no attempt to give a survey of epitaph features and how they changed over time. The focus will be on the narrative voice and setting (physical and figurative) of the deceased in epitaphs, especially those which have poeticizing/poetic features to analyze the (self) representation of the dead. In addition to actual grave inscriptions, I examine illusory epitaphs in Latin poetry as both grave and textual markers and as limited and limitive narratives and reading experiences in ancient and modern settings. I close my discussion of the animation of the dead with the (self) representation of the dead in elegiac texts which leads to a reciprocity between epitaphs and poetic texts in which the dead take control of their own authorial agenda and future commemoration.

Commemoration of the dead, through the recording of the accomplishments of one's military or political career through epitaphs, or through portraiture, would have a multigenerational audience in an urban setting.[3] In the case of public figures like Sulla, the record of one's character or accomplishments would shape later interpretation and also be politically relevant since one's career could provide the basis of later emulation. The actual words of Sulla's epitaph do not survive; Plutarch, however, records that it was written by Sulla himself and that it emphasized this character (hence political) trait: no friend surpassed him in kindness, no enemy in mischief.[4]

From the perspective of the viewer/emulator, the deceased becomes an *exemplum* represented by former deeds and current statue/inscription. Pliny, *Epistulae* 2.7.5–7 describes his reaction to a decreed statue of Cottius and the didactic value of displaying the portraits and records of the dead in public spaces. To Pliny, the statue of Cottius is an object of contemplation that will inspire both a physical and an emotional interaction with him (*Ep.* 2.7.6–7):

Erit ergo pergratum mihi hanc effigiem eius subinde intueri subinde respicere, sub hac consistere praeter hanc commeare. Etenim si defunctorum imagines domi positae dolorem nostrum levant, quanto magis hae quibus in celeberrimo loco non modo species et vultus illorum, sed honor etiam et gloria refertur![5]

Therefore, it will be especially pleasing for me to look at his statue, turning back frequently to look at it, standing before it, and walking past it. Truly do the *imagines* of the dead placed in the home lighten our sorrow; all the more do they in a public place not only to recall the appearance and portraits of men but also their honor and fame!

Imagines in the home are inspirational, but statues and records of the dead in public spaces are more inspirational still since they can reach a wider audience and encourage the emulation of the virtuous or valorous behavior of the dead. These memorials are not tombs that contain the remains of the deceased, rather, they are figurative and epigraphic tributes to the dead.[6]

The familiar trope of invoking the dead (*evocatio mortuorum*) in a forensic setting could also blur the distinction between the living and the dead in an urban setting and extend the figurative life of a historic figure. Cicero was aware of the dramatic potential of alluding to the dead as sentient personages since he refers, elsewhere, to the *manes* of the dead conspirators, in a forensic setting.[7] In the *Pro Caelio,* Cicero resurrects the dead Appius Claudius Caecus the Censor to pass judgment on the scandalous sexual behavior of Clodia.[8] In addition to recalling to Clodia the great position of her family, Appius compares her lurid ways to the virtuous actions of her female ancestors, such as Q. Claudia who saved the image of Cybele and Claudia the Vestal who saved her father. Perhaps Cicero's most wicked use of this grand figure was to have him condemn his descendant's lasciviousness in the words of a stern censor:

'Cur te fraterna vitia potius quam bona paterna et avita et usque a nobis cum in viris tum etiam in feminis repetita moverunt? Ideone ego pacem Pyrrhi diremi, ut tu amorum turpissimorum cotidie foedera ferires, ideo aquam adduxi, ut ea tu inceste uterere, ideo viam munivi, ut eam tu alienis viris comitata celebrares?'

"Why did a brother's vice move you more than your father's or your ancestors' which have been handed down since my time not only by the men but by the women? Was it for this that I tore up the peace of Pyrrhus, so that you might enter into compacts with your shameful lovers on a daily basis? Was it for this that I drew water to Rome so that you might use it lewdly, for this that I built a road so that you might loiter accompanied by the husbands of other women?"

This character assassination is damning due to the force of Cicero's rhetorical skill in conjuring up a seemingly realistic person or rather a portrait of the deceased in a familial context of chiding a child for shameful behavior. Cicero claims Appius is scolding in the stern old style, rather than the new gentle method, thereby drawing even more attention to Appius' words and Clodia's immorality. Moreover, resurrecting the dead as a witness in forensics is effective since the dead are not open to cross-examination and they also represent an earlier morality which was guaranteed, in the rhetoric of Rome's moral degeneration, to draw a sharp contrast with the amorality of the present age.

If the dead could attack the living, then the living could also attack the dead. In his *Satires,* Juvenal chose his targets wisely and attacked the dead rather than risk offending the living:

> [. . .] experiar quid concedatur in illos
> quorum Flaminia tegitur cinis atque Latina
>
> [. . .] I shall try what I may against those whose ashes
> are covered along the Flaminia and Latina. (*Sat.*1.170–71)

As satiric targets, the dead cannot defend themselves against attacks on their former characters and actions. As metonymic targets, however, Juvenal can criticize an anonymous contemporary for the same behavior once committed by the deceased who is mentioned by name.

The deceased remain in an urban landscape as commemoration replaces demarcation of their remains.[9] On a figurative level, the dead repopulate the boundaries of the city on whose roads, outside of the walls, they greet those who approach and leave as they transform the urban topography into a metaphorical landscape of death. The Etruscan necropolis, perhaps conceived as a reproduction/model of the world of the living but juxtaposed and separated from that world as though a parallel or even mirror image that is within view but separate and distinct has been replaced in the city of Rome with a figurative necropolis. Superimposed on the city with the deceased living among the current inhabitants, it shares the same urban and domestic space, and continues to affect the livings' behavior through the visual and epigraphic recollection of the dead's identities and achievements.

Epitaphs and Self-representation of the Dead

Mark the spot

Graves and epitaphs of the *hic est ille situs* type give directions for a viewer to look in a specific spot and identify the person buried there. Thus, they perform a deictic and a semantic function. Identification of the deceased is linked to memorialization of their accomplishments as Varro points out in his definition of a *monimentum* (*De lingua latina* 6.49):

> Meminisse a memoria, cum <in> id quod remansit in mente rursus move-tur; quae a manendo ut manimoria potest esse dicta. Itaque Salii quod cantant: Mamuri Veturi, significant memoriam veterem. Ab eodem monere, quod is qui monet, proinde sit ac memoria; sic monimenta quae in sep-ulcris, et ideo secundum viam, quo praetereuntis admoneant et se fuisse et illos esse mortalis. Ab eo cetera quae scripta ac facta memoriae causa monimenta dicta.[10]

> To remember comes from the word memory, since that which has remained in the mind is recalled; just as when something that has remained can be called a memory. So the Salii when they sing, *Mamuri Veturi,* they mean an ancient memory. From this comes the word to remind, since when one reminds, it is from memory. Thus the memorials on graves and even along the road admonish those passing by that they themselves were mortal and that the living, too, are mortal. From this other things that are written and done for the sake of memory are called monuments.

Funeral monuments, according to Varro, perform many functions that are physical and associative: mark the spot of burial; communicate the accom-plishments of the deceased to a passerby who interprets the grave marker as a commemoration of the deceased's accomplishments and a generic message on the brevity of life.

In first-person narratives on epitaphs that address a visitor or passerby, the tomb represents and conveys the words of the deceased and initiates a dialogue with the viewer that stops short when the epitaph cannot con-tinue the conversation beyond an initial address. Portraits of the deceased on their funerary monument make the engagement with a passerby more dynamic: the first-person narrative of the inscription (self) represents both the deceased and the tombstone and even competes with the deceased.[11] Particularly engaging are funerary altars, like that of Cornelia Glyce, now in the Cortile Ottagono of the Vatican Museums (figure 1), that contain a portrait of the deceased within a window-like frame that gives the impression of occupancy within a house, rather than a burial within an altar.[12] The deceased is a double presence (actual corpse and allusion to the corpse) that engages the solitary viewer. To each visitor, however, the deceased takes on a new personality; therefore, both the deceased and the visitor are constantly changing.

Both the tombstone and the viewer/reader are important for reification. But what about the actual dead whose presence is assumed beneath the gravestone and whose identity is subsumed by the inscription? Even if a proper name were recorded, the actual personality and appearance of the deceased, known to those who knew them in their lifetime, cannot be recovered by those reading an epitaph generations after their death. Photographs of the deceased are now common on tombstones; but often the physical information they provide can be of limited use if the deceased died in old age but is commemorated by a picture taken in their youth or even in their old age since, in either scenario, only a snapshot of a specific moment of life is captured. Despite the presence of biographical detail, whether in a photograph or in an inscription, a "type" or abstraction of their former selves seems to be memorialized more than a specific "individual." Epitaphs give an "illusion of personality" since the words seem to belong to the deceased, but, in reality, we do not know who composed them. Thus, the writing and reading of epitaphs test the limits of self-representation and commemoration as a limited versus limitive narrative and reading experience.[13] Juvenal (*Sat.* 10.142–46) mocks human vanity through the nonpermanence of stone inscriptions:

> patriam tamen obruit olim
> gloria paucorum et laudis titulique cupido
> haesuri saxis cinerum custodibus, ad quae
> discutienda valent sterilis mala robora fici,
> quandoquidem data sunt ipsis quoque fata sepulcris.[14]

> The pursuit of glory by a few men
> has before crushed a country: out of desire for
> praise and a title that clings on stones that guard their ashes,
> which the evil strength of a barren fig tree can crush,
> since a lifespan has been given even to their graves.

Representation of the deceased involves a similar dynamic of association: a

Figure 1. Funerary altar of Cornelia Glyce (ca. 80 CE)
Vatican Museums. Rome. Photo: M. Erasmo

portrait, whether accurate or not, represents yet competes with the deceased who no longer looks like his representation although an incription or recognition of features perpetuates the identification.[15] The representational possibilities and limitations of the deceased self-identifying with their portrait appear in the poet Ennius' epitaph:

aspicite, o cives, senis Enni imaginis formam.
  hic vestrum panxit maxima facta patrum.

Behold, o citizens, the appearance of the image of old Ennius.
  He recorded the greatest deeds of your fathers.

Ennius' *imago* is used as a rhetorical device. Ennius invites the viewer to look upon the appearance of his *imago*. Thus, the second-person address to the viewer turns Ennius from figurative interlocutor to the object of the viewer's gaze, as subjective self-representation competes with objectification of the subject. Ennius is both absent and present in the multiple representation of his image to the solitary viewer.

The custom of having the dead address a visitor to their grave or a passerby, who is too busy or too young to ponder the brevity of life and the inevitability of death, is found in Greece; however, many examples from Italy reinforce specific Roman ideals. Epitaphs include descriptions in the first and or third person of their former identities that stress moral character, accomplishments, and social station in life with greetings and warnings to the living, whether a descendant or a passerby, with the effect that the dead speak for themselves in tomb inscriptions. We often find the same information included on epitaphs in the third person. While biographic elements varied, in ancient epitaphs the deceased's concern about their reputation in death among the living and the dead is uniquely Roman. The dead engage the living in a way which causes one to question their status as "dead."

The epitaph belonging to a Claudia, for example, dates to around 135–120 BCE and was inscribed on a tablet or pillar found at Rome, now lost (*CIL* 1.2.1211). The epitaph is written in the senarius, a conversational meter from the stage, one that gives this epitaph an informal and colloquial air, as though the deceased were actually conversing with the passerby:

Hospes, quod deico paullum est; asta ac pellage.
Heic est sepulcrum hau pulcrum pulcrai feminae.
Nomen parentes nominarunt Claudiam.
Suom mareitom corde deilixit souo.
Gnatos duos creavit, horunc alterum
in terra linquit, alium sub terra locat.
Sermone lepido, tum autem incessu commodo.
Domum servavit, lanam fecit. Dixi. Abei.

Stranger, what I say is brief: stay and read it.
This is the unattractive tomb of an attractive woman.
Her parents gave her the name Claudia.
She loved her husband with all her heart.
She bore two sons, of these one she leaves
on earth, the other she has placed below the ground.
She was charming in conversation but proper in her behavior.
She kept house, she made wool. I have spoken. Depart.

Stylistic features suggest a writer other than the deceased, giving the epitaph an archaic feel that contrasts with the colloquial and informal meter: archaic spellings are found on line 1, *deico* for *dico;* line 2, *heic* for *hic* and *pulcrai* for *pulcrae*, (h is missing for *pulcrum*, too); line 4, *mareitom* for *maritum* and *souo* for *suo*. In addition, all lines end in a period except for line 5, and line 4 contains a *figura etymologica: nomen nominarunt* which is a feature of archaic Latin poetry. Line 2 also attempts to make an etymological pun on the word *sepulcrum* with the phrase *hau pulcrum* since both the prefix *se-* and the adverb *hau(d)* can both mean "not." The adjective *pulcrai* to describe Claudia's physical appearance forms a nice contrast to the unattractiveness of the tomb which the tomb itself expresses.

Whoever the author of the epitaph was, the narrative voice belongs to Claudia.[16] The epitaph opens and closes with first-person addresses by Claudia but her biographical details appear in the third person; thus, there are two narrative voices/speakers in an epitaph which Claudia apparently narrates herself (*dixi*). The combination of self-representation and presentation of her personality reflects her selfless personality by progressing in subject matter from her parents, to her husband, to her children, and finally to herself and her modesty by praising her virtues in the third-person narrative voice. The generic address to a passerby is here made personal through a combination of narrative voices that emphasize and even demonstrate Claudia's character.[17]

The dynamic between presentation and self-representation on epitaphs is most apparent in texts that include a poeticizing/poetic narrative which is concerned with the form and content of expression that reveals as much about the deceased as it does about the narrative voice. If an epitaph represents and competes with the deceased, then a poetic presence adds a third narrative voice that imposes a narrative structure on the words of both the deceased and the epitaph. The tomb visitor who wishes to learn the identity of the deceased becomes engaged in a narratological exercise in which competing narrative voices (and visual elements) vie for attention.

The visitor/passerby as reader (*lector*) construct appears in the epitaph of Herennia Crocine from Gades (modern Cadiz), Spain that dates to the first century BCE (*CIL* 2.1821):

> Ave! / Herennia Crocine / cara sueis inclusa hoc
> tumulo. / Crocine cara sueis. Vixi ego / et
> ante aliae vixere puellae. / Iam satis est.
> Lector discedens, / dicat 'Crocine sit tibi
> Terra / levis.' Valete superi.

> Hail! Herennia Crocine, dear to her own, is buried
> in this tomb. Crocine, dear to her own. I lived even
> as other girls lived before me. That is enough.

Let the reader say while departing, "Crocine, lightly
rest the earth on you." Farewell to those who live above ground.

Herennia's first-person address to the passerby reveals little beyond her age.
The extent of her accomplishments is summed up by *vixi ego*–I lived just as
other girls before me. Her individuality seems to reside in her appreciation
of the inevitable fact that she shares in the collective fates of other girls. In
her request of the passerby she wishes for a generic hope expressed by the
proverb *sit tibi terra levis* / "lightly rest the earth on you.' Crocine speaks
these words on the passerby's behalf and thus dramatizes a conversation/
exchange with strangers who continually wish her a peaceful repose. Thus,
the passerby is a reader and a speaker through reification of the tomb and
the epitaph.

The epitaph of Helvia Prima (*CIL* I, 2. 1732), in elegiac couplets, which
dates to around 45 BCE and was found at Beneventum, is a variation on the
passerby theme:

Tu qui secura spatiarus mente viator
    et nostri voltus derigis inferieis,
Si quaeris quae sim, cinis en et tosta favilla,
    ante obitus tristeis Helvia Prima fui.
Coniuge sum Cadmo fructa Scrateio,
    concordesque pari viximus ingenio.
Nunce data sum Diti longum mansura per aevum,
    deducta et fatali igne et aqua Stygia.

Passerby, you who walk past with carefree mind and
    glance on my funeral gifts,
If you ask who I am, look at my ashes and burnt embers,
    I was Helvia Prima before my sad death.
I enjoyed my marriage to Cadmus Scrateius,
    we lived one in heart with equal disposition.
Now I have been given to Dis to remain an eternity,
    led down by fatal fire and the Styx's water.

Helvia invites the passerby to identify her by looking at her cremated remains
by which she identifies herself. She does not mention a profession or her age,
only that she enjoyed a happy marriage. The contrast between the apparent
good health of the passerby and the death of the deceased is exaggerated
here with Helvia Prima's emphasis on her cremated remains. The passerby

in line 1 physically measures out his steps as he passes Helvia's tomb. On a figurative level, he also measures out his life on earth free from care (*secura spatiarus mente*), perhaps meaning that he is too confident in youth. In line 7, Helvia Prima claims that she too will measure out her (after)life, but this will be below the earth (*longum mansura per aevum*). Helvia's description of her loving relationship with her husband, Cadmus Scrateius, is common in Latin epitaphs and is the focus of her life's accomplishments. The theme of marriage is also contained in the final two lines of the epitaph—Helvia has been given to the god of Death, Dis (*data sum Diti*), in much the same way that her father/patron gave her once to her husband, Cadmus. This figurative double marriage emphasizes Helvia's character as a devoted and congenial wife. Thus, poetic elements are used as a means of expressing Helvia's character and (self) representation.

A poetic consciousness is apparent from the earliest Latin epitaphs that come from the Tomb of the Scipios near the Via Appia Antica in Rome. The anonymous authors of these inscriptions peppered their epitaphs with archaic language more appropriate to an earlier age, and yet this language was consciously at odds with the poetic style of the epitaph. We find modern spellings and contemporary concepts together with archaic forms, but we also find archaisms in epitaphs whose poetic style betrays a later date when the language does not. This archaizing style produced an eclectic if not jarring effect: like reading a contemporary obituary written in Elizabethan or Victorian verse or reading a Victorian obituary reworked in modern slang. However odd this may seem to us, descendants wished their ancestors to be portrayed in a favorable contemporary light, that is, Hellenized through a Greek education (even when this seems historically unlikely), but in language that was solemn and grounded in Italic tradition. While these epitaphs have already received much attention for their language and (emerging) poetic sensibilities, I would like to focus on self-representation and the effects of a poetic identity (super)imposed, literally and figuratively, on both the deceased and the tombstone.[18]

The earliest two epitaphs are literal palimpsests—reworked versions of the originals of which only the first line or two of each survives. As the first-known epitaphs of ancient Rome, they are pre-conventional but they are also conventional in that the reworked versions reveal more about later attitudes toward burial customs and epitaphs. Both the original and reworked versions identify the deceased in relation to his father. The reworked versions give political and military accomplishments, making the epitaphs highly personal and specific in their recording of aristocratic virtues. The epitaphs were written by an unknown author or authors (tradition claims the poet Ennius but the evidence is inconclusive). The first-person voice, however, was intended to represent the (self-representational) words of the deceased. The reworked inscriptions were written for a contemporary reader who wanted to self-identify with his ancestors, but also for his ancestors to self-identify with his own ideals. It is unclear how these epitaphs influenced later Roman epitaphic tradition since these tombs were in a family vault presumably accessible only to family members. In other words, we cannot answer the question of how poetic elements on epitaphs became normalized, especially considering the wide variety of objects (tombstone, plaque, vase, sarcophagus, etc.) upon which epitaphs were inscribed.

The earliest of the Scipio epitaphs is that of Lucius Cornelius Scipio Barbatus (consul 298, censor 290 BCE; *CIL* 1.2.6–7):

a) [L. Cornelio] Cn. f. Scipio
b) Cornelius Lucius Scipio Barbatus
Gnaivod patre prognatus, fortis vir sapiensque,
quoius forma virtutei parisuma fuit,
consol censor aidilis quei fuit apud vos,
Taurasia Cisauna Samnio cepit
subigit omne Loucanam opsidesque abdoucit.

a) Lucius Cornelius Cn. f. Scipio
b) Cornelius Lucius Scipio Barbatus
son begat by Gnaeus, a brave and wise man,
whose beauty matched his bravery,
he was a consul, censor, and aedile among you,
he captured Taurasia, Cisauna, and Samnium,
he subdued all of Loucania and took hostages.

The epitaph appears on Barbatus' sarcophagus in two different versions: an original (painted) line survives as line a which provides the name of the deceased in a traditional ordering of names. The reworked and inscribed inscription is section b. A poetic treatment of the reworked inscription is apparent in the first line which rearranges the traditional format of a Roman name, as it appears in line 1 of the original inscription. In line 2, *fortis vir sapiensque* is a reference to a Hellenic education, for which Barbatus is historically too early, but a trait traditionally ascribed to his famous descendant (great-grandson) Scipio Africanus. The Greek emphasis on physical beauty as an indication of inner virtue is apparent in line 3 and is another anachronistic cultural detail superimposed on stone and onto the character and

Figure 2. Sarcophagus of Scipio Barbatus. Vatican Museums.
Rome. Photo: M. Erasmo

personality of the deceased. Barbatus' elected offices are listed in line 4 while
the tribes he conquered are listed in the final two lines. Modern spellings
are evident in the list of offices: *consol* for archaic *cosol; censor* for archaic
cesor. Archaic elements include the spelling of *Gnaeus* in line 2 as *Gnaivod,
parisuma* in line 3 for *parissima,* and *quei* in line 4 for *qui.* The epitaph is
composed in the Saturnian meter which predates hexameter verse at Rome
and was used in epitaphs until at least the mid-first century BCE, long after
its disappearance as a literary meter (except in the earliest books of Lucilius'
Satires). Therefore, this epitaph contains a fusion of Greek (content) and
traditional Roman/Italic elements (content/form).

The content of the epitaph is now as eclectic as its appearance and current location. The sarcophagus recalls Greek altar designs from South Italy
with Ionic and Doric decorative elements, but it also shares general characteristics with Etruscan sarcophagi (figure 2). It was moved from the Tomb of
the Scipios on the Via Appia Antica to the Vatican Museums where it now

Figure 3. Sarcophagus of Scipio Barbatus (background). Vatican Museums. Rome. Photo: M. Erasmo

sits in a niche along a busy corridor across from a satellite gift shop that sells
posters of the Sistine Chapel, gift items, and museum publications (figure
3). Large tour groups that pass through the corridor make it almost impossible to stop long enough to read Barbatus' epitaph or to read the epitaph
of his son Lucius Cornelius Scipio which hangs directly above Barbatus'
sarcophagus. To read the father's epitaph is a challenge, but to read the son's
requires a museum visitor to step back and stand firm against the crowds
rushing past unaware of the tomb or the historically important epitaphs. Not
only is the tomb out of its ritual context, so too has the commemoration
of the deceased changed if the act of reading an epitaph designed to grab
a passerby's attention is made impossible because of Barbatus' new (nonfunerary) surroundings. To museum visitors rushing past the sarcophagus en
route to or from the Sistine Chapel and only vaguely aware of the objects
in their peripheral vision, there is no time or interest to commemorate the
dead; instead, a funerary marker has become an itinerary marker to get one's
bearings between exhibition halls.

The following epitaph of Barbatus' son, Lucius Cornelius Scipio (consul
259, censor 258 BCE; *CIL* 1.2.8–9) is the second oldest and also of historic
and linguistic interest:

a) [L.] Cornelio L.f. Scipio

[a]idiles cosol cesor

b) Honc oino ploirume cosentiont R[omai]

duonoro optumo fuise viro

Luciom Scipione. Filios Barbati

consol censor aidilis hic fuet a[pud vos].

hec cepit Corsica Aleriaque urbe

dedet Tempestatebus aide mereto[d].

a) [L.] Cornelius L. f. Scipio

aedile, consul, censor

b) Most would agree that he excelled all men at Rome,

Lucius Scipio. The son of Barbatus,

he was consul, censor, and aedile among you.

he captured Corsica and the city Aleria,

he dedicated to the Goddesses of Weather a temple, by merit.

This epitaph is more recent than that of the elder Scipio, but the archaizing elements evoke the language of an even earlier date. The language is at odds with its innovative poetic style and the result is an epitaph that is at once archaizing and modern. The effect of this lingustic/artistic contradiction is to obscure the (self) representation of the deceased in the original epitaph. The imposition of an aesthetic on an epitaph reveals more about Scipio's descendants' representation of their ancestor and self-representation of their own eclectic tastes.

Two lines survive from the original inscription in section a, and the reworked epitaph appears in section b. We can see from the original inscription that Scipio's name is given in the traditional word order in the first line and the public offices which he held in the second line. In the reworked version, *Cornelius* is dropped and the second *L* for *Lucius* to signify his father's name is changed to *Barbatus*. Scipio's name does not appear until line 3 where the traditional order of *Lucius (Cornelius) Barbati Filios Scipio* is given a poetic treatment so that his name is rearranged and divided in two by a period, thereby separating the epitaph into roughly two halves.

The epitaph is full of archaisms: in line 1, we find *honc* for *hunc; oino* for *unum, ploirume* for *plurimi; consentiont* for *consentiunt* and *Romai* for *Romae*. In line 2, *duonoro . . . viro* substitutes for *bonorum virorum,* and *fuise* replaces *fuisse*. The offices held in line 4, *consol, censor, aidilis,* are properly written and replace the archaisms of the original line 2 which do not have an n for *consol* and *censor*. In line 5, *hec* replaces *hic*. The reason for the change

in spelling between *hic* in line 4 and *hec* in line 5 is unclear; *hic* replaces
the relative pronoun *quei* which we find in Scipio's father's epitaph, line 4,
and points to a deliberate break with the previous sentence (epitaph 1 puts
the titles and the names of the conquered places in the same sentence); fhe
final m is not written for the accusatives *Corsica Aleriaque urbe.* In line 6,
Tempestatebus replaces *Tempestatibus* and is a personification of Weather goddesses. The final m is missing for *aide.*

There were many generations buried at the Tomb of the Scipios, including Gn. Cornelius Scipio Hispanus (c 135 BCE; *CIL* 1.2.15), whose epitaph
is remarkable for its poetic form and content:

> Cn. Cornelius Cn. f. Scipio Hispanus pr. aid. cur.
> q. tr. mil. II Xvir sl. iudik. Xvir sacr. fac.
> Virtutes generis mieis moribus accumulavi,
> progeniem genui, facta patris petiei.
> Maiorum optenui laudem, ut sibei me esse creatum
> laetentur; stirpem nobilitavit honor.

> Gnaeus Cornelius, son of Gnaeus, Scipio Hispanus, praetor, curule aedile,
> quaestor, tribune of soldiers twice; member of the Board of Ten for
> Judging Lawsuits; member of the Board of Ten for Making Sacrifices.
> By my virtue, I increased the virtue of my clan,
> I begat offspring and sought to rival my father's deeds.
> I upheld the praise of my ancestors, so that they may be happy
> that I was created with themselves; my honor ennobled my stock.

The epitaph is written in elegiac couplets (alternating lines of hexameter
and pentameter verse), which are the earliest surviving examples. The first
two lines appear to be aimed at the living while the two elegiac lines appear
to be aimed at his ancestors. Hispanus' emphasis on his ancestors mirrors
the ancestor worship that would be found in the home, and he furthermore
strives to be worthy of similar praise by employing, in the Latin, archaisms
(*mieis; petiei; sibei*) that would have been used by his ancestors a century
earlier. That his dead ancestors would be happy (*laetentur*) with his moral
character illustrates a readership joined, rather than separated, by death.
Thus, the epitaph reflects a need for accuracy since self-representation would
have an objective assessment by ancestors who now form the contemporary
family of the deceased, as would his descendants who will join him and
their ancestors and face a similar reckoning of their accomplishments and
virtues.

The arrangement of the epitaph's information contrasts strongly with the previous two. The first two lines contain the deceased's name and the names of the public offices which he held. His special offices are listed in line 2. Abbreviations are given for his offices and their minimalization here serves to emphasize the importance of the elegiac portion of the epitaph. With line 3, the elegiac portion opens with the word *virtutes* while line 6 ends with the word *honor*. In other words, the verses open and close with the personal qualities of Hispanus. In line 3, *accumulavi* replaces the third-person voice of the first two epitaphs. We find poetic features: alliteration of m's, p's, g's, and t's throughout which adds an archaic sound to the epitaph. A *figura etymologica* (the side-by-side placement of a noun and verb derived from the same root), in line 4: *progeniem genui*. The line emphasizes three generations of Hispanus' family: his children, his parents, and himself. Line 5 contains three elisions and ends in an enjambment while the other lines end in a period. Therefore, this epitaph represents a departure from the first two epitaphs in its poetic form and content: seemingly paradoxically, it preserves archaic forms and poetic features side by side that give it, at once, both an archaic and a contemporary flavor to reflect Hispanus' stated audience of the dead and the living. Despite the highly poetic character of the epitaph, poetry emerges as a vehicle for self-representation of the deceased rather than the poet.

So far, I have examined select epitaphs in which the words describing the deceased have been changed in a later rewriting of the epitaph or in which the deceased is (self) represented on a tombstone that competes for narrative attention. The presence of a poetic/poeticizing voice complicates the narrative of epitaphs and engages a visitor, who is interested in learning the identity of the deceased, in an interpretative challenge. The epitaph that the poet Laberius composed for his wife illustrates this challenge: the narrating poet and the deceased share the tomb's narrative only to have Laberius replaced by the narrative voice of an unknown writer who composes Laberius' own epitaph:

> Bassa, vatis quae Laberi coniuga, hoc alto sinu
> frugae matris quiescit, moribus priscis nurus.
> animus sanctus cum maritost, anima caelo reddita est.
>
> Parato hospitium; cara iungant corpora
> haec rursum nostrae, sed perpetuae, nuptiae.
> In spica et casia es, benedora stacta et amomo.
> inde oro gramenue novum vel flos oriatur,

unde coronem amens aram carmenque meum et me.
purpureo varum vitis depicta racemo
quattuor amplesast ulmos de palmite dulci.
scaenales frondes detexant hinc geminam umbram
arboream procaeram et mollis vincla maritae.

Hic corpus vatis Laberi, nam spiritus ivit
    illuc unde ortus. quaerite fontem animae.

Quod fueram non sum, sed rursum ero quod modo non sum.
    ortus et occasus vitaque morsque itidest.[19]

Bassa, wife of the poet Laberius, rests here in the
deep lap of fruitful Earth, a wife of ancient morals.
Her revered thoughts are with her husband, her soul has returned to
        heaven.

Prepare a suite; let our marriage vows unite our beloved
bodies again, but forever.

You are in saffron and cinnamon, fragrant myrrh and balsam.
From there I pray a plant or a flower may grow, with which,
grief stricken, I may wreath the altar, my verses, and myself.
The vine colored with the purple bunches of grapes has
embraced four elm trees with their dear tendrils.
Let the scenic greenery weave here a twin shadow,
the tall tree and the bonds of their tender spouse.

Here lies the body of the poet Laberius, for his spirit returned
    whence it came. Seek the fountainhead of the soul.

What I was, I am not now, but I will be again what I am not now.
    Rising and setting, life and death are the same.

Laberius identifies his wife in relation to himself and his role of poet (*vates*). The wife occupies various physical and figurative locations: her remains are buried below the earth which is personified as a giving mother while her soul is in heaven. Her (cremated?) remains are surrounded by spices and fragrant greens which the poet hopes will grow into a new herb or flower to mark her altar and wear as a physical sign of his grief. The new herb or flower will also signal the content and emotion of his dirge.

The thought of being figuratively surrounded by his wife through the flowers that she would give life to turns Laberius' thoughts to the physical setting of the tomb. The epitaph describes the appearance of the tomb which is a *cepotaphium:* four elm trees which are supporting grape vines are paired like spouses and their interwoven branches form a theatrical backdrop (*scaenales frondes*) to the tomb, altar, and epitaph. The branches also recall the romantic pastoral setting of Daphnis' tomb in Vergil's *Eclogue* 5, thus further transforming the tomb's location into an intertextual space. Laberius' tribute to his wife turns the act of reading an epitaph for the identity of the deceased into an intertextual experience that involves his self-identification as a poet in a physical and figurative landscape with her remains (actual and metaphorically transformed). In its original setting, the epitaph that describes the figurative metamorphosis of the tomb's setting was also part of the landscape it described, thus serving as a botanical marker common in public gardens today that allow a visitor to "read" the epitaph for the identity of the deceased against its setting.

Laberius' third-person narrative voice of his wife is replaced by the third-person narrative of an unknown author. This added narrative voice does not add to the biographical and self-identifying information contained in Laberius' epitaph to his wife; rather, the epitaph simply marks the location of Laberius' remains without reference to his wife and informs the passerby that his soul has returned to its source. The identity of the first-person narrative voice in the final two lines of the epitaph is unclear: Laberius? his soul? The universalizing statement of birth, life, and death is reminscent of tragedy, and if the reader understands them as belonging to Laberius, they would be words full of gravity and pathos from a poet famous for his mimes.

Survivors of the deceased can also impose their presence and narrative voices onto epitaphs that turn the focus away from the deceased and even the poetic voice toward the survivor expressing their grief. Even in the following damaged epitaph, the marking of a son's death, for example, gives the deceased's mother an opportunity to mourn his death and lament the sad circumstances of her own life:

> filio
> infelicis]sim\<a\> mater
> [aetatis pri]mo qui mihi flore perit [perit]
> percussus cornu, bubus dum pascua ponit;
> ad quem dum curro, dum miser ante perit.

infelixs genetrix Diti tria funera duxsi;
    lugebam natas cum mihi natus obit.
quod superest matri saltem concedite, Manes,
    ut sint qui voltus post mea fata premant.
M. Octavi Pulli f. Rufi.[20]

       to her son
a most unfortunate mother
    who in the first bloom of youth was taken [taken] from me
gored by a horn as he was laying out fodder for the oxen;
    the poor boy died even as I was running to him.
I, an unlucky mother, have led three funerals to Dis.
    I was mourning my daughters when my son died.
Manes, at least allow a mother to keep what is left
    so that there may be those who can close my eyes after death.
Marcus Octavius Rufus, son of Pullus.

The epitaph is remarkable for the manner in which the deceased, Marcus Octavius Rufus, died while in the farm fields and for the prominent role in the narrative that his mother occupies. The son shares his epitaph with sisters who predeceased him. Therefore, the tombstone marks the location/ identity of her son, but it also represents and marks the grief of his mother who also expresses a wish for the future that someone will survive her and give her a burial.

In another epitaph, a grave is used as the memorial to the grief of a man who lost his wife and son when their ship sank. The husband/father's grief dominates the epitaph and overshadows the personalities of his wife and son:

Heu crudele nimis fatum. dua funera maerens
    plango vir et genitor flebile mersa deo.
sat fuerat, Portmeu, cumba vexsisse maritam
    abreptamque mihi sede iacere tua.
adiecit Chloto iteratum rumpere filum,
    ut natum raperet tristis, ut ante, mihi.
me decuit morti prius occubuisse suppremae
    tuque mihi tales, nate, dare exsequias.
ad tu ne propera, simili qui sorte teneris,
    dunc annos titulo, nomina ut ipse legas.
illa bis undenos vixit, natus quoque senos;

nomen huic Probus est, huic quidem Athenaidis.
quas ego, quas genitor pro te dabo, nate, querellas,
 raptum que(m) Stygio detinet unda lacu!
quam bene bis senos florebas, parve, per annos,
 credebantque deis vota placere mea!
stamina ruperunt subito tua candida Parcae
 apstuleruntque simul vota precesque mihi.
cum te, nate, fleo, planctus dabet Attica aedo
 et comes ad lachrimas veniet pro coniuge Siren,
semper et Alcyone flebit te voce suprema
 et tristis mecum resonabet carmen et Echo
Oebaliusque dabit mecum tibi murmura cycnus.[21]

Alas, my too cruel fate. Mourning, I weep for two deaths,
 as husband and father, sadly drowned by fate.
It would have been enough, Charon, for you to have carried
 my wife in your boat, and once taken, to rest in your home.
Clotho took part and broke a second thread, so that, as before,
 she, sullen, could snatch my son from me.
It was proper for me to be laid out in final death before you
 and for you to offer such funeral tributes to me.
But do not hasten to read the names yourself, you who are grasping a
 similar fate, until
 you read the years on the epitaph.
She lived twenty two years, my son twelve;
 his name was Probus, hers was Athenais.
What laments, my son, will I your father give you whom the
 water of the Stygian stream detains, snatched from me?
How well you lived, child, for your twelve years, and
 they thought my vows were pleasing to the gods!
Suddenly, the Parcae cut your white thread and, at the same time,
 robbed me of my vows and prayers.
When I weep for you, my son, the Attic nightingale will give a lament
 and the Siren will come as companion to the tears for my wife,
and Alcyone will weep for you with her final cries and sad Echo
 will repeat the funeral song with me
and the Spartan swan will lament you with me.

The narrative voice (= a Probus based on the son's name) mourns his losses
in his dual roles as husband and father. The unknown author/poet of the

epitaph not only poeticizes Probus' grief, but also identifies himself as a poet, as he links himself with mythological birds associated with death, in particular with the dying swan which is common as a metaphor for a poet's last song. The highly poeticized expression of his grief, however, is at odds with the numerous grammatical mistakes that pepper the epitaph. The comparison of the shipwreck that took the lives of both wife and son to the boat of Charon, at the beginning of the epitaph, is relevant but also signals that the expression of grief will be highly figurative and less likely to reflect the actual self-expression of the husband/father.

Illusory Epitaphs

Mark the spot?

How should we interpret graves of the *hic est ille situs* type, like the one given to Pompey in Lucan's *Bellum Civile,* which do not mark the location of the deceased's remains? My own experience with my father's grave illustrates the danger of interpreting epitaphs literally, but even with the knowledge that the deceased is not buried where an epitaph specifies, how should a viewer/ reader interpret information contained in an epitaph, like that of Scipio Barbatus now in the Vatican Museums, that no longer serves its original purpose in announcing and demarcating where the deceased is buried? From a physical perspective, this results when a grave marker is moved but not the deceased (or remains of the deceased are disturbed and also relocated, but not where the grave marker is located); thus the epitaph no longer demarcates the location of a corpse. The location of its new surroundings takes on a new aesthetic context that replaces the former religious/sociological one.

Cicero, for example, in planning a memorial park for his daughter Tullia, advises Atticus to decorate the grounds with Greek and Roman (funeral) monuments:

> de fano illo dico, de quo tantum quantum me amas velim cogites. equidem neque de genere dubito (placet enim mihi Cluati) neque de re (statutum est enim), de loco non numquam. velim igitur cogites. ego, quantum his temporibus tam eruditis fieri potuerit, profecto illam consecrabo omni genere monimentorum ab omnium ingeniis sumptorum et Graecorum et Latinorum.[22]

> I refer to that temple, about which I wish you to think about as much as

you esteem me. I have no hesitation at all about the form (indeed, the plan of Cluatius pleases me), nor about the idea (since it is already decided), but I sometimes do about the location. Therefore, I wish for you to think about it. I, as much as it will be possible in these informed times, will consecrate to her every kind of memorial supplied from the masterpieces of the Greeks and Latins.

Although Cicero is still in search of a site, the landscape design has already been planned by an architect who will (super)impose his design on the site which will itself be an imposition/physical sign of Cicero's grief on the landscape. The mixture of Greek and Roman monuments to decorate the gardens represents a further recontextualizing of the original objects as funeral markers in a new landscape setting.

Today, epitaphs on museum walls are decorative items and mark a shift from the topography of death where the dead are buried to the decoration with death in a secular setting, where the objects of death ritual from epitaphs, urns, sarchopaghi, to grave goods are displayed. At the Capitoline Museums in the Palazzo Nuovo, for example, to the right of the entrance to the alcove containing the Capitoline Venus, is the epitaph of a certain Rufus (figure 4) that is powerful and full of pathos in its simplicity:

D.M.

RUFO

RUFILLA•MATER

FILIO•CARISSIMO

FECIT

D.M.

To Rufus

His mother Rufilla

for her dearest son

made this.

The inscription is brief like many epitaphs that have just D.M. (= *dis manibus,* i.e., to the divine shades), and the name of the deceased, but this one also contains the name of the deceased's mother. No family name of a *gens* or clan is given, perhaps signifying the epitaph of a freedwoman. Furthermore, the inscription is painted on a small plaque with few words and was therefore inexpensive to produce. Rufilla informs the reader of her relationship to her dead son, but we do not know whether her husband is already dead

Figure 4. Epitaph of Rufus. Capitoline Museums # 4520. Rome.
Photo: M. Erasmo

or indeed, whether she had even been married since the boy seems to be named after her and not his father. Rufus is defined by his mother's affection for him, rather than by his own attributes or accomplishments, therefore suggesting that this is an epitaph to a dead child. Rufilla does not, however, dominate the epitaph in the same way as does the mother of Marcus Octavius Rufus. The syntax also conveys information in an iconic reading of the epitaph: the datives *Rufo* and *filio carissimo* are separated by *Rufilla mater* and *fecit,* the placement of which words evokes a maternal caress and reflects the centrality of the mother's role in her son's life. On lines 2 and 3, we also have an enjambment, a line that carries over into another line without punctuation, with *mater* and *filio* separated by lines 3 and 4 that poignantly signifies that a mother is close to her son even though separated by death. Rufus' mother could not have known that her memorial would be in a museum someday, especially as a peripheral attraction to a famous statue.

The juxtaposition between Rufus' epitaph (just one of many along the same wall) and the Capitoline Venus is interesting. A cordon blocks the entrance to the alcove and the viewer stands at the entrance with funeral plaques on the walls on either side. (figure 5). The cordon separates both the museum visitor and the epitaphs of the Roman dead from Venus, spatially and temporally, but it also unites them as mortals, past and present. The primary focus of attention is the statue, but it is visible through the

Figure 5. Capitoline Venus. Capitoline Museums. Rome. The epitaph of Rufus is on the bottom of the row of epitaphs to the right of the alcove entrance. Photo: M. Erasmo

peripheral vision of death memorials: Venus, on her pedestal, represents an artistic ideal that has outlasted the mortality of generations of Romans and which continues to be perpetuated. Nonfunerary art competes with or is complemented by memorials, depending on the perspective of the viewer, of the Roman dead who are not buried in the museum, but whose presence is nonetheless suggested or even advertised along its walls.

Venus preparing for her bath behind the cordon, however, may not be safe from misinterpretation. If the placement of Rufus' epitaph in a museum elevates it to the status of "art," the placement of Venus' statue among funerary markers may turn it into a funerary statue by assimilation: to museum visitors familiar with second-century CE portraits of wealthy Romans modeled after Venus (especially of the Capua type), and imitated in the funerary portrait reliefs of freedwomen, Venus may be misinterpreted as a portrait of an ancient Roman woman depicted as Venus.[23] The mistake would be facilitated if a museum visitor noticed the portrait of a Flavian Woman as Venus, located in the same corridor as Rufus' epitaph but along the other wall, before approaching the alcove of the Capitoline Venus (figure 6). This portrait statue was found in Rome near the Basilica and Catacombs of San Sebastiano, which suggests a funerary context among the tombs along the

Figure 6. Portrait of Flavian Woman as Venus. Capitoline Museums. Rome. Photo: M. Erasmo

Via Appia Antica.[24] The pose of this Venus is less modest than that of the Capitoline Venus *pudica* type; nonetheless, the contrast between the Venus-like body and the Roman face of the woman commands attention.

Paradoxically, through assimilation, the Capitoline Venus, herself the model for funeral portrait types, would become a copy of herself adapted for funerary commemoration in an alcove that enshrines (or entombs) its famous model. Through falsely advertising the location of their remains, the epitaphs of Rufus and the other Roman dead lining the corridor of the Palazzo Nuovo turn funerary art into art and art into funerary art in an interpretive exercise that requires a museum visitor to contemplate an object, whether epitaph or portrait, within the contexts of its original function in its former location and its new (aesthetic) function in its new (nonfunerary) location.[25]

Mark the text

Epitaphs in a literary passage, like their museum counterparts, are also removed from their original ritual contexts and express a similar deception or paradox: a corpse is not buried where the text indicates. The *viator* was a *lector* at an actual tombstone, but now the *lector* becomes a *viator* through the reading of texts that are encoded with epitaphs. A grave marker functions as a narrative marker since the text is literally encoded with an epitaph (versus an actual tombstone which encodes a landscape). Just as an epitaph on a tombstone represents and competes with the narrative voice of the deceased, epitaphs in literary texts compete with the narrative voice of the author. Actual and figurative epitaphs both provide narrative closure: an epitaph on a tombstone represents biological and biographical closure, but an epitaph in a literary text may frustrate an expectation or imitation of that closure when the death is just a fiction for a character (or author) who continues to live beyond the narrative of the epitaph and its literary setting.

Dido, for example, in the speech which Seneca quoted in condemning Pacuvius' mock funerals, delivers her own epitaph in the *Aeneid* (4.653–58). Immediately prior to her suicide on a funeral pyre, which she constructed with objects of sentimental value that Aeneas had given to her, Dido lists her life's major accomplishments:

> vixi et quem dederat cursum Fortuna peregi,
> et nunc magna mei sub terras ibit imago.
> urbem praeclaram statui, mea moenia vidi,
> ulta virum poenas inimico a fratre recepi,
> felix, heu nimium felix, si litora tantum
> numquam Dardaniae tetigissent nostra carinae.

> I lived and what course Fortune gave, I completed,
> and now my great *imago* will go below the earth.
> I founded a famous city and saw my city walls,
> I avenged my husband from his enemy, my brother,
> happy, more than happy I would have been if the
> Dardanian fleet had never reached our shores.

Dido represents herself and her accomplishments with emphasis on verbs in the first person, but she does not identify herself explicitly. Emphasis is placed on survival, revenge, and unhappiness (since the repetition of *felix* in line 4 is part of a conditional clause). Dido does not give any details of her relationship with her husband and significantly, she does not see or describe herself as *pia,* a common epithet for women on tombstones.

As a self-represented character, Dido's narrative voice competes with Vergil's. She does not make any direct references to her relationship with Aeneas; rather, the narrative of her epitaph and of her life's accomplishments ends with the arrival of the Trojans to Carthage. Until Anna arrives to find her sister dying on a burning pyre, Dido is her own funeral director, corpse, and mourner/audience. The pathos of the scene is increased by reading/hearing Dido recite her own epitaph since she has consciously separated herself from her body and the living as though a stranger reads and interprets what she is, in fact, reciting about herself. The epitaph serves as a textual marker of the location of Dido's suicide and cremation, but it also foreshadows Dido's reappearance in the text in Book 6. Dido's epitaph provides closure and nonclosure to the narrative: the conceit that she expresses that she will continue to live on in death in the Underworld is common on actual epitaphs, but here is programmatic (to readers who remember the epitaph when she reappears in the epic or on a rereading of the poem).[26]

The frequent allusions to and inclusion of epitaphs in epic, which formed part of the narratives of funerals from Vergil to Statius, encode the shared narrative landscape of epic, but they also serve as authorial and emotional markers in elegiac poetry. While the origins of Latin elegiac poetry are obscure, its themes of love and death share features with epitaph verse from the shared elegiac meter of alternating hexameter and pentameter verse for the arousal of pathos.[27] As a literary genre, however, elegy is related to death and Propertius uses death and the dead as theme and interlocutor to deemphasize the distinctions between life and death and assert the originality of his poetry. In elegy 1.7. 21–26, for example, the poet states his preference for elegiac over epic poetry and imagines his readers discussing his artistic legacy as though visiting his tomb:

> tum me non humilem mirabere saepe poetam,
>   tunc ego Romanis praeferar ingeniis;
> nec poterunt iuvenes nostro reticere sepulcro
>   'Ardoris nostri magne poeta, iaces.'
> tu cave nostra tuo contemnas carmina fastu:
>   saepe venit magno faenore tardus Amor. [28]

> Then you will often marvel at me, not an obscure poet,
>   and I will be preferred to all the talents of Rome:
> Nor will young men be able to stay silent at my tomb:

"Great poet of our passions, you lie buried."
Be careful not to despise our poems with your arrogance:
    often, Love comes late at great cost.

Propertius projects his fame beyond his death to promote the quality of his
poetry in the present. The *lector* of his poetry is also the *scriptor* of his illusory
epitaph, which extends the narrative presence of Propertius in death.

Propertius exploits the epitaph tradition in elegies 1.21 and 1.22, dating to 41–40 BCE, in which he describes the dying words of his kinsman
Gallus, who had fought at the siege of Perugia. It soon becomes apparent,
however, that the poem is spoken not by a dying, but rather an already dead
Gallus. By employing an epitaph form, Propertius can give the ostensible
words of Gallus after his death. Emotion and the expression of sentiments
are exchanged between the living and the dead as though death were no
impediment:

'Tu, qui consortem properas evadere casum,
    miles ab Etruscis saucius aggeribus,
quid nostro gemitu turgentia lumina torques?
        pars ego sum vestrae proxima militiae.
sic te servato ut possint gaudere parentes,
    ne soror acta tuis sentiat e lacrimis:
Gallum per medios ereptum Caesaris ensis
    effugere ignotas non potuisse manus;
et quaecumque super dispersa invenerit ossa
    montibus Etruscis, haec sciat esse mea.'

"You who hasten to avoid a companion fate,
    a soldier wounded on the Etruscan ramparts,
why do you turn your eyes welling with tears to my groans?
    I am your closest comrade-in-arms.
So save yourself so that your parents may rejoice,
    and my sister not guess these deeds from your tears:
that Gallus stole out from the midst of Caesar's swords,
    but was not able to flee the hands of someone unknown;
and whatever bones she may find scattered atop
    Etruscan mounds, let her know that these are mine."

The words on the epitaph self represent both Gallus and his words which
continue in death. The epitaph marks the location where Gallus' remains are

located, but the final lines inform the passerby that his remains are not all buried but rather, are scattered around the battle site. Therefore, the epitaph does not mark the spot where Gallus is buried, even though the narrative serves as a physical and textual marker for his sister who will search for his tomb and his unburied remains. The illusory epitaph as the self-represented words of Gallus requires the passerby/reader to question whether or not Gallus is dead or alive and buried or unburied. The epitaph is both limited and limitive to the addressee/*lector* who seems to be reading an epitaph, but is actually reading a poem modeled on an epitaph for a character who is already dead but addressing the reader as though he were still alive.

In elegy 22, Propertius responds to the previous poem and again uses the death of his kinsman to comment on contemporary politics. The poem is not an epitaph, but rather a description of Gallus' family's connection to Perugia and the losses it sustained, measured in both life and land. Lines 6–8 make it clear that the Gallus of elegy 21 never received a burial:

> Qualis et unde genus, qui sint mihi, Tulle, Penates,
> > quaeris pro nostro semper amicitia.
> si Perusina tibi patriae sunt nota sepulcra,
> > Italiae duris funera temporibus,
> cum Romana suos egit discordia civis,
> > (sic mihi praecipue, pulvis Etrusca, dolor,
> tu proiecta mei perpessa es membra propinqui,
> > tu nullo miseri contegis ossa solo),
> proxima supposito contingens Umbria campo
> > me genuit terris fertilis uberibus.

> Of what sort and from where, Tullus, are my Penates
> > you are constantly seeking on behalf of our friendship.
> If the Perusine tombs of our homeland are known to you,
> > and the deaths of Italy in harsh times,
> when Roman civil war drove on her own citizens
> > (this is an especial grief to me, Etruscan dust, that
> you have endured the bones of my relative to be flung away.
> > With no soil do you cover his wretched bones),
> fertile Umbria, where she touches closest to the adjoining fields,
> > bore me among fruitful lands.

The contrast drawn in the final lines between the unburied body of Propertius' kinsman and the Etruscan soil as the source of his own birth emphasize earth as both the starting and ending points of life. It thus adds to the pathos of Gallus' death, in that his body was never buried and hence he could not be found by his relatives, despite the illusory epitaph providing a physical and textual marker to identify his remains. From the perspective of death ritual, the absence of a grave epitaph also means that Gallus could not converse with passersby as they reanimate his personality by reading his epitaph aloud, despite the narrative conceit that elegy 1.21 preserved the text of both tomb and the deceased.

If a poet can turn a reader of his elegies into a *scriptor* and *lector* of epitaphs, he can also reverse the exchange through imitation of a deceased addressing a passerby/*lector* on an epitaph that does not mark the figurative location of his remains. The poet furthermore plays dead in imitation of epitaphs in the first-person narrative voice. In his second (verse) preface to the *Parentalia,* written in the 4th c CE, the Christian Ausonius, for example, introduces his collection of epitaphs (*epicedes*) with a poem that is itself modeled upon epitaphs:

Nomina carorum iam condita funere iusto,
    fleta prius lacrimis, nunc memorabo modis,
nuda, sine ornatu, fandique carentia cultu:
    sufficit inferiis exsequialis honos.
nenia, funereis satis officiosa querellis,
    annua ne tacitum munera praetereas
quae Numa cognatis sollemnia dedicat umbris,
    ut gradus aut mortis postulat aut generis.
hoc satis est tumulis, satis et telluris egenis:
    voce ciere animas funeris instar habet.
gaudent compositi cineres sua nomina dici;
    frontibus hoc scriptis et monumenta iubent.
ille etiam, maesti cui defuit urna sepulchri,
    nomine ter dicto paene sepultus erit.
at tu, quicumque es, lector, qui fata meorum
    dignaris maestis commemorare elegis,
inconcussa tuae percurras tempora vitae
    et praeter iustum funera nulla fleas.[29]

The names of loved ones already buried in a proper ritual,
    already mourned with tears, I now commemorate in verse,
plain, without ornament and lacking polished turns of phrase:
    a funereal tribute is sufficient for the dead.

Dirge, ever dutiful in funeral laments,
    do not forget the annual gifts for the silent ones
which Numa established as annual rites for kindred shades,
    as the distance or relation of the dead demands.
This is enough for the dead, those buried and those lacking earth:
    calling upon the dead by name is similar to a funeral.
Buried ashes are gladdened when their own names are spoken;
    even their graves order this on their inscribed fronts.
Even that man, for whom the urn of a sad burial is lacking,
    will be as though buried when his name is said three times.
But you, Reader, whoever you are, who think it worthwhile to
      commemorate
    the deaths of my relatives in sad verses,
may you pass the span of your life unharmed and
    may you never mourn a death unless it is natural. (1–18)

Ausonius addresses the reader of his poems (*lector,* 15), as though he were a self-represented narrating voice of an epitaph that is addressed to a passerby. Ausonius does not use the address to predict his poetic immortality, but rather he asks the reader to participate in his tribute to his dead relatives. The animated dead will rejoice at the voicing of their names by the reader and even the unburied will be honored as buried if the reader says their name three times: *gaudent compositi cineres sua nomina dici;* / *frontibus hoc scriptis et monumenta iubent* (11,12). Thus the reader of Ausonius' poems is the figurative *lector* of an epitaph who himself becomes a second narrative presence to the dead through a reading process that simultaneously addresses and pleases the dead honorand.[30]

Ausonius refers to the *Parentalia* as *nenia* (line 5) and as *elegea* (7.1), but the collection is unique as a literary genre since it combines elements of illusive epitaphs and elegy (*epicede*) in theme and poetic format. *Epicede,* borrowed from Greek literature, included the voicing of grief and the offering of consolation, was a very popular theme in both Roman poetry and prose.[31] Epicede in verse occurs as early as Homer and the dirge-like laments of the tragic stage and bucolic song provided much for Romans to emulate in poetry and prose for expressing grief or offering consolation to a survivor after the death of a loved one. Grief and consolation are addressed to the deceased and to the living: In 106, Catullus mourns the death of his brother; Horace consoles Vergil in *Odes* 1.24 following the death of Quinctilius Varus; Ovid, in *Amores* 3.9, offers a lamentation on the death of Tibullus; the unknown author of the *Consolatio ad Liviam* offers sympathy to Livia on the death of her son Drusus in 9 BCE. Other examples can be culled from the letters of Cicero, Seneca, and Pliny, the epigrams of Martial, and the *Silvae* of Statius.

Ausonius' poems were written as poetic tributes that imitate the offerings to the dead normally given at their tombs during the festival *Parentalia* and were probably composed soon after his *Epicedion in Patrem*.[32] Although a Christian, Ausonius draws on the ancient pagan funerary festival called the *Dies Ferales* or *Dies Parentales,* observed between the Ides of February (13th) and February 21, during which the dead were honored at their graves. Religious differences are not explored, but rather the focus is on the ongoing communion between the poet and his dead family which connects pagan and Christian funerary practice.

As figurative offerings to the dead, the poems turn the reading process into a ritualized experience. To Statius, Vergil's tomb was a source of poetic inspiration that literally and figuratively encoded his poetry. Ausonius, by contrast, uses the Roman festival of the dead as a pretext and text for his collection that transforms the reader into a participant in the commemoration who figuratively visits the tombs of his relatives and recites Ausonius' text. Thus, Ausonius uses allusion to death ritual to transform his readers into grave visitors who will recite his words to his own relatives: the more the poems are read, the more Ausonius' relatives (and not those of the reader) will be commemorated.

As a symbolic ritualized narrative, the poems differ from Ovid's description of the *Parentalia* in his *Fasti* (2.533–70) and his narrative of other people's observance of ritual (2.571–616).[33] Ovid describes the proper rites for the worship and commemoration of the dead of the *Parentalia,* the origin of which he assigns to Aeneas (2.533–46):

> Est honor et tumulis, animas placare paternas,
>   parvaque in exstructas munera ferre pyras.
> parva petunt manes: pietas pro divite grata est
>   munere; non avidos Styx habet ima deos.
> tegula porrectis satis est velata coronis
>   et sparsae fruges parcaque mica salis,
> inque mero mollita Ceres violaeque solutae:
>   haec habeat media testa relicta via.
> nec maiora veto, sed et his placabilis umbra est:
>   adde preces positis et sua verba focis.
> hunc morem Aeneas, pietatis idoneus auctor,
>   attulit in terras, iuste Latine, tuas.

ille patris Genio sollemnia dona ferebat:
    hinc populi ritus edidicere pios. [34]

There is honor even for graves: to placate your ancestral souls,
    bring small offerings to the constructed pyres.
The shades seek small gifts: instead of an expensive one, piety
    is cherished; deepest Styx does not have greedy gods.
A clay tile covered with a laid wreath is sufficient,
    sprinkled fruit and small grains of salt,
and Ceres softened in wine and scattered violets:
    let a clay urn left in the middle of the road hold these.
I do not forbid greater gifts, but a shade is placated with these things.
    Add prayers and familiar words to the raised hearth.
Aeneas, the fitting author of piety, brought this custom
    to your lands, righteous inhabitant of Latium.
He offered sollemn gifts to the Genius of his father:
    from him the rites were taught to the pious populace.

Ovid's description of the rituals associated with the *Parentalia* double as
a prescription of those rituals to the reader as he advises simple gifts and
sincerity as the most necessary elements to honor the dead, including the
temporary suspension of rites such as marriage to give the dead their due.
The aitiology of the ritual which assigns to Augustus' mythological ancestor Aeneas the pious commemoration of the dead also serves as a warning
for those neglecting the festival.[35] The dead are animated recipients of the
offerings (*parva petunt manes,* 535), but later in the description of the feast,
they actually repopulate the earth (as they did once when their rites were
neglected, 547 ff.) during the course of the festival: *nunc animae tenues et
corpora functa sepulcris / errant, nunc posito pascitur umbra cibo* (565–66).
Whereas Ovid advises the reader on the proper observance of the festival,
Ausonius transforms his readers into figurative participants in the festival
through the reading process.

    A reader approaching Ausonius' *Parentalia* for the first time, however,
cannot anticipate the content based on Ovid's *Fasti* nor the order of the
poems. The collection begins with poems addressed to Ausonius' parents and
next come poems addressed, in a seeming random order, to his uncle, grandfather, grandmother, aunt, two more uncles, his father-in-law, his wife, son,
grandson, sister, brother, son-in-law, brother-in-law, nephew's wife, nephew,
another brother-in-law, sister-in-law, another nephew, another sister-in-law
and brother-in-law, his son's father-in-law, his niece's son and daughter, his

sister's son-in-law, three aunts, a cousin, another sister, and his son's mother-
in-law.[36] There is no teleological order to the list, progressing as it does from
direct relations to relations related by marriage or vice versa, since the poems
addressed to his wife and son follow poems addressed to his grandparents,
aunt, uncles, and father-in-law. In *Parentalia* 3.1–5, for example, Ausonius
struggles with his decision to place his uncle after his father. The last word
of the collection is Ausonius' own name which functions as a *sphragis* and
echoes line 1 of the first poem dedicated to his father in which his name,
also Ausonius, appears.

Ausonius could have arranged the poems in any order and there is a certain artistry apparent in the haphazard arrangement that reflects the uncer-
tainty of life and death since members of a family do not die in a set order
or symmetrical pattern. The effect is like a visit to a cemetery where one
encounters tombstones in a random order, depending on the date of death or
the date the tomb or burial plot was purchased, even in areas where members
of the same family are buried. Since the poems perform a ritualistic function
as commemorative tributes read by the reader, the order of the collection
also serves as a legend or map for a reader to negotiate the various tombs
and even the various dead who are animated recipients of the poems.

In *Parentalia* 1, Ausonius praises his father for his moderation and phi-
losophy which accounted for his sastisfying life:

> Primus in his pater Ausonius, quem ponere primum,
>   etsi cunctetur filius, ordo iubet.
> cura dei, placidae functus quod honore senectae
>   undecies binas vixit Olympiades;
> omnia quae voluit qui prospera vidit; eidem
>   optavit quicquid, contigit ut voluit,
> non quia fatorum nimia indulgentia, sed quod
>   tam moderata illi vota fuere viro;
> quem sua contendit septem sapientibus aetas,
>   quorum doctrinam moribus excoluit,
> viveret ut potius quam diceret arte sophorum,
>   quamquam et facundo non rudis ingenio,
> praeditus et vitas hominum ratione medendi
>   porrigere et fatis amplificare moras.
> inde et perfunctae manet haec reverentia vitae,
>   aetas nostra illi quod dedit hunc titulum:
> ut nullum Ausonius quem sectaretur habebat,
>   sic nullum qui se nunc imitetur habet.[37]

First among these is my father Ausonius, whom nature orders
    to be placed first even if his son should hestitate.
He was a care to God, since he enjoyed the honor of a serene
    old age and lived for twice eleven Olympiads.
all that he wanted, he saw as hoped; likewise, whatever he
    hoped for, he acquired just as he wanted,
not because of overindulgence on the part of the Fates, but because
    his prayers were so reasonable;
whom his own age compared to the seven sages,
    whose teaching he followed in his habits,
since he would rather live by the rule of wisdom than profess it,
    although he was not unskilled in eloquence;
he was gifted in the knowledge of healing the lives of men
    and to stretch out and lengthen delays for the Fates.
Therefore, this reverence remains of his life that has passed,
    that our age has given this epitaph to him:
Just as Ausonius had no one whom he could follow,
    so he has no one who now could imitate him.

Ausonius emphasizes the primacy of position of his father, in terms of relationship and position within the poetic collection with the repetition of
primus and *primum* in line 2. The poem glosses over details of his father's
life given in the longer *Epicedion in Patrem,* in particular his father's career in
oratory (9–10) which is here the subject of a debate between art and innate
ability (lines 11–12).

Ausonius' poem ends with an epitaph (*titulus*) in praise of his father's
uniqueness but it does not list major life achievements. The two balanced
lines offer seemingly generic praise. As a *titulus,* the epitaph does not mark
the location of his father's remains and it gives a generic rather than a biographical description of his father's life.

In the first half of *Parentalia* 4 to his grandfather, Ausonius describes
how his grandfather was exiled after he fell out of political favor with Vic-
torinus. He also describes his grandfather's marriage to Aemilia, who was
poor despite his own financial misery.[38] Ausonius' address to his grandfather
in the second half (lines 17–32) imitates the details found on an epitaph:

tu caeli numeros et conscia sidera fati
    callebas, studium dissimulanter agens.
non ignota tibi nostrae quoque formula vitae,
    signatis quam tu condideras tabulis,
prodita non umquam, sed matris cura retexit

sedula quod timidi cura tegebat avi.
tu novies denos vitam cum duxeris annos,
    expertus Fortis tela cavenda deae,
amissum flebas post trina decennia natum
    saucius—hoc laevo lumine cassus eras—
dicebas sed te solacia longa fovere,
    quod mea praecipuus fata maneret honos.
et modo conciliis animarum mixte priorum
    fata tui certe nota nepotis habes
sentis quod quaestor, quod te praefectus, et idem
    consul honorifico munere commemoro.

You knew the measurements of heaven and about stars
    knowing of fate, following this pursuit secretly.
Nor was the pattern of my life unknown to you,
    which you had recorded on sealed tablets,
never brought forward, but the care of my mother uncovered
    what the persistent care of my shy grandfather concealed.
When you had lived out your life of ninety years,
    you knew well the dangerous arrows of the goddess Chance,
you wept, wounded, for a son who died in his thirtieth year
    —you were void of light by this calamity—
you used to say that you cherished a far off consolation,
    because high honor was waiting for my fates.
Now that you have joined the assemblies of those former lives,
    surely you have noted the fortunes of your grandson.
You perceive that I, a quaestor, a prefect, and likewise a
    consul, commemorate you with the honor of a tribute.

Ausonius mentions that the loss of his uncle was a source of grief for his grandfather, but that his own success provided solace and pride in his old age. Rather than end the poem with the accomplishments or offices attained by his grandfather that are typical on tombstones, Ausonius lists his own political positions: quaestor, prefect, and consul, which are more appropriate to his own epitaph.

The final word *commemoro* emphasizes the primacy of Ausonius and his accomplishments within his grandfather's epitaph as though a tribute to him. It also emphasizes the narrating and reading processes that turn the poems into ritualized experiences. Like the mother of Marcus Octavius Rufus in the epitaph to her son and Probus' epitaph for his wife and son, Ausonius the poet supplants the dead as the narrative focus. But unlike as in

actual epitaphs, he does so within a fictionalized ritual context: the illusory
epitaph does not mark where the grandfather is buried.

Ausonius' poem to his wife (*Parentalia* 9) is touching since Ausonius
describes moments from a typical day that reinforce his loneliness without
her:

> Hactenus ut caros, ita iusto funere fletos,
> > functa piis cecinit nenia nostra modis.
> nunc dolor atque cruces nec contrectabile fulmen,
> > coniugis ereptae mors memoranda mihi.
> nobilis a proavis et origine clara senatus,
> > moribus usque bonis clara Sabina magis,
> te iuvenis primis luxi deceptus in annis
> > perque novem caelebs te fleo Olympiades.
> nec licet obductum senio sopire dolorem;
> > semper crudescit nam mihi poena recens.
> admittunt alii solacia temporis aegri;
> > haec graviora facit vulnera longa dies.
> torqueo deceptos ego vita caelibe canos,
> > quoque magis solus, hoc mage maestus ago.
> vulnus alit, quod muta domus silet et torus alget,
> > quod mala non cuiquam, non bona participo.
> maero, si coniunx alii bona, maereo contra,
> > si mala: ad exemplum tu mihi semper ades.
> tu mihi crux ab utraque venis, sive est mala, quod tu
> > dissimilis fueris, seu bona, quod similis.
> non ego opes cassas et inania gaudia plango,
> > sed iuvenis iuveni quod mihi rapta viro:
> laeta, pudica, gravis, genus inclita et inclita forma,
> > et dolor atque decus coniugis Ausonii.
> quae modo septenos quarter impletura Decembres,
> > liquisti natos, pignora nostra, duos.
> illa favore dei, sicut tua vota fuerunt,
> > florent, optatis accumulata bonis,
> et precor ut vigeant tandemque superstite utroque
> > nuntiet hoc cineri nostra favilla tuo.

> So far our dirge, performed in pious measures, has sung
> > of our dear ones mourned at the completion of their full lives.
> Now, a grief and a misery and a wound that cannot be touched—

the untimely death of my wife must be commemorated by me.
Noble in her lineage and from an illustrious line of senators,
    Sabina was more renowned for her good character,
I wept for you in my youth deceived in early years
    and through these thirty six years, unwedded, I weep for you;
nor, in my old age, is it possible to lull my prolonged grief;
    for always does it grow raw as a fresh pain for me.
Others find release through the pain filled solace of time;
    but the length of days makes my wounds more heavy.
I tear my grey hairs that are mocked by my unwed life,
    and the more that I am alone, the more lonely I am.
My wound is fed because my quiet house is silent and my bed is cold,
    and because I share my troubles or joys with no one.
I am saddened, if one has a good wife, and saddened likewise, if
    another has a bad one: you are always the paragon before my eyes.
You are my pain and from either type you come to mind, if one is bad
    since you were dissimilar, or if good, since you were the same.
I do not weep for useless wealth or for empty joys,
    rather that, in your youth, you were taken from your young husband:
Cheerful, modest, respected, famous for high birth and famed for beauty,
    you were both the grief and glory of your husband Ausonius.
Before you completed your twenty-eighth December,
    you left our two children, the pledges of our love.
By the grace of god, just as were your prayers,
    they prosper surrounded by an abundance of hoped-for goods,
and I pray that they may thrive so that, at last, my embers
    will announce to your ashes that they still live.

This follows the poem dedicated to his wife's father, which Ausonius ends with a declaration of his devotion as a widower and son-in-law (8.15–18):

et nunc perpetui sentis sub honore sepulcri,
    quam reverens natae quamque tui maneam.
caelebs namque gener haec nunc pia munera solvo:
    nam et caelebs numquam desinam et esse gener.

And now beneath your eternal tomb you perceive with honor
    how I have remained devoted to your daughter and to yourself.
For unwed, I, your son-in-law, now complete my pious pledges:
    that I will never stop being unwed or your son-in-law.

Thus the reader is already aware of Ausonius' devotion to his wife before reading the poem, yet it does not prepare the reader for the extent of the loneliness which fills Ausonius years after her death.[39] The expressions of love in this poem evocative of Vergilian intertexts (*dolor decusque* recalls *Aen.* 10.57: Aeneas' apostrophe to the dead Pallas) also form the epilogue of the vibrant love between the couple described in epigram 20 which is playful and romantic.

The final third of the poem (line 21 ff.) is an epitaph to Ausonius' wife and contains typical elements such as the love between spouses, a listing of her virtues, her age, and Ausonius' hope of being reunited with her after death. Ausonius and Sabina are united through marriage and their surviving children whom Ausonius will announce as thriving to her as soon as they are rejoined through the cremation process: the embers burning his remains will reunite with her burnt ashes in a physical communion to replace the figurative communion that existed when only one spouse was dead.

Thus, Ausonius combines epitaph with epicede to produce a poetic genre that is both highly personal and yet communal, since Ausonius' poems transform the reader into a performer of ritual commemoration of his relatives. The dead are animated as they hear Ausonius' tributes to them, which are also his meditations on the effect of their deaths on him. The dead are not where the epitaphs claim they are; rather the epitaphs serve as textual markers that distinguish each of Ausonius' dead relatives and effect the same reification as an epigram on an actual tombstone for an ongoing communion with the dead.

Reviving the Dead

In T. S. Eliot's "Little Gidding" (No. 4 of *Four Quartets*), the narrator describes an encounter with a dead teacher who summarizes life's lessons as he simultaneously causes the narrator/reader to question the validity of previous thoughts, words, and actions. The poem erases the distinction between beginning and end, life and death, and the living in the dead:

> Every phrase and every sentence is an end and a beginning,
> Every poem an epitaph. And any action
> Is a step to the block, to the fire, down the sea's throat
> Or to an illegible stone; and that is where we start.
> We die with the dying:
> See, they depart, and we go with them.

We are born with the dead;
See, they return and bring us with them.[40]

Poetry is a vehicle for self-expression, which, like an epitaph, marks an end
that is destined to be lost to the living. The living are inseparable from the
dead who give the living the paradigm and pattern of death.

Eliot's blurring of the boundaries between life and death from the perspective of one who is dead but recognizable by one who is living adds
pathos to the reunion, since the dead figuratively assume their former identities and (literally) communicate with the living more effectively than they
can through epitaphs. Somewhat different than a poem (epicede) or a prose
passage voicing grief or expressing consolation to a mourner or the figurative
repopulation of the dead among the living during the *Parentalia,* is the inclusion of the dead as a literary character (like Eliot's teacher), or the ostensible
poetic voice in a poem of those who continue to represent themselves to
an author/interlocutor/ reader as they console them. This reversal of roles
animates the dead and redirects the focus and narrative flow of poems and
epitaphs. The dead Julia, for example, in Lucan's *Bellum Civile,* addresses
Pompey in a dream, while standing on a burning funeral pyre (3.12–34):

'[. . .] coniuge me laetos duxisti, Magne, triumphos:
fortuna est mutata toris, semperque potentis
detrahere in cladem fato damnata maritos
innupsit tepido paelex Cornelia busto.
haereat illa tuis per bella per aequora signis,
dum non securos liceat mihi rumpere somnos
et nullam vestro vacuum sit tempus amori
sed teneat Caesarque dies et Iulia noctes.
me non Lethaeae, coniunx, oblivia ripae
immemorem fecere tui, regesque silentum
permisere sequi. veniam te bella gerente
in medias acies. numquam tibi, Magne, per umbras
perque meos manes genero non esse licebit;
abscidis frustra ferro tua pignora: bellum
te faciet civile meum.'[41]

"[. . .] With me as your wife, Magnus, you led happy triumphs home:
your fortune changed with your wedding bed, and Cornelia,
your concubine, always damned by fate to drag down powerful
husbands into disaster, married into a warm tomb. Through war

and the deep seas, let her cling to your standards, as long as I can
disturb your sleepless nights, and there is no spare time for
your love, but let Caesar own your days, and Julia your nights.
The oblivion of Lethe's shore, husband, has not made me forgetful
of you, and the Kings of the Dead allowed me to pursue you.
While you wage war, I will come into the lines of battle. Never,
Magnus, by my ghost and by my shade, will you stop being his
son-in-law; in vain do you cut your family pledges with your sword:
civil war will make you mine."

Julia's speech reverses the narrative flow from narrator to character and from
the living to the dead. Julia is described in terms that make her physical appearance a decreasingly recognizable and visible form as though her
apparition begins to fade the moment she begins to speak: *imago* (3.9);
manes (3.32); and *umbra* (3.35). The continuation of family strife, in the
underworld, reinforces the civil war between her former husband (Pompey) and her father (Caesar) as she represents herself as Pompey's widow
and Caesar's daughter. Julia uses the imagery of cremations to illustrate the
doomed marriages of her successor Cornelia, whose life can be measured
by the time that elapses between the cremations of her husbands. The dead
occupy the world of the poet, the interlocutor, and reader thus, blurring the
distinctions and boundaries between the living and the dead who continue
to represent themselves.

Today, communion with the dead continues literally and figuratively via
the Internet which is changing contemporary mourning and communication options with the dead and, in some cases, for the dead themselves. The
location of one's keyboard is replacing traditional venues such as churches
and funeral homes to pay one's last respects and to offer condolences to the
family of the deceased. Web guest books, for example, on the *World Wide
Cemetery* allow one to post messages any time of the day without leaving
home or actually viewing the deceased or attending a funeral service in person. Online postings, which do not expire, also outlast the permanence of
a traditional condolence card.

The Internet is also changing the dynamic between the deceased and
(self) representation of epitaphs that allows for reciprocity of communication between the living and the dead. The website, My-last-e-mail.com, for
example, allows the dead to send a final email on the day of their death
to both friends and enemies. Another site, www.tomylovedones.com, is
reserved for messages to family and friends and messages are sent after the
company receives a death certificate, so messages may arrive a month after

a death, rather than on the day of one's death. Although the messages were composed while the dead were still alive, the website allows the dead to continue to communicate with the living who may not be expecting further communication with the dead. The conversation is one-sided and the dead get the final word, so to speak, since the recipient of their last email cannot send a reply. The sending of unintentional emails to the dead whose email addresses are still included in distribution lists is awkward, but the effect is less jarring than the receipt of an email intentionally sent from the deceased, especially with malicious intent. Thus, just as epitaphs and tombs compete with the identity and narrative voice of the deceased, the "cyber dead" extend the lives and impact of their embodied alter egos.

In Poem 2.13b discussed in chapter 1, Propertius, playing dead, addressed Cynthia to chide her for her inattention. The motif of a dialogue with a character who is not actually dead but who has an imagined conversation with a beloved after death, is similar to 4.7 in which Cynthia's ghost communicates with Propertius in a dream following her cremation and burial.[42] The poem reverses the narrative direction of 2.13b, but neither character is actually dead in the fictional reality of the elegies. In Poem 4.11, however, Propertius animates the dead, rather than imagines himself or Cynthia dead, to dramatize the advice which the dead Cornelia, daughter of Augustus' former wife, Scribonia, gives to her grieving husband Paullus (L. Aemilius Lepidus Paullus).[43] In form it is much like the anonymous poem "The Unquiet Grave," in which a deceased wife urges her husband, from her grave, to stop grieving and either return to the living or join her with the dead.[44] The effect is similar to reading the messages of the "cyber dead" in that the reader cannot respond to Cornelia. But the words she speaks are those given to her by Propertius; therefore, the effect, while dramatic, is less effective than receiving an actual email message from someone dead.

In Propertius, the tomb (*sepulcrum,* 1) serves as the setting of the dialogue and also as a representation of the dead Cornelia who describes the barriers between the living and the dead which she subsequently bridges through an epicede to her husband and a summation, before the gods of the underworld, of her ancestry and life accomplishments (27–36):

'ipsa loquor pro me: si fallo, poena sororum
    infelix umeros urgeat urna meos.
si cui fama fuit per avita tropaea decori,
    Afra Numantinos regna loquuntur avos:
altera maternos exaequat turba Libones,
    et domus est titulis utraque fulta suis.

mox, ubi iam facibus cessit praetexta maritis,
    vinxit et acceptas altera vitta comas,
iungor, Paulle, tuo sic discessura cubili:
    in lapide hoc uni nupta fuisse legar.'[45]

"I plead on my own behalf: if I lie, let the unhappy
    urn, the punishment of the Sisters, crush my shoulders.
If to anyone was the fame of honor through ancestral trophies,
    African kingdoms speak of my Numantine ancestors:
the crowd on the other side, my maternal Libones, is balanced,
    and either house is propped up by their own honors.
Early, when my bordered robe gave way to marriage torches,
    and I bound my gathered hair with parting fillets,
thus was I joined to your bed, Paullus, soon to leave it:
    on this stone, I shall be recorded as the wife of one man."

Cornelia represents herself in giving the poet (*ipsa loquor pro me*) the text of her epitaph. Only when Cornelia self-identifies as a *univira* (36) and remarks that a reference to her sole marriage is inscribed on her tomb is the reader made aware of a competing text on her epitaph that is visible to Paullus in the poem.[46] The poem does not make clear, however, whether other details contained in Cornelia's epitaphic summary of her life are modeled upon the epitaph. Thus, her self-representation may elaborate or even contradict details inscribed on her fictional epitaph (which was composed by Paullus after her death?) As a self-represented character, Cornelia also vies with the poetic voice of the elegy.

    Cornelia places emphasis on her faithfulness as a wife and her noble virtue: *viximus insignes inter utramque facem* (46). She claims that she speaks the truth and hopes that her urn will weigh heavily on her (49) if she does not, in a reversal of the *terra tibi levis sit* formula. The tone of the poem is different from 2.13b which was intended to rejuvenate Propertius' affair with Cynthia; thus the elegiac lover/mistress model is here exchanged for a husband/wife model. The wife is also presented as a mother and Cornelia emphasizes to her daughter the virtues appropriate to women, such as faithfulness to her husband (68)—an ideal antithetical to elegy but which is contextualized by Propertius into the moral climate of Augustan Rome (57–74):

maternis laudor lacrimis urbisque querelis,
    defensa et gemitu Caesaris ossa mea.

ille sua nata dignam vixisse sororem
    increpat, et lacrimas vidimus ire deo.
et tamen emerui generosos vestis honores,
    nec mea de sterili facta rapina domo.
tu, Lepide, et tu, Paulle, meum post fata levamen,
    condita sunt vestro lumina nostra sinu.
vidimus et fratrem sellam geminasse curulem;
    consule quo, festo tempore, rapta soror.
filia, tu specimen censurae nata paternae,
    fac teneas unum nos imitata virum.
et serie fulcite genus: mihi cumba volenti
    solvitur aucturis tot mea facta meis.
haec est feminei merces extrema triumphi,
    laudat ubi emeritum libera fama rogum.
nunc tibi commendo communia pignora natos:
    haec cura et cineri spirat inusta meo.

I am praised with maternal tears and public mourning,
    and my bones are honored even with Caesar's groans.
He laments me who lived as worthy sister to his own daughter,
    and I saw the tears of a god flow.
Nevertheless, I earned the noble honors of my matron's stole,
    nor was I snatched by death in a sterile home.
You, Lepidus, and you, Paullus, my comfort in death,
    my eyes were closed in your embrace.
I saw my brother twice earn the curule chair;
    in whose consulship, a happy time, his sister died.
Daughter, born as the mirror of your father as censor,
    be sure, in imitation of me, that you keep to one husband.
Extend, even, our lineage: the ferry awaits and I willingly go,
    so many of my good deeds left to those who will grow them.
This is the supreme reward of a woman's triumph,
    that a shameless reputation should praise her deserving grave.
Now I entrust to you our children, our common pledge:
    this care breathes, unburned, among my ashes.

Fidelity and a good reputation (symbolized by Cornelia's adoption of a *stola* to symbolize the bearing of at least three children and an honourable burial) are equated with a military triumph. The concern for one's reputation even after death (*laudat ubi emeritum libera fama rogum*, 72) recalls the epitaph to her ancestor Hispanus, discussed above, in which he imagines his ancestors judging his character from the underworld. The presence of Augustus at her funeral is further witness to Cornelia's lineage and character and the emphasis on honor and family. Concern for her children is still felt in death and is equated with the heat that burns the ashes of her pyre (74). This is an anachronistic reference since she has already been cremated and buried, but the metaphor is effective in animating Cornelia and placing her in a constantly changing liminal state between corpse, funeral recipient, and living interlocutor.

Cornelia addresses the judges of the Underworld in the final lines of her speech as though on trial in order to defend her former virtue:

> causa perorata est. flentes me surgite, testes,
>   dum pretium vitae grata rependit humus.
> moribus et caelum patuit: sim digna merendo,
>   cuius honoratis ossa vehanter avis.

> My speech is ended. Arise, you witnesses who weep for me
>   while the welcoming earth rewards the value of my life.
> To virtue, heaven lies open: may I seem deserving to
>   be among the shades of my honored ancestors. (99–102)

Cornelia's final words contain intertextual references to Ennius' *Elogium* of the Scipios. The expression at line 101, *moribus et caelum patuit,* alludes to the words of her ancestor Scipio Africanus, who emphasizes the reward of immortality for his virtue in Ennius' *Elogium of the Scipios:*

> a sole exoriente supra Maeotis paludes
> <next two lines missing>
>   nemo est qui factis aequiperare queat.
> si fas endo plagas caelestum ascendere cuiquam,
>   mi soli caeli maxima porta patet.[47]

> By the rising sun above the Maeiotian marshes
> . . . .
>   there is no one who is able to be equal with the deeds.
> if it is sanctioned for anyone to rise to the regions of the gods
>   the greatest gate of the sky lies open to me alone.

Thus, Cornelia connects her own virtue with that of Scipio Africanus by adapting the last line of Ennius' *Elogium.* By emphasizing this connection,

Cornelia and Scipio are connected in life through common blood and in death through common virtue. Cornelia expresses the idea common on epitaphs that through one's conduct while alive, one must earn respect from dead ancestors. The striking image of the gates of heaven lying open to virtue led to further imitation of the Ennian passage by Silius Italicus, who adapts the line in his *Punica*. Indeed, the epigram was adapted on an actual tombstone illustrating the reciprocity between epitaphs and poetic texts.[48]

Reciprocity between poetry and actual epitaphs is further illustrated by the epitaph of M. Lucceius Nepos, which is Flavian in date and similar to the narrative features of Propertius 4.11, in which the buried dead communicate with the living through speech and epitaph. This is an actual tombstone in which Nepos is figuratively animated by his epitaph and at the site of his burial through poetic intertexts, such as Ennius, Catullus, Vergil, Propertius, Ovid, Tibullus, and Lygdamus, that mythologize the deceased and present him as a god. The unidentified narrative voice of the epitaph converses with the dead Nepos, his kinsman, who self-represents himself as divine (*desine flere deum*, 16), and therefore asks his interlocutor to stop mourning. In lines 1–12, of which only half lines survive, the narrator insists that the vision is not part of a dream but is the deceased himself: *non fuit illa quies, / sed verus iuveni color et sonus, at status ipse / maior erat nota corporis effigie* / "it was not a dream, / but the true appearance and sound of the youth, but his height was greater than the usual form of his body" (10–12).[49] The rest of the poem consists of a dialogue between M. Lucceius Nepos and his unidentified kinsman (13–46):

> ardentis oculorum orbes umerosq(ue) nitentis
> ostendens roseo reddidit ore sonos:
> 'adfinis memorande, quid o me ad sidera caeli
> ablatum quereris? desine flere deum,
> ne pietas ignara superna sede receptum
> lugeat et laedat numina tristitia.
> non ego Tartareas penetrabo tristis ad undas,
> non Acheronteis transuehar umbra vadis,
> non ego caeruleam remo pulsabo carinam
> nec te terribilem fronte timebo, Charon,
> nec Minos mihi iura dabit grandaeuus et atris
> non errabo locis nec cohibebor aquis.
> surge, refer matri ne me noctesque diesque
> defleat ut maerens Attica mater Ityn.
> nam me sancta Venus sedes non nosse silentum
> iussit et in caeli lucida templa tulit.'

erigor et gelidos horror perfuderat artus;
    spirabat suavi tinctus odore locus.
die Nepos, seu tu turba stipatus Amorum
    laetus Adoneis lusibus insereris,
seu grege Pieridum gaudes seu Palladis [arte,
    omnis caelicolum te chor[u]s exc[ipiet.
si libeat thyrsum gravidis aptare co[rymbis
    et velare comam palmite, Liber[eris;
pascere si crinem et lauro redimire [u—que
    arcum cum pharetra sumere, Ph[oebus eris.
indueris teretis manicas Phrygium [que u—x,
    non unus Cybeles pectore vivet a[mor.
si spumantis equi libeat quatere ora [lupatis,
    Cyllare, formosi membra vehes e[quitis.
sed quicumque deus, quicumque vocaber[is heros,
    sit soror et mater, sit puer incolu[mis.
haec dona unguentis et sunt potiora c[orollis
    quae non tempus edax, non rapi[t—u u x. [50]

Showing the blazing orbs of his eyes and gleaming shoulders
    he uttered words from his rosy lips:
"Kinsman, who mourns me, why do you lament that I have been
    abducted to the stars of the sky? Stop mourning a god,
that your devotion may not mourn me unaware that I have been
      welcomed
    into that place above and insult a god by your sorrow.
I will not sadly approach the streams of Tartarus,
    nor will I be conveyed across the waters of Acheron as a shade.
I will not inch the sea-blue boat forward with my oar,
    nor will I fear you, Charon, menacing in your looks,
nor will Minos, the ancient one, pass judgment on me; I will not
    roam in the dark places nor be constrained by those waters.
Rise, tell my mother not to weep for me night and day
    just as the Attic mother mourns for Itys.
Sacred Venus has forbidden me to know the places of the silent ones
    and has brought me to the bright shrines of heaven."
I jumped back and fear had taken hold of my cold limbs;
    the place was filled with a sweet perfume.
Divine Nepos, whether you are surrounded by a crowd of cupids,
    or you have happily joined the games of Adonis,

whether you delight in the company of the Muses or in the skill of
    Minerva,
    the whole chorus of heavenly dwellers will welcome you.
If it should please you to wrap a thyrsus with ripe ivy-berries
    or to cover your hair with vine shoots, you will be Liber;
if it should please you to grow your hair out and tie it with laurel,
    and to take up the bow and quiver, you will be Pheobus.
Wear fine sleeves and a Phrygian cap, and not one
    love will burn in the heart of Cybele.
If it should please you to shake the mouth of a foaming horse in
    reins, Cyllarus, you will carry the limbs of a handsome rider.
But whatever god, whatever hero you will be called,
    may your sister and mother and your child be free from harm.
These gifts, which greedy time cannot snatch [. . .], are more
    important than perfumes and garlands.

Poetic and mythological intertexts define and distinguish Nepos from
the other dead: he will not cross the river Styx, be judged by Minos, nor
face a fate similar to Itys' (20–26). Venus has made Nepos immortal and
transported him to heaven (27–28). The role of Venus in the immortaliza-
tion of humans recalls the funerary portraiture of women, like the portrait
of the Flavian woman as Venus in the Capitoline Museums, which signify
an apotheosis through representation and assimulation as Venus. Nepos'
apotheosis (28) also recalls narratives in Ennius' *Annales* and Ovid's *Fasti,*
which describe the apotheosis of Romulus. Nepos' kinsman idealizes his
ascent and integration into heaven, with excessive imagery that evokes the
anticipated and hyperbolic arrival of Augustus among the constellations in
the *Georgics.*

To Nepos' family, his apotheosis is not in question, only the nature of his
metamorphosis. In addition to the content of the epitaph which celebrates
the apotheosis of the deceased, rather than mark the location of the burial
of his formerly human remains, the epitaph, as poetic (inter) text, also functions as an illusory epitaph. It recalls the speech of Cornelia in Propertius
4.11 and the ghost of Cynthia in 4.7, and illustrates the reciprocity between
epitaphs and elegies as related genres that influence each other's themes and
language. The (self) representation of the dead also points to the ongoing
communion between the living and the dead who take control of their
commemoration through their figurative participation in their own funerary
ritual. The divine presence of Nepos leaves behind a fragrance, a detail which
adds to the figurative encounter between the living and the dead (29–30).

This chapter has focused on the narrative voice and setting (physical and figurative) of the deceased in epitaphs, especially those which have poeticizing/poetic features to analyze the (self) representation of the dead. In addition to actual grave inscriptions, I examined illusory epitaphs in Latin poetry as both grave and textual markers and as limited and limitive narrative and reading experiences. The animation of the dead through their figurative (self) representation in elegiac texts highlights the reciprocity between epitaphs and poetic texts, in particular the reciprocal communication between the living and the dead. The figurative revival of the dead to console the living in elegies reverses the narrative voice of epicedes and includes the narrative of the deceased's own epitaph in an ongoing communion with the living.

CONCLUSION

WHAT STARTED out as a search for the personal meaning of an inscribed stone marking where my father is buried has led me to an examination of the figurative significance of death ritual, ancient and modern. My reading strategy for reading death in ancient Rome focused on the associative reading process that revealed various and often competing authorial agendas from narrators, characters, and even the dead themselves. I explored the extent to which literary texts allude to funeral and burial ritual, the narrative role played by the allusion to recreate a fictive version of the ritual (to turn reading, in some cases, into a performative and ritualistic act), and how the allusion engages a reader's knowledge of the ritual or previous literary intertexts. The ongoing communion between the living and the dead results in a participatory theater in which the distinctions between life and death are blurred and increasingly irrelevant as the dead repopulate the physical and figurative landscape of ancient Rome.

I began my study by focusing on the semiotic and moral implications of the living corpse. Propertius' self-representation as a corpse at his own funeral and the funeral rehearsals of Pacuvius and Trimalchio illustrated how allusions to funerary ritual become part of an authorial agenda to blur the boundary between life and death. The blurring, however, not only casts doubt on the character's mortality, but it also allows the reader to consider the moral implications of a character's appearance or behavior as a living corpse. In the case of figuratively dead widows, the Widow of Ephesus and Seneca's widow Paulina, the ambiguity of their mortality and their abuse of funerary ritual allows both author and reader to condemn their behavior as immoral.

Actors and audiences in literary texts introduced an examination of the dramatizing of death ritual as (self) concious theater: the dramaturgical and moral implications of playing dead, death ritual as spectacle within a play and reassembling the dead, and the inherent theatricality of funerary ritual that resulted in a figurative cast of corpses. The reciprocity between theatricality and funerary rituals turns a funeral into a theater of the dead to make viewing and reading performative and ritualistic acts: the revival of the dead as actor and audience further enhances reading as participatory theater, as the dead participate in their own and others' funerals before a spectator reader/audience. The funeral of Julius Caesar, for example, turned his cremation into a spectacle and representations of Caesar into actors performing before a mourning audience. The inherent theatricality of funerals leads to reciprocity with the theater in which characters play dead and death ritual is used as spectacle, as in Seneca's *Troades.* The reassembling of the dead in Seneca's *Phaedra,* and the theatricalizing of funerary ritual results in a cast of corpses, such as representations of Augustus at his funeral and a reader who assumes the changing roles of spectator and mourner.

The symbolic significance of funerary ritual, which can simultaneously communicate different meanings to various audiences, reflects the allusive quality of death ritual as text and intertext in the epics of Vergil and Ovid. Successive treatments of the epic trope of funerals and cremations increase the intertextuality between and within texts, but they become increasingly distant from the reality and the experiences of the reader. The narrative of Hecuba's sorrows in Ovid's *Metamorphoses,* for example, is presented as a tragedy within the epic that turns pathos into bathos as Hecuba prepares Polyxena's corpse for burial only to corrupt the ritual when she find Polydorus' corpse on the shores of Troy. The cremation of Julius Ceasar and his apotheosis serve as the teleological focus of the poem, although Ovid leaves out many historic details, thus distancing his readers further in a text that describes funerary rituals removed from their experience or memory of an historical event. Caesar's transformation into a god foreshadows Ovid's own immortality, effected through his poetry, and expressed through funerary ritual to emphasize the transformative power of cremation to destroy and resurrect life.

Successive treatments of the epic trope of funerals and cremations further engage and frustrate the reader's (and character's) experience with those rituals and their familiarity with the trope. Lucan's description of the death and cremation of Pompey takes Ovid's narrative style to more grotesque levels. Narratives such as the cremation of Opheltes in Statius' *Thebaid* engage more with literary intertexts than associations with actual funerary ritual.

Argia and Antigone's search for the corpses of Polynices and Eteocles, and also Statius' abandonment of his description of the funeral and cremation of Creon, served as a metaphor for the trope which was in search of a narrative. Readers of these descriptions of cremations and burials in post-Vergilian and Ovidian epic become further distanced as participants or readers who can identify elements of the ritual as realistic, as they simultaneously sympathize with the narrative (mis)treatment of the deceased's death and funeral.

What if the dead continued to engage the living and communicate their own authorial agendas in unexpected settings, both literary and actual? This question guided my final chapter, in which I analyzed epitaphs as grave and textual markers, actual and illusory, for the (self) representation of the dead, and implications on the viewing/interpretative process when the dead are not buried where the grave indicates, in texts and in modern settings of ancient funerary monuments, such as the epitaph of Rufus and the portrait of the Flavian Woman as Venus in the Capitoline Museum, and the sarcophagus of Cornelius Scipio Barbatus in the Vatican Museums. The revival of the dead in elegiac texts leads to reciprocity with epitaphs that gives the dead further opportunity to take control of their representation and commemoration. The blurring of the boundaries between the living and the dead also leads to a performative exchange in the *Epigrams* of Ausonius in which reading becomes a ritualistic act through the reification of an illusory epitaph.

Narratives of funerary ritual have come full circle as the dead are not actually dead and descriptions of their disposal and commemoration contribute to the illusion when various authorial voices compete for a text and an audience, and both characters and readers are participants in fictive recreations of funerals and burials, fictional and historic, that allude to actual rituals and literary descriptions of those rituals. These changing roles and scripts make reading death a participatory reading experience that challenges the reader's experiences as mourner and reader in narratives that blur the distinctions between the living and the dead.

NOTES

Introduction

1. It is the second version of the Louvre painting that appears on this book's cover. See Lee 1989, 89–95 for a discussion of the "Et in Arcadia ego" motif in pastoral poetry and Panofsky 1982, chapter 7: "*Et in Arcadia Ego:* Poussin and the Elegiac Tradition" for an analysis of the various versions of the painting by Poussin and Guercino and the impact of death on the shepherd's landscape.

2. Recent studies have taken a variety of reading and writing strategies to analyze the relationship between epitaph and reader; tomb and viewer: Bodel 2001, 1–72; Petrucci 1998: "The Tomb and Its Signs," 1–4; "From the Sign to the Text," 5–9; "The Order of Memory," 15–23; Sourvinou-Inwood 1995, chapter 3: "Signs of the Dead: "The Grave Monument in Homer and the Archaic Age," 108–297; chapter 4: "Reading (Death) Otherwise: The Case Study of an Archaic Epigram," 362–412, in particular her discussion about classification of signs: indexical and symbolic, 112–122; Morris 1992, chapter 6: "Famous Last Words: The Inscribed Tombstone," 156–73; and Shaw 1991, 66–90.

3. Cited is the text of Green 1999, 83. For an analysis of this epigram, see also Kay 2001, 48–49, 153–56.

4. See Fowler 2000, chapter 9: "The Ruin of Time: Monuments and Survival at Rome," 193–217 for an epistemological analysis of monuments in Latin literature, including Ausonius *Epigram* 37 and the death of Turnus in the *Aeneid.*

5. On the relationship between epitaphs and the viewer, see Carroll 2006, 53–58.

6. Toynbee 1971; rpt. 1996, 94–100 examines *cepotaphia* as contractual obligations for the maintenance of tombs and the commercial growing of crops at enclosed grave orchards or vineyards, whereby the deceased effectively became an "absentee landlord" since these contracts were legally enforceable. See more recently, Gregori 1987–1988, 175–88 and Purcell: 1987, 25–41.

7. For parallels in the reception of English gardens, see Dixon Hunt 1992, in particular 179–81, for a discussion of the associative meanings of ruins in a landscape and page 186 for the reading of a landscape's syntax.

8. I cite the Latin text of Shackleton Bailey 2003, 348, 350.

9. Pliny (*H.N.* 7.1.5) observes that anxiety over burial is a human trait: *uni animantium luctus est datus, uni luxuria et quidem innumerabilibus modis ac per singula membra, uni ambitio, uni avaritia, uni inmensa vivendi cupido, uni superstitio, uni sepulturae cura atque etiam post se de futuro.* (ed. Rackham 1969, 508). For a discussion of the lack of commemoration associated with anonymous graves, see Carroll 2006, 59–85.

10. The line is preserved in Seneca, *Ep.* 92.34–35. For an analysis of the line, see Avallone 1945, 85, 89–95 and Avallone 1962, 279, 282–86.

11. For a discussion of the location and the funeral sculptures in Maecenas' garden, see Bell III 1998, 295–314.

12. For a detailed analysis of the cultural memory of space in the city of Rome, see Davies 2000a, 121–35, and Edwards 1996, in particular 28–29 for her discussion of cultural memory and the synchronicity of memory and the theories of Freud and Bakhtin.

13. Ed. Ogilvie 1974. Elsewhere, Ogilvie cites inscriptional evidence that suggests the Gallic Pyres were located at the foot of the Capitoline Hill. See Ogilvie 1965, 737.

14. The construction of tombs and tomb complexes in the Campus Martius, such as Augustus' mausoleum with the text of his *Res Gestae,* moved the dead (and their self-representation) closer to the inhabited areas of the city in the late Republic that turned representations and commemoration of the dead into propagandistic viewing experiences that emphasized the dynastic ambitions of the deceased and his surviving family members. On the transformative effect (topopraphic and figurative) of imperial funeral monuments on the city of Rome, see Davies 2000a, chapter 6: "The Power of Place," 136–71, and Davies 2000b, 27–44. For the physical and figurative visual effects of recarved or removed statues of those suffering *damnatio memoriae,* see Varner 2000a, 9–26, and Kleiner 2000a, 45–57. Flower 2000, 58–69 analyzes the effect of a *damnatio memoriae* on epigraphic texts. See Howarth 2007, 19–34 for recent examples of the blurring of the distinctions between the living and the dead and their continuing impact on the social and topogaphic landscape. See in particular page 31 for a discussion of the commemoration of the dead at the site of their death, such as roadside memorials rather than the place where they are buried: "[. . .] this location is not only, or even necessarily, viewed primarily as the place of death but it is also the place where the person was last *alive*" (emphasis in original). Thus, the dead can be commemorated in multiple locations simultaneously and expand their presence upon the world of the living.

15. On the religious importance of burial, see Toynbee 1996, 43: "All Roman funerary practice was influenced by two basic notions—first, that death brought pollution and demanded from the survivors acts of purification and expiation; secondly, that to leave a corpse unburied had unpleasant repercussions on the fate of the departed soul"; Morris 1989, 296–320 and 1992; Jupp 2006, 3: "The shadows thrown by death affect more than the contemporary and the present. Death crosses time barriers. It involves both memorialisation and expectation; and in that setting, religions have a profound part to play. Because death begs questions about the hereafter, and the fate of individuals and their bodies, to decay or extinction, to resurrection, immortality or reincarnation, the whole issue of the disposal of the dead has deep theological implications. For many, especially in the past, the fate of the dead in relation to the afterlife was a matter of

anxiety." On the moral imperative to provide burial, see Pollmann 2004, 32–33 for an analysis of ancient and modern sources.

16. For a detailed analysis of references to death ritual in the *De legibus,* see the recent commentary of Dyck 2004. For the sacrifice of a pig, see Toynbee 1996, 50 and 291–92, note 176.

17. On the complex subject of religious pollution occasioned by contact with corpses or the improper burial of the dead, see most recently, Lindsay 2000, 152–73, and Bodel 2000, 128–51, in particular 133–35 for a discussion of the burial of the poor in Rome as a matter of pragmatism rather than religious pollution.

18. Plutarch (*Pompey* 1.1–2) opens his account of Pompey's life with an anecdote about the abuse of the corpse of Strabo, Pompey's father, to illustrate that the father was hated as much as the son was loved by Romans. Abuse of Strabo's corpse whether on its way to the pyre or once it was placed on it (text is unclear about timing) is a violation of funeral ritual, as offensive to the living and an insult to the dead, since the cremation process was underway with the construction of a pyre and the (seeming) placement of Strabo's corpse upon it. Plutarch uses details surrounding the death ritual of Strabo to introduce Pompey to his readers: the reference to Strabo at the beginning of Pompey's biography connects Pompey genealogically to his father; however, details surrounding his cremation distinguish Pompey politically and morally from him. Fear of defilement after death is attested for prominent Romans: Sulla, whose family practiced inhumation, wanted to be cremated after death to avoid defilement/mutilation of his corpse (as had been done to the corpses of the elder and younger Marius: Cicero, *De leg.* 2.22.56–57; Granius Licinianus 36.25; Pliny *H.N.* 7.187). For fear of defilement after death, see Seneca, *Ep.* 92.5 and Noy 2000, 186–196, in particular, 190–91; and Hope 2000, 112–25 for the abuse and mutilation of corpses and interference with burial.

19. *De legibus* 2.22.57: *nam prius quam in os iniecta gleba est, locus ille, ubi crematum est corpus, nihil habet religionis; iniecta gleba tum et illis humatus est, et gleba, vocatur, ac tum denique multa religiosa iura conplectitur* (2.22.57).

20. Cicero does not quote laws dealing with the abuse of funerary ritual or graves but Catullus 59 uses the amoral corruption of funerary ritual to further delineate the character of Rufa:

> Bononiensis Rufa Rufulum fellat,
> uxor Meneni, saepe quam in sepulcretis
> vidistis ipso rapere de rogo cenam,
> cum devolutum ex igne prosequens panem
> ab semiraso tunderetur ustore.

> Rufa from Bononia sucks off Rufulus,
> Menenius' wife, whom you have often seen
> among the tombs stealing a meal from the pyre itself,
> chasing a bread loaf that has fallen down from the flames,
> pounded meanwhile by the half-shaven cremator.

Text of Mynors 1958, rpt. 1989. On interpreting violations of grave monuments, see Carroll 2006, 79–83 and Nappa 1999, 329–35 for an analysis of the poem as a graffito that uses voyeurism both to draw in and attack the reader.

21. See Sumi 2005, 299 notes 36 and 37.

22. For the dead as symbols, see Hope 2000, 125–26: "The corpse could become a potent symbol which was open to abuse and manipulation. Who possessed the corpse, buried the corpse, commemorated the corpse and subsequently had access to it were crucial issues both within the family and wider power structures. [. . .] Yet, in speaking of the relationship between the living and the dead in terms of power and control, there is perhaps a risk of losing sight of individuality and that every corpse was unique. In fact individuality was the very key to this process; to honour the corpse or to abuse it was tied to the preservation or destruction of individual identity."

23. Elsner 1998, 145 focuses on the reciprocity of identity between the deceased and survivors through funerary ritual: "It is especially in death that a lifetime's social position and identity came to be defined through the last rites and commemorative images. The art of death is a kind of summation of, and a visual eulogy on, the life which has passed away. It is also a testimony to the inheritance and status of the survivors—marking out the identities of the living through the portrayal of their dead."

24. For the religious significance of Greek burial rituals, see Kurtz and Boardman 1971; Vermeule 1979, rpt. 1981,1–41; Humphreys 1980, 96–126; Garland 1985; Sourvinou-Inwood 1995; Wickkiser 1999, 65–74; and Oakley 2004.

25. Ed. Volpilhac-Lenthéric 1984.

26. In his note on the summary of foreign funerals, however, Duff 1934, rpt. 1968, 238 comments that the summary is irrelevant to its literary context and even repellent to good taste: "The digression about funeral customs that follows (11. 468–487) is so out of place here and so unworthy of the writer that some editors have expelled it from the text." Volpilhac-Lenthéric 1984, 248 describes Scipio's description of foreign funerals as, "un hors-d'oeuvre purement didactique."

27. Cicero, in describing the antiquity of inhumation burials (*De leg.* 2.22.56), also uses the metaphor: *At mihi quidem antiquissimum sepulturae genus illud fuisse videtur, quo apud Xenophontem Cyrus utitur; redditur enim terrae corpus et ita locatum ac situm quasi operimento matris obducitur.* See Dyck 2004 *ad loc.,* for Cicero's paraphrasing of Xenophon, *Cyropaedia* 8.7.25 and examples from Servius for Vergil's use of the metaphor at *Georg.*2.268; *Aen.* 3.96; and *Aen.* 12.209 and Corbeill 2004, chapter 3: "Blood, Milk, and Tears: The Gestures of Mourning Women," 67–106 for an analysis of women's mourning rituals that recreate figuratively the birthing process.

28. See Fowler 2000, 115–37 for a discussion of ekphasis and intertextuality, and Hinds 1998, 10 ff., "Reversing the trope" for an analysis of the intertexuality of the tree-cutting trope (Vergil and Ennius) to which can be added Silius' own contribution when Hannibal orders the construction of pyres to bury the Carthaginian dead following the Battle of Cannae:

> tum munera iussa,
> defessi quamquam, accelerant sparsoque propinquos
> agmine prosternunt lucos: sonat acta bipenni
> frondosis silva alta iugis. hinc ornus et altae
> populus alba comae, validis accisa lacertis,
> scinditur, hinc ilex, proavorum consita saeclo.
> Devolvunt quercus et amantem litora pinum
> ac, ferale decus, maestas ad busta cupressos.

Although exhausted, they make haste with their ordered duties
and lay low the nearby wood with a scattered band.
The forest, with its tall leafy branches, rings out as it is struck
with the double axe. Here the mountain-ash and the silver poplar
of lofty foliage is cut down, felled by mighty arms,
here the holm-oak, planted in the time of their ancestors.
They send headlong the oak trees and the pine that hug the shore
and the gloomy cypress as an offering for the funeral pyre. (10.527–34)

29. Feeney 1998, 122.

Chapter 1

1. Stillinger 2003, 481 dates this poem toward the end of 1819, but it was not published until 1898 (Forman's edition). The poem was written on the same sheet that Keats used to draft stanzas 45–51 of *The Jealousies*.

2. Ed. Eussner 1908.

3. *Imagines* are often translated variously as death masks, funeral masks, and ancestor masks, but the terms are not synonymous. Flower 1996, 1–3 details these important distinctions: *imagines* were made during the lifetime of the deceased, were never buried with the deceased, and were displayed in the home and worn by actors at funerals to imitate the deceased. As Sallust, *Iug.* 4.5–6 (ed. Ahlberg 1957) makes clear, the function of the masks was commemorative—to recall the character and accomplishments of the deceased to the memory of the living:

> Nam saepe ego audivi Q. Maxumum, P. Scipionem, praeterea civitatis nostrae praeclaros viros solitos ita dicere, quom maiorum imagines intuerentur, vehementissume sibi animum ad virtutem adcendi. scilicet non ceram illam neque figuram tantam vim in sese habere, sed memoria rerum gestarum eam flammam egregiis viris in pectore crescere neque prius sedari, quam virtus eortum famam atque gloriam adaequaverit.

> For I have often heard that Quintus Maximus, Publius Scipio, and other prominent men of our country were accustomed to say that, when they looked upon the *imagines* of their ancestors, their hearts would burn exceedingly for the pursuit of virtue. Of course they did not mean that the wax or portrait had such a power over them, but rather it is the memory of great deeds that kindles this flame in the hearts of noble men that cannot be supressed until their own virtue has equalled the fame and glory of their ancestors.

4. Sallust's description of the dying Catiline becomes an important interext for Lucan's description of the dying Pompey (see chapter 4) and Tacitus' description of the dying Tiberius: *iam Tiberium corpus, iam vires, nondum dissimulatio deserebat . . .* (*Ann.* 6.50.1) which attributes a hypocritical appearance to the dying emperor. This and subsequent citations to Tacitus' *Annales* refer to the text of Fisher 1981. I agree with

Edwards 2007, 30 that, "The death of Catiline is of critical importance to the assessment of his character," but would add that the description of his corpse is important to that assessment.

5. Ed. Grummere 1979, 70. For an analysis of Pacuvius' mock funeral, see Bodel 1999, 262.

6. Edwards 2007, 174–76 compares Pacuvius' funeral rehearsal to Trimalchio's in the *Satyricon* but offers different interpretations. Grottanelli 1995, 66–67 considers Pacuvius' mock-funeral within the wider context of Syrian and Oriental *carpe diem* themes.

7. For analyses of current trends in the modern funeral industry, see Howarth 1996 and Kearl 1989 and his website: www.trinity.edu/~mkearl/death-3.html for latest trends in funerary services and symbolic immortality. Bodel 2000, 135–44 discusses undertakers and their marginalization in ancient Rome.

8. Other metamorphoses available to the deceased include: turning into a reef (Eternal Reefs) or even a gem made from the carbon of the deceased (Life Gem). For the artistic, "cremains" can be turned into works of art. Also, Capuchan friars at the church of Santa Maria della Concezione in Rome decorate the church with the bones of the deceased and mix their remains with those of other monks to produce art that is constantly updated when deteriorated bones must be replaced, thus mixing the combined body parts of various generations of friars.

9. A similar tension between the aesthetics of mortality and morality surround Gunther von Hagens's exhibition "Body Worlds," which includes corpses, preserved by a process called plastination, that enables him to remove skin to reveal muscles and veins to pose corpses in various ways. Corpses, therefore, play dead in a way that calls their mortality into question and also the morality of treating corpses as works of art. Other similar exhibits such as "Bodies . . . the Exhibition" by Premier Exhibitions attract controversy because prior permission to use the corpses was not obtained in the lifetime of the deceased since their bodies were not claimed after dying a natural death.

10. I cite the text of Barber 1990, 47–49 who divides poem 13 into two parts. For a discussion of the relation of the first part to the second, see Camps 1967, 115. Dufallo 2007, 89–98 discusses the role of funerary ritual in the poems of Propertius as an example of restored behavior.

11. On the act of eating as metacommentary on the writing process in Neronian Rome, see Gowers 1994: 131–50 and Rimell 2002, 185–89. Goddard 1994, 67–82 examines literary descriptions of Nero's eating habits as symptomatic of his reign. For the complexity of Petronius' narrative strategy, see Slater 1990, Conte 1996, and Courtney 2001. On Trimalchio's lack of wit as emblematic of the dinner, see Hutchinson 1993, 110.

12. See chapter 5 for an extended discussion of the *Parentalia.*

13. All citations to the *Satyricon* refer to the text of Sage and Gilleland 1969.

14. Edward Courtney 2001, 121–122 draws a parallel between Trimalchio and Pacuvius' mimicking of the *Parentalia.*

15. I cite from the text of P. T. Eden 1984, 52.

16. The bibliography of the tale is extensive and I cite recent studies that have served as focal points for further discussion: Pecere 1975; Bakhtin 1981, 221–24; Huber 1990; Conte 1996; McGlathery 1998, 313–36; and Rimell 2002, 123–39.

17. See Courtney 2001, 168 for a discussion of Percere 1975, 52 who notes that the

husband is laid on a marble slab rather than placed in a sarcophagus to expedite the soldier's involvement in the scene since he would not need to remove the lid.

18. Rimell 2002, 129 summarizes the effect of epic intertextuality on a reader's interpretation of the tale: "This story does not simply displace epic, but incorporates it, ensuring that Eumolpus' penultimate performance is not totally satisfying and cathartic but potentially disturbing and difficult to read."

19. Compare the family suicide of Lucius Antistius Vetus, his mother-in-law Sextia and daughter Antistia Pollitta (*Ann.* 16.9 ff.), in particular how the morally virtuous and unpretentious suicides contrast with those of Seneca and Paulina.

20. All citations to the *Annales* refer to the text of Fisher 1981.

21. For analyses of Tacitus' narration of the suicide, see Hutchinson 1993, 263–68; Griffin 1976, 367–83; and Edwards 2007, 109–12 for philosophical implications. For other narrative accounts of Seneca's suicide, see Dio Epitome 62.25: Seneca wished his wife to commit suicide and he cut her veins as well as his own. Since Seneca's death was slow, soldiers hastened his demise. Paulina still had not died at the time of Seneca's death and so lived on, but no mention of Nero's intervention. Dio mentions that Seneca finished writing a book before his suicide. Suetonius, *Nero* 35 mentions the suicide in passing and does not refer to Paulina.

22. Lepida ludorum diebus qui cognitionem intervenerant theatrum cum claris feminis ingressa, lamentatione flebili maiores suos ciens ipsumque Pompeium, cuius ea monimenta et adstantes imagines visebantur, tantum miseri cordiae permovit ut effusi in lacrimas saeva et detestanda Quirinio clamitarent, cuius senectae atque orbitati et obscurissimae domui destinata quondam uxor L. Caesari ac divo Augusto nurus dederetur.

On the day of the games, which interupted her trial, [Aemilia] Lepida entered the theatre accompanied by distinguished women. With tearful lamentation, she called upon her ancestors including Pompey himself whose monuments and portraits stood visible to all. She roused such sympathy from the crowd that they poured tears and hurled violent and hateful insults against Quirinius to whose old age, childlessness, and undistinguished family she was being sacrificed—a woman who was once intended as the wife of Lucius Caesar and daughter-in-law of the divine Augustus. (*Annales* 3.23.1)

See O'Gorman 2000, 60 and 69 for the role of Aemilia as an iconic woman who herself evokes an *imago* as she appeals to the *imagines* of her ancestors.

23. For a different interpretation of Paulina's survival of her suicide attempt, see Hutchinson 1993, 267 on how Paulina's aim for glory is frustrated.

24. See Edwards 2007, 198–99 for an analysis of Octavia's suicide that serves as a contrast to that of her mother Messalina.

25. Hutchinson 1993, 321 compares the narrative of Pompey's death in Lucan with Tacitus' description of Seneca's suicide which is interrupted by Paulina's attempted suicide and subsequent survival. See chapter 4: "Cremating Pompey in Lucan's *Bellum Civile*" for futher discussion of how the narrative prolongs the death of Pompey.

26. See Edwards 2005, 13–22 and 2007, 109–112 for an analysis of Tacitus' narrative and its emphasis on Seneca's appearance.

27. Seneca's suicide is mocked by the later description of Petronius' suicide (*Ann.* 16.19), who treats his suicide flippantly and as a condemnation of pompous stoic suicides of his contemporaries, and paradoxically as an inconvenience and vehicle for conviviality. Edwards 2007, 176–78 examines Petronius' suicide as a self-conscious rejection of Socrates' suicide in Plato's *Phaedo* in favor of a Lucretian model.

Chapter 2

1. This and subsequent citations of Suetonius refer to the text of Rolfe 2001.

2. The shift from the exterior to the interior of the Temple is also significant as a response to earlier criticism of Caesar's regal ambitions when he received an embassy of senators before the Temple without rising (Suetonius, *Divus Iulius* 78), since placement within the Temple now evoked the quasi-divine status of a quasi-king. Caesar's future official deification ensured him his own temple which gave, in turn, the same dynastic and divine connections as Venus' temple to his successors.

3. See Bodel 1999, 272–75 and Sumi 2002, 566–72 for a discussion of the features and sources of Caesar's funeral; Weinstock 1971, 346–55 for details surrounding Caesar's funeral that evoked divine worship. Was Caesar's body concealed by a wax image? Tacitus *Ann.* 3.5 mentions images but it is not clear whether these were used only when the deceased died far away and therefore the corpse could not be brought expediently to Rome, or whether this ceremony was merely an interim one until the real funeral could take place.

4. Sumi 2002, 559–66 examines the historiographic evidence for the participation of mimes at Roman funerals that he also discusses more recently in Sumi 2005. See Erasmo 2004a, 96–101 for a discussion of theater activities and the quotation of tragedy at Caesar's funeral. Theatricalizing of the public's grief was connected with political expression during and after the funeral: in chapter 85, Suetonius reports that the public turned against Caesar's assassins after his funeral.

5. At *Phil.* 2.91, Cicero describes Caesar's corpse as *sem(i)ustilatus.* Elsewhere (*Pro Mil.* 33), Cicero claims that Clodius' corpse was half cremated (*semiustilatus*). Noy 2000, 191 argues against interpreting Cicero's language as meaning Caesar's corpse was not ceremoniously cremated (as argued by Lacey 1986, 224), but that Cicero's claims should be taken literally, even though they are inaccurate, as attacks against those in charge of the cremations, Sex. Clodius and Antony, for failing in their duty to the deceased. Noy 2000, 189–90 compares evidence (Velleius 2.119.5 and Florus 2.30.38) for the seemingly contradictory accounts of mutilation of Varus' half-burnt corpse. See *AP* 7.401 for half-burning of a corpse as an insult to the dead.

6. See Noy 2000, 192–93 for his rejection of theories that posit that even a complete burning of a corpse may not have constituted a proper cremation, in particular, Prieur 1991, 13 who argues that a purification rite was necessary for proper cremation, and Estiez 1995, 104, who argues that a symbolic inhumation was necessary for a cremation to be considered complete. Elsewhere, Suetonius reports a public desire to give Tiberius a partial cremation deliberately (*Tib.* 75).

7. Plutarch, *Brutus* 20 also reports Antony's waving of Caesar's bloody robe and that the mob erected an impromptu pyre and took half-burnt brands from it to set on fire the houses of his murderers. There is no mention of the wax image or of the mechanical device used to display it. Sumi 2005, 107–8 imagines Mark Antony punc-

tuating his *laudatio* by pointing to the appropriate actor playing Caesar at various points in his speech. See also Dufallo 2007, 60; 143n. 22 for a discussion of Antony's actions at Caesar's funeral.

ὧδε δὲ αὐτοῖς ἔχουσιν ἤδη καὶ χειρῶν ἐγγὺς οὖσιν ἀνέσχε τις ὑπὲρ τὸ λέχος ἀνδρείκελον αὐτοῦ Καίσαρος ἐκ κηροῦ πεποιημέ–
νον. τὸ μὲν γὰρ σῶμα, ὡς ὕπτιον ἐπὶ λέχους, οὐχ ἑωρᾶτο. τὸ δὲ ἀνδρείκελον ἐκ μηχανῆς ἐπεστρέφετο πάντῃ, καὶ σφαγαὶ τρεῖς καὶ εἴκοσιν ὤφθησαν ἀνά τε τὸ σῶμα πᾶν καὶ ἀνὰ τὸ πρόσωπον θηριωδῶς ἐς αὐτὸν γενόμεναι. τήνδε οὖν τὴν ὄψιν ὁ δῆμος οἰκτί–
στην σφίσι φανεῖσαν οὐκέτι ἐνεγκὼν ἀνῴμωξάν τε καὶ διαζωσα–
μενοι τὸ βουλευτήριον, ἔνθα ὁ Καῖσαρ ἀνῄρητο, κατέφλεξαν καὶ τοὺς ἀνδροφόνους ἐκφυγόντας πρὸ πολλοῦ περιθέοντες ἐζήτουν, οὕτω δὴ μανιωδῶς ὑπὸ ὀργῆς τε καὶ λύπης, ὥστε τὸν δημαρχοῦντα Κίνναν ἐξ ὁμωνυμίας τοῦ στρατηγοῦ Κίννα, τοῦ δημηγορήσαντος ἐπὶ τῷ Καίσαρι, οὐκ ἀνασχόμενοί τε περὶ τῆς ὁμωνυμίας οὐδ' ἀκοῦσαι, διέσπασαν θηριωδῶς, καὶ οὐδὲν αὐτοῦ μέρος ἐς ταφὴν εὑρέθη. πῦρ δ' ἐπὶ τὰς τῶν ἄλλων οἰκίας ἔφερον, καὶ καρτερῶς αὐτοὺς ἐκείνων τε ἀμυνομένων καὶ τῶν γειτόνων δεομένων τοῦ μὲν πυρὸς ἀπέσχοντο, ὅπλα δ' ἠπεί–
λησαν ἐς τὴν ἐπιοῦσαν οἴσειν.

I cite the text of White 1979.

9. On the representation of Caesar, see Flower 1996, 103–4, 125–26. For the self-representation of characters in Senecan drama, see Littlewood 2004 and Boyle 1997, in particular 114, and my discussion below for examples from Seneca's *Troades*.

10. Sumi 2005, 108 uses the phrase *deus ex machina* to describe the wax image. Sumi places the image within the context of the growing theatricality of funeral spectacle, but points to its unprecedented use as it is used here and questions the presentation of the body in a bloody and wounded state as effective advertising for Caesar's divinity. Weinstock 1971, 361 less convincingly argues that the function of the image was to represent Caesar and not his wounds and that the use of the mechanical device was not to turn the image around. The image, however, preserves the condition of Caesar's body at the time of his murder and seems designed to remind mourners of that event and to incite more passionate emotions. For the role of Antony at the funeral and the political implications of the image, see Osgood 2006, 12–14.

11. See the discussion in chapter 3 of Ovid's suppression of details surrounding Caesar's funeral in order to advance his own narrative agenda.

12. For the theatricalizing of death as punishment, see Coleman 1990, 44–73 for the term fatal charade and ancient sources, in particular Tertullian, on the features and interpretations of incorporating the killing of criminals within and as theater spectacle; Kyle 1998 for an analysis of fatal charades and the punishment of *noxii* through spectacles and their disposal from the late Republic to the Christian era; and Hutchinson 1993, 306–14 for literary texts that present death as spectacle.

13. The populace's visual association that connected Caesar with the wax image also led to the incorrect verbal/homonymic association between the tribune Cinna and the praetor Cinna and led to the former's impromptu execution.

14. See Fitch 2002, 169–70 for dramatic sources of the play. Since many dramatic

precursors do not survive, gauging Seneca's originality is difficult, especially his inclusion of Hector's tomb as Astyanax's hiding place. At least in the case of Accius' *Astyanax* we can see Seneca's departure since in that play Andromache hides Astyanax in the hills.

15. See Fantham 1982, 78: "More than any other of Seneca's tragedies, the *Troades* is dominated by contemplation of death and by the dead, not only as objects of mourning and glorification, but paradoxically as agents and motivators of the dramatic action."

16. All citations of Seneca's *Troades* in this chapter refer to the text of Fitch 2002 which is sensitive to the funereal implications of the text. Translations are my own.

17. I find a parallel with Harrison 2003 and his analysis in chapter 7 (72–89) of the first Easter Sunday from a "*Hic non est*" perspective as a variation of tomb language and Astyanax's temporary or borrowed tomb, but it is especially relevant when his mangled corpse is described, thereby producing a visual antinomy: here/not here; alive/not alive; dead/not dead; Hector/not Hector, etc.

18. For a discussion of the irrationality of Andromache's speech, see Boyle 1994 *ad loc.*, 192.

19. For the metaphor that compares a tomb to a womb, see Cicero, *De leg.* 2.22.56 quoted in the Introduction.

20. Ovid, *Met.* 13.415–17, describes Astyanax as a child when he is thrown from the tower; therefore, he is a passive participant of his death, but pathos is elicited by connecting the tower to a time when Andromache held the child while watching Hector in the battlefield: *mittitur Astyanax illis de turribus, unde / pugnantem pro se proavitaque regna tuentem / saepe videre patrem monstratum a matre solebat.*

21. For Andromache's continuing preference for Hector over Astyanax, see Fantham 1982, 375. On the wording of the epitaph, Boyle 1994, 228 points out the incongruity of Andromache's remarks in that the comparision of a son to his father is usually a cause for celebration. Littlewood 2004, 249 discusses the impropriety of Andromache's witticism.

22. Andromache does not explicitly say farewell to Hector's tomb in the play. At Ovid, *Met.* 13.423–28, Hecuba is discovered among the *sepulcra* of her children and dragged away, but she is only able to rescue Hector's ashes andd leave a lock of her hair on his tomb.

23. Seneca's emphasis on back-to-back spectacles viewed from the same vantage point reminds me of Pliny's description of C. Scribonius Curio's famous temporary theater, built in 53 BCE, which was an amphitheater designed to pivot and form two back-to-back theatrers in which simultaneous plays could be presented. At *H.N.* 36.117–120, Pliny describes the grand opening of the theater in which some spectators remained seated as the amphitheater was turned into the two separate theaters, thus also turning this conversion into a form of entertainment in its own right.

24. On the dramaturgical role played by the tombs, see Boyle 1994, 228 re: line 1121 Achilles' tomb: "the tomb of Ach. (*tumulus,* 1121, 1164, *bustum,* 1150) dominates the ending of the *Tro.* as it had the second act 9 (*tumulus,* 180, 196, 288, *bustum* 330, 361)—and again through narrative. Hector's tomb (*tumulus,* 1087), which had physically controlled the stage and its action throughout the centre of the play (371–813), is not mentioned in this final speech. Its role in this final act is as an object of incidental and pathetic reference (profaned by a 'callous spectator,' *ferus spectator,* 1087) in the narrative build-up to the spectacle of Ast.'s death."

25. See Boyle 1994, 229 for theater language that transforms the onlookers into spectators and for a discussion of how Seneca includes *to miaron* ("the repulsive") in the audience's viewing experience, which Aristotle considered alien to tragedy (*Poet.* 1452b34–36) when the virtuous encountered disaster, and Boyle 2006, 213–15 on the metatheatricality of the deaths of Astyanax and Polyxena.

26. The pivotal viewing experience of a double tragedy is reminiscent of Ovid, *Met.* 13.490 ff where Hecuba witnesses the corpses of Polyxena and Polydorus in rapid succession. See chapter 3 for an analysis of Ovid's "tragedy" of Hecuba.

27. See Fitch and McElduff 2002, 18–40 and Littlewood 2004, *passim* for the self-representation of characters in Senecan tragedy.

28. See Littlewood 2004, 252 for an extended analysis of the episode as a play within a play. Pseudo-Seneca describes Octavia's wedding day as her funeral day.

29.   perge, thalamos appara.
   taedis quid opus est quidve sollemni face,
   quid igne? thalamis Troia praelucet novis.
   celebrate Pyrrhi, Troades, conubia,
   celebrate digne: planctus et gemitus sonet.

   Quickly, prepare the
   marriage bed. What use are torchlights, the nuptial torch, or fire?
   Troy will illuminate this unheard-of wedding. Celebrate the
   marriage of Pyrrhus, Trojan women, celebrate appropriately:
   let the beating of breasts and groans resound. (898–902)

30. cum subito thalami more praecedunt faces
   et pronuba illi Tyndaris, maestum caput
   demissa. "Tali nubat Hermione modo"
   Phryges precantur, "sic viro turpi suo
   reddatur Helena."

   when, suddenly, torches pass in procession, like a wedding,
   with Helen, daughter of Tyndareus, as the bride's
   attendant, hanging her head in grief.
   "May Hermione have such a wedding," the
   Phrygians pray, "Like this may shameful
   Helen be returned to her husband!" (1132–36)

31. For the dramatic roles played by Polyxena and Astyanax, see Littlewood 2004, 254: "She and Astyanax perform affectingly for their audience, but this audience's superficiality does not diminish the morally more significant heroism which another audience might obscure."

32. Tarrant 1985, repr. 1998, 194 *ad loc.* compares the young Tantalus with Polyxena. Littlewood 2004, 235 draws a parallel between the postmortem actions of Polyxena and the young Tantalus. Polyxena's paradigm shift also points to a *contaminatio* of roles in a play that combines the double plots of Polyxena and Astyanax.

33. Polyxena the character may also be aware of her intertext's actions at Catullus 64.362–70 in which her sacrifice at Achilles' tomb and the actions of her corpse after

death are predicted by the Parcae: *alta Polyxenia madefient caede sepulcra; / quae, velut ancipiti succumbens victima ferro, / proiciet truncum summisso poplite corpus* (368–70). Cited is the text of Mynors 1989.

34. For the dramatic sources of Polyxena's sacrifice, see Fitch 2002, 169–70. For nondramatic intertexts, in addition to Catullus 64, 362–70, see Lucretius, *DRN* 1. 80–101, for the corruption of Iphigenia's wedding into her funeral, but there is no emphasis, as there is in Seneca, on theatricality. See Morisi 2002, 177–90 for an extended analysis of the Catullan and Lucretian intertexts of the myth. Compare with Ovid, *Met.* 13. 439ff., where after a lengthy speech, Polyxena covers up her bared body as she dies; therefore, Seneca focuses on Polyxena's anger rather than her modesty. See chapter 3 for an extended discussion of this passage, especially 13.451–52: *fortis et infelix et plus quam femina virgo / ducitur ad tumulum diroque fit hostia busto.*

35. Ovid, *Met.* 15.490–546 relates the details of his accident and how he was cured by Aesculepius and turned into the god Virbius in Italy; thus Ovid avoids Hippolytus' death and cremation.

36. This and subsequent citations to the *Phaedra* refer to the text of Fitch 2002.

37. See Erasmo 2004a, 129–34 for a discussion of the intertextuality between Seneca's account of Hippolytus' death and the account in Ovid, *Met.* 15.521–29. In Lucan, *BC* 2.166–68, parents try to identify the faceless corpses of their sons.

38. Cicero, *De leg.* 2.22.55 refers to *os resectum*. Varro, *L.L.* 5.23, however, describes *os exceptum*. For the archaeological evidence concerning *ossilegium,* see Becker 1987, 25–32; Toynbee 1996, 49, 50; and Carroll 2006, 4–8, 67–68, 163–64. In Vergil, *Aen.* 6.228, Misenus' remains are collected following his cremation: *ossaque lecta cado texit Corynaeus aeno.* See the discussion in chapter 3 of Pompey's cremation in Lucan's *BC* for further literary allusions to the ritual.

39. Cited is the text of Ogilvie 1974.

40. Compare with Apuleius, *Met.* 7.26 where a muleteer is reassembled for burial. See Enk 1957, 305.

41. Pentheus' severed head is displayed to the audience in Euripides' *Bacchae,* but it is not rejoined with the rest of his body on stage. See Plutarch, *Crass.* 3.3 for a performance of the play in Carrhae in which Crassus' head was incorporated into a dramatic production as Pentheus' severed head. On the semiotic implications of this performance and its relevance to the theatricality of Roman tragedy, see Erasmo 2004a, 32–33 and Boyle 2006, 157. It is unclear whether body parts were incorporated into pantomimic productions of the Kronos or Thyestes myths in which a character literally becomes a tomb of the eaten body parts.

42. Seneca's intertextuality with elegiac poetry finds a parallel in his *Thyestes* where he alludes to Greek lyric intertexts in his description of Tantalus in the Underworld in the first choral ode. See Erasmo 2006a, 185–98.

43. I cite the text of Barber 1990.

44. See chapter 5 for a discussion of this poem as an illusory epitaph.

45. Goold 1990 *ad loc.* prints a colon.

46. Text of Postgate 1990.

47. See Coffey and Mayer 1997, 5–10, for various versions of the myth.

48. My translation of Dio (here and below) is based on the text of Cary 1981:

ταῦτα μὲν αἱ ἐντολαὶ εἶχον, μετὰ δὲ τοῦτο ἡ ἐκφορὰ αὐτοῦ

ἐγένετο. κλίνη ἦν ἔκ τε ἐλέφαντος καὶ χρυσοῦ πεποιημένη καὶ
στρώμασιν ἁλουργοῖς διαχρύσοις κεκοσμημένη. καὶ ἐν αὐτῇ
τὸ μὲν σῶμα κάτω που ἐν θήκῃ συνεκέκρυπτο, εἰκὼν δὲ δή τις
αὐτοῦ κηρίνη ἐν ἐπινικίῳ στολῇ ἐξεπηαίνετο. καὶ αὕτη μὲν ἐκ
τοῦ παλατίου πρός τῶν ἐς νέωτα ἀρχόντων, ἑτέρα δὲ ἐκ τοῦ
βουλευτηρίου χρυσῆ, καὶ ἑτέρα αὖ ἐφ' ἅρματος πομπικοῦ ἤγετο.
καὶ μετὰ ταύτας αἵ τε τῶν προπατόρων αὐτοῦ καὶ αἱ τῶν
ἄλλων συγγενῶν τῶν τεθνηκότων, πλὴν τῆς τοῦ καίσαρος
ὅτι ἐς τοὺς ἥρωας ἐσεγέγραπτο, αἵ τε τῶν ἄλλων Ῥομαίων
τῶν καὶ καθ' ὁτιοῦν πρωτευσάντων, ἀπ' αὐτοῦ τοῦ Ῥωμύλου
τοῦ μεγάλου εἰκὼν ὤφθη, τά τε ἔθνη πάνθ' ὅσα προσεκτήσατο,
ἐπιχωρίως σφίσιν ὡς ἕκαστα ἀπηκασμένα ἐπέμφθη. κἀκ τούτου
καὶ τὰ ἄλλα αὐτοῖς, ὅσα ἐν τοῖς ἄνω λόγοις εἴρηται, ἐφέσπετο.
προτεθείσης δὲ τῆς κλίνης ἐπὶ τοῦ δημηγορικοῦ βήματος, ἀπὸ
μὲν ἐκείνου ὁ Δροῦσός τι ἀσέγνω, ἀπὸ δὲ τῶν ἑτέρων ἐμβόλων
τῶν Ἰουλιείων ὁ Τιβέριος δημόσιον δή τινα κατὰ δόγμα λόγον
ἐπ' αὐτῷ τοιόνδε ἐπελέξατο.

49. See Sumi 2005, 256–61 for an analysis of Dio's account of Augustus' funeral, in particular as a conversion of republican aristocratic funeral practices into imperial ritual ceremony and how the funeral procession is an evocation of a military triumph. Sumi recreates the topography traversed by the images of Augustus and suggests that the image of Augustus in a chariot and the ancestors originated their procession from the Forum of Augustus although Dio's narrative is not explicit about the route taken by this Augustus to meet up with the other images at the rostra. See Beacham 1999, 151–53 for an analysis of the funeral procession and cremation.

50. See Bodel 1999, 271–72 for the *imagines* at Augustus' funeral and the use of *imagines* in the first century CE and Flower 1996, 245–46 for a discussion of the importance of *imagines* to the political program of Augustus' funeral.

51. This ambiguity is furthermore reflected in funerary art. Funerary monuments such as sarcophagi that depict scenic productions (actors on stage) may commemorate an actual performance event associated with the deceased's own funeral and were, perhaps, intended for the continued enjoyment of the deceased even in death, as we find with Etruscan tombs which include banqueting scenes. See Bieber 1961 for the connection between productions of tragedies and tomb decoration, in particular, 157, fig. 570 (marble relief from Naples with Perseus and Andromeda); fig. 571 (wall painting from Pompeii with Perseus and Andromeda). Also, 162, fig. 588 for a terra cotta relief adorning the tomb of P. Numitorius Hilarus with scenes from tragedy including Andromache holding Astyanax and Odysseus. Bieber argues, 163, "The relief probably illustrates a scene from the *Astyanax* of Accius, based on Sophocles. The tragedies of Accius, just as those of Pacuvius, were still given in the first century B.C. Somewhat later Seneca, who knew Accius, has a similar scene in his *Troades* (vv. 705 ff)." Tragic scenes also adorn the tombs from Rome (Columbarium in the Villa Doria Pamphili), Bieber, 163, fig. 589; Ostia, 163, fig. 560; and Herculaneum with a depiction of Phaedra and her nurse,164, fig. 591.

52. The inherent dangers of reading funerary symbolism as a shared reception of meanings are many and there are parallels in the scripting and multiple reception of

symbolism with royal funerals of later historical periods. I share the cautious approach
of Woodward 1997, 11: "My own analysis similarly recognises that the power of ritual
lies in its multivocality and identifies the use of symbols as the means of achieving it.
Symbols, whether visual or choreographic, operate through multivalency, multivocality
and ambiguity, qualities that enable them to draw together the multifarious experiences
of individuals, emotional and intellectual, shaping them into the homogeneity that is
required on ritual occasions."

53. A further connection between the theater audience and the Dead is made figuratively by Seneca who in the *Hercules Furens* compares the crowds of the dead in the
Underworld to the excited populus of Rome at the premiere performance of a play in
a new theater:

Quantus incedit populus per urbes
ad novi ludos avidus theatri . . .

As much as the populace hastens through cities
anxious for the plays of a new theater. (838–39)

54. Τιβέριος μὲν ταῦτα ἀνέγνω, μετὰ δὲ τοῦτο τήν τε κλίνην οἱ
αὐτοὶ οἵπερ καὶ πρότερον ἀράμενοι διὰ τῶν ἐπινικίων πυλῶν
κατὰ τὰ τῇ βουλῇ δόξαντα διεκόμισαν, παρῆν δὲ καὶ συνεξέ—
φερεν αὐτὸν ἥ τε γερουσία καὶ ἡ ἱππάς, αἵ τε γυναῖκες αὐτῶν
καὶ τὸ δορυφορικόν, οἵ τε λοιποὶ πάντες ὡς εἰπεῖν οἱ ἐν τῇ
πόλει τότε ὄντες. ἐπεὶ δὲ ἐς τὴν πυρὰν τὴν ἐν τῷ Ἀρείῳ πεδίῳ
ἐνετέθη, πρῶτοι μὲν οἱ ἱερῆς πάντες περιῆλθον αὐτήν, ἔπειτα δὲ
οἵ τε ἱππῆς, οἵ τε ἐκ τοῦ τέλους καὶ οἱ ἄλλοι, καὶ τὸ ὁπλιτικὸν
τὸ φρουρικὸν περιέδραμον, πάντα τὰ νικητήρια, ὅσα τινὲς
αὐτῶν ἐπ' ἀριστείᾳ ποτὲ παρ' αὐτοῦ εἰλήφεσαν, ἐπιβάλλοντες
αὐτῇ. κἀκ τούτου δᾷδας ἑκατόνταρχοι, ὥς που τῇ βουλῇ ἐδό—
κει, λαβόντες ὑφῆψαν αὐτήν. καὶ ἡ μὲν ἀνηλίσκετο, ἀετὸς δέ
τις ἐξ αὐτῆς ἀφεθεὶς ἀνίπτατο ὡς καὶ δὴ τὴν ψυχὴν αὐτοῦ ἐς
τὸν οὐρανὸν ἀναφέρων. πραχθέντων δὲ τούτων οἱ μὲν ἄλλοι
ἀπηλλάγησαν, ἡ δὲ δὴ Λιουία κατὰ χώραν πέντε ἡμέραις μετὰ
τῶν πρώτων ἱππέων μείνασα τά τε ὀστᾶ αὐτοῦ συνελέξατο καὶ
ἐς τὸ μνημεῖον κατέθετο.

55. On the release of an eagle as a symbol of apotheosis, see Davies 2000a, 10–11;
Sumi 2005, 260; and Cumont 1949, 293–302.

56. Sulla was the first to receive a public funeral which included unusual elements
such as his procession in which statues of Sulla carved from frankincense and cinnamon
trees were carried on wheelbarrows overflowing with spices. On the relation between
Sulla's funeral and Julius Caesar's, see Weinstock 1971, 348–49, 360–61.

57. My translation is based on the Greek text of Paton 1972:

Ὅταν γὰρ μεταλλάξῃ τις παρ' αὐτοῖς τῶν ἐπιφανῶν ἀνδρῶν,
συντελουμένης τῆς ἐκφορᾶς κομίζεται μετὰ τοῦ λοιποῦ κόσμου
πρὸς τοὺς καλουμένους ἐμβόλους εἰς τὴν ἀγορὰν ποτὲ μὲν
ἑστὼς ἐναργής, σπανίως δὲ κατακεκλιμένος. πέριξ δὲ παντὸς

τοῦ δήμου στάντος, ἀναβὰς ἐπὶ τοὺς ἐμβόλους, ἂν μὲν υἱὸς
ἐν ἡλικίᾳ καταλείπηται καὶ τύχῃ παρών, οὗτος, εἰ δὲ μή, τῶν
ἄλλων εἴ τις ἀπὸ γένους ὑπάρχει, λέγει περὶ τοῦ τετελευτηκότος
τὰς ἀρετὰς καὶ τὰς ἐπιτετευγμένας ἐν τῷ ζῆν πράξεις. δι' ὧν
συμβαίνει τοὺς πολλοὺς ἀναμιμνησκομένους καὶ λαμβάνοντας
ὑπὸ τὴν ὄψιν τὰ γεγονότα, μὴ μόνον τοὺς κεκοινωνηκότας τῶν
ἔργων, ἀλλὰ καὶ τοὺς ἐκτός, ἐπὶ τοσοῦτον γίνεσθαι συμπαθεῖς
ὥστε μὴ τῶν κηδευόντων ἴδιον, ἀλλὰ κοινὸν τοῦ δήμου φαί-
νεσθαι τὸ σύμπτωμα. μετὰ δὲ ταῦτα θάψαντες καὶ ποιήσαντες
τὰ νομιζόμενα τιθέασι τὴν εἰκόνα τοῦ μεταλλάξαντος εἰς τὸν
ἐπιφανέστατον τόπον τῆς οἰκίας, ξύλινα ναΐδια περιτιθέντες. ἡ
δ' εἰκών ἐστι πρόσωπον εἰς ὁμοιότητα διαφερόντως ἐξειργασμέ-
νον καὶ κατὰ τὴν πλάσιν καὶ κατὰ τὴν ὑπογραφήν. ταύτας δὴ
τὰς εἰκόνας ἔν τε ταῖς δημοτελέσι θυσίαις ἀνοίγοντες κοσμοῦσι
φιλοτίμως, ἐπάν τε τῶν οἰκείων μεταλλάξῃ τις ἐπιφανής,
ἄγουσιν εἰς τὴν ἐκφοράν, περιτιθέντες ὡς ὁμοιοτάτοις εἶναι
δοκοῦσι κατά τε τὸ μέγεθος καὶ τὴν ἄλλην περικοπήν. οὗτοι δὲ
προσαναλαμβάνουσιν ἐσθῆτας, ἐὰν μὲν ὕπατος ἢ στρατηγὸς
ᾖ γεγονώς, περιπορφύρους, ἐὰν δὲ τιμητής, πορφυρᾶς, ἐὰν δὲ
καὶ τεθριαμβευκὼς ἤ τι τοιοῦτον κατειργασμένος, διαχρύσους.
αὐτοὶ μὲν οὖν ἐφ' ἁρμάτων οὗτοι πορεύονται, ῥάβδοι δὲ καὶ
πελέκεις καὶ τἆλλα τὰ ταῖς ἀρχαῖς εἰωθότα συμπαρακεῖσθαι
προηγεῖται κατὰ τὴν ἀξίαν ἑκάστῳ τῆς γεγενημένης κατὰ τὸν
βίον ἐν τῇ πολιτείᾳ προαγωγῆς ὅταν δ' ἐπὶ τοὺς ἐμβόλους
ἔλθωσι, καθέζονται πάντες ἑξῆς ἐπὶ δίφρων ἐλεφαντίνων. οὗ
κάλλιον οὐκ εὐμαρὲς ἰδεῖν θέαμα νέῳ φιλοδόξῳ καὶ φιλαγάθῳ.
τὸ γὰρ τὰς τῶν ἐπ' ἀρετῇ δεδοξασμένων ἀνδρῶν εἰκόνας ἰδεῖν
ὁμοῦ πάσας οἷον εἰ ζώσας καὶ πεπνυμένας τίν' οὐκ ἂν παρα-
στήσαι; τί δ' ἂν κάλλιον θέαμα τούτου φανείη.

58. On the spectacle of the ceremony described by Polybius, see Flower 1996, 36–
38; Beacham 1999, 17–19; Bodel 1999, 262–67, who refers to the funeral cortege as
"participatory spectacle" and discusses theatrical elements in Lucian's *De luctu;* and
Dufallo 2007, 25–26, 134 n.33 for a discussion of the role of actors. In Erasmo 2004a,
3, I cautioned against using the term "theatrical" as a synonym for spectacle unless
direct parallels to the theater or a theatrical production were implied.

59. Parts of this section contain adaptations of my earlier discussion of funerals in
Erasmo 2004a, 75–79.

60. The *Amphitryon* contains a pun based on the *imagines* mask and the comic and
tragic masks worn by actors. Sosias, looking at Mercury who is wearing a mask resembling Sosias' own face, exclaims:

nam hicquidem omnem imaginem meam, quae antehac fuerat, possidet.
vivo fit quod numquam quisquam mortuo faciet mihi.

This man has got hold of my total image, which used to be my own! My
image is carried around now that I am alive, more than anyone will do
so when I'm dead. (458–59)

Thus in the play, we have an actor imitating a god who in turn is seen to be imitating a dead actor.

61. The evidence for *ludi scaenici* in the forum comes from Livy 31.50.4: *Et ludi funebres eo anno per quadriduum in foro mortis causa M. Valeri Laevini a Publio et Marco filiis eius facti, et munus gladiatorium datum ab iis; paria quinque et viginti pugnarunt.* On the forum as the site of funeral games see, Saunders 1913, 93–94, and Hanson 1959, 17. See Richardson 1992, 380, for arguments against the location.

62. See Hanson 1959.

63. For the symbolic use of the throne by Caesar *in absentia* and in procession of the *sellisternia* and *lectisternia,* see Dio 44.6.3. For the honor of having a throne in the theater, see Weinstock 1971, 281–82; Hanson 1959, 82 ff. Only once while alive did Caesar occupy a visible place in the theater with regal attributes with divine connotations. This was at the Lupercalia of 45 BCE, where Caesar caused a scandal by wearing a crown and dressed in triumphal robes while seated upon a gold throne on the rostra (Plutarch, *Caes.* 61). For the ivory statue, see Dio 43.45.2. By decree, it was to be kept in the Capitoline Temple, dressed in triumphal robes and carried in the procession of the gods in the *pompa circensis.* The statue was first used in the *pompa* when Caesar was still in Spain.

64. See Cicero, *Ad Att.* 15.3.2 (May 22, 44 BCE); Appian, *B.C.* 3.28.105 ff, where the tribunes prevent Octavian from bringing Caesar's golden throne into the theater, to the delight of Cicero and the Equites. For the second occasion (July), see Dio 45.6.5; Appian, *B.C.* 3.28.107. For successful installations, see Dio 50.10.2 and 56.29.1. It is ironic that Augustus' own death was portended when a mime actor sat on Caesar's throne at the horseraces at the Augustalia in 13 BCE., and actually put the crown that had been placed on the throne on his own head (Dio, 56.29.1).

65. Suetonius, *Div. Jul.* 76.1 refers to a *suggestum* in the orchestra, and also to the *pulvinar.*

66. See Fishwick 1991, 555.

67. Suetonius, *Aug.* 43.5: *rursus commissione ludorum quibus theatrum Marcelli dedicabat, evenit ut laxatis sellae curulis compagibus caderet supinus.* Augustus was then 52 years old.

68. Suetonius, *Aug.* 45.1. All of his grandchildren and step-grandchildren except, it seems, the future emperor Claudius, whom Augustus would not allow to attend the Games of Mars out of fear he would embarrass the Imperial family (Suetonius, *Claud.* 4.3).

69. For Germanicus, see Weinstock 1957, 144–54.

70. See Fishwick 1991, 555–56.

71. See Purcell 1999, 181–93 for a discussion of the identity and role of mimes in Roman funerals.

72. I translate Diodorus Siculus *World History* (*Bibliotheca*) 31.25 from the text of Walton 1968:

τῶν γὰρ Ῥομαίων οἱ ταῖς εὐγενείαις καὶ προγόνων δόξῃ
διαφέροντες μετὰ τὴν τελευτὴν εἰδωλοποιοῦνται κατά τε τὴν
τοῦ χαρακτῆρος ὁμοιότητα καὶ κατὰ τὴν ὅλην τοῦ σώματος
περιγραφήν, μιμητὰς ἔχοντες ἐκ παντὸς τοῦ βίου παρα-
τετηρηκότας τήν τε πορείαν καὶ τὰς κατὰ μέρος ἰδιότητας

τῆς ἐμφάσεως. παραπλησίως δὲ καὶ τῶν προγόνων ἕκαστος προηγεῖται τοιαύτην ἔχων διασκευὴν καὶ κόσμον ὥστε τοὺς θεωμένους διὰ τῆς ἐκ τούτων ἐμφάσεος γινώσκειν ἐφ' ὅσον ἕκαστοι τιμῆς προήχθησαν καὶ μετέσχον τῶν ἐν τῇ πολιτείᾳ καλῶν.

73. Pertinax was honored with a *funus imaginarium et censorinum* by Septimius Severus (*Script. Hist. Aug. Vit. Pert.* 15.1). For an analysis of Pertinax's funeral, see Weinstock 1971, 361; Davies 2000a, 8, 10, 125; and Sumi 2005, 108.

74. My translation is based on the Greek text of Cary 1982:

ἡ δὲ δὴ ταφὴ καίτοι πάλαι τεθνηκότος αὐτοῦ τοιάδε ἐγένετο. ἐν τῇ ἀγορᾷ τῇ Ῥωμαίᾳ βῆμα ξύλινον ἐν χρῷ τοῦ λιθίνου κατεσκευάσθη, καὶ ἐπ' αὐτοῦ οἴκημα ἄτοιχον περίστυλον, ἔκ τε ἐλέφαντος καὶ χρυσοῦ πεποικιλμένον, ἐτέθη, καὶ ἐν αὐτῷ κλίνη ὁμοία, κεφαλὰς πέριξ θηρίων χερσαίων τε καὶ θαλασ- σίων ἔχουσα, ἐκομίσθη στρώμασι πορφυροῖς καὶ διαχρύσοις κεκοσμημένη, καὶ ἐς αὐτὴν εἴδωλόν τι τοῦ Περτίνακος κήρινον, σκευῇ ἐπινικίῳ εὐθετημένον, ἀνετέθη, καὶ αὐτοῦ τὰς μυίας παῖς εὐπρεπής, ὡς δῆθεν καθεύδοντος, πτεροῖς ταῶνος ἀπεσόβει. προκειμένου δ' αὐτοῦ ὅ τε Σεουῆρος καὶ ἡμεῖς οἱ βουλευταὶ αἵ τε γυναῖκες ἡμῶν προσῄειμεν πενθικῶς ἐσταλμένοι. καὶ ἐκεῖναι μὲν ἐν ταῖς στοαῖς, ἡμεῖς δὲ ὑπαίθριοι ἐκαθεζόμεθα. κἀκ τούτου πρῶτον μὲν ἀνδριάντες πάντων τῶν ἐπιφανῶν Ῥωμαίων τῶν ἀρχαίων, ἔπειτα χοροὶ παίδων καὶ ἀνδρῶν θρηνώδη τινὰ ὕμνοι ἐς τὸν Περτίνακα ᾄδοντες παρῆλθον. καὶ μετὰ τοῦτο τὰ ἔθνη πάντα τὰ ὑπήκοα ἐν εἰκόσι χαλκαῖς, ἐπιχωρίως σφίσιν ἐσταλμέ- να, καὶ τὰ ἐν τῷ ἄστει αὐτῷ γένη, τό τε τῶν ῥαβδούχων καὶ τὸ τῶν γραμματέων τῶν τε κηρύκων καὶ ὅσα ἄλλα τοιουτό- τροπα, ἐφείπετο. εἶτ' εἰκόνες ἧκον ἀνδρῶν ἄλλων, οἷς τι ἔργον ἢ ἐξεύρημα ἢ καὶ ἐπιτήδευμα λαμπρὸν ἐπέπρακτο, καὶ μετ' αὐ- τοὺς οἵ τε ἱππεῖς καὶ οἱ πεζοὶ ὡπλισμένοι οἵ τε ἀθληταὶ ἵπποι καὶ τὰ ἐντάφια, ὅσα ὅ τε αὐτοκράτωρ καὶ ἡμεῖς αἵ τε γυναῖκες ἡμῶν καὶ οἱ ἱππεῖς οἱ ἐλλόγιμοι οἵ τε δῆμοι καὶ τὰ ἐν τῇ πόλει συστήματα ἐπέμψαμεν. καὶ αὐτοῖς βωμὸς περίχρυσος, ἐλέφαντι τε καὶ λίθοις Ἰνδικοῖς ἠσκημένος, ἠκολούθει. ὡς δὲ παρεξῆλθε ταῦτα, ἀνέβη ὁ Σεουῆρος ἐπὶ τὸ βῆμα τὸ τῶν ἐμβόλων, καὶ ἀνέγνω ἐγκώμιον τοῦ Περτίνακος. ἡμεῖς δὲ πολλὰ μὲν καὶ διὰ μέσου τῶν λόγων αὐτοῦ ἐπεβοῶμεν, τὰ μὲν ἐπαινοῦντες τὰ δὲ καὶ θρηνοῦντες τὸν Περτίνακα, πλεῖστα δὲ ἐπειδὴ ἐπαύσατο. καὶ τέλος, μελλούσης τῆς κλίνης κινηθήσεσθαι, πάντες ἅμα ὠλοφυράμεθα καὶ πάντες ἐπεδακρύσαμεν. κατεκόμισαν δὲ αὐτὴν ἀπὸ τοῦ βήματος οἵ τε ἀρχιερεῖς καὶ αἱ ἀρχαὶ αἵ τε ἐνεστῶσαι καὶ αἱ ἐς νέωτα ἀποδεδειγμέναι, καὶ ἱππεῦσί τισι φέρειν ἔδοσαν. οἱ μὲν οὖν ἄλλοι πρὸ τῆς κλίνης προῄειμεν, καί τινες ἐκόπτοντο ἑτέρων πένθιμόν τι ὑπαυλούντων. ὁ δ' αὐτοκράτωρ ἐφ' ἅπασιν εἵπετο, καὶ οὕτως ἐς τὸ Ἄρειον πεδίον ἀφικόμεθα. ἐπεσκεύαστο

δὲ ἐν αὐτῷ πυρὰ πυργοειδὴς τρίβολος, ἐλέφαντι καὶ χρυσῷ
μετὰ ἀνδριάντων τινῶν κεκοσμημένη, καὶ ἐπ' αὐτῆς τῆς ἄκρας
ἅρμα ἐπίχρυσον, ὅπερ ὁ Περτίναξ ἤλαυνεν. ἐς οὖν ταύτην τὰ
ἐντάφια ἐνεβλήθη καὶ ἡ κλίνη ἐνετέθη, καὶ μετὰ τοῦτο τὸ εἴδωλον
ὅ τε Σεουῆρος καὶ οἱ συγγενεῖς τοῦ Περτίνακος ἐφίλησαν. καὶ ὁ
μὲν ἐπὶ βῆμα ἀνέβη, ἡμεῖς δὲ ἡ βουλὴ πλὴν τῶν ἀρχόντων ἐπὶ
ἰκρία, ὅπως ἀσφαλῶς τε ἅμα καὶ πολεμικὰς διεξόδους διε—
λίττοντες διεξῆλθον. εἶθ' οὕτως οἱ ὕπατοι πῦρ ἐς αὐτὴν ἐνέβα—
λον. γενομένου δὲ τούτου ἀετός τις ἐξ αὐτῆς ἀνέπτατο. καὶ ὁ
μὲν Περτίναξ οὕτως ἠθανατίσθη.

75. For analyses of the program of the opening of Pompey's theater, see Beacham 1999, 63–65; Erasmo 2004a, 83–91; and Boyle 2006, 155–57.

76. Howarth 2000, 134.

77. These are: Naevius' *Clastidium* for Marcellus' battle in 222BCE; Ennius' *Ambracia* (after 189 BCE which is the starting date of campaign); and Pacuvius' *Paullus* for L. Aemilius Paullus (in 160 BCE?).

78. For discussions of the possible performance occasions of *fabulae praetextae*, see Dupont 1985, 219ff; Flower 1995, 170–90, in particular 178–81; Manuwald 2001, 110–30; and Erasmo 2004a, 71–80 in particular for the semiotic implications of performances at which the honoree may have been in the audience or actually was as in the case of Cornelius Balbus at the performance of his *Iter*.

79. See Erasmo 2004a, 91–101 for an extensive analysis of the play and its intertextual value as propaganda in the late Republic.

Chapter 3

1. Cited is the text of Volpilhac-Lenthéric 1984.

2. Hutchinson 1993, 289–94 analyzes the narrative of Paullus' death which, like Lucan's description of the death of Pompey, is prolonged for narrative effect.

3. Livy (22.52.6) gives few details of Paullus' actual funeral.

4. For a parallel use of death ritual as epic intertext, see Holt 1992, 319–31 for an examination of Ajax' inhumation burial.

5. This and future citations to the *Aeneid* refer to the text of Mynors 1990.

6. The pyre is described as *altos . . . rogos* (4.645–46) and *rogus* (4.676). Ovid *Fasti* 3.549–50 contains reference to Dido's epitaph and pyre.

7. For the funeral games of Anchises in Book 5 serving as a dual ceremony for Dido also, see Anderson 1969, 52 and Pavlovskis 1976, 195.

8. Servius, *ad loc: cupressus adhibetur ad funera, vel quod caesa non repullulat, vel quod per eam funestata ostenditur domus, sicut laetam frondes indicant festae.* In addition, Servius cites Varro who claims that cypress trees surrounding the pyre would lessen the odor of the pyre (*ustrina*) for onlookers who remained until the body burned and the remains were collected: *Varro tamen dicit pyras ideo cupresso circumdari propter gravem ustrinae odorem, ne eo offendatur populi circumstantis corona, quae tamdiu stabat respondens fletibus praeficae, id est principi planctuum, quamdiu consumpto cadavere et collectis cineribus diceretur novissimum verbum 'ilicet,' quod ire licet signficant [. . .]* . Text of Thilo and Hagen 1961. See Austin 1977, 102–8 for an extended analysis of the passage.

Servius' comments are intended for a readership unfamiliar with cremation customs practiced two centuries earlier. While some comments seem summaries of information contained in the *Aeneid*, others seem drawn from other sources to place those elements of funerals and cremations found in the poem in a wider cultural context.

9. Servius, *ad loc.*, claims that the phrase *lavant frigentes et ungunt* comes from Ennius' description of the washing and anointing of Tarquin's corpse by a *bona femina: Exin Tarquinium bona femina lavit et unxit* (Book 3, Skutsch 1986, ix). For a discussion of the intertextuality between these passages and the possible identity of the *femina* as Tanaquil (according to Donatus), see Skutsch 1986, 303.

10. Servius, *ad loc: unde et funus dictum est. per noctem autem urebantur: unde et permansit ut mortuos faces antecedant).* On the occurrence of cremations at night, Servius, at *Aen.* 11.186: *more tulere patrum,* claims that some people burn bodies during the day, as in the mass cremations of Trojans and others at night and cites the cremation of Pallas as an example, but the text does not state the time of day explicitly. Noy 2000, 187 reviews the evidence for nocturnal funerals, in particular Arce's suggestion (1988, 22) that public funerals beginning at dawn would allow a cremation to be completed by nightfall. Rose 1923, 191–94 argues against the view that cremations at Rome only took place at night. Vergil does not refer to the custom (mentioned at Pliny, *HN* 11.150) of opening the eyes of a corpse prior to the lighting of a pyre.

11. Servius, *ad loc.,* claims that ashes had to be sorted since nobles were never cremated alone but were burned with a horse, dog, or a slave.

12. Servius, *ad loc.,* claims that the olive, now considered a tree of good omen, used to be considered funereal like the laurel before Augustus, according to Donatus, forbade the use of laurel in funerals (*ad officium lugubre*) so that it could be used to crown triumphators.

13. Servius, *ad loc.,* cited above. The calling of the deceased by name is mentioned in other literary passages: Vergil, *Aen.* 4.674: *morientem nomine clamat;* Horace, Ode 2.20.23–24: *compesce clamorem ac sepulcri / mitte supervacuos honores;* and Propertius, 1.17.21–26: *illic si qua meum sepelissent fata dolorem, / ultimus et posito staret amore lapis, / illa meo caros donasset funere crines / mollitur et tenera poneret ossa rossa; / illa meum extremo clamasset pulvere nomen, / ut mihi non ullo pondere terra foret.*

14. Homer, *Iliad* 23.117–20

> But when they came to an outcrop of many-springed Ida
> Right away they cut the high-crested oaks with the long-edged bronze
> and the trees fell with a great crash . . .

Compare with *Iliad,* 24. 778ff (Priam orders wood for Hektor's pyre) and Stesichorus, P. Oxy. 3876 fr 61–62.

15. Ennius *Annales* (Book 6: Skutsch 1986):

> Incedunt arbusta per alta, securibus caedunt,
> percullent magnas quercus, exciditur ilex,
> fraxinus frangitur atque abies consternitur alta,
> pinus proceras pervertunt: omne sonabat
> arbustum fremitu silvai frondosai.

Austin 1977, 93–95 examines the intertextuality between Ennius and Vergil.

16. Sequence of events in Hector's funeral held during a twelve-day truce: women wail (Andromache, Hecuba, Helen); Priam orders wood for pyre to be set up in city (24.778 ff), after collecting wood for nine days, Trojans bury Hector on the tenth day, bones collected on the eleventh day, bones placed in urn and set in a grave covered by close set stones and a grave mound, feast.

17. Servius, *ad loc.*, 64; ibid. vol. 2, p. 484, but also used of Misenus' bier.

18. See Gransden 1991, *ad loc.*, 67, p. 75 who makes this observation.

19. The term *ustrinum* does not occur in literary descriptions of pyres. See Polfer 2000, 30 for a discussion of Festus' definition (*De significatu verborum, s.v. bustum*) of an *ustrinum: bustum proprie dicitur locus, in quo mortuus est combustus et sepultus [. . .]; ubi vero combustus quis tantummodo, alibus vero est sepultus, is locus ab urendo ustrina vocatur.*

20. Noy 2000, 187–89 cites scientific studies that calculate the average length of time for a cremation by Roman standards would be 7 to 8 hours (McKinley 1989, 67), or even 10 hours based on an experimental burning of a complete skeleton on a pyre (Piontek 1976, 278: "The process of cremation and its influence on the morphology of bones in the light of results of experimental research" (English summary). A second cremation might be necessary, on the following day if the corpse did not burn completely under ideal conditions of sufficient time, fire temperature, meteorological conditions, and air flow. On the funeral rituals of youths in Rome and the provinces, see Martin-Kilcher 2000, 63–77, in particular 73–75 for a discussion on the difficulty in identifying the tombs of young men and differences between Roman and German practices surrounding the burial of young men.

21. Gransden 1991, *ad loc.*, points out the erotic quality of the passage that seems to transform Pallas' bier into a marriage couch. If Vergil suggests a substitution of rituals from a funeral to a marriage, then the subtext of the passage suggests a closer relationship between Aeneas and Pallas than the text elsewhere explictly attests. Vergil does not specify how long Pallas'corpse was laid out. If Vergil's readers were accustomed to a seven-day laying-out period for the corpse (Serv. *ad Aen.* 5.64; 6.218), then the still youthful appearance of Pallas, without any signs of physical decay, would be remarkable.

22. Servius, *ad loc.* 66: *obtentu frondis inumbrant veluti cameram quandam capulo ramorum extensione fecerunt.*

23. Cf. *Ecl.* 5.3, for example, where Menalcas invites Mopsus to sit under interwoven branches: *hic corylis mixtas inter consedimus ulmos?* The description of the setting also evokes the bed of Adonis in Theocritus, *Idylls* 15.

24. See Toynbee 1996, 62–63 and Courtney 1995, 375 for the funereal significance of roses and violets, which were associated with the spilt blood of Attis, at the festival of the Rosalia.

25. *Ecl.* 3.62–63: *Et me Phoebus amat; Phoebo sua semper apud me / munera sunt, lauri et suave rubens hyacinthus.*

26. For a discussion of Vergil's manipulation of the pastoral landscape to include death, see Lee 1989, 90.

27. In his *Life of Vergil*, Suetonius claims that Vergil lamented the death of his brother Flaccus under the name of Daphnis: *[. . .] cuius exitum sub nomine Daphnidae deflet* (14).

28. Cf. 5.64: *'deus, deus ille, Menalca!'* See Putnam 1970, 188 ff. and Rose 1942,

124ff and 130 ff for a discussion of the problems of associating the apotheosis of Daphnis with that of Julius Caesar.

29. *Ecl.* 5. 38–39: *pro molli viola, pro purpureo narcisso / carduus et spinis surgit paliurus acutis.*

30. See Putnam 1970, 172 ff for an analysis of how the landscape mourns the death of Daphnis.

31. Compare with Lucan, *BC* 8 where the reader becomes a voyeuristic audience to Pompey's cremation.

32. At *Aen.* 5.47–48 (and Servius *ad loc.*), Vergil mentions the burial of Anchises' bones: *ex quo reliquias divinique ossa parentis / condidimus terra maestasque sacravimus aras,* thus providing an epilogue to the mysterious circumstances surrounding his death. For an extended analysis of Anchises' burial, see the discussion of Caieta's epitaph in Ovid's *Metamorphoses* in the following section.

33. Servius, *ad loc.*, cites Asinius Pollio's observation on Vergil's use of passages that denote personification of the day expressions to foreshadow and reflect the context of narratives. In addition to this example, Pollio cited *Aen.* 4.585: *Tithoni croceum linquens Aurora cubile* to comment on forthcoming events in the relationship between Aeneas and Dido.

34. *Annales* 14, Skutsch frag ix: *Omnes occisi occensique in nocte serena.* cf. Lucan, *BC* 7.787 ff where Caesar refuses to burn the dead after Battle of Pharsalus.

35. At Lucan, *BC* 8. 778–79, Pompey's cremated remains are gathered at dawn, but at Silius Italicus, *Punica* 10.540–43 the pyres of the Carthaginian dead are lit at dawn.

36. Servius, *ad Aen.* 11.185: *pyra est lignorum congeries; rogus cum iam ardere coeperit dicitur; bustum vero iam exustum vocatur.* Servius further defines *busta* at 11.201: *bustum dicitur in quo mortuus conbustus est, ossaque eius ibi iuxta sunt sepulta. alii dicunt, ubi homo combustus est, nisi ibidem humatus fuerit, non esse ibi bustum, sed ustrinum.*

37. Toynbee 1996, 55 gives a brief outline of features of a *funus militare* and cites Livy 27.2.9: *congestos in unum locum (Romani) cremavere suos;* and the Roman dead following Varus' defeat in Teutoberg.

38. Servius, *ad Aen.* 11.210: *tertia lux: mos enim erat tertia die ossa crematorum legi.*

39. The heavy cost of war would also be felt back at home. On the effect of military mortality on Italy's agrarian culture, in particular in the late 3rd and 2nd centuries BCE, see Rosenstein 2004, 107–69.

40. Ovid's narrative seems indebted to Euripides' *Hecuba,* but as discussed in chapter 2 in connection with Seneca's *Troades,* there were many Greek and Latin versions that include varying elements and emphases of the death of Astyanax, the sacrifice of Polyxena, the visiting ghost/returning corpse of Polydorus, and allusions to Hecuba's transformation into a dog.

41. In Ovid's description of Niobe's turning to stone (*Met.* 6.303–12), he compares the stone-like facial features of Niobe to an *imago: nihil est in imagine vivum* (6.305).

42. See Hinds 1998 107–11 for points of similarity and departure between the narrative role played by Caieta in the *Metamorphoses* and Vergil's in the *Aeneid* as a narrative bridge to Homer's *Odyssey.*

43. At *Aeneid* 3.709–11, Aeneas unexpectedly laments: *heu, genitorem, omnis curae casusque levamen, / amitto Anchisen. hic me, pater optime, fessum / deseris, heu tantis nequiquam erepte periclis!* It is only after Vergil describes the burial of Anchises' remains

in Sicily does the reader realize that the whole time that Aeneas was living with Dido in Carthage in Book 4, Anchises' remains (*ossa*) were in an urn there, too. Vergil, however, does not specify where Anchises was cremated or where his cremated remains were kept while Aeneas was in Carthage. Thus Aeneas conveys Anchises for a second time, as he did from burning Troy, when he arrives in Sicily. As Anchises' remains are buried in a tumulus tomb, Aeneas says farewell with language that evokes an epitaph. Aeneas, however, emphasizes Anchises' failure to share in his own fated future rather than his life's accomplishments: *'salve, sancte parens, iterum: salvete recepti / nequiquam cineres animaeque umbraeque paternae. / non licuit finis Italos fataliaque arva / nec tecum Ausoniam, quicumque est, quaerere Thybrim'* (5.80–83). See Barchiesi 1986, 77–107 for Vergilian intertexts that inform the *Metamorphoses* as both points of contact and departure.

44. For textual markers other than cremations that affect a reading of Book 15, see Barchiesi 1997b, 181–208 for episodes such as the transformations of Hippolytus-Virbius and Cipus, and Asclepius' arrival in Rome and its relation to Augustus, that anticipate and relate to the ending of the poem; Hardie 1993, 6 for Cipus' transformation into a scapegoat to prevent becoming another Romulus; and Feeney 1991.

45. At *Met.* 14.820–28, Mars plucks Romulus up from the earth and his earthly body dissolves and is replaced by a divine form. Compare with Livy 1.16.4 and Ovid *Fasti* 2.491 ff, where Mars plucks Romulus during a tempest. Livy also relates a second version in which Romulus was murdered by senators during an assembly. For the apotheosis of Romulus, see Wiseman 1995; Fox 1996, 109–12; and Weinstock 1971, 347, 357.

46. According to Dio 41.14.3; 43.45.3, Caesar wore clothing that imitated Romulus' and had a statue of himself installed in the Temple of Romulus on the Quirinal Hill. Augustus' attempts to associate himself with Rome's legendary founder go further: according to Dio 53.16 he considered adopting the name Romulus (Suet. *Aug.* 7.2 reports that the actual proposal was made by unnamed supporters, although it is difficult not to see Augustus' involvement in such an important propaganda measure, but that Plancus' suggestion of Augustus was accepted as more honorable with religious implications). For further examples of Augustus' assimilation with Romulus and implications for his mausoleum, see Davies 2000a, 139–40.

47. Divine observance of human funeral ritual contrasts with emerging rituals of Julio-Claudians that advertised divine associations: at the funeral of Agrippa, Agrippa's sons (Augustus' adopted sons) did not wear black at the funeral games (Dio 55.8.5); at Augustus' funeral, Tiberius and Drusus did not dress in mourning to advertise that they were not touched by death and Tiberius asked the senate for absolution for having touched Augustus' corpse (Dio 56.31.3); Tiberius chided Germanicus for handling corpses following Roman defeat at Teutoburg (Tac. *Ann.* 1.62); and when delivering the oration at his son Drusus' funeral, Tiberius had his corpse veiled from his sight. Gaius, however, broke with with protocol when he dressed in mourning to accompany Tiberius' corpse to Rome from Misenum (Suet. *Gaius* 13).

48. See Gradel 2002, 54–72, and Weinstock 1971, 281–310 for detailed discussion of evidence for deification prior to Caesar's assassination. The actual moment of apotheosis is difficult to pinpoint: at time of death or cremation? See Davies 2000a, 10 for a discussion of cremation and apotheoses of emperors; Allara 1995, 69–79, in particular, p. 70 for a discussion on cremation as the moment that the soul definitively

left the body; Weinstock 1971, 356–63 for details surrounding Caesar's ascension. Suetonius, *Aug.* 100.4 reports that a witness to Augustus' cremation claimed that he saw a
likeness of the emperor rise to heaven: *Nec defuit vir praetorius, qui se effigiem cremati
euntem in caelum vidisse iuraret.* Suetonius does not give details surrounding the burning of Augustus' body, but he does give details of what happened after the cremation:
Augustus' cremation remains were collected by equestrians in ungirt tunics and placed
in his mausoleum. Augustus used his mausoleum for political purposes: Suetonius *Aug.*
101.3 reports that he banned his daughter and granddaughter Julia's corpses from his
mausoleum: *Julias filiam neptemque si quid iis accididisset, vetuit sepulcro suo inferri.*
See Davies 2000a, 102–19 for an extended discussion of the role played by Augustus'
mausoleum under successive emperors and the commemoration of empresses.

49. See Davies 2000a, 9–11 for a summary of typical elements of Imperial funerary
ritual; Boatwright 1985, 485–97 for the location of Hadrian's *ustrinum,* in particular,
p. 494 ff for ceremonies that accompanied Imperial cremations; Polfer 2000, 30–37 for
varying features of *ustrina* in the provinces; and Gualtieri 1982, 475–81 for an analysis
of pyre characteristics and ritual features of Lucanian funerary ritual. In what follows, I
follow Sumi 2005, 97–120, "Caesar ex Machina: Ceremony and Caesar's Memory" in
his analysis of the ancient sources (incl. Appian and Dio) concerning theatrical elements
in Caesar's funeral and Weinstock 1971, 346–55 for the chronology of events.

50. Portraits that pre- and postdate Caesar's apotheosis would have been visible in
the city at the same time, so contemporaries would have been constantly reminded of
his changed status from mortal to god and the rarity, historical and representational, of
such an apotheosis. Another change to occur is a kind of rejuvenation since postumous
images seem, generally, to be more youthful and idealized.

51. The statue is now in the Braccio Nuovo of the Vatican Museums. On the portraiture of Augustus, see Kleiner 1992, 61–72.

52. Wickkiser 1999, 113–42 discusses intertexts and argues against a heavily polemical reading of the *sphragis* and interprets the final lines as a positive statement that expresses Ovid's dependence on Augustus' success for the success of his own poetic fame.
For further discussion of Ovid's *sphragis,* see the discussion below about the ending of
Statius' *Thebaid.* See Erasmo 2006b, 369–77 for an analysis of Horace's transformation
into a swan (Ode 2.20) as a metapoetic statement on the immortality of his poetry and
its relation to earlier intertexts.

53. On the competiveness of Ovid's demarcation of his fame, see Wickkiser 1999,
136: "The precedent had been set by Vergil, yet Ovid placed himself rather than Augustus in the super-celestial realm."

54. Cited is the text of Owen 1980.

55. See Dufallo 2007, 125–26 for Ovid's exile as funeral procession.

Chapter 4

1. The tattoo and quote come from an article that appeared in The Associated
Press, April 11, 2007. Through the irony of Parsons's cremation recipe, however, one
can detect anxiety about his mortality which Parsons himself admits. "I'm not afraid of
death. I'm afraid of life," he said, "I'm afraid of living and not being able to take care
of myself."

2. All citations to Lucan's *De bello civili* refer to the Teubner edition of Shackleton Bailey, 1988. An earlier version of this section appeared as Erasmo 2005, 344–60, which focused on the audience's sympathy for Pompey which the text elicits through its repulsive narrative of the abuse of his corpse, from death to cremation.

3. See Mayer 1981, 172–73 for the washing of wounds with tears and absurd variations in Latin poetry.

4. For the irony of recognition through unrecognizable features, see Mayer 1981, 67: "One expects a headless body to be unrecognizable, hence Virgil's *sine nomine corpus;* but Lucan fancies that the loss of his head is the very thing that identifies Pompey." See also Hutchinson 1993, 318, n. 50.

5. Mayer 1981, 324 recognizes the sympathizing yet polarizing effect of the narrative: "Lucan seeks to move us, but also to repel, distance, and entertain."

6. *Aen.* 2.557–58: *iacet ingens litore truncus, / avulsumque umeris caput et sine nomine corpus.* On the parallels between the Lucan and Vergilian passages, see Narducci 1973, 317–25 and Hinds 1998, 8–10 for a discussion of the Priam/Pompey allusion in Vergil as a reflexive annotation of Vergil's own pre-Lucan borrowing from Roman history. Marpicati 1999, 191–202 considers Silius Italicus' polemical use of the intertext. For examples illustrating how the theme of the death and disfigurement of Pompey was moving to the Roman reader, Mayer 1981, 169 cites: Val. Max 1.8.9; *Aen.* 2. 557–58; Propertius 3.11.33–36; and Manilius 4.50 ff.

7. Compare 2.175–87 where M. Marius Gratidianus' corpse is cut up: *Vix erat ulla fides tam saevi erimus, unum / tot poenas cepisse caput.* See Morford 1996, 53 for a discussion on how Gratidianus' mutilated corpse (2.187–90) anticipates Pompey's corpse rolling on shore.

8. See Bartsch 1997, 91 ff; Leigh 1997 for extensive analyses of the two narrative voices of Lucan that express both cynicism and partisanship, and O'Hara 2007, 121–42 for a discussion of inconsistency in the epic as part of a wider narrative strategy in epic poetry.

9. Recent examinations of Book 8 focus on the poetic outbursts that frame descriptions of Pompey's killing and decapitation to provide an outlet for the reader to commiserate with the narrator. See Paratore 1982, 43–84 for an extended analysis of the death of Pompey, in particular, the role of digressions and the narrative role played by Cornelia; and Hutchinson 1993, especially 316 ff for an analysis of the relation between the poetic outbursts and narrative descriptions.

10. On the unifying theme of Pompey's burial, see Mayer 1981, 168: "But [Lucan] will go further and use burial as a linking theme, a structural device that binds together the closing scenes of the seventh, eighth, and ninth books." Lucan's use of death as a unifying theme between and within books is echoed in Tacitus' *Annales,* in particular in the narrative tension between the annalistic format and the thematic division of events. Descriptions of deaths, for example, coincide with the ending of books: Book 2 ends with the death of Germanicus, Book 11 with Messalina's execution, Book 12 with Claudius' murder; Book 14 opens with Agrippina's assassination and ends with the death of Octavia, and Book 15 ends with the executions and suicides of the Pisonian conspirators. On the dramatic effects of Tacitus' narrative arrangement of deaths, see Walker 1952, 35–49 and Mellor 1993, 118–22.

11. On the use of Pompey's death to frame the opening and closing of Book 9, Mayer 1981, 168: "Book IX opens with a calm and glorified Pompey, but closes with the mockery of an extravagent and useless burial of his embalmed head"; and Morford

1996, 14. Compare with Plutarch's *Life of Pompey* which opens with a description of the desecration of Pompey's father's corpse.

12. Mayer 1981, 169: "But as time passed, Pompey became less of a reality and more of a rhetorical *exemplum,* and Lucan has poured out his enthusiasm upon a *nominis umbra.*"

13. See Leigh 1997, chapter 7: "A View to a Kill: Lucan's Amphitheatrical Audience," 234–91, in particular 235 ff, for a discussion of the amphitheater as a metaphor for civil war.

14. Leigh 1997, 246, however, does not refer specifically to the decapitation of Pompey in Book 8: "The notion that Lucan makes accessible to his reader a mode of response to suffering akin to the sadistic disengagement of the amphitheatre is disturbing. In particular, it suggests a radical contrast to what is traditionally taken as the pathetic sensibility of Vergilian epic." See Leigh's analysis (247) of battle scenes in the *Aeneid* that questions Vergil's arousal of pathos and argues, instead, for a disengaged narrative. Most 1992, 391–419, examines the frequency and narrative emphasis of memberment in Neronian poetry. Varner 2003, 130–31 discusses the grotesque as a feature of daily life under Nero.

15. For further analysis of the decapitation as a moral act, see Mayer 1981, 162 and Hutchinson 1993, 320: "The first section of the account of the killing reduces emphasis on the actual stabbing, which appears in a subordinate clause (619 f): this subordination is both mannerist and expressive. What matters more than that action is Pompey's conquest of it. His covering of his head, seen as it were from without in Dio and Plutarch, in Lucan is intensely imagined from within: we feel Pompey's physical and mental apprehension and his victorious effort to prevail morally through his physical bearing."

16. Varner 2005, 67–82 analyzes the reciprocity between the mutilation of real bodies and the portraits of the condemned. For further analyses of the literary and archeological evidence for *damnatio memoriae,* see Davies 2000b, 27–44; Varner 2001, 45–64; and Varner 2004.

17. See Hardie 1993, 38 for an analysis of Achillas as substitute for Caesar.

18. At *Aen.* 12.915–17, Turnus reads the scene of his impending death more successfully: he is aware of the presence of the Rutulians and the city, but also of the absence of his chariot and Juturna.

19. For the narrative focus on Pompey's head, see Hutchinson 1993, 324: "The head itself is made the focus of Pompey's grandeur, of pathos, horror, and grotesqueness. This accumulation upon a single object serves expressive purposes; but it also emphasizes the multiplicity of tone, and creates strange effects."

20. Appropriately, Achillas is later killed as a sacrificial victim to Pompey (10.523–24) in an even more brief description.

21. Ironically, Pompey anticipates his decaptation: *spargent lacerentque licebit* (8.629).

22. See Hutchinson 1993, 321 for a discussion of how the narrative reflects Pompey's prolonged death, especially his comparison of Lucan's narrative with Tacitus' description of Seneca's suicide (*Ann.* 15.60.2–65), which is interrupted with the account of Paulina's attempted suicide and survival.

23. Hutchinson 1993, 323 *ad loc:* "But Lucan has such obvious pleasure in delaying the short, crucial, and improbably horrid *diu* 'for a long while,' that it is hard to be simply shocked."

24. On the jarring effect of citing unnamed witnesses in a narrative that projects immediacy, see Mayer 1981, 163: "It seems to be an apology or even guarantee for a statement that is 'strange but true.'"

25. See Hutchinson 1993, 322–23: "Pompey's actual death is hideously deferred: he has still not quite died when his head has been cut off and is being put on a stake. . . . The moment of death itself is left unstated; this is made more curious by the incidental description of the near-final stages in Pompey's impossibly extended decease (682f.)."

26. On the irony of Pompey's boast, see Bartsch 1997, 77.

27. Butrica 1993, 342–47 highlights Lucan's altering of historical fact, such as his placement of Pompey's murder on the shore rather than on a skiff.

28. For Claudius Quadrigarius' account, see Aul. Gell 9.13: *Ubi eum evertit, caput praecidit, torquem detraxit eamque sanguinulentam sibi in collum inponit. Quo ex facto ipse posterique eius Torquati sunt cognominati.* Claudius describes the beheading succinctly and the emphasis is on the torque rather than the beheading. Livy's narrative of the beheading, in imitation of Claudius, is equally terse, but it is preceded by more graphic language describing how Manlius stabs the Gaul in the stomach and the groin: *Iacentis inde corpus ab omni alia vexatione intactum uno torque spoliavit, quem respersum cruore collo cirumdedit suo.* Ed. Walters and Conway 1979).

29. Hardie 1986, 152: "For a Roman of the time of Augustus, it was certainly the wounded gladiator who provided the most accessible spectacle of death in arms, and there is a strong feeling of the gladiatorial about the death of Turnus: the sense that these two awesome warriors are fighting for their lives in total isolation, despite and because of the huge audience of spectators." More recently, Hardie 1993, 38 connects Pompey's death with the death of Turnus by pointing out similarities between Achillas and Achilles. See Leigh 1997, 236 ff for an analysis of the metaphor of the epic warrior to a gladiator, with reference to Hardie 1986, 152 ff on the duel in Livy between Torquatus and the Gaul and the duel between Aeneas and Turnus.

30. Turnus dies with an audience of Trojans, their allies, Rutulians, their allies and nature mourning his imminent death (12.928–29): *consurgunt gemitu Rutuli totusque remugit / mons circum et vocem late nemora alta remittunt.* Ed. Mynors 1990.

31. Mayer 1981, 164 discusses the pathos of Pompey dying in solitude without his last rites.

32. See Flower 1996, 91–127 for an analysis of the ancient evidence for the inclusion of *imagines* in funerary contexts.

33. Compare with Tacitus' description of the dying Tiberius: *iam Tiberium corpus, iam vires, nondum dissimulatio deserebat . . . (Ann.* 6.50.1). Ed. Fisher 1981, 210.

34. For the embalming of Poppaea's corpse, see Dio 62.27 and Tacitus, *Ann.* 16.6.1: *corpus non igni abolitum, ut Romanus mos, sed regum externorum consuetudine differtum odoribus conditur tumuloque Iuliorum infertur* (Fisher 1981, 383). Toynbee 1996, 41 discusses the rarity of embalming at Rome. Slater 1996, 33–40 analyzes the historiographic evidence and semiotic significance for Nero's wearing of a mask of his own and of the dead Poppaea while appearing on stage.

35. Mayer 1981, 665 *ad loc.* prefers the ms. reading of *iratum* over the common emendation of *placatam* and lists several passages dealing with fixed facial features in death: Diod. Sic. 17.58; Lucretius 3.654 ff.; Statius, *Theb.* 3.94; *Herc. Oet.* 1608, 1684, 1726.

36. For the features and prevalence of pauper burials in Rome and Italy, see Toynbee 1996, 101–3 and Bodel 1986, 38–54. Mayer 1981, 167–170 places Pompey's burial in the context of Latin poetry.

37. Plutarch, *Pompey* 80.1–4, claims Pompey was buried by his freedman (Philippus) and an old soldier who chanced by the corpse. Lucan, however, uses Cordus, a literary invention, to increase the pathos of the scene by having the accomplished and famous Pompey cremated and buried by a single figure to whom Lucan assigns the rank of quaestor. See Johnson 1987, 83–84 for Lucan's elaboration of the historical evidence and Thompson 1962, 339–55 for the significance of Cordus' rank, in particular how the rank of quaestor is to a general what a son is to his father.

38. On the anti-heroic sensibility when compared to tree fellings of Vergil (*Aen.* 6.179–82; 11.134–38) and Ennius (*Ann.* 6.1x, Skutsch), and Homer discussed above, see Mayer 1981, 169: "In fine, the expectation of a reader who is acquainted with traditional epic accounts is baulked at every point, and his pity should be awakened by the sense of contrast."

39. See Noy 2000, 186–96 for contexts in which a corpse may receive partial cremation due to time constraints in an attempt to disfigure a corpse to prevent its identification and mutilation. See, in particular, 190–191 for Cordus' cremation of Pompey and Lucan's knowledge of the mechanics of cremation.

40. It is ironic that earlier at 4.803–4, Caesar refuses to cremate the Pharsalus dead (Pompey's men) in a collective cremation.

41. Ovid, *Met.* 8.640–45:

> Baucis
> inque foco tepidum cinerem dimovit et ignes
> suscitat hesternos foliisque et cortice sicco
> nutrit et ad flammas anima producit anili
> multifidasque faces ramaliaque arida tecto
> detulit et minuit parvoque admovit aeno . . .

> Baucis
> scattered the warm ashes on the hearth and
> roused yesterday's fire and fed it with leaves
> and dry bark. She blew her old woman's breath
> toward the flames and took split wood and dry
> twigs down from the roof, broke them and placed
> them under her little pot.

42. Mayer 1981, 179 notes that *congesta . . . clausit humo* (788–89), is verbally echoed by Tacitus in describing Agrippina's burial at *Ann.* 14.9.2: *neque . . . congesta aut clausa humus.*

43. The same corruption of funerary ritual would again play itself out figuratively before Caesar's gaze: Plutarch records that Brutus' ashes were returned to his mother (*Brutus* 53.4.7), but his head was sent to Rome to be thrown at the base of Caesar's statue (Suet. *Aug.* 13).

44. By referring to Pompey's name on the epitaph as sacred (*sacrum . . . nomen,* 792),

Lucan suggests that this pauper burial should be treated as a shrine. See Bartsch 1997, 80 for the use of *sacer* and the author's growing adulation of Pompey and Johnson 1987, 81–82 for the irony of the epitaph.

45. See Mayer 1981, 167, 168 for the theme of Pompey's epitaph as the subject of a literary exercise in the *Anthologia Latina* and Martial 5.74.

46. Text of Fisher 1981, 377–78. See Tucker 1987, 330–37 and Hutchinson 1993, 314, n. 44 for the historical context of Lucan's death and the historicity of Tacitus' passage: "One might best see defiance of the suppressor of his poetry, and a certain magnificent frivolity." Furneaux 1907, repr. 1974, 408 discusses the conjecture that the passage in question was from *Phars.* 3.635–46 which describes a character bleeding to death. There is no evidence to connect this passage with Tacitus' account.

47. Suetonius, *De poetis* 31.31–34: *Codicillos ad patrem de corrigendis quibusdam versibus suis exaravit, epulatusque largiter brachia ad secandas venas medico praebuit.*

48. On the complexity and intertextuality of Statius' narrative, see Coleman 2003, 9–23, especially 15–23; Hinds 1998, in particular, 135–44 for a discussion of Ovidian intertexts in Statius' *Achilleid* which is relevant to my discussion of Ovidian allusions in the *Thebaid;* Hutchinson 1993, 73–76; Hardie 1990: 3–20; and Williams 1978, 254–61. My focus is on the first half of Book 6; for Statius' use of intertexts and intratexts in the second half of Book 6; see Lovatt 2005.

49. See Smolenaars 1994, xxvii–xxviii for Statius' supplementing of primary intertexts with secondary intertexts.

50. At 5.313–19, Hypsipyle builds a sham pyre in her courtyard for her father Thoas, whom she rescued from the Lemnian women's slaughter of all male inhabitants on Lemnos, to avoid detection of her plot. When the other women discovered that Thoas was still alive and ruling on the island of Chios (5.486ff), Hypsipyle fled Lemnos and was brought to Thebes by pirates. For inter- and intratextual narrative analyses of Hypsipyle's sham pyre, see Pagán 2000, 436–38; Nugent 1996, 46–71; Vessey 1970, 44–54.

51. Cited is the text of Shackleton Bailey 2003.

52. See Lesueur 1991, 144, n. 4 for his observation of the increasing value of the objects as their levels rise and for a parallel description of sacrificial offerings at Statius, *Silvae* 2.1.157–62.

53. At Cat. 64.251, *parte ex alia* signals a narrative shift from the description of Theseus' return to Athens after killing the Minotaur and Bacchus' discovery of Ariadne on Naxos. Statius alludes to both epics: Vergil for thematic similarity of the descriptions of two pyres and Catullus for narrative shift signaled by the refocusing of the reader's narrative gaze. See Hinds 1998, 125–26 for Statius' allusion to Catullus 64 in his *Achilleid* as a mythological source and as a work of poetry.

54. See Lesueur 1991, 146, n. 14 for echoes from *Aeneid* 11.152, Evander's lament for Pallas; 11.45 Aeneas' lament for Pallas; and Catullus 64.139 from Ariadne's complaint of Theseus to which can be added Ennius, *Annales* 51. Another Vergilian allusion in Eurydice's speech occurs at line 6.159 which echoes *Aen.* 11.164.

55. Text of Fitch 2004.

56. For the significance of circumbulation in funerary rituals, see Davies 2000a, 125–28, in particular for analysis of the frieze decoration of Trajan's Column which turned the act of viewing into a simultaneous act of commemoration.

57. See Pollman 2004, 44–48 for Argia as a new epic paradigm.

58. For the contrast between Hypsipyle and Argia and Antigone, see Pagán 2000, 436–38.

59. For the moral imperative to bury the dead in the *Thebaid,* see Pollmann 2004, 32–36.

60. For intertextuality with literary precursors, see Pollmann 2004, 53–57.

61. Pollmann 2004, 103–4; 136 argues for a reference to the uncremated dead (here and at 12.191–93).

62. See Pollmann 2004, 189–90 for poetic intertexts to divided smoke and flames, esp. Silius, *Punica,* 16.533–48 and 12.440–41: *cernisne ut flamma recedat / concurratque tamen? vivunt odia improbia, vivunt* and Hardie 1993, 45–46 for the continuation of the brothers' mutual enmity through their embodiment of the Furies.

63. Like Sophocles, Statius uses death ritual to highlight the tyrannical personality of Creon in his denial of a universally held ritual. See Pollmann 2004, 35–36 for an extended discussion of the traits of Creon's tyranny.

64. On recent interpretations of the poem's ending, in particular how Book 12 relates to the *Aeneid* and to the *Thebaid* as a whole, see Pollmann 2004, 53–57; Coleman 2003, 21–22; Pagán 2000, 423–52 considers the ending from the perspective of "aftermath narrative"; Hardie 1997, 139–62, especially 151–56; Braund 1996, 1–23, esp. 16–18 for an analysis of the poem's ending as a series of supplemental readings after line 781; and Hardie 1993, 48.

65. For Statius' allusion to poetic intertexts, see Pollmann 2004, 280 for Statius' allusion to the end of the *Georgics;* Hardie 1997, 156–58 for a discussion of Ovid and Ennius as intertexts that provides more closure to the *Thebaid* than does the *Aeneid;* Braund 1996, 7–8; Dominik 1994, 174; and Henderson 1991, 30–80 for intertextuality with Horace and Ovid.

66. See Hinds 1998, 91–98 for Statius' authorial claims of inferiority, especially to Vergil, and textual markers that should make the reader hesitate before accepting them.

67. See Pollmann 2004, 288 for a discussion with recent bibliographical references.

68. Cited is the text of Shackleton Bailey 2003. For Statius' use of death/death ritual to express his literary debt to Lucan, see Malamud 1995, 1–30.

69. Vergil's first attested literary work was a mock epitaph of the schoolmaster Ballista (Suet. *Vita* 17), thus the composition of his own epitaph provides a nice ring composition to his poetic career: *Monte sub hoc lapidum tegitur Ballista sepultus: / nocte die tutum carpe, viator, iter.*

70. Aulus Gellius, who preserves the epigrams of Naevius, Plautus, and Pacuvius, states that they were recorded on epitaphs: *trium poetarum inlustrium epigrammata, quae ipsi fecerunt et incidenda sepulchro suo reliquerunt . . . (N.A.* 1.24). The names of these poets appeared on their tombs with various literary intertexts:

Naevius:
Inmortales mortales si foret fas flere,
flerent divae Camenae Naevium poetam.
itaque postquam est Orchi traditus thesauro,
obliti sunt Romae loquier lingua Latina.

Plautus:

Postquam est mortem aptus Plautus, Comoedia luget
scaena [est] deserta; dein Risus Ludus Iocusque
et Numeri innumeri simul omnes conlacrimarunt.

Pacuvius:
Adulescens, tametsi properas, hoc te saxulum
rogat ut se aspicias, deinde quod scriptum est legas.
hic sunt poetae Pacuvi Marci sita
ossa. hoc volebam nescius ne esses. vale.

Text of Courtney 1993, 47. Pacuvius' epitaph was imitated in the inscription of the tomb of L. Maecius Philotimus (*CIL* 1, 2.1209). Massaro 1992, 12–18 discusses Pacuvius' epitaph in relation to Philotimus' and other actual epitaphs. Ennius' epitaph was placed on his statue which was located in the Tomb of the Scipios: *aspicite, o cives, senis Enni imaginis formam. / hic vestrum panxit maxima facta patrum.* The epitaph of Callimachus (*Epigram* 23) combines a record of his poetic accomplishments and the Muses' benevolence—a combination which would influence the epitaphs of Roman poets.

71. Not only does Augustus pay tribute to Alexander the Great, but he also "resurrects" and "reburies" Alexander who had been taken out of his tomb for Augustus' inspection, thus giving him power over the living and the dead. By adding control of the underworld to his control of land and the sea, Augustus embodies the powers of Pluto, Jupiter, and Neptune.

Chapter 5

1. Cited is the text of Rolfe 2001, 170. For interpretations of the quote, see Gyles 1962, 193–200 and Frazer 1966, 17–20. Unfortunately, the narrative of Tacitus' *Annales* breaks off during the events of 66 CE and there is no description of his burial in Dio. See Davies 2000a, 19 for details surrounding the disposal of Caligula's half-burnt remains and the burial of Nero's ashes.

2. The word that Suetonius uses to describe the pit (*scrobem*), normally refers to a hole dug in the ground for the planting of trees and, less commonly, for descriptions of a pit in which to bury the dead (*OLD,* 1712). Tacitus is the only other historian who uses the word: at *Ann.* 1.61 for Germanicus' inspection of the remains of slaughtered soldiers at the scene of Varus' defeat and *Ann.* 15.67 where a pit is dug to receive the beheaded corpse of Subrius Flavus, who was executed for the role he played in the Pisonian conspiracy. For an analysis of *Ann.* 1.61, see Pagán 2000, 428–30 within the literary tradition of post-battle narratives and Woodman 1979, 143–55; Williams 1978, 254–61 for intertextual and post-Vergilian narrative features.

3. See McWilliam 2001, 74–98 and Carroll 2006, 48–53 on the public nature of Roman funerary monuments.

4. Plutarch, *Sulla* 38.4.

5. Ed. Radice 1972, 100.

6. See Kleiner 1987, 23–24 for commemorative altars (*cippi*) that formed part of the tomb complexes that lined the roads leading out of Rome.

7. Cicero, in the *In Pisonem* (7.16), mentions the *coniuratorum manes mortuorum.*

8. *Pro Caelio* 14.34. Appius' speech is actually a rhetorical figure called, *prosopopoeia,* which is an imagined speech of a person "in character." For an extended analysis of death ritual in Ciceronian oratory, see Dufallo 2007, chapters 1–3.

9. See Koortbojian 1996, 231–32 for the viewing of the "street of tombs" as a cumulative experience.

10. Ed. Kent 1967, 216. Aicher 2004, xvii–xviii situates memorials in a broad architectural context: "What Varro stresses here is the importance of public architecture in its capacity to provoke memory, to occasion the exchange between past and present that was such a pressing concern for the Romans. It is interesting that Varro identifies tomb structures as the word's original sense; then, as now, the primary function of tomb architecture is to remind, as our noun "memorial" stresses in a nice parallel to the Latin etymologies. But for the Latin speaker, the same word for a tomb memorial extends to other public architecture as well, defining their essential function as "memorials" of the past, even if, as is often the case, the dominant daily use of a structure—as an archive or treasury, for instance—tends to obscure this function."

11. For a discussion of 'speaking images,' see Koortbojian 1996, 233.

12. See Kleiner 1987, 33–34 for characteristics of portraits on the main body of an altar that are placed in a window-like frame and 138–39 for an analysis of Cornelia Glyce's funeral altar.

13. For the terms limited and limitive, see Fowler 2000, chapter 9, "The Ruin of Time: Monuments and Survival at Rome," 193–217.

14. Cited is the text of Clausen 1992, 126

15. See Huskinson 1998, 129–58 for a discussion of interpretive strategies occasioned by portrait heads that were perhaps left intentionally unfinished.

16. See Massaro 1992, 78–114 for an extensive analysis of Claudia's epitaph.

17. Lattimore 1962, 230–37 collects Greek and Latin examples of epitaphs addressed to a wayfarer.

18. See Lattimore 1962, 270–72; Courtney 1995, 40–43, 216–29; Flower 1996, 166–80; Petrucci 1998, 15–16; Goldberg 1995, chapter 3, "Saturnian Aesthetics," 58–82, especially 62–64 for versification of the Scipio texts; and Erasmo 2004b, 69–72. Coarelli 1996, 217–32 argues against three phases of inscription on Barbatus' sarcophagus (and two for his son) based on letter forms.

19. Courtney 1995, 178–79, 389–90: Epitaph 188 = *CIL* 6.13528.

20. Courtney 1995, 180–81, 393: Epitaph 191 for his commentary on the epitaph.

21. Ed. Courtney 1995 Epitaph 187: 176–77 = *CIL* 6.25063. See 387–88 for Courtney's commentary which focuses on the grammar and mythological allusions.

22. Cicero, *Ad Att.* 12.18.1. Cited is the text of Shackleton Bailey 1999, 286.

23. For the mythological portraiture of Imperial women and those imitating them, based on Venus statue types, including the Venus of Capua (best represented by a statue in the Naples Archeological Museum), see Bieber 1977, 43–58 and 65–66 for portraits based on the Capitoline Venus type in particular and D'Ambra 1996, 219–32. For mythological portraiture of imperial women, wealthy women, and the imitation of the mythological portraiture of imperial women by freedwomen in their funerary portrait reliefs, see Werde 1981; Kleiner 1981, 512–44; Kleiner 1987, 83, 85; Kleiner 1992, 75–78, "Female Portraiture in the Age of Augustus"; 177–79, "Flavian Female Portraiture"; 277–80, "Female Portraiture under the Antonines—the Faustinas," in particular 280 for a discussion of three statuary groups based on the Venus of Capua

and Ares Borghese types; 280–283, "Private Portraiture under the Antonines" for the funeral portrait reliefs of freedwomen who imitated the mythological portraiture of women in the imperial circle,"as a form of private deification in funerary contexts," 281.

24. See D'Ambra 2000, 101–14, in particular 105–6 for an extended analysis of this portrait which dates from 100–120 CE. D'Ambra's description of the effect of her pose, "The pose [. . .] asserts a sense of self-possession and, perhaps, self-consciousness," 106, restores animation to the portrait which would have been even more effective, perhaps even disarming, in her original funerary context.

25. When looking at the large number of headless portraits of Venus in museums, I wonder if they, too, had a funereal context now difficult to recover. Were "Roman" heads removed intentionally from statues, rather than broken off accidentally through a fall, to negate the original funereal context (location and portrait head of the deceased) by a collector of art, whether in antiquity or the renaissance who preferred a headless portrait of Venus to statues like the Flavian woman as Venus in the Capitoline Museums?

26. The trope of including epitaphs within a poem is mocked by Ovid in *Amores* 2.6 in which he describes the death of Corinna's parrot. The poem ends with an imagined epitaph on the bird's tomb: *Colligor ex ipso dominae placuisse sepulchro: / ora fuere mihi plus ave docta loqui.* Catullus 3 does not contain an epitaph; therefore, it is an epicede only.

27. See Massaro 1992, 38–50 for a discussion, with examples, of the metrical features of elegiac epitaphs in the late Republic.

28. All citations to Propertius refer to the text of Barber 1990.

29. Ed. Green 1999, 75.

30. See Elsner 1998, 71–99 for an analysis of the Christian burial monuments and the reading strategy necessary for understanding the emerging Christian iconography of the fourth century CE.

31. The dirges in the *Iliad* following the death of Hector illustrate the early and far-reaching influence of the epicede genre in Greek and Latin literature.

32. For the relative dating of the two poetic works and a discussion of recent bibliography of the *Parentalia,* see Green 1991, 298–300. For a more recent examination of the *Parentalia,* see Lolli 1997.

33. Following the *Parentalia,* Ovid describes the festival of the *Caristia Comitialis* (2.617–38), in which the living turn from commemoration of their dead relatives to appreciation of their living relatives. See Littlewood 2001, 916–35 for Ovid's manipulation of Roman funerary ritual to include Remus within the foundation legend of Rome without compromising Romulus.

34. Cited is the text of Alton, Wormell, and Courtney 1985, 42–43. For recent bibliography on the narrative features of the *Fasti,* see Herbert-Brown 2002; Barchiesi 2001; Barchiesi 1997b and Miller 1991.

35. See Feeney 1998, 132–33 for his discussion on multiple aitiologies of Roman ritual in the *Fasti.*

36. See Lolli 1997, 22–25 for a discussion of the ordering of the poems.

37. This and future citations to the *Parentalia* refer to the text of Green 1999. See Green 1991, 302–3 and Lolli 1997, 60–65 for a commentary on the poem.

38. For an analysis of this poem, see Green 1991, 306–9 and Lolli 1997, 86–93.

39. See Green 1991, 312–14 for his commentary, in particular, Vergilian intertexts of lines 7–9 with Dido (*Aen.* 4.17, *deceptam* by the death of her husband) and line 24 with Vergil's apostrophe to the dead Pallas (*Aen.* 10.507), and Lolli 1997, 124–30.

40. For an analysis of Eliot's poem and an analysis of common themes and narrative elements of elegy, see Schenck's introduction, "Every Poem an Epitaph" 1988, 1–18.

41. Ed. Shackleton Bailey 1988, 51–52.

42. For a detailed study of the poem, see Warden 1980; the commentary of Camps 1965, 114–25; Johnson 1997, 163–80; Dufallo and McCracken 2006, for an extended analysis of Propertius 4.7; and Dufallo 2007, 7–8 for a discussion of *prosopopoeia,* an author's assumption of the dead's identity, and 74–98 for an analysis of this poem and Augustan elegy as examples of "restored behavior." For the ancient belief in ghosts and ghost story narratives, see Felton 1999.

43. My analysis of the poem benefited from the commentary of Camps 1965, 153–67; Johnson 1997, 163–80; and Dufallo 2007, 74–98. In 2.34.89–90, Propertius mentions that Licinius Calvus wrote an elegy on the death of Quintilia, but it is unclear whether Calvus' elegy was written as an imaginary dialogue with the dead Quintilia. Calvus' elegy is also mentioned at Catullus 96.

44. For the text of this poem, see Enright, ed. 1983, 120–21. This poem also appears in an adapted form as a ballad under the title, "How Cold the Wind Doth Blow."

45. Cited here and the following passages is the text of Barber 1990.

46. An earlier section of the narrative (4.11.13: *non minus immitis habuit Cornelia Parcas*) alludes to *Aen.* 12.150: *Parcarumque dies et vis inimica propinquat.* See Massaro 1992, 171–72 for a discussion of a similar line in the late Republican epitaph of the freedwoman Eucharis Licinia: *infstae Parcae deposuerunt carmine* and 147–48 for a discussion of epitaphs that contain references to the poetry of Ovid.

47. I cite the text of Courtney 1993, 40–42. Ennius modeled his *Elogium* after Alcaeus of Messene's epigram in praise of Philip V of Macedon (*AP* 5.518).

48. Silius Italicus, *Punica: at quis aetherii servatur seminis ortus / caeli porta patet* (15.78–9). The tomb of Vettius Agorius Praetextatus (*CLE* 111.19) adapts Ennius' epigram: *cura sofarum, porta quis caeli patet.* See Courtney 1993, 41–42, and Skutsch 1985, 147–48.

49. The larger-than-life appearance echoes the description of Creusa: *nota maior imago* (*Aen.* 2.773) and recalls Cicero's description of Africanus' ghost (*Rep.* 6.9–26): *Africanus se ostendit ea forma, quae mihi ex imagine eius quam ex ipso erat notior; quem ubi agnovi, equidem cohorrui [. . .] .* The description of Nepos' eyes: *ardentis oculorum orbes* (13) quote the actual words used to describe Turnus' eyes: *ardentis oculorum orbes* (*Aen.* 12.670).

50. Courtney 1995: 170–173; 381–384: Epitaph 183 = *CIL* 6.21521. For a detailed analysis of poetic intertexts, see Bömer 1982–1984: 275–281 and Lissberger 1934: 97–98 for literary intertexts.

WORKS CITED

Ahlberg, A. W., ed. 1991. *C. Sallusti Crispi Catilina Iugurtha Fragmenta Ampliora.* Leipzig.

Aicher, Peter J. 2004. *Rome Alive: A Source-Guide to the Ancient City.* Vol. 1. Wauconda, IL.

Allara, A. 1995. "*Corpus et cadaver,* la 'gestation' d'un nouveau corps." In F. Hinard, ed. *La mort au quotidien dans le monde romain,* 69–79. Paris.

Alton, E. H., D. E. W. Wormell, and E. Courtney. 1985. *P. Ovidi Nasonis Fastorum Libri Sex.* Leipzig.

Anderson, W. S. 1969. *The Art of the Aeneid.* Englewood Cliffs, NJ.

Arce, J. 1988. *Funus imperatorum: los funerales de los emperadores romanos.* Madrid.

Austin, R. G. 1977. *P. Vergili Maronis Aeneidos Liber Sextus.* Oxford.

Avallone, Riccardo. 1945. *Mecenate. I frammenti.* Salerno.

———. 1962. *Mecenate.* Napoli.

Bakhtin, M. M. 1981. *The Dialogic Imagination: Four Essays.* Edited by Michael Holquist. Austin.

Barber, E. A. 1990. *Sexti Properti Carmina.* Oxford.

Barchiesi, Alessandro. 1986. "Problemi d'interpretazione in Ovidio: continuità delle storie, continuazione dei testi." *MD* 16: 77–107.

———. 1997a. *The Poet and the Prince.* Berkeley and Los Angeles.

———. 1997b. "Endgames: Ovid's Metamorphoses 15 and Fasti 16." In Deborah H. Roberts, Francis M. Dunn, and Don Fowler, eds., *Classical Closure. Reading the End in Greek and Latin Literature,* 181–208. Princeton, NJ.

———. 2001. *Speaking Volumes. Narrative and intertext in Ovid and Other Latin Poets.* London.

Bartsch, Shadi. 1994. *Actors in the Audience: Theatricality and Doublespeak from Nero to Hadrian.* Cambridge, MA.

———. 1997. *Ideology in Cold Blood: A Reading of Lucan's Civil War.* Cambridge, MA.

Beacham, Richard C. 1999. *Spectacle Entertainments of Early Imperial Rome.* New Haven.

Becker, Marshall Joseph. 1987. "The Contents of Funerary Vessels as Clues to Mortuary Customs: Identifying the *Os Exceptum.*" In *Proceedings of the 3rd Symposium on Ancient Greek Art and Related Pottery,* 25–32. Copenhagen.

Bell, Malcolm, III. 1998. In Cima and La Rocca, eds., 295–314.

Bergmann, Bettina, and Christine Kondoleon, eds. 1999. *The Art of Ancient Spectacle.* New Haven.

Bieber, Margarete. 1961. *The History of the Greek and Roman Theater.* Princeton, NJ.

———. 1977. *Ancient Copies: Contributions to the History of Greek and Roman Art.* New York.

Boatwright, Mary T. 1985. "'The *Ara-Ditis-Ustrinum* of Hadrian' in the Western Campus Martius and Other Problematic Roman *Ustrina.*" *AJA* 89: 485–97.

Bodel, J. 1986. "Groves and Graveyards: A Study of the *Lex Lucerina.*" *AJAH* 11: 38–54.

———. 1999. "Death on Display: Looking at Roman Funerals." In Bettina Bergmann and Christine Kondoleon, eds., 259–81. New Haven.

———. 2000. "Dealing with the Dead: Undertakers, Executioners and Potter's Fields in Ancient Rome." In Valerie M. Hope and Eireann Marshall, eds., *Death and Disease in the Ancient City,* 128–51. London and New York.

———. 2001. "Epigraphy and the Ancient Historian." In John Bodel, ed., *Epigraphic Evidence: Ancient History from Inscriptions,* 1–72. London.

Bömer, F. 1982–1984. "Der Klassiker Ovid. Bermerkungen zu CE 1109." *Acta Antiqua Academiae Scientiarum Hungaricae* 30: 275–81.

Boyle, A. J., ed. 1990. *The Imperial Muse: Flavian Epicists to Claudian.* Bendigo.

———. 1994. *Seneca's Troades: Introduction, Text, Translation and Commentary.* Leeds.

———. 1997. *Tragic Seneca. An Essay in the Theatrical Tradition.* London and New York.

———. 2006. *Roman Tragedy.* London and New York.

Braund, Susanna Morton. 1996. "Ending Epic: Statius, Theseus and a Merciful Release." *PCPS* 42: 1–23.

Butrica, J. L. 1993. "Propertius 3.11.33–38 and the Death of Pompey." *CQ* 43.1: 342–47.

Camps, W. A. 1965. *Propertius: Elegies Book IV.* Cambridge.

———. 1967. *Propertius: Elegies Book II.* Cambridge.

Carroll, Maureen. 2006. *Spirits of the Dead: Roman Funerary Commemoration in Western Europe.* Oxford.

Cary, Ernest. 1982. *Dio's Roman History.* Vol. 7. Cambridge, MA and London.

CIL. *Corpus Inscriptionum Latinarum.* Berlin, 1863–present.

Cima, Maddalena, and Eugenio La Rocca, eds. 1998. *Horti Romani: Atti del Convegno Internazionale Roma, 4–6 maggio 1995,* Bulletino Della Commissione Archeologica Communale di Roma. Rome.

Clausen, W. V. 1992. *A Persi Flacci et D. Iuni Iuvenalis Saturae.* Oxford.

Coarelli, Filippo. 1996. *Revixit Ars: Arte e ideologia a Roma. Dai módelli ellenistici alla tradizione republicana.* Rome.

Coffey, Michael, and Roland Mayer. 1997. *Seneca Phaedra.* Cambridge.

Coleman, Kathleen M. 1990. "Fatal Charades: Roman Executions Staged as Mythological Enactments." *JRS* 80: 44–73.

———. 2003. "Recent Scholarship on the Epics." In D. R. Shackleton Bailey, ed., *Statius Thebaid, Books 1–7,* 9–29. Cambridge, MA and London.

Conte, Gian Biago. 1996. *The Hidden Author: An Interpretation of Petronius' Satyricon.* Translated by Elaine Fantham. Berkeley and Los Angeles.

————. 2007. *The Poetry of Pathos. Studies in Virgilian Epic.* Oxford.

Cooley, Alison E., ed. 2000. *The Epigraphic Landscape of Roman Italy.* London.

————. 2000. *The Afterlife of Inscriptions.* London.

Corbeill, Anthony. 2004. *Nature Embodied: Gesture in Ancient Rome.* Princeton, NJ.

Courtney, Edward. 1993. *The Fragmentary Latin Poets.* Oxford.

———— 1995. *Musa Lapidaria. A Selection of Latin Verse Inscriptions.* Atlanta.

———— 2001. *A Companion to Petronius.* Oxford.

Cumont, F. 1949. *Lux Perpetua.* Paris.

D'Ambra, Eve. 1996. "The Calculus of Venus: Nude Portraits of Roman Matrons." In Natalie Boymel Kampen, ed., *Sexuality in Ancient Art: Near East, Egypt, Greece, and Italy,* 219–32. Cambridge.

————. 2000. "Nudity and Adornment in Female Portrait Sculpture of the Second Century AD." In Diana E. E. Kleiner and Susan B. Matheson, eds., *I Claudia II: Women in Roman Art and Society,* 101–14. New Haven.

Davies, Penelope J. E. 2000a. *Death and the Emperor. Roman Imperial Funerary Monuments from Augustus to Marcus Aurelius.* Cambridge.

————. 2000b. "'What Worse Than Nero, What Better Than His Baths?' *Damnatio Memoriae* and Roman Architecture." In Varner a, 27–44.

Dixon, Susan, ed. 1992. *The Roman Family.* Baltimore.

Dixon, Suzanne, ed. 2001. *Childhood, Class, and Kin in the Roman World.* London and New York.

Dixon Hunt, John. 1992. *Gardens and the Picturesque. Studies in the History of Landscape Architecture.* Cambridge, MA and London.

Dominik, W. 1994. *The Mythic Voice of Statius: Power and Politics in the Thebaid.* Leiden.

Duff, J. D. 1968. *Silius Italicus Punica.* Cambridge, MA and London.

Dufallo, Basil, and Peggy McCracken, eds. 2006. *Dead Lovers: Erotic Bonds and the Study of Premodern Europe.* Ann Arbor.

Dufallo, Basil. 2007. *The Ghosts of the Past: Latin Literature, the Dead, and Rome's Transition to a Principate.* Columbus, OH.

Dupont, Florence. 1985. *L'Acteur-roi ou le théâtre dans la Rome antique.* Paris.

Dyck, Andrew R. 2004. *A Commentary on Cicero, De Legibus.* Ann Arbor.

Eden, P. T. 1984. *Seneca Apocolocyntosis.* Cambridge.

Edwards, Catharine. 1996. *Writing Rome. Textual Approaches to the City.* Cambridge.

————. 2005. "Archetypically Roman? Representing Seneca's Ageing Body." In Andrew Hopkins and Maria Wyke, eds., *Roman Bodies. Antiquity to the Eighteenth Century,* 13–22. London.

————. 2007. *Death in Ancient Rome.* New Haven and London.

Elsner, Jaś, and Jamie Masters, eds. 1994. *Reflections of Nero: Culture, History, and Representation.* Chapel Hill and London.

Elsner, Jaś, ed. 1996. *Art and Text in Roman Culture.* Cambridge.

————. 1998. *Imperial Rome and Christian Triumph. The Art of the Roman Empire AD 100–450.* Oxford.

Enright, D. J. 1983. *The Oxford Book of the Death.* Oxford.

Erasmo, Mario. 2001. "Among the Dead in Ancient Rome." *Mortality* 6.1: 31–43.

————. 2004a. *Roman Tragedy: Theatre to Theatricality.* Austin.

————. 2004b. *Archaic Latin Verse.* Newburyport.

————. 2005. "Mourning Pompey: Lucan and the Poetics of Death Ritual." *Studies in Latin Literature and Roman History: Collection Latomus 12*. Vol. 287: 344–60.

————. 2006a. "Enticing Tantalus in Seneca's *Thyestes*." *MD* 56: 185–98.

————. 2006b. "Birds of a Feather?" *Latomus* 65.2: 369–77.

Estiez. O. 1995. "La *translatio cadaveris*. Le transport des corps dans l'antiquité romaine." In F. Hinard, ed., *La mort au quotidien dans le monde romain*, 101–8. Paris.

Eussner, Adam. 1908. *C. Sallusti Crispi Catilina Iurgurtha Ex Historiis Orationes et Epistulae*. Leipzig.

Fantham, Elaine. 1982. *Seneca's Troades*. Princeton, NJ.

Feeney, Denis. 1986. "History and Revelation in Vergil's Underworld." *PCPhS* 32: 1–24.

————. 1991. *The Gods in Epic: Poets and Critics of the Classical Tradition*. Oxford.

————. 1998. *Literature and Religion at Rome: Cultures, Contexts, and Beliefs*. Cambridge.

Felton, D. 1999. *Haunted Greece and Rome: Ghost Stories from Classical Antiquity*. Austin.

Fisher, C. D. 1981. *Cornelii Taciti Annalium ab Excessu Divi Augusti Libri*. Oxford.

Fishwick, Duncan. 1991. *The Imperial Cult in the Latin West*. Leiden.

Fitch, John G. 2002. *Seneca Tragedies VIII*. Cambridge, MA and London.

————. 2004. *Seneca Tragedies IX*. Cambridge, MA and London.

————, and S. McElduff. 2002. "Construction of the Self in Senecan Drama. *Mnemosyne* 55: 18–40.

Flower, Harriet I. 1995. "*Fabulae Praetextae* in Context: When Were Plays on Contemporary Subjects Performed in Republican Rome?" *CQ* 45: 170–90.

————. 1996. *Ancestor Masks and Aristocratic Power in Roman Culture*. Oxford.

————. 2000. "*Damnatio Memoriae* and Epigraphy." In Varner a, 58–69.

Fowler, Don. 2000. *Roman Constructions. Readings in Postmodern Latin*. Oxford.

Fox, Matthew. 1996. *Roman Historical Myths. The Regal Period in Augustan Literature*. Oxford.

Frazer, R. M., Jr. 1966. "Nero the Artist-Criminal." *CJ* 62: 17–20.

Furneaux, Henry. 1974. *The Annals of Tacitus*. Oxford.

Garland, B. 1985. *The Greek Way of Death*. Ithaca, NY.

Goddard, Justin. 1994. "The Tyrant at Table." In Jaś Elsner and Jamie Masters, eds., *Reflections of Nero: Culture, History, and Representation*, 67–82. Chapel Hill and London.

Goldberg, Sander M. 1995. *Epic in Republican Rome*. New York and Oxford.

Goold, G. P. 1990. *Propertius Elegies*. Cambridge, MA.

Gowers, E. 1994. "Persius and the decoction of Nero." In Elsner and Masters, eds., 131–50.

Gradel, Ittai. 2002. *Emperor Worship and Roman Religion*. Oxford.

Gransden, K. W. 1991. *Virgil Aeneid Book XI*. Cambridge.

Gregori, G. L. 1987–1988. "Horti sepulcrales e cepotaphia nell inscrizioni urbane." *Bcomm* 92: 175–88.

Gregory, A. P. 1994. "'Powerful Images:' Responses to Portraits and the Political Uses of Images in Rome." *JRA* 7: 80–99.

Green, R. P. H. 1991. *The Works of Ausonius. Edited with Introduction and Commentary*. Oxford.

————. 1999. *Decimi Magni Ausonii Opera*. Oxford.

Griffin, M. 1976. *Seneca: A Philosopher in Politics*. Oxford.

Grottanelli, Cristiano. 1995. "Wine and Death—East and West." In Oswyn Murray and Manuela Tecuşan, eds., *In Vino Veritas*. London.

Grummere, Richard M. 1979. *Seneca IV: Ad Lucilium Epistulae Morales*. Cambridge, MA and London.

Gualtieri, Maurizio. 1982. "Cremation among the Lucanians." *AJA* 86: 475–81.

Gyles, M. F. 1962. "Nero: *Qualis Artifex?*" *CJ* 57: 193–200.

Habinek. T. N. 2005. *The World of Roman Song: From Ritualized Speech to Social Order*. Baltimore.

Hanson, J. A. 1959. *Roman Theater-Temples*. Princeton, NJ.

Hardie, Philip. 1986. *Virgil's Aeneid: Cosmos and Imperium*. Oxford.

————. 1990. "Flavian Epicists on Virgil's Epic Technique." In A. J. Boyle, ed., *The Imperial Muse. Ramus Essays on Roman Literature of the Empire: Flavian Epicists to Claudian*, 3–20. Bendigo.

————. 1993. *The Epic Successors of Virgil. A Study in the Dynamics of a Tradition*. Cambridge.

————. 1997. "Closure in Latin Epic." In Roberts, Dunn, and Fowler, eds., 139–162.

Harrison, George W. M., ed. 2003. *Seneca in Performance*. London.

Harrison, Robert Pogue. 2003. *The Dominion of the Dead*. Chicago and London.

Henderson, J. 1991. "Statius' *Thebaid* / Form premade." *PCPS* 37: 30–80.

Herbert-Brown, Geraldine, ed. 2002. *Ovid's Fasti. Historical Readings at Its Bimillenium*. London.

Hexter, Ralph, and Daniel Selden, eds. 1992. *Innovations of Antiquity*. New York.

Hinard, F., ed. 1995. *La mort au quotidien dans le monde romain*. Paris.

Hinds, Stephen. 1998. *Allusion and Intertext. Dynamics of Appropriation in Roman Poetry*. Cambridge.

Holt, Philip. 1992. "Ajax's Burial in Early Greek Epic." *AJP* 113: 319–31.

Hope, Valerie M. 2000. "Contempt and Respect: the Treatment of the Corpse in Ancient Rome." In Hope and Marshall, eds., 104–27.

Hope, Valerie M., and Eireann Marshall, eds. 2000. *Death and Disease in the Ancient City*. London and New York.

Hopkins, Andrew, and Maria Wyke, eds. 2005. *Roman Bodies. Antiquity to the Eighteenth Century*. London.

Howarth, Glennys. 1996. *Last Rites: The Work of the Modern Funeral Director*. Amityville, NY.

————. 2000. "Dismantling the Boundaries between Life and Death." *Mortality* 5.2: 127–38.

————. 2007. "The Rebirth of Death: Continuing Relationships with the Dead." In Margaret Mitchell, ed., *Remember Me: Constructing Immortality. Beliefs on Immortality, Life, and Death*, 19–34. New York and London.

Huber, G. 1990. *Das Motif der 'Witwe von Ephesus.'* Tübingen.

Humphreys, S. C. 1980. "Family Tombs and Tomb Cult in Ancient Athens: Tradition or Traditionalism?" *JHS* 100: 96–126.

Huskinson, J. 1998. "Unfinished Portrait Heads on Later Roman Sarcophagi: Some New Perspectives." *PBSR* 66: 129–58.

Hutchinson, G. O. 1993. *Latin Literature from Seneca to Juvenal*. Oxford.

Johnson, W. R. 1987. *Momentary Monsters: Lucan and His Heroes.* Ithaca and London.
———. 1997. "Final Exit: Propertius 4.11." In Roberts, Dunn, and Fowler, eds., 163–80.
Jupp, Peter C. 2006. *From Dust to Ashes. Cremation and the British Way of Death.* Houndsmills, Basingstoke, Hampshire and New York.
Jupp, Peter C., and Glennys Howarth, eds. 1997. *The Changing Face of Death. Historical Accounts of Death and Disposal.* Houndsmills, Basingstoke, Hampshire, London and New York.
Kampen, Natalie Boymel, ed. 1996. *Sexuality in Ancient Art: Near East, Egypt, Greece, and Italy.* Cambridge.
Kay, N. M. 2001. *Ausonius Epigrams: Text with Introduction and Commentary.* London.
Kearl, Michael. 1989. *Endings: A Sociology of Death and Dying.* Oxford.
Kent, Roland G. 1967. *Varro, On the Latin Language.* Cambridge, MA.
Kertzer, David I., and Richard P. Saller, eds. 1991. *The Family in Italy from Antiquity to the Present.* New Haven.
Keyes, Cllinton Walker. 1977. *Cicero in Twenty-Eight Volumes.* XVI: *De Republica De Legibus.* Cambridge, MA and London.
Kleiner, Diana E. E. 1981. "Second-Century Mythological Portraiture: Mars and Venus." *Latomus* 40: 512–44.
———. 1987. *Roman Imperial Funerary Altars with Portraits.* Rome.
———. 1992. *Roman Sculpture.* New Haven.
———. 2000a. "Now You See Them, Now You Don't. The Presence and Absence of Women in Roman Art." In Varner a, 45–57.
———, and Susan B. Matheson, eds. 2000b. *I Claudia II: Woman in Roman and Art and Society.* New Haven.
Koortbojian, Michael. 1995. *Myth, Meaning, and Memory on Roman Sarcophagi.* Berkeley and Los Angeles.
———. 1996. "*In commemorationem mortuorum:* Text and Image along the 'Streets of Tombs.'" In Jaś Elsner, ed., *Art and Text in Roman Culture,* 210–33. Cambridge.
Kurtz, D. C., and J. Boardman. 1971. *Greek Burial Customs.* Ithaca, NY.
Kyle, Donald G. 1998. *Spectacles of Death in Ancient Rome.* London and New York.
Lacey, W. K., ed. 1986. *Cicero: 2nd Philippic Oration.* Warminster.
Lattimore, Richmond. 1962. *Themes in Greek and Latin Epitaphs.* Urbana.
Lesueur, Roger. 1991. *Stace: Thébaïde Livres V–VIII.* Paris.
Lee, M. Owen. 1989. *Death and Rebirth in Virgil's Arcadia.* Albany.
Leigh, Matthew. 1997. *Lucan: Spectacle and Engagement.* Oxford.
Lindsay, Hugh. 2000. "Death-Pollution and Funerals in the City of Rome." In Hope and Marshall, eds., 152–83.
Lissberger, Ewald. 1934. *Das Fortleben der römischen Elegiker in den Carmina Epigraphica.* Stuttgart.
Littlewood, C. A. J. 2004. *Self-Representation and Illusion in Senecan Tragedy.* Oxford.
Littlewood, R. J. 2001. "Ovid among the Family Dead: The Roman Founder Legend and Augustan Iconography in Ovid's *Feralia* and *Lemuria.*" *Latomus* 60: 916–35.
Lolli, Massimo. 1997. *D. M. Ausonius: Parentalia. Inroduzione, testo, traduzione e commento.* Brussels.
Lovatt, Helen. 2005. *Statius and Epic Games: Sport, Politics, and Poetics in the* Thebaid. Cambridge.

Malamud, M. 1995. "Happy Birthday, Dead Lucan: (P)raising the Dead in *Silvae* 2.7." *Ramus* 24: 1–30.

Manuwald, Gesine. 2001. *Fabulae praetextae: Spuren einer literarischen Gattung der Römer.* Munich.

Marpicati, Paolo. 1999. "Silio 'delatore' di Pompeio (*Pun.* 5,328 ss.; 10, 305 ss.)." *MD* 43: 191–202.

Martin-Kilcher, Stefanie. 2000. "*Mors immatura* in the Roman World—A Mirror of Society and Tradition." In John Pearce, Martin Millet, and Manuela Struck, eds., *Burial, Society and Context in the Roman World,* 63–77. Oxford.

Massaro, Matteo. 1992. *Epigrafia Metrica Latina di Età Repubblicana.* Bari.

Mastidoro, M. 1991. *Corcordanza dei Carmina Latina Epigraphica.* Classical and Byzantine Monographs 21. Amsterdam.

Mayer, R. 1981. *Lucan Civil War VIII.* Warminster.

McGlathery, D. B. 1998. "Petronius' Tale of the Woman of Ephesus and Bakhtin's Material Bodily Lower Stratum." *Arethusa* 31: 313–36.

McKinley, J. I. 1989. "Cremations: Expectations, Methodologies and Realities." In C. A. Roberts, F. Lee, and J. Birtliff, eds. *Burial Archaeology. Current Research, Methods and Development.* BAR British Series 211.

McWilliam, Janette. 2001. "Children among the Dead: The Influence of Urban Life on the Commemoration of Children on Tombstone Inscriptions." In Dixon, ed., 74–98.

Mellor, Ronald. 1993. *Tacitus.* New York and London.

Miller, John F. 1991. *Ovid's Elegiac Festivals. Studies in the Fasti.* Bern, New York, and Paris.

Mitchell, Margaret, ed. 2007. *Remember Me: Constructing Immortality. Beliefs on Immortality, Life, and Death.* New York and London.

Morford, M. P. O. 1996. *The Poet Lucan: Studies in Rhetorical Epic.* 2nd ed. London.

Morisi, Luca. 2002. "Ifigenia e Polissena (Lucrezio in Catullo)." *MD* 49: 177–90.

Morris, Ian. 1989. "Attitudes toward Death in Archaic Greece." *CA* 8: 296–320.

———. 1992. *Death-Ritual and Social Structure in Classical Antiquity.* Cambridge and New York.

Most, Glenn. 1992. "*Disiecti membra poetae:* The Rhetoric of Dismemberment in Neronian Poetry." In Ralph Hexter and Daniel Selden, eds., *Innovations of Antiquity,* 391–419. New York.

Murray, Oswyn, and Manuela Tecuşan, eds. 1995. *In Vino Veritas.* London.

Mynors. R. A. B. 1989. *C. Valerii Catulli Carmina.* Oxford.

———. 1990. *P. Vergili Maronis Opera.* Oxford.

Nappa, Christopher. 1999. "Catullus 59: Rufa among the Graves." *CP* 94: 329–35.

Narducci, E. 1973. "Il trunco di Pompeo." *Maia* 25: 317–25.

Norman, Naomi J. 2002. "Death and Burial of Roman Children: The Case of the Yasmina Cemetery at Carthage, Part 1, Setting the Stage." *Mortality* 7.3: 302–23.

———. 2003. "Death and Burial of Roman Children: The Case of the Yasmina Cemetery at Carthage, Part II, The Archaeological Evidence." *Mortality* 8.1: 36–47.

Noy, David. 2000. "'Half-Burnt on an Emergency Pyre': Roman Cremations Which Went Wrong." *Greece and Rome* 47: 186–96.

Nugent, S. G. 1996. "Statius' Hypsipyle: Following in the Footsteps of the *Aeneid.*" *Scholia* 5: 46–71.

Oakley, John H. 2004. *Picturing Death in Classical Athens: The Evidence of the White Lekythoi*. Cambridge.

Ogilvie, R. M. 1965. *A Commentary on Livy Books 1–5*. Oxford.

———. 1974. *Titi Livi Ab Urbe Condita*. Oxford.

O'Gorman, Ellen. 2000. *Irony and Misreading in the Annals of Tacitus*. Cambridge.

O'Hara, James J. 2007. *Inconsistency in Roman Epic. Studies in Catullus, Lucretius, Vergil, Ovid and Lucan*. Cambridge.

Oliver, G. J., ed. 2000. *The Epigraphy of Death: Studies in the History and Society of Greece and Rome*. Liverpool.

Osgood, Josiah. 2006. *Caesar's Legacy: Civil War and the Emergence of the Roman Empire*. Cambridge.

Owen, S. G., ed. 1980. *P. Ovidi Nasonis Tristium Libri Quinque Ibis Ex Ponto Libri Quattuor Halieutica Fragmenta*. Oxford.

Pagán, Victoria E. 2000. "The Mourning after: Statius *Thebaid* 12." *AJP* 121: 423–52.

Panofsky, Erwin. 1982. *Meaning in the Visual Arts*. Chicago.

Paratore, Ettore. 1982. *Lucano*. Roma.

Paton, W. R. 1968. *Diodorus Siculus World History (Bibliotheca)*. London and Cambridge, MA.

———. 1972. *Polybius: The Histories*. London and Cambridge, MA.

Pavlovskis, Zoja. 1976. "*Aeneid* V: The Old and the Young." *CJ* 71: 193–205.

Pearce, John, Martin Millet, and Manuela Struck, eds. 2000. *Burial, Society and Context in the Roman World*. Oxford.

Pecere, O. 1975. *Petronio, la novella della matrona de Efeso*. Padua.

Petrucci, Armando. 1995. *Le scritture ultime: Ideologia della morte e strategie dello scrivere nella tradizione occidentale*. Giulio Einaudi editore s.p.a.

———. 1998. *Writing the Dead. Death and Writing Strategies in the Western Tradition*. 1998. Translated by Michael Sullivan. Stanford.

Piontek, J. 1976. "The Process of Cremation and Its Influence on the Morphology of Bones in the Light of Results of Experimental Research" (English summary). *Archeologia Polski* 21: 277–280.

Polfer, Michael. 2000. "Reconstructing Funerary Ritual: The Evidence of *Ustrina* and Related Archeological Structures." In Pearce, Millet, and Struck, eds., 30–37.

Pollmann, Karla F. L. 2004. *Statius, Thebaid 12*. Paderborn.

Postgate, J. P. 1990. *Tibulli Aliorumque Carminum Libri Tres*. Oxford.

Prieur, J. 1991. *La morte nell' antica Roma = La mort dans l'antiquité romaine*. Genoa.

Purcell, N. 1987. "Tomb and Suburb." In von Hesberg and Zanker, 25–41.

———. 1999. "Does Caesar Mime?" In Bergmann and Kondoleon, eds., 181–93.

Putnam, Michael C. J. 1970. *Virgil's Pastoral Art*. Princeton, NJ.

Rackham, H. 1969. *Pliny: Natural History*. Cambridge, MA.

Radice, Betty. 1972. *Pliny: Letters and Panegyricus*. Vol. 1. Cambridge, MA and London.

Richardson, L. R., Jr. 1992. *A New Topographical Dictionary of Ancient Rome*. Baltimore.

Rimell, Victoria. 2002. *Petronius and the Anatomy of Fiction*. Cambridge.

Roberts, Deborah H., Francis M. Dunn, and Don Fowler, eds. 1997. *Classical Closure. Reading the End in Greek and Latin Literature*. Princeton, NJ.

Rolfe, J. C. 2001. *Suetonius*. Vols. 1–2. Cambridge, MA and London.

Rose, H. J. 1923. "Nocturnal Funerals in Rome." *CQ* 17: 191–94.

———. 1942. *The Eclogues of Vergil.* Berkeley and Los Angeles.

Rosenstein, Nathan. 2004. *Rome at War. Farms, Families, and Death in the Middle Republic.* Chapel Hill.

Sage, Evan T., and Brady B. Gilleland. 1969. *Petronius: The Satyricon.* New York.

Saller, R., and Brent M. Shaw. 1984. "Tombstones and Roman Family Relations in the Principate: Civilians, Soldiers, and Slaves." *JRS* 74: 124–56.

Saunders. C. 1913. "The Site of Dramatic Peformances at Rome in the Times of Plautus and Terence." *TAPA* 44: 87–97.

Schenck, Celeste Marguerite. 1988. *Mourning and Panegyric. The Poetics of Pastoral Ceremony.* University Park and London.

Seale, Clive. 1998. *Constructing Death. The Sociology of Dying and Bereavement.* Cambridge.

Shackleton Bailey, D. R. 1988. *M. Annaei Lucani de Bello Civili Libri X.* Stuttgart.

———. 1999. *Cicero Letters to Atticus.* Vol. 3. Cambridge, MA and London.

———. 2003. *Statius Thebaid, Books 1–7.* Cambridge, MA and London.

Shaw, Brent. 1991. "The Cultural Meaning of Death: Age and Gender in the Roman Family." In Kertzer and Saller, eds., 66–90.

Scheidel, Walter. 2001. *Death on the Nile. Disease and the Demography of Roman Egypt.* Leiden, Boston, and Cologne.

Sigismund Nielsen, Hanne. 2001. "The Value of Epithets in Pagan and Christian Epitaphs from Rome." In Suzanne Dixon, ed., *Childhood, Class, and Kin in the Roman World,* 165–77. London.

Skutsch, Otto. 1985. "On the Epigrams of Ennius." *LCM* 10: 146–48.

———. 1986. *The Annals of Quintus Ennius.* 2nd ed. Oxford.

Slater, Niall W. 1990. *Reading Petronius.* Baltimore and London.

———. 1996. "Nero's Masks." *CW* 90: 33–40.

Smolenaars, J. J. L. 1994. *Statius, Thebaid VII: A Commentary.* Mnemosyne Suppl. 134. Leiden, New York, and Cologne.

Sourvinou-Inwood, Christiane. 1995. *Reading Greek Death.* Oxford.

Stillinger, Jack, ed. 1982. *John Keats: Complete Poems.* Cambridge, MA.

Sumi, Geoffrey S. 2002. "Impersonating the Dead: Mimes at Roman Funerals." *AJP* 123: 559–85.

———. 2005. *Ceremony and Power. Performing Politics in Rome between Republic and Empire.* Ann Arbor.

Susini, G. C. 1973. *The Roman Stonecutter.* Trans. A.M. Dabowski. Oxford.

Tarrant, R. J. 1998. *Seneca's Thyestes: Edited with Introduction and Commentary.* Atlanta.

Thilo, G., and H. Hagen. 1961. *Servii Grammatici Qui Feruntur in Vergilii Carmina Commentarii.* Hildesheim.

Thompson, L. A. 1962. "The Relationship between Provincial Questions and Their Commanders-in-Chief." *Historia* 11: 339–55.

Toynbee, J. M. C. 1996. *Death and Burial in the Roman World.* 2nd ed. Baltimore and London.

Tucker, Robert A. 1987. "Tacitus and the Death of Lucan." *Latomus* 46: 330–37.

Varner, Eric R., ed. 2000a. *From Caligula to Constantine: Tyranny and Transformation in Roman Portraiture.* Atlanta.

———. 2000b. "Tyranny and Transformation of the Roman Visual Landscape." In Varner, ed., 9–26.

———. 2001. "Punishment after Death: Mutilation of Images and Corpse Abuse in Ancient Rome." *Mortality* 6: 45–64.

——— 2003. "Grotesque Vision: Seneca's Tragedies and Neronian Art." In George W. M. Harrison, ed., *Seneca in Performance*. London.

———. 2004. *Mutilation and Transformation:* Damnatio Memoriae *and Roman Imperial Portraiture*. Leiden.

———. 2005. "Execution in Effigy: Severed Heads and Decapitated Statues in Imperial Rome." In Andrew Hopkins and Maria Wyke, eds., *Roman Bodies. Antiquity to the Eighteenth Century*, 67–82. London.

Vermeule, Emily. 1981. *Aspects of Death in Early Greek Art and Poetry*. Berkeley and Los Angeles.

Vessey, D. 1970. "Notes on the Hypsipyle Episode in Statius, *Thebaid* 4–6." *BICS* 17: 44–54.

Volpihac-Lenthéric, J. 1984. *Silius Italicus La Guerre Punique Tome III Livres IX–XIII*. Paris.

von Hesberg, H., and P. Zanker. 1987. *Römische Gräberstrassen, AbhMünchen N.F.* 16.

Walker, B. 1952. *The Annals of Tacitus*. Manchester.

White, Horace. 1995. *Appian Roman History*. Vol. 3. Cambridge, MA and London.

Warmington, E. H. 1988. *Remains of Old Latin*. Vols. 1, 2, and 4. Cambridge, MA and London.

Walters, C. F., and R .S. Conway. 1979. *Titi Livi Ab Urbe Condita*. Oxford.

Walton, Francis R. 1968. *Diodorus of Sicily*. London and Cambridge, MA.

Warden, John. 1980. *Fallax Opus: Poet and Reader in the Elegies of Propertius*. Phoenix Suppl. 14. Toronto.

Weinstock, Stefan. 1957. "The Image and the Chair of Germanicus." *JRS* 47: 144–54.

———. 1971. *Divus Julius*. Oxford.

Werde, Henning. 1981. *Consecratio in Formam Deorum: Vergöttlichte Privatpersonen in der römischen Kaiserzeit*. Mainz am Rhein.

West, D., and A. J. Woodman, eds. 1979. *Creative Imitation and Latin Literature*. Cambridge and New York.

Wickkiser, Bronwen L. 1999. "Famous Last Words: Putting Ovid's *Sphragis* Back into the *Metamorphoses*." *MD* 42: 113–42.

———. 1999. "Speech in Context: Plato's *Menexenus* and the Ritual of Athenian Public Burial." *RSQ* 29: 65–74.

Williams, G. 1978. *Change and Decline: Roman Literature in the Early Empire*. Berkeley and Los Angeles.

Wiseman, T. P. 1995. *Remus. A Roman Myth*. Cambridge.

Wolff, Étienne. 2000. *La poésie funéraire épigraphique à Rome*. Rennes.

Woodman, A. J. 1979. "Self-Imitation and the Substance of History: Tacitus, Annals 1.61–5 and Histories 2.70, 5.14–15." In West and Woodman, eds., 143–55.

Woodward, Jennifer. *The Theatre of Death. The Ritual Management of Royal Funerals in Renaissance England 1570–1625*. Woodbridge, Suffolk and Rochester, NY.

Zwierlein, Otto. 1988. *L. Annaei Senecae Tragoediae*. Oxford.

INDEX

A

Achaemenides, 98
Achillas, 111–12
Achilles, 40–42, 46, 49–53, 74,
    83–84, 86, 92–95, 97, 149
L. Aemilius Paullus, 75–76
L. Aemilius Paullus, son of L. Aemilius
    Lepidus Paullus, 197
L. Aemilius Paullus Macedonicus, 68
Aeneas, 77, 82, 84–91, 110, 136,
    148–49, 181–82, 187–88, 194
Aesculapius, 100
aesthetics of morality, 2, 34, 41, 53, 61
aesthetics of mortality, 2–3, 34, 61
Agrippina, mother of Nero, 27
Agrippina, wife of Germanicus, 55, 67
Alexander the Great, 109, 152–53
altar, 159, 167, 173
Ambarvalia, 10
American funerary culture, 15–16,
    108, 160, 196–97
Anaxarete, 100
Anchises, 106
Anius, 97–98
Andromache, 40–49, 86
Antigone, 140–41, 145, 147–48
Apollo, 85, 91
Appian on Caesar's funeral, 38–40
Argia, 140–41, 144–45, 147–48
Astyanax, 40–53, 74, 139

B

Baucis, 118
bier, 38–39, 61, 63, 75–76, 78–79,
    81–82, 84–85, 87, 130–31, 136,
    140
Britannicus, 67
bucolic, 84–91
bustum, busta, 17, 37, 42, 44, 90, 94

C

Caieta, 98–99
Campus Martius, 36–37, 50, 63–64
Capitoline Museums, 177–80, 179
    (fig. 3), 203
Capitoline Venus, 178–80
carmen, 86, 98, 126, 132–33, 172, 175
Catiline, 14, 115, 123
Catullus, 85–86, 186, 201
cemetery, 5, 189, 196
cepotaphia, 2–3, 20, 173

A

Atreus, 137–38
Augustus: 98, 100–101, 103–7, 121,
    152–53, 197; funeral, 11, 55,
    61–64, 66, 69, 73; mausoleum,
    155; triumph, 62
Aurora, 96–97, 102
Ausonius, 12; *Epigrams,* 1–2; *Parenta-*
    lia, 185–94

Cicero: *De legibus*, 6–7; *Epistles*, 187;
Pro Caelio, 157–58; on Tullia's
memorial, 176–77
Claudii, *gens*, 64
Ap. Claudius, 7–8
Ap. Claudius Caecus, 157–58
Nero Claudius Drusus, son of Livia, 67
Claudius, Emperor, 22–23
Claudius Quadrigarius, 114
Cleopatra, 103
Clodia, 157–58
commemoration, 22
Cordus, 110, 116–17, 120–21, 125
Cornelia, daughter of Scribonia,
197–201
Cornelia, wife of Pompey, 111–12,
120–22, 124, 196
Cornelia Glyce, 159–60, 161 (fig. 1)
P. Cornelius Scipio Aemilianus, 7, 9,
200–1. *See also* Scipio Africanus
Cornelii, *gens*, 6
Coronis, 91
Cottius, 156–57
Creon, 109, 140, 143–44, 146–50
Curia of Pompey, 37
cyber dead, 197
Cynthia 16–19, 57–59

D

damnatio memoriae, 111
Daphnis, 85–86, 150
dead, the: as actor, 61; agents of
transformation, 3; living, 13, 14,
33, 162, 196, 201–3; participants
at funerals, 9, 11, 15, 39, 74, 182;
playing dead, 10, 11, 14–16, 19,
22, 24, 26, 30, 34, 41, 68–69, 74,
185; reviving the dead, 194–204;
self-representation of, 12, 72, 153,
156, 161–62, 170–71, 194–204;
as symbols, 7, 158
death ritual: as spectacle, 11, 20, 24,
50–51, 53, 61, 73; theatricalization of, 10–11, 13, 15–16, 33–34,
37–39, 40–41, 55, 61–74
Dido, 25–26, 79–80, 131, 181, 182
Dies Ferales, 187

Dies Parentales, 187
Dio Cassius on Augustus' funeral,
62–64; Pertinax' funeral, 69–72
Diodorus Siculus on L. Aemilius Paul-
lus Macedonicus' funeral, 68
Domitii, *gens*, 155

E

effigy, 62–63, 71, 121
elegea, 186
Eliot, T. S., 194–95
elogium, 201
embalming, 7
Ennius, 76, 82, 89, 105, 135, 152;
Annales, 76, 83, 89, 203; *Elogium
of the Scipios*, 200–201; epitaph,
161–62
epicede, 186
epitaph: of Claudia, 162; of L.
Cornelius Scipio Barbatus, 166,
167 (fig. 2), 168 (fig. 3), 176; of
L. Cornelius Scipio, 168–70; of
Gn. Cornelius Scipio Hispanus,
170–71, 200; as grave marker,
1–3, 12, 20–21, 76, 159–76; of
Helvia Prima, 164–65; of Herennia Crocine, 163–64; of Gaius
Hostius Pamphilus, 3; illusion of
personality, 160; illusory, 176–80;
of Laberius and his wife Bassa,
171–73; M. Lucceius Nepos, 201–
203; M. Octavius Rufus, 173–74,
191; of Probus' wife, 174–76, 191;
of Rufus, 177, 178 (fig. 4), 179; as
textual marker, 1–3, 5, 12, 19–21,
31–32, 49, 87, 98, 106, 124–26,
154–57, 181–94
Erictho, 116
Eteocles, 97, 109, 127, 140–41, 143,
146–47, 150, 153
Eurydice, 131, 136
Evander, 77, 136

F

fabulae praetextae, 73
Faustina Minor, 68

Feeney, Denis, 9–10, 18,
feretrum, 75, 77, 81, 82, 84, 99,
	129–30
Flavian woman as Venus, 179, 180
	(fig. 6), 203
foreign burial rituals, 7–9
funerary ritual: carrying out the dead,
	89; cremation, 5–7, 53–55, 57–61,
	63, 71–72, 75–77, 80–84, 86–89,
	90–109, 117–21, 127–44, 146,
	148–49, 153, 196–97; (prohibi-
	tion), 9, 22, 37; embalming, 7;
	figurative, 7, 9, 10; final words,
	82, funeral games, 83; inhuma-
	tion, 6, 9, 22, 23, 197; invoking
	the dead, 157–58; nonburial, 5, 6;
	offerings, 75, 79, 80–81, 83, 88,
	90, 135, 144; as text and intertext,
	9–12, 83–87, 109, 124–41, 153,
	155–56, 201

G

Gallic Pyres, 5, 6
Gallus, 183–85
Germanicus 55, 67
grave: definition, 6–7. *See also* tomb

H

Hannibal, 75–76
Hector, 40–44, 49–51, 53, 144, 149
Hecuba, 11, 40, 77, 92–100, 107,
	110, 127, 145
Hercules, 91, 100, 144
Hills of Rome: Capitoline, 5, 37, 103;
	Esquiline, 5; Velian, 7
Hippolytus, 54–57, 60–61, 124, 128,
	138
Homer, 27, 76, 80, 82–84, 135, 149,
	186
Horace, 105, 121, 151, 153, 186
Howarth, Glennys, 72–73
Hypsipyle, 128, 139–40

I

Iliad, 80, 83–84, 89, 91, 97

imago, 14, 30, 38, 62–63, 65–66, 69,
	76, 102, 115, 157, 161–62, 181,
	196
imperial ritual, 67–68
Iphis, 100

J

Julia, daughter of Caesar, 195–96
Julii, *gens*, 64
Julius Caesar: 111, 116, 122–25, 196;
	apotheosis, 77, 97, 100–107; cre-
	mation/funeral, 11, 35–40, 61–62,
	64, 69, 73, 74, 91, 100
L. Junius Brutus, 73
D. Junius Brutus Callaicus, 73
Jupiter, 97, 102, 105
Juvenal, 158, 160

K

Keats, John, 13–14

L

Lamian Gardens, 5, 155
landscape of death, 2–3, 5, 158. *See
	also* topography of death
Latinus, 99
laudatio, 37–38
Lavinia, 99
Leigh, Matthew, 111
Linus, 131
Livia, wife of Augustus, 55, 63–64,
	186–87
Livy, 6, 67, 114
Lucan, 12, 140, 142, 153; *Bellum
	Civile*, 109–26, 195; death of,
	126–27
Lycurgus, 136
Lygdamus, 201
ludi, 37, 66–67
lustratio, 35

M

Macareus, 98
Maecenas, 5

Manlius Torquatus, 114
Marcellus: nephew of Augustus, 67;
    Theater of, 67
Marius, 6
Mark Antony, 37–39
Memnon, 96–97, 102
Menoecus, 143–44
metatheater, 41, 51, 53, 61, 74
Mettius Fufetius, 55
Misenus, 80–84, 89–91, 127, 130,
    135
mock funeral, 14–15, 19, 20–23
monument, 2, 20, 159
Morta, 90
mourning, 4, 53, 90

N

Naevius, 152
Naples, 151
Narcissus, 91
nenia, 186
Neoptolemus, 93–94
Nero, 27, 29, 154–56
Niobe, 96
Numa, 6

O

Opheltes, 127–40, 143, 150, 153
ossilegium, 6, 22, 31, 54–55, 57–61,
    64, 72, 74, 82–83, 124
Octavia, daughter of Claudius, 30–31
Odyssey, 27
Orion, 97–98
Ovid, 11–12, 76–77, 140, 142, 153,
    186, 201; Fasti, 187–88, 203;
    Metamorphoses, 91–107, 118,
    127–28, 145, 151; Tristia, 106–7

P

Pacuvius, 38, 152
Pacuvius: governor of Syria, 14–15,
    22–33, 181
Pallas, 76–80, 82–87, 89–91, 129,
    131, 135–36, 194
Parentalia, 6, 12, 15, 20, 22, 185–95

Parsons, Russell, 108, 125
Patroklos, 83–84, 86, 89, 96
Paulina, wife of Seneca, 27–33
Pelops, 133
Pertinax, 69–72
Petronius on Trimalchio, 20–23;
    Widow of Ephesus, 23–27
Phaëthon, 145–46
Philemon, 118
Plautus, 152
Pliny, Epistles, 156, 187
Plutarch, 156
Polybius on Roman aristocratic funer-
    als, 64–67
Polydorus, 92–93, 96
Polynices, 97, 109, 127, 140–41,
    145–47, 150, 153
Polyxena, 27, 40–41, 47, 49–53, 74,
    92–96, 139, 145
pomerium, 6
pompa, 64–65
Pompey: 109–26, 176, 195–96; tri-
    umph, 62
Poppaea Sabina, 31
Pothinus, 119
Poussin, Nicolas, 1
Priam, 40, 94, 110
Propertius, Elegies: 16–19, 57–60,
    182–85, 197–201
pyra, pyre, 42, 71, 75–76, 80–85,
    87–89, 94, 128, 130–33, 135–39,
    143–44, 146, 148, 181, 195
Pyramus, 91

R

rogus, 35, 59, 89, 120, 131, 138,
    143–45, 147, 199
Roman Forum, 37, 66, 69, 71
Romulus, 62, 100, 203

S

S. Maria del Popolo, 155
S. Sebastiano, 179
Sabina, wife of Ausonius, 192–94
Sallust on the death of Catiline, 14,
    115, 123

Sappho, 85
Scipio Africanus 7, 9, 200–201
Scribonia, 197
sema, 42
Seneca, 27–33; *Apocolocyntosis,* 22–23;
    Epistles, 8–9, 14–15, 181, 187;
    Phaedra, 53–61, 124, 138, 140;
    Thyestes, 118, 137–38, 140;
    Troades, 40–53, 128–29
Septimius, 111–12, 116
Septimius Severus, 69–72
sepulchrum, sepulcrum, 6–7, 42–43
Silius Italicus on foreign burial prac-
    tices, 7–9; Hannibal's cremation
    of L. Aemilius Paullus, 75–76;
    intertextuality, 201
Socrates, 32–33
Solon, 7
Sophocles, 148
spectacle, 24, 47, 50, 53
sphragis, 105–7, 121, 140–41, 149,
    151, 153, 189
Statius: 11, 182; father's tomb, 3–5;
    Silvae, 3–5, 187; *Thebaid,* 109,
    127–53
stramen, 75, 77, 84, 129, 131
Suetonius on Augustus at Alexander's
    tomb, 152–53; Julius Caesar's
    apotheosis, 103–4; Julius Caesar's
    funeral, 35–36; Nero's burial,
    155; Nero's directions for his
    grave, 154; Vergil's epitaph, 152;
    Vespasian's funeral, 69
Sulla, 6, 156

T

Tacitus on death of Lucan, 126–27;
    death of Octavia, 30–31; Seneca's
    suicide, 27–29
Tarquins, 73
Temple: of Venus Genetrix, 36, 39
theater 10–11, 47, 51
theatricality, 11, 15, 51, 103

Theocritus, 85–86
Theseus, 54, 56, 124, 140, 148–49
Thetis, 96–97
Thisbe, 91
Thucydides, 9
Thyestes, 138
Tiberius, 63, 68
Tibullus, 10, 186, 201
titulus, 190
tomb: 2, 9, 43–44, 49, 50, 85, 125,
    152–53, 187, 189, 197. *See also*
    grave
Tomb of the Scipios, 166, 170
tombstone, 2, 5, 160, 191
topography of death, 1–3, 5–6, 41
torus, 84, 129, 130, 136, 192
Trimalchio, 19–23
tumulus, 5, 42–44, 46, 83, 93
Turnus, 77, 79–80, 91, 99, 114,
    148–49
Twelve Tables, 6–7

V

Valerii, *gens,* 7
Varro, 82
Q. Varus, 186
Vatican Museums, 160, 167, 176
Venus, 98, 100, 102, 105, 179–80,
    203; Capua type, 179. *See also*
    Capitoline Venus
Vergil, 3, 11, 105–7, 110, 135, 151–
    53, 182, 186, 194, 201; *Aeneid,* 4,
    14, 25–27, 76–91, 129, 132, 141,
    143, 149, 151; *Eclogues,* 85–86;
    epitaph, 152; *Georgics,* 150–51;
    tomb, 3, 106, 187
Vespasian, 69
Via: Appia, 125, 165, 167, 180; Fla-
    minia, 156, 158; Latina, 158

W

Widow of Ephesus, 23–27